CLIMATE CHANGE AND INTERNATIONAL POLITICS

CLIMATE CHANGE AND INTERNATIONAL POLITICS

Dr. Narottam Gaan

PUBLICATIONS

KALPAZ PUBLICATIONS

DELHI-110052

Climate Change and International Politics

Rs. 900

ISBN: 81-7835-641-4

Published in 2008 in India by
Kalpaz Publications
C-30, Satyawati Nagar,
Delhi-110052
E-mail: kalpaz@hotmail.com
Phone : 9212729499

Lasser Type Setting by: Quick Media, Delhi
Printed at : Vishal Kaushik Printers, Delhi

Dedication

to

My worshipful father who returned to the Eternal Abode on 4th April, 2007 and was the instrument chosen by God for my coming to this earth and for what I am today, and who must revel in unbounded joy to see this consecrated at his lotus feet with love and reverence.

CONTENTS

Preface

Until Newtonian view of the universe, scientific discoveries and inventions ushered in to provide the ontological foundation to Political Science, the climate was not factorized into the realm of international politics. It was just an Aristotle and Montesquieu's confinement of climate to its impact on human nature, and character. When industrial revolution began catching the imagination of humans about a thawing of a new world and possibilities of a different kind of development, a Newtonian and Cartesian view of the universe emerged to dominate the policy makers, statesmen and scientists of the west. A split between matter and spirit took place giving a quietus to the traditional wisdom of seeing both as one and always in unity. The world was nothing but matter, a cornucopia of lifeless raw materials to be harnessed for the development of human beings. Science opened the eyes of the state to the new possibilities and vistas of different primrose ways of life purely based on materialistic aggrandizement. Here science and political science shared the same ontological foundation. Political Science utilized Science to set the goals for human beings to provide a good life to individuals. Good life was defined in terms of providing a commodious and luxurious living.

The scientific determinism of what constitutes "a good life" was rationalized by both Hobbes and Locke into scripting the epithet of liberalism based on possessive individualism. It helped in the growth of an atomistic rich industrialized class occupying the reins of state to exploit the nature and the other for a commodious living. Thus, wealth production and a commodious living premised on an inordinate life style and exorbitant consumption became the guiding metaphor for the emergence of a liberal market based political and economic order setting the tone and tenor of what is defined as development for the west and then, for the entire world.

Thus, "development of matter" was considered significant for the fulfillment of the goals set for human beings in this political and economic order. It was separated from the concept of "development of human beings". Rather, development of matter in various forms by scientific inventions and their application to the attainment of human goals set by the liberal political order, got a premium over the development of human beings. Not refinement and limitation of human limitless desires but their exponential expansion soared with materialistic bonanza unveiled by science from underneath the Earth. The more matter is explored, developed, harnessed and transformed into different forms for the commodious living, wealth production and inordinate life style of human beings, the more human beings and the nations are considered modern, developed and civilized. The different civilizations and cultures' ancient wisdom of looking at nature as nothing but a part of the larger self, a separate subjectivity woven into the coordinated whole of the entire being, were sacrificed at the altar of science's deification of matter. The nature and other living human and non-human beings and non-living elements are treated as "the other" to be exploited for the attainment of end set by both science and state. This gave rise to the emergence of power by which the rich propertied class remaining at the helm of affairs arrogated to themselves the rightness of authority in the form of the sovereign state to do so. With this view dominating and founding the epistemological copingstone of the western notion of what constitutes development. This became gradually the Bible of development for all nations of the world. As a primary requirement of this development, nature came under the fury of human exploitation. Nature no longer remained the guiding determinant of human being's way of life, social, economic and political structure and functions. It remained subordinate and hostage to the western view of defining life and development. Translated into reality, this rightness of action over nature and others as the sine qua non of development became the synonym for power and when legitimized by the consent of the governed for the attainment of the goals, and confined to a territorial exclusivity, became the modern sovereign state. The unimpeded right to abundant economic growth, wealth production and inordinate life style becoming the premise of modern liberal state resulted in a dominant rich class having the reins of authority. This became the ruling class within a state and the imperialist power in interstate relations having the sole authority by military and economic power to extract the resources from anywhere in the world. When this class spread its liberal market economy and logic to all parts of the globe through its controlled MNC and TNC, it resulted in globalization. By this process, the nature was exploited and despoliated as this could provide the raw materials for development based on fossil fuel technology and industrialization. Development thus understood in the western liberal lexicon constituted the benchmark and the ultimate lodestar for all the nations of the world. Thus, ethno-science and ethnoliberal political economy forming the ontological foundation of development resulted in the destruction of nature and its devastating consequences upon the humankind. What was once at the fringe of human concern now leapfrogs to the center stage of political thinking and policy making. The result of this western paradigm of development has been devastation of environment manifesting in the form of land degradation, desertification, water scarcity, global warming, sea level rise, ozone layer depletion and extinction of species, flora and fauna. The most horrifying and destructive among these is the climate change due to development based on fossil fuel technology, which has been solely responsible for limitless emission of Carbon Dioxide and other greenhouse gases to the atmosphere.

There have been no definitive statements on what level of global mean temperatures change might be regarded as an acceptable risk, or, in the words of the Framework Convention on Climate Change, what might be regarded as dangerous anthropogenic interference with the climate system. The reasons for this uncertainty are very clear. How climate change will impact at the local or regional level and at what magnitude is uncertain. Perception of what constitutes an acceptable risk depends on location, coping capacity and who is making the assessment. Nevertheless, there is an emerging consensus that if global mean temperature rises can be contained to around 2.0°C an increase of this order can be managed without undue risk to international security. But confidence in this statement plummets sharply once the rise exceeds 2.0°C. In April, 2006, Sir David King, the UK Chief Scientist, warned that the temperatures will probably rise by at least 3.0°C, which will cause severe droughts, put 400 million people at risk from hunger and jeopardize water supplies for up to 3 billion people.

A few dissident climatologists and meteorologist contest the IPCC assessments on two main grounds. Some question the reliability and consistency of the temperature and atmospheric data gathered for use in understanding the climate system and validating climate change models, particularly satellite observations. While accepting that concentrations of greenhouse gases have increased and the surface of the planet is warming, they argue that these rises are not demonstrably penetrating the upper atmosphere. If substantial climate change is occurring, warming should be evident throughout the 12 kilometer deep troposphere. Sceptics also claim that the amplifying effect on global warming predicted by the IPCC may be minimal because water vapour feedback may not reach the upper atmosphere and greenhouse enhancing water vapour in the atmosphere could actually decrease because of the physics of cloud formation.

A subsequent review by the IPCC showed that temperature trends from weather balloons since 1958 for the lowest 8 km of the atmosphere and at the surface are in good agreement with a warming of about

0.1°C per decade. After errors in the processing of the satellite data were rectified, both satellite and balloon observations have since provided clear supporting evidence of surface observations showing an increase in surface temperature extending right through to the atmosphere.

A second argument advanced by sceptics is that observations showing temperature change are based on meteorological records taken by weather services around the world and that the sites for these thermometers have been influenced by the so called "heat island" effect where the growth of urban development, particularly large, high rise buildings tend to artificially raise temperatures and block natural atmospheric mixing. But climate scientists are well aware of this anomaly and have developed methods for filtering out the distorting effects of urban sites. Observations from meteorological stations and satellites have been supplemented and compared with those obtained from deep-ocean measurements and analysis of the isotopic composition of ice, tree rising growth and borehole temperatures. The integration of all these measurements is providing a much clearer and richer picture of the history of our climate, enabling scientists to predict future temperature and sea level rises with greater certainty and accuracy. Other independent reports by leading climatologists have endorsed the basic findings of the IPCC and the evidence for global warming has become more compelling since 1995 and 2001 Assessment Reports. The IPCC Report for 2007 came out with greater accuracy and certainty about global warming and impacts on region wise. Despite the skeptics doubting the underlying assumptions and the veracity of data, evidence that human activities are significantly warming up the planet is now irrefutable, even if there are still uncertainties about the precise and exact rate of global warming and sea level rise.

Climate change is no longer abstract, a myth or hoax, as American President Bush used to advocate depending on the skeptics. The climate change with ramifying implications upon social, political, economic life of human beings has pitch-forked itself into the center stage of political thinking. Till now no less a person than American President who used to cock a snook at the scientific certainty about global warming as a myth, has come to grips with the problem. As revealed by Mark Townsend and Paul Harris in New York Sunday February 22, 2004, Observer, a secret report suppressed by US defence chiefs by the Observer, warns that major European cities will be sunk beneath rising seas as Britain is plunged into a Siberian climate by 2020. Nuclear conflict, mega droughts, famine and widespread rioting will erupt across the world. The document predicts that abrupt climate change could bring the planet to the edge of anarchy as countries develop a nuclear threat to defend and secure dwindling food, water and energy supplies. The threat to global stability eclipses that of terrorism.

The report commissioned by influential Pentagon defence adviser Andrew Marshall and authored by Peter Schwartz, CIA consultant and former head of planning at Royal Dutch/ Shell Group, and Doug Randall of the California based Global Business Network, says that climate change "should be elevated beyond a scientific debate to a US national security concern" An eminent scenario of catastrophic change is plausible and would challenge United States national security in ways that should be considered immediately. As the report says, as early as next year widespread flooding by a rise in sea levels will create major upheaval for millions. Bush administration came under heavy fire from a large body of respected scientists who claimed that it cherry picked science to suit its policy agenda and suppressed studies that it did not like. Suppression of this report was a further glaring example of the White House trying to bury the threat of climate change. It was in congruence with American established practice of jettisoning every bit of scientific findings about the climate change as a concocted fiction. It felt no contrition in rejecting the Kyoto protocol, which was the result of the deep concern and efforts of nations to mitigate the climate change. Many climatologists believe that their verdicts could prove the catalyst in forcing President Bush to accept climate change as a real and happening phenomenon. Their hope that the catastrophic climate change will convince the United States to sign up to global treaties to reduce the rate of climatic change is yet to be fulfilled.

The climate change - the irrefutable result of anthropogenic interference into the atmosphere in terms of limitless emission of Carbon Dioxide and other greenhouse gases by the industrialized North countries since the very inauguration of industrial revolution to the present and later on by the populous developing countries like India, China and Brazil - is in reality an issue of mitigation. Sincere efforts were made by the nations of the world while responding to the consensual verdict of a bevy of scientists, to reduce the emission of Carbon Dioxide to the atmosphere, which culminated in the signing of the historic Kyoto protocol setting the target for the rich industrialized countries. Though America was a signatory to this, it out rightly rejected it being influenced by its industrial lobby on the plea that without meaningful participation from the developing countries, it would not abide by the treaty. Unfortunately, America remained impervious to its own historic deed of emitting Carbon Dioxide and other greenhouse gases to the atmosphere, which it has been doing on the principle of inequity. But, when the question of mitigating the problem crops up, what comes as a sign of American double standard is that it insists on the principle of equity. It is North countries' inordinate life style and exorbitant consumption, in sum, their luxury emission is kept at par with the survival emission of the developing countries. The arguments adduced by the developing countries that binding them to the obligations of the global treaty on mitigation on the American stated principle of equity, will certainly put a cap on their right to development on western path of fossil fuel based industrialization, seem ethically and logically sound yet remain a hornet's nest in the furtherance of the Kyoto protocol ahead. The resentment of the developing countries against American stance could be seen from the remark once made by President Yoweri of Uganda that global warming is "an act of aggression by the rich against the poor". Similarly, "the culprits pay or atone for" what they have wrought to the atmosphere, seems ethical and logical yet continues to remain at the core of the debate on mitigation issues.

It can be indubitably said that cutting the use of fossil fuels would be the worthwhile step to stem the tide of climate change. The ball is in the court of the North countries. It is a wake up call to them to rethink their inordinate life style and consumption. It may compromise their uncontested living standard, but in keeping in view the onslaught of climate change on humanity, the future generations' right to live on this planet and inter-species accountability and responsibility, there appears to be no other alternative. Alternative energy resources should be explored as fossil fuels are finite and going to be emptied. It is the rich people who must usher in an ethical awakening in them about how to limit one's desires, moderate one's consumption and be awakened to the need for inter-generational responsibility and future generations' right to live on this planet.

Since the climate change has already outstripped the lukewarm mitigation efforts of the nations, the issue of how to adapt to the catastrophic consequences of climate change looms large in the present context. As predicted by IPCC fourth assessment report, the worst sufferers and victims would be the poor of the developing countries more particularly, in Asia and Africa. Since the developing countries lack the necessary scientific, technological and financial wherewithal to meet the challenges, the North should come forward providing the necessary adaptation strategies and resources to the South and the poor to meet the challenges. Both rich and poor - all are going to be islanders or coastal dwellers one way or another. Living far from sea level is not going to keep anyone safe from climate change effects, including the indirect effects of the raising sea level. Climate change is a security issue but it is not a matter of narrow national security defined in realistic parlance.

It has a new dimension. This is about collective security in a fragile and increasingly interdependent world where the catastrophic repercussions of climate change will percolate to all parts of the globe transcending national boundaries exposing again the brittleness of territorial impregnability supposedly maintained by militarization to the onslaught of climate change.

Climate change offers humanity an opportunity for a quantum leap from the atomistic, possessive individualistic proclivities to an enlarged consciousness, a thought poet John Donne contributed to the collective consciousness of the Westerners. No man is an island, as no part of the Nature is an enclave or the other or the separate objectivity to be exploited. All are to be seen as subjectivities woven eternally in the divine web, and as manifested larger self affirming the wisdom of Indian Upanishads: Thou art that (Tat Tvam Asi). It is again a question of reviewing the Newtonian and Cartesian view of the universe and the split between matter and spirit. Keeping in view the recent developments in Physics toward realizing on the part of scientists the dissolution of the split in a consciousness that is what in East held as divine, a new foundation for a rethinking of the very concept of development, outlook and vision of man about the universe can be laid down. As Danah Zohar in his Quantum Self pointed out:

> "The quantum world view transcends the dichotomy between mind and body, or between inner and outer, by showing us that the basic building blocks of mind (bosons) and the basic building blocks of matter (fermions) arise out of a common quantum substrate (the vacuum) and are engaged in a mutually creative dialogue whose roots can be traced back to the very heart of reality creation".

It is no surprising that the new vision of reality is in harmony with the visions of spiritual traditions. The ecological paradigm requiring a spiritual revolution in man is rooted in a perception of reality that goes beyond the scientific framework to an awareness of the oneness of all life, the interdependence of its multiple manifestations, and its cycles of change and transformation. The part is in the whole and the whole is in the part. All are interwoven in the cosmic web of divinity to form the being of both nature and human beings.

This book no doubt a great endeavour in this direction to analyze the crisis of climate change in these above dimensions, will succeed in amplifying the desideratum for a new vision and opening up the "Third Eye" and marking the shift in values from a mechanical world view to a cosmic world view to develop a new found respect for nature's arsenal of retaliatory responses.

Narottam Gaan

Acknowledgements

Another long intellectual stride commenced from the day I conceived of inking a book on Climate Change and International Politics taking not only my own ideas but also ideas and facts from various conferences and seminars abroad and in India I attended, imbibing new thinking, approaches and views from scholars I met, and from books I rummaged through, getting articles, and papers published in various journals of international repute, and reached its logical conclusion when all these variant strands of ideas seeped through my in-depth analytical acumen and rigour of scientific scrutiny to be blended nicely into a synthesized and pithy tapestry. If the collections from others are likened to bricks, mine is the architectural design, adding blood and flesh to the structure and shaping the ultimate monument in the form of this book. But for the help and cooperation from others it could not have been possible to bring out this book in the present form. My unbounded thanks and gratitude flow from the core of my heart to a galaxy of scholars to name a few like Come Carpentier De Gourdon, Dr. Arthur H. Westing, Dr. Thomas F Homer Dixon of Toronto University, Dr. Richard A Matthew of California University, Galtung, and Ben Wisner, Maureen Fordham and others who have played a key role in shaping my views and vision about the multidimensional aspects of climate change and security threats to humanity from different perspectives. I am also extremely grateful to WBGU, German Advisory Council on Global Change for their report entitled "World in Transition: Climate Change as a Security Risk", which I used in my study. From the abyss of my heart I always convey my sense of gratification to a host of erudite scholars for the materials, articles and books they have provided me without exhibiting even a shred of evidence of their being hesitant. I will fail in my duty if I do not give my heart rendering thanks to the authorities of European University Center for Peace Studies, (EPU), Stadtschlaining, Austria and the Austrian Government for having privileged me with a much coveted scholarship to go to Austria and Hungary and to have higher studies on International Relation. This helped me a lot come in contact with a number of great scholars like Arthur H. Westing, Gunther Bachler and Galtung whom I consider as yet the very prominent authorities to have provided me different perspectives to my work. I also thank the authorities of Jawaharlal Nehru University Library, Indian Council of World Affairs,

Teenmurti Library, United Nations Library and American Centre for having allowed me to work and collect materials.

My words are inadequate to express my humble gratitude and indebtedness to Prof. Mahendra Prasad Lama, Vice Chancellor, Sikkim University and former chairperson, South Asian Studies, School of International Studies, Jawaharlal Nehru University, Dr. S.D. Muni and Dr. S. R. Chakravarty, former professors in JNU, New Delhi, Prof. Annpurna Nautiyal of HNB University, Garhwal, Srinagar, my teachers Dr. Benudhar Pradhan, Director, Gandhian Institute for Peace Research and Action, and Dr. Asha Hans, former Professor in Political Science, Utkal University, Vanivihar, Bhubaneswar and S. N. Girish, I.A.S., a man of honesty, exemplary probity and humanist, and P.K. Choudhury, a great social activist for their inspiration, kind words and choicest good wishes kept in store for me. I must put in record my gratitude to my classmate and intimate friend Shanti, for her standing me in good stead. Mahesh and Sitakanta, two promising young scholars of JNU, New Delhi and Narayan Dash deserve my love and gratitude for their ungrudging help.

I am extremely grateful to my parents, my life companion Reena in our eternal journey, and my two loving beautiful flowers Tattwamasi and Yogeswar Krishna who have always spurred me inspiringly to the ethos of trailblazing and emerging shining, and withstood difficulties in the preparation of the book. My eldest son, Tattwamasi deserves all credit, my love and blessings for having computerized the entire work to my utmost satisfaction. From the inner cavern of my heart secrets my reverence and love to Swami Samarpanananda Giri and Swami Sudhananda Giri, two great divine and realized souls for their constant blessings and inspiration. Behind all these and the sole doer, but for who it is not possible to write such a book are Paramahamsa Prajnanananda and my Gurudev Paramahamsa Hariharananda. I deem it a God given privilege to sing in paeans of their Beatific Bliss and Glory in this humble work, which I consecrate at their Lotus Feet.

1

Introduction : Climate as a Factor in International Politics

There is no dearth of examples in history to demonstrate that climate shifts or extremes of weather triggering conflict and even contributing to the rise and fall of civilizations and nations. In assessing the significance of climate change for international security, it is worthwhile to recognize that climate is in a state of flux. This has little resemblance to the climate prevailing in pre-historic ages. None of the temperatures or climate fluctuations in terms of cold temperature lower average mean temperature five degrees colder prevailing in 20,000 B.C. or 10,000-15000 years ago, has nothing to do with human activity but is primarily the consequences of Earth's celestial heat beat - the variations in its orbit around the sun and the obliquity and wobble of its axis. The effects are typically measured in hundreds of thousands or million of years, although some fluctuations occur over much shorter time scales because of decadel variations in solar radiation, periods of greater or lesser volcanic activity and the internal features of the coupled ocean-atmosphere-biosphere system producing, for example, the El Nino and La Nina effects. Changes to the biology of the planet can also influence climate by causing feedback loops, enhancing the magnitude of climatic fluctuations during colder phases.

The climate is determined by the balance between solar energy that arrives at the outer limits of the atmosphere and the proportion that is reflected or re-radiated back to space by clouds, aerosol particles and the Earth's surface, with the amount of snow and ice being particularly important because of their reflective qualities. So called greenhouse gases - mainly carbon dioxide, methane, nitrous oxide and chlorofluorocarbons also play a role by preventing the unimpeded escape of heat from the Earth to space. Of far more immediate concern, is the now irrefutable evidence that human activities are heating up the planet at a rapid rate. This anthropogenic warming could have profound implications for human security and way of life. The reason is that air pollution from industrial emissions, automobile exhausts, the burning of carbon based fuels, changes in land use, agriculture and the large scale destruction of forest cover has resulted in a build up of greenhouse gases in the Earth's atmosphere. These gases have grown significantly in concentrations since the industrial revolution that took place in West, and fully to the point of being destructive of human civilization by the rich industrialized nations before the developing and poor countries came in with their population, and determined will to follow the western path of development.

The reality is that climate change of the order and time frame predicted by climate scientists poses more fundamental questions of human security, survival and the stability of nations, which necessitates judgments about political and strategic risk as well as economic cost. The central problem is the rate at which temperatures are increasing rather than the absolute size of differential warming. Spread over several centuries, or a millennium, temperature rises of several degrees could probably be managed without political instability or major threats to agriculture, commerce and other infrastructures. Compressed within the space of a single century, global warming will prove more vulnerable and far more daunting challenges of human and biological adaptation, especially for natural ecosystems, which typically evolve over hundreds of thousands and million of years. None other than the western political and economic system and the way of life ubiquitously imitated by all and firmly entrenched in fossil fuel technology, faces the greatest challenges for review, when the question of mitigation and adaptation to the climate change crops up.

The disastrous threats posed by climate change are in relation to the development of matter or the objective world outside the man by the application of science and technology. It is the human activities by science and technology on matter or nature seen as lifeless raw materials that disturbed the stability in climate change. This kind of analysis wholly resting on exploitative activities of man on nature for deciphering the caused of climate change is in tune with the current scientific and technological advancement. Going beyond this scientific analysis, the ancient wisdom of the East delineates the indelible impacts of humans' evil nature such as avarice, cruelty, atomic selfishness and other inhuman qualities upon the climate, as these interfere with the operation of God's cosmic laws, which in turn, threatens mankind with its fury. "The vibrations of evil that mankind leaves in the ether upset the normal harmonious balance of the earth. When the earth becomes very heavy with disease and evil, these etheric disturbances cause the world to give way to earthquakes, floods, and other natural disasters."[1] Thus, the advocacy of spiritual resurgence in human beings is considered significant in order to have a review of their inordinate and commodious life style, which has brought in the dangers of climate change to the doorstep.

It is enunciated in Taitariya Upanisad[2] (II, I-3) that first there was space, from space came air, from air came fire, from fire came water, and from water came the earth, then all living beings. So all these elements of creation are found immanent within human beings, the latest and last creation of God. Nature constituted of both living and nonliving is the external manifestation of what is found in microform in human beings. Inextricably correlated and symbiotically related, both nature and human beings seem to be part of the same Universal Self, the creator of the universe. Delineated as such in India philosophy, culture and religion this does not jibe with the mainstream of western thinking which views that both nature and human beings are two separate, disjointed and unconnected categories and extraneously related only when the former is held subordinate, the lifeless other, and solely exists for the purpose of the latter.

The relationship between nature and human beings was shot into prominence only recently when the disastrous impacts of the decline in quality and quantity of the flora and fauna of nature on human beings, their social relationship and political – economic fabric were seriously felt and factorized into explaining many of the political events, crises and conflicts. It was a divagation from what was conventionally held in post Second World War mainstream of International Relation that social events were to be explained by social factors or causes.

Notwithstanding this differentiated view of nature, the very fact that the natural environment shapes human behaviour and political institutions finds acceptability in every age. Natural environment, which was a neglected area of study, has occupied in recent years center stage in national and international politics with literatures proliferating on environmental security and conflict to explain the environmental causes of conflict.

The very analysis of nature as a cause of political outcome can be harked back to Aristotle and Montesquieu. The Greek geographer-Philosopher Strabo during 64 BCE-23 CE believed that geography was destiny, even that particular geographical circumstances conducted to certain political orders. Aristotle famously remarked, in the Politics, on the impact of climate on men's characters and, ultimately, their politics. The ancients were true ecologists, for they assumed a strong organic relationship between environment and society. Long before 'green house effect' came to limelight, let alone having to come to grips with politics, Montesquieu had declared the "empire of climate is the first and greatest empire."

Contrary to what Jean Bodin writing in 1566, said reason as exercised by statesmen could overcome the tyranny of geography, Napoleon Bonaparte stated that "the politics of a state is its geography".[3] Long before the term "geopolitics" was coined by Swedish academic Rudolf Kjellen, political scientists tried to understand nature as a cause of political events. With nature coming back into the arena of political analysis, Political Science returns to its earliest and most basic theories.[4]

Nature as Cause of Social Events

That nature is the cause of social and human events has become the main focus of naturalist theorists, which are though of various types such as cosmic naturalism, analogical naturalism, anthropological naturalism and functional-materialistic naturalism.

Cosmic naturalism believes in cosmic astrology to be the guiding factor of human events. Astrologists locate the cause of human events in astronomical patterns. Here the links between causes and consequences are mysterious and not subject to scientific or empirical investigation.

The analogic naturalism agrees with analogous linkage between the human social processes and natural ones, but does not claim that non-human physical nature is the cause of human outcomes. By borrowing various metaphors, languages, images and models from nature, these theorists try to understand the logic of human social systems. This borrowing has been mutual, for example, Charles Darwin applied" the doctrine of Thomas Malthus... to the whole animal and vegetable kingdoms".[5]

Deudney states "there is no convincing reason to believe that deeply recurrent patterns in non human nature…must serve as a model for human interactions, because human beings differ in so many important ways from other *animals* and all plant life".[6]

Sometimes a close resemblance between human brings and animals is struck. Human beings are endowed with a rare power of discrimination and wisdom without which humans are just like animals. There is no dearth of literature to demonstrate an analogy between human beings and plants. In the Bhagavad-Gita it is said

Urdhvamulam adhahsakham asvattham prahur avyayam'
Chandamisi yasya parnani yas tam veda sa vedavit."

(Chap XV, I)

They (The wise) likened human life to an imperishable Asvattha tree with its root above and branches below. It leaves are the Vedas; he who knows it is the knower of Vedas. Paradoxically, though the ashvattha tree is here referred to as eternal, the word itself in one commonly accepted derivation means that which does not remain tomorrow, from a-svas. The metaphorical ashvattha tree in this sense alludes to the world of transitoriness and its beings, which are ever in the process of change-nothing remaining the same from the present moment to the next.[7]

So allegories and metaphors are derived from plant kingdom to understand the philosophy of human life and unravel the mystery behind the creation. The halo of sacredness that is strewn around the planet kingdom has something to say about that transcendental stage of human life where he/she does not find *any* distinction between human beings, animals and plants and realizes the eternal immanent in them like the life and seed of the ashvattha tree being eternal. In order to make the planet earth worth living in, what this school of thought suggests is to find a symbiotic and organic relationship that exists between human beings, animals and plants and all elements of the creation.

The anthropological naturalist theories discover the causes of human behaviour in intrinsic human nature – factors such as race, intelligence, genetic endowment, and deep psychology.[8] Though such theories have largely disappeared from the domain of international relations and political science, but have strong footholds in other social sciences.

Functional-materialist naturalist theories are very much relevant to the issues of environmental security and conflict. The interaction of human beings with the non-human natural environment results in specific human behaviour and institutions about which these theories provide behavioural social scientific propositions. These theories try to forge a link or bond between specific physical constraints and opportunities provided by nature with alternatives in the performance of very functional tasks of human beings. The very nature and process of human activity towards survival, sustenance or development in the form of organizing society, group and political institutions and human behaviour is very much shaped by the diverse ways in which the differing material environments present themselves to human beings.

It is not only the presentations of specificity of natural environment to human beings, but also the very understanding of the intricacies of nature and its relation with human beings in particular historical and cultural contexts that set the goal, objectives and nature of human activity. As such theories are not exclusively about political outcomes, but encompass sociological, economic and cultural outcomes as well.[9]

The main objectives of these early theories *are* to demonstrate that the natural environment and its resources are independent variables such as climate, soil, water, mineral resources, topography and population to shape patterns of human political life in many important and recurrent ways.

Nature Absent in Social Sciences

In the late nineteenth and early twentieth century and more particularly after the Second World War, the development and researches in the realm of social science witnessed expulsion of nature from their studies. Whereas the naturalist social scientists were wont to explaining human activities and political tendencies in terms of nature as causal variables, the social scientists sought social causes of social outcomes. Thus, the absence of nature in the explanatory analysis of social scientists made the social science denatured. This occurred at a time when Western liberalism, pattern of development, and masculine understandings of power understood the nature as "the other" a repository of lifeless raw materials to be harnessed for the betterment of human beings. But in this pattern of development, cultural hegemony and thinking was expressed a little concern for the natural environment. The speed with which the global environment is deteriorating and catapulting the attention of policy makers to the center stage of reviewing the hegemonic cultural pattern and developmental thinking requires the earliest back of nature into the realm of social sciences. Thus, what was at the earliest a natural social science needs to be appended to the present social- social science.

The proclivity of social scientists to give a short shrift to natural variables in favour of human institutions and historical variables has strengthened after the Second World War. As the sociologist Samuel Klausner has observed, "in part social science has asserted its independence as a discipline by demonstrating the limited explanatory power of physical concepts of human behaviour".[10] The analysis of natural environment as an independent and causal variable is largely absent in the field of international relations, which is defined as a branch of political science. Kenneth Walz finally sealed the ouster of natural environment from the realm of social science as found in his "three images" typology of theories of the causes of war.[11] First image explanations locate the causes of international outcomes, say the cause of war, "in the nature and behaviour of men, wars result from selfishness, from misdirected aggressive impulses, from stupidity."[12] Second image explanations locate causes in the internal structure of the state. Imperialism, for example results from a particular internal economic structure like capitalism; similarly, international peace results from a particular form of government like democracy.[13] In order to explain what the actors will do in international relations, then in addition to looking at the attributes of the actors, we must also look to the constraints that define the strategic settings in which the actors interact. The third image locates causes within the state system.[14]

Marking a departure from the actor centered history and also from the tendency of the present social scientists, some historians like Fernand Braudel, William McNeill, Alfred Crosby and G. Barraclough pronounced in their writings the intimacy of human beings with their environment. As Geoffrey Barraclough observed, "the prevalent tendency is to adopt a broadly materialistic position in the sense that their central theme is man's conflict with his environment."[15] Similarly, depicting a historian's enterprise, Braudel described the mountain as more important than the ruler. His study encompasses the entire material realities of "man in his intimate relationship to the earth, which bears and feeds him."[16]

Nature Deterministic or Puppet?

At one extreme of geopolitical theorists is found a tight and inevitable relation between the material forces and institutional structure. Human beings are held as the puppets of material forces. At the other extreme is Lucian Febvre's concept of possibilism, which emphasized human freedom in responding to material forces.[17] According to this view material forces are of marginal importance in explaining human affairs.

Between the two extremes can be made a middle synthesized view, which holds that natural environment significantly defines the consequences of the choices humans make, but *does* not dictate which choice they desire or pursue. It is also inevitable that they will bear the consequences of not making an appropriate choice. Human institutions are not passive before nature, or the puppets of nature, but it is nature and not humanity that significantly determines whether human actions achieve their goals.

Geopolitical Theory: Role of Climate in Shaping the Fate of Nations

Prior to industrial revolution climate was a prominent topic in geopolitical theory. Hippocrate's Airs, Waters, and Places[18] attested to such a view followed by Aristotle and Montesequieu. In his Politics Aristotle delineates three zones and argues that people in cold northern regions were prone to an excess of spiritedness (thumos) and as a result were ungovernable, but free.[19] At the other extreme, people in the torrid zones of Asia and Africa were prone to an excess of bodily desire (eros). Pursuing wants of the body, Asian and Africa lived in a condition of material sophistication. But the absence of spiritedness made them relatively passive politically, and more willing to accept despotic rule. In Aristotle's view the middle temperate zone is the golden mean between two extremes. The Greeks living in it could enjoy the benefits of material civilization without despotism. Carrying further the arguments, Aristotle stated that the Greeks had a natural prosperity and right to rule over lesser peoples. On the basis of this natural factor, he explained why one group of humans dominated the other groups.[20]

Later on, Montesquieu's views stand just a restatement of what Aristotle had said about the impact of climate upon the temperament of human beings, which in turn affects the type of custom and law of society. Unlike Aristotle, who emphasized the superiority of balanced or middle climatic conditions, Montesquieu argued that colder Northern conditions are most conducive to the advance of civilization. Like Aristotle, Montesquieu linked colder climates with a love of liberty, and argued that warmer climates retard material progress, induces political prosperity and a predisposition towards despotism. Like Aristotle, Montesquieu did not attribute all political outcomes to climate.

This natural social science based on nature as the causes of social outcomes declined giving rise to social science that gave importance to social causes of social outcomes in the 19th century. Few researches like Markham and Huntington continued the Aristotelian tradition and argued that tropical regions of the world are economically and politically retarded relative to the temperate regions because of the enervating effects of humidity and heat.[21]

The above analysis relates to arguments about the deterministic role of climate in shaping the character and destiny of the nation. Nature remained an independent variable or factor to explain political and social behaviour of human beings.

Development in the field of science and technology reduced natural environment to a repository of raw materials to be exploited for the betterment of human beings. Nature no longer remained independent or deterministic rather became a puppet in the hands of the human beings. Today, a country is considered more advanced, progressed or civilized, having highest rates of economic growth, only because it has overexploited the resources of the earth at the expense of other nations, or other peoples, and overtaxed the atmosphere by emitting carbon dioxide more than what other nations put together had done to the atmosphere. Ironically, the polluters in the world today to the utmost are the richest. The pattern of development, life style and consumption as decided by the western people since the day of industrialization and development of science, based on burning of fossil fuels has been responsible for global climate change with disastrous consequences like global warming, sea level rise, ozone hole and other changes upon survivability and existence of not only human beings but of the entire creation. As yet, no other change to the environment has been more challenging to the existing dominant pattern of development, way of life, political and economic thinking than the climate change.

Nature in an Unequal World

Geopolitical theories about the role of environmental factors in shaping the very uneven patterns of economic and political development during the emergence of global system remain relevant. Emergence of Europe over the last half millennium as the dominant *power* in world history has been the most far-reaching development. Through its network of trade, exchange and interaction on a worldwide scale Europe occupied almost all the earth. With the end of colonialism, the European dominance ended, but a "great rift" between the North and South continues to be one of the salient features of the world politics.[22]

According to Deudney, three clusters of arguments can be launched to explain the disparity and great hiatus between the North and South. Out of these, two arguments are both social-social scientific in the sense that these put emphasis on social causes for explaining social outcomes. The third one is geopolitical. External social systemic explanations based on Marxism and World-system theory argue that North's progress is based on explanations and plundering of the rest of the world. Most arguments on the "development of underdevelopment" emphasize that the source of South's impoverishment is external and located in the logic of a world system of capitalism and imperialism dominated by the North.[23] The internationalist social systemic theories argue that domestic institutional and cultural factors, market institutions and incentives, cultural disposition towards work and savings are of crucial importance for development.

These two clusters of arguments do not give credence to the geopolitical theory that nature is important. Pushed to the marginal status by the decay of geopolitics in Political Science, the third clusters of arguments hold that the great difference in the pattern of development and economic growth can be explained as the product of ecological and climatic factors.

The environmental degradation in all sectors of nature with its disastrous impact on existence and survival of the living beings on earth has again brought to fore the importance of ecological factor in political analysis. What was once neglected and given a low status comes to be considered important in view of the fact that the environmental degradation due to human activities has come in challenging the conventionally understood political theories and ideas on security, development and political organization etc. The social science's ascent on social causes of social outcomes needs to be supplemented by returning to the natural-social science approach. The impact of natural environment and human – nature interactions remain the basis on which such a journey back to the geopolitical traditions should take place. That does not mean that natural environment is always independent of social practice, but a rethinking of the role of nature in social practice and human evolution needs to take place. In the words of Deudney, "unfortunately, the recent turn of social theory away from structuralism to an emphasis on the socially constructed nature of reality, while offering many insights and correctives to mechanistic structural arguments could exacerbate the incapacity of social science to deal with environmental issues."[24] It is western view of life, political and economic constructions that have perceived nature in a particular way and accordingly being acted upon for its social purpose. Such a social construction of nature has been at the root of the environmental crisis afflicting the entire globe. So such a particularistic perception and construction of nature and weaved into its political and economic design has been universalized and hegemonic at the cost of other's perception and construction. Social science theories guided by this particularistic turned universalistic logic and arguments in their social construction of nature and weaving into their overall socio-politico design *have* been impervious to the other aspects of the diversely enriched human life, as well to the beauty and bounty of nature. "Social constructions inevitably shape how nature is perceived and acted upon, but nature itself is not socially constructed, and any social science that assumes so will inevitably be blind to important aspects of human life. Nature constitutes a structuring reality for human beings that is not socially constructed."[25]

The relationship between nature and civilization harks back to the day the creation came into being on this .earth. But the arrogance with which the human beings- the dominant creature of the universe - wreak havoc on its nature is a very recent phenomena and started with industrial age. Rachel Carson's controversial 1962 bestseller "Silent Spring" highlighting the impact of pesticides on human health and her moral outrage at the rapacious behaviour of Homo sapiens could foresee a revolutionary change in the manner in which the relationship between nature and civilization would henceforth be perceived. No longer could nature be regarded as simply a compendium of lifeless raw materials- "the other" - to be endlessly transformed by human ingenuity and labour into commensurable commodities. The relationship was more complex and beyond the mechanical portrayal of the Newtonian age. Succinctly put, the environmental life support system upon which all life depends is being depleted and degraded by human actions- at stake is the future of humankind.

The scientific world during 16th and 17th century through its enormous discoveries and inventions promised the human beings the heavenly city to be brought down to the earthly city by inclining humans to materialistic aggrandizement, goods driven pleasures, exorbitant consumptions, inordinate life style. In its endeavour it partly succeeded but failed in that it became unwittingly an accomplice in the hands of human beings in destroying the nature. The faith of the science in ingenuity of human beings to create a heavenly city on earth came to be reviewed with its being not able to find alternative or other roads to what so far has been defined as development. In the early euphoric ambience of industrial revolution and march of science, could not be heard the murmurs, protestations and concerns about the deleterious impact of industrial pollution, and fears of scarcity-induced conflict and misery. Even the environmentalist Lester Brown's arguments for a redefinition of national security in 1977 and six years later Richard William's support to this initiative created little interests *among* the students of world politics. These voices for a second look were silent springs but could not be washed away completely by turbulent waters of the imperatives of cold war. Environmental issues were placed squarely on the agenda of world politics at the United Nations Conference on the Environment held in Stockholm in 1972. Through the creation of the United Nations Environment Programme at this conference, an officially recognized institutional setting was accorded to environmental issue. Public concern about the immediate and cumulative effects of environmental change compelling state officials to take environmental issues seriously reached its crescendo when Brundtland Commission released its report, "Our Common Future" in 1987, established by the United Nations General Assembly. The findings of the report caught the immediate attention of the policymakers because its redefinition of development was designed to meet the needs of the present without compromising the ability of future generations to meet their own needs. By the late 1980s and early 1990s, environmental security became a broad movement Numerous environmental advocates including Michael, Renner, Jesica Tuchman Mathews, Norman Myers and Gwyn Prins wrote in favour of redefining national security to encompass resources and environmental threats. Homer Dixon and others brought out a link between environmental degradation and conflict. With the end of cold war, the environmental movement got prominence and moved into the political mainstream and gained legitimacy in the academic world.

Arguments about climate as an important cause of cultural, social, economic and political life took a downslide as natural history gave way to modern social- social science in the nineteenth century. But there are a very few exceptional scholars who tried to continue these arguments. Climate found a prominent place in Arnold Toynbee's elaborate theory of civilization and history. These theories of climate determinism have tried to connect variations in climate with variations in human behaviour by the intervening variable of energy. Markham[26] and Huntington[27] argue that tropical regions of the world are economically and politically retarded relative to the temperate regions because of the enervating effects of humidity and heat. To anyone from a temperate climate who has spent time in the tropics, this theory has intuitive appeal, and has been supported by studies of physiology and behaviour. But as comprehensive explanation for relative levels of civilizations, Huntington's theories have been severely criticized and discredited in the field of geography[28].

A major theme of twentieth- century theoreticians of climate geopolitics is that the development of man made techniques of microclimatic control such as space heating and air conditioning expand the areas of Earth's surface habitable by energetic peoples. S. F. Markham argues that the expansion of civilization into the northern parts of the temperate zone resulted from the development of coal as a source of energy. So the Western pattern of development premised on fossil fuel technology is the culmination of the use of coal and other fossil fuels as a principal source of energy. In the present century more particularly during the last two decades the consequences of this kind of development on climate change in terms of global warming, sea level rise, ozone layer depletion and weather pattern are seriously felt. The more advanced a country is in terms of industrialization, the more it happens to be the polluter of the atmosphere through emission of Carbon Dioxide and other greenhouse Gases. The industrialized countries of the North home to 25% populations of the world have usurped 75% of the atmosphere at the cost of the majority 75% populations of the world and driving them to the brink. The devastating consequences of the climate change as found in IPCC reports in terms of survival of species, agricultural decline, decline in food productions, health hazards and other effects on humanity put the greatest challenges to the established frame of mind about human security, development and state structures and way of life.

This book is an endeavour in the direction of the putting the challenges; the environmental crisis more importantly climate change. In stead of confining itself to the periphery of the crisis, diagnosing the symptoms it goes deep into the crisis and strikes at the very root to start building anew the conventionally understood theories with insights and thoughts derived from time immemorial civilized values and ethics. It calls for a review of the core western centric and liberal assumptions upon which the normative structure of the contemporary international society is based. A moral and ethical reconstruction of society and human beings is emphasized upon in their awareness of the transcendental that unites all the animate and inanimate, the present and future, with the bond of divine. It carries human beings beyond the standardized normative structure of western determined global market society and its values. It questions the very conception of the world as a complex of phenomena controlled by certain scientifically identifiable laws. The solution to the climate change, it does not seek in some technical tricks but in the ethical resurgence of human beings with a transcendental vision and wisdom.

This book delineates the politics of climate change and its challenges to the sovereign state system, established economic and political thinking, and way of life. It shows how the present climate change talks, negotiations and treaties remain ineffective before the adamancy of the United States. Unless and until the western concept of development based on burning fossil fuels, pattern of life and consumption style gets reviewed; all hopes and aspiration of humanity fixed on a treaty will remain chimerical.

References

1. Paramahansa Yogananda, The Divine Ronance, (New Delhi: Oxford and IBH Publishing Co., Pvt. Ltd., First Indian Print 1992), p. 61.
2. Eight Upanisads Vol. I translated by Swami Gambhirananda (Calcutta: Advaita Ashrama, 1998), fourth edition, pp. 323-25.
3. Quoted in Adam Garfinkle, Geopolitics: Middle Eastern Notes and Anticipations, ORBIS Vol. 47, No. 2, Spring 2003, p. 264.
4. *Ibid.*
5. Charles Darwin, The Origin of Species (Original 1859), (New York: Oxford University Press, 1979).
6. Daniel H. Deudney, "Bringing Nature Back in: Geopolitical Theory from the Greeks to the Global Era," in Daniel H. Deudney and Richard A. Matthew ed., Contested Grounds (Albany: State University of New York Press, 1999), p. 28.
7. Sri Sri Paramahansa Yogananda, God Talks With Arjuna, The Bhagavad Gita: Royal Science of God realization Vol. II, Kolkata: Yogada Satsanga Society of India, 2002), p. 927.
8. Melvin Konner, The Tangled Wing: Biological Constraints on the Human Spirit (New York: Harper and Row, 1982); Mary Midgley, Beast and Man: The Roots of Human Nature (Ithaca, N.Y.: Cornell University Press, 1978).

9. Marvin Harris, Cultural Materialism: The Struggle for a Science of Culture (New York: Random House, 1979); and Martin F. Murphy and Maxine L. Margolis, eds., Science, Materialism, and the Study of Culture (Gainescille University Press of Florida, 1995).
10. Samuel Z. Klausner, "Social Science and Environmental Quality", The Annals, of the American Academy of Political and Social Science Vol.389, May 1970, p. 4.
11. Kenneth Waltz, Man, the State and War (New York: Columbia University Press, 1959).
12. *Ibid.,* p. 16.
13. *Ibid.,* pp. 80-164.
14. *Ibid.,* p. 12.
15. Geoffrey Barraclough, Main Trends in History (expanded and updated by Michael Burns) (London: Holmes & Meier, 1991), p. 158.
16. Fernand Braudel, On History, trans, Sarah Matthews (Chicago: University of Chicago Press, 1980), p. 185.
17. Lucian Febvre, A Geographical Introduction to History (London: Kegan, Paul, 1925).
18. Hippocrates, "Airs, Waters and Places", in G.E.R. Lloyd ed, Hippocratic Writings (London: Penguin, 1978).
19. Aristotle, The Politics. Barker ed., (Oxford: Oxford University Press, 1948), Paragraph 1327, p. 298.
20. See David Livingstone, The Geographical Tradition (Oxford: Blackwell, 1993), pp. 1-32, 216-59; and David Arnold, The Problem of Nature: Environment, Culture and European Expansion (Oxford: Blackwell, 1996)
21. Ellsworth Huntington, Civilization and Climate (New Haven, Conn.: Yale University Press, 1915); Ellsworth Huntington, The Mainsprings of Civilization (New York: John Wiley and Sons, 1945).
22. L.S. Stavrianos, Global Rift (New York: Morrow, 1981).
23. See Thomas Richard Shannon, An Introduction to the World System Perspective (Boulder, Colo.: Westview Press, 1989).
24. Daniel H. Deudney, "Bringing Nature Back in Geopolitical Theory from the Greeks to the Global Era", *op. cit.,* p. 50.
25. *Ibid.*
26. Ellsworth Huntington, Civilization and Climate (New Haven, Conn.: Yale University Press, 1915); Ellsworth Huntington, The Mainsprings of Civilization (New York: John Wiley and Sons, 1945).
27. F.S. Markham, Climate and the Energy of Nations (London: Oxford University Press, 1947).
28. Stephen Visher, " Ellsworth Huntington: Human Ecologist", Journal of Human Ecology, Vol. 2, 1952, pp. 1-27.

2

Greenhouse Gases and Climate Change

The Earth's Atmosphere

Air surrounds the Earth and extends as far as 1600 kilometers above the surface. This air is called the atmosphere. Nitrogen makes up about 78 percent of the atmosphere and oxygen makes up about 21 percent. The remaining one percent consists mainly of Argon and small amount of other gases such as Carbon Dioxide and trace amounts of Hydrogen, Ozone, Methane, Carbon monoxide, Helium, Neon, Krypton and Zenon. Air also contains water vapor and particles of dust. The air gets thinner the farther it is from the Earth. About 1600 Kilometers above the Earth the atmosphere gradually fades into space. The atmosphere is made up three layers.

The troposphere is the lowest layer extending to about 17 kms. above the Earth's surface. It contains most of the planet's air and is where greenhouse effect takes place. Windstorms, most clouds and weather features all take place in the troposphere. The stratosphere extends from about 17 km. to about 50 km above the Earth's surface. The upper most part of this layer contains the Ozone layer. The thermosphere is the upper most layer of the Earth's atmosphere and extends from about 50 km. to 64 km. above the Earth's surface.

Energy from the sun mainly in the form of visible light drives the Earth's weather and climate, and heats the Earth's surface. In turn Earth radiates energy in the form of infrared radiation (thermal radiation) back into space. "greenhouse Gases" in the troposphere such as water vapor, Carbon Dioxide, Ozone, Methane, and Nitrous Oxide, block some of the infrared radiation from escaping into space. This heat trapping ability of the atmosphere is called the greenhouse effect. Without this natural greenhouse effect temperature would be much lower than they are now and life on Earth as we know it today would not have been possible. Without greenhouse effect the average of the Earth's temperature would be 18°C instead of its hospitable 15°C.

Emission of Carbon Dioxide, Methane and certain other gases intensifies the greenhouse effect of the atmosphere and thus causes long-term climate change primarily a rise in temperature. Some of the gases in the Earth's atmosphere more particularly water vapor and Carbon Dioxide *have* an ability to absorb infrared radiation (heat). They do not prevent sun light from reaching the Earth's surface and warming it, but they do trap some of the infrared radiation emitted back into the space by the Earth. In other words they work in roughly the same ways, as the glass in a greenhouse. The surface of the planet would be utmost 35°C colder than it is now. Greenhouse gases have always been present in the atmosphere but now concentrations of several of them are rising as a result of human activities intensifying the greenhouse effect[1].

The Earth's climate system depends on the planet's receiving and disposing of energy from the sun. The Earth's surface receives all energy originating from the sun except for a small fraction of heat from its inner core. The Earth receives only about one/ two billions of the energy emitted by the sun that heats the Earth, drives the ocean and creates the weather patterns[2].

Greenhouse Gases (GHGs) are those gases, which retain a part of the sun's energy reflected back from the Earth's surface in the Earth's atmosphere. This effect along with energy absorbed by the Earth's surface affect the long-term energy balance of the Earth and its atmosphere, which fundamentally controls the Earth climate. Incoming radiation from the sun mainly in the form of visible light is absorbed at the Earth's surface and in the atmosphere above and on average absorbed radiation is balanced by the amount of energy returned to the space in the form of infrared "heat" radiation. The greenhouse gases trap some heat in the lower part of the Earth's surface and water vapor and Carbon Dioxide as well as cloud and small particles called aerosols[3].

Many chemical compounds found in the Earth's atmosphere act as "greenhouse gases". These gases allow sunlight to enter the atmosphere freely, when the sunlight strikes the Earth surface some of it is reflected back towards space as infrared radiation (heat), greenhouse gases absorb this infrared radiation and trap the heat in the atmosphere. Overtime the amount of energy sent from the sun to the Earth should be about the same of the amount of energy radiated back into space leaving the temperature of the Earth's surface roughly constant[4].

Earth's atmosphere is composed of many different gases, three of which make up about 99-95% of the atmosphere nitrogen (78.08%) oxygen (20.95%) and argon (0.92%). However, it is the gases that comprise the other 0.05% of the atmosphere (often called "trace" gases) that have concerned scientists. Two trace gases in particular Carbon Dioxide and Methane have very important attributes. While being virtually transparent to the shorter wavelengths of energy received from the sun, these gases readily absorb the longer wavelengths of energy given off by the Earth. Thus, a portion of the energy from the Earth that would normally be released to space is absorbed by these trace gases and is then transmitted back towards the Earth. Therefore these trace gases have been termed "greenhouse gases". That is they allow the sunlight but they prevent much of the energy from radiating back through[5].

The greenhouse effect is one of the major areas of concern to the world and it certainly will have a significant effect on much of planets resources relating to the biodiversity, water forests, land and of course the oceans. A greenhouse acts as a heat trap when a portion of the sun's heat coming in through its glass walls is prevented from escaping out side and results in the temperature inside the glass house to be higher than what it is outside. The greenhouse effect then gets its name because of a similar phenomena occurring on a global scale. A number of gases on the Earth's atmosphere like the glasses in a greenhouse let solar radiation pass to the surface of the Earth, while trapping infraradiation that is remitted from the surface of the Earth. The trapping of the infraradiation that would have otherwise escaped to space results in increased global temperature, and is referred to as the greenhouse effect.[6]

Without any disputation there is scientific consensus over the fact that certain gases cause so called "greenhouse effect" on the Earths surface and the lower atmosphere. Basically these gases, which are generally called greenhouse gases, do not have much if any influence in the incoming short wave radiation it passes through the Earth's atmosphere.[7] Scientists know from actual measurements that the amount of solar energy absorbed by Earth is in close balance with the amount of energy radiated back into space as infrared. Some of the radiation is being trapped in the atmosphere before it is reradiated back to space. It is fairly easy to measure how much solar heat energy the various greenhouse gases absorb and what parts of the spectrum they do or do not absorb. Absorption of infrared by the greenhouse gases is adequate to explain the heat trapping effects given that the reality of the "natural" greenhouse effect is well established. It is logical to conclude that increase in atmospheric concentrations of greenhouse gases will cause an increase in greenhouse warming.

The Earth absorbs light from the sun and most of the heat is then radiated back to the space. Gases as ozone and small percentage of

Carbon Dioxide create a shield which trap some of the heat and keeps the Earth warm without these umbrella cover made of the ozone, the planet would be lifeless and freeze with an average surface temperature of 20°C. The ozone shield is like a glass roof in a greenhouse which has indoor planets, pollutants particularly gases such as Methane, Chlorofluorocarbons, Sulphur Dioxide that come out of factory chimneys cause pollution gases and less heat escapes through the atmosphere because of the build of the these gases[8].

Infrared (IR) active gases principally water vapor (H_2O), Carbon Dioxide (CO_2) and Ozone (O_3) naturally present in the Earth's atmosphere absorb thermal IR radiation emitted by the Earth's surface and atmosphere. The atmosphere is warmed by this mechanism and invites its IR radiation with a significant portion of this energy acting to warm the surface and the lower atmosphere. As a consequence, the average surface air temperature of the Earth is about 30°C higher than it would be without atmospheric absorption and reradiation of IR energy. This phenomenon is popularly known as the "greenhouse effect" and the IR active gases responsible for the effect are likewise referred to as "greenhouse gases". The rapid increase in the concentration of greenhouse gases since the industrial period began, has given rise to concern over potential resultant climate changes[9].

Climate change is a change in the "average weather" that a given region experiences. Average weather includes all the features associated with the weather such as temperature, wind patterns and precipitation, greenhouse gases including Carbon Dioxide, Methane, water vapor and Nitrous Oxide. They appear naturally but are also made through industrial process. CFCs are another form of greenhouse gases but are only produced in industrial processes. greenhouse gases allow radiation from the sun to pass through the atmosphere of Earth. The Earth absorbs the radiation then reflects it back. But in doing so, the wavelength of the radiation is changed. When this outgoing radiation meets particles of a greenhouse gas, the radiation is absorbed by the particles. This makes the particles wobble and stretch and when shiver that motion warms up the greenhouse gas. So on a large scale all the greenhouse gases around the Earth form a warm blanket around the planet raising global temperatures. This is known as greenhouse effect. These greenhouse gases absorb some of the sun's energy, warming the atmosphere near the Earth's surface. This keeps the Earth warm enough to support life. But the scientists believe that increased emission of greenhouse gases is causing too much energy to be trapped, increasing global temperature.[10]

The atmosphere around the Earth is made up gases. Some of these gases functions like the panes of a greenhouse. They let some radiation from the sun in but also retain heat in the atmosphere, that is they do not let all radiation back out. As a result of this natural effect, it is warmer on Earth than it would be without these heat trapping gases. Human contribution of certain gases to the atmosphere has increased this greenhouse effect[11]. The concentration of Carbon Dioxide, with Methane and Nitrous Oxide allows sunrays (short wave length) to enter the atmosphere and reach the surface of the Earth but prohibit the heat radiation from the Earth (Long wave length) to escape thus, leading to an increase in global temperature within a century. The planet has already been warmed by 0.8 to 2.5°C and going to be hotter by 3 to 5°C within the next century[12].

The principal greenhouse gases comprise Carbon Dioxide (CO_2), Water vapor (H_2O), Methane (CH_4), Nitrous Oxide (N_2O) and Chlorofluorocarbons (CFCs). All of these gases except for the CFCS are natural constituents of the atmosphere that is a vital greenhouse effect. This naturally occurring greenhouse keeps Earth's surface and lower atmosphere constant without which human life on the Earth would be horrible. The climate of the Earth is constantly changing. Changes in the past have been attributed to natural changes though at the current time the term climate change refers to changes in the climate as a result of human behaviour. Climate change and greenhouse effect are inextricably linked. The greenhouse effect is also a natural process without which life on Earth could not be sustained. The problem occurs when excess greenhouse gases which are produced by human activity trap outgoing radiation. This results in the Earth warming more than it would naturally leading to a variety of problems including flash floods and droughts[13]. The sun, which has a temperature of approximately 11000°F, emits its energy in short wave lengths (wave lengths that can easily penetrate the Earth's atmosphere). The Earth absorbs this energy, warm up and then releases this energy. One of the primary mechanisms for releasing this energy is through radiation in wavelengths that are relatively low compared to those of the sun. If the Earth did not release this energy the Earth surface would become very hot and would be unable to support life[14].

Over the last twenty years concern has been hovering on the fact that concentration of certain trace gases in the atmosphere are gradually increasing and may lead to a warming of the Earth's surface and to drastic climatic changes. The enhanced greenhouse effect is the result of increases of the GHGs in the atmosphere. A number of gases in the Earth's atmosphere like the glass in a greenhouse let solar radiation pass to the surface of the Earth. It is due to excessive use of chemicals like Feron (CCl_2F_2) and burning of fossil fuels excessive build up of CO_2 takes place in the atmosphere, which allows less and less heat escape through the atmosphere. This causes the temperature of the Earth to rise. Thus, the shield has the same effect of the glass in a greenhouse. The prediction that the greenhouse effect which keeps the Earth warm would one day get out of control.

The concentrations of greenhouse gases in the atmosphere have been steadily increasing since the industrial revolution almost 250 years ago. The greenhouse effect is neither new nor necessarily bad. In fact it is observed that without greenhouse effect, life as we know it would probably not exist on the Earth. The levels of trace gases in the atmosphere have been increasing rapidly over the past century paralleling the rapid growth of industrialization and urbanization. The primary source of the increased level of Carbon Dioxide in the atmosphere can be found in the burning of fossil fuels such as coal, oil and natural gases. However, the regional decline of boreal and tropical forests is also important because there areas that once removed Carbon Dioxide from the atmosphere are now a source of Carbon Dioxide as they are cut down and burned. The increased level of Methane in the atmosphere comes from a variety of sources, which include rice, paddies (rice is the most abundant crop world wide), the digestive tracks of bovine and termites produce a long lasting haze of sulfuric acid droplets. Owing to the rise in atmospheric Carbon Dioxide caused by modern industrial societies with their excessive and intensive combustion of fossil fuels (coal, oil and natural gases) the greenhouse effect on Earth may be intensified and long-term climatic changes may result. An increase in atmospheric concentrations of other trace gases such as Chlorofluorocarbons (Ferons, Nitrous Oxide and Methane) due again largely to human activity may also aggravate greenhouse conditions. The first of these gases receiving attention was CO_2 and latter three were brought into the scientific debate in the mid 1970s. All of these gases except for CFCs are natural constituents of the atmosphere that is there is a natural greenhouse effect. These naturally occurring greenhouse gases keep the Earth's surface and lower atmosphere about 33°C warmer than it would be without them. Without the natural greenhouse effect the surface of the Earth would be inhospitable. The CO_2 level in the atmosphere has been steadily increasing from about 280 ppmv (parts per million lay volume) in the preindustrial period to about 335 ppmv in 1992. The concentration of CH_4 increased from 700ppbv to 1714 ppbv over the same time span.

There is no denial of the fact that human activities are responsible to add more and more gases to the atmosphere. All most all greenhouse gases reached their highest recorded levels in the 1990s and continue to increase. Atmospheric Carbon Dioxide (CO_2) and Methane (CH_4) have varied substantially during glacial and interglacial periods over the past 42,000 years but even the longest of these values are much less than their current atmospheric concentrations. In terms of radiative forcing by greenhouse gases emitted through human activities, CO_2 and CH_4 are the 1st and 2nd most important gases respectively. From the year 1750 to 2000 the concentration of CO_2 increased by 31$\pm$4% and that of CH_4 raise by 15$\pm$25%. These rates of increase are unprecedented in climatic system. As fossil fuels in the form of oil gas and coal are burned, more than 6 billion tons of carbons are released into the atmosphere raising the concentration of Carbon Dioxide in the atmosphere. Throughout the 1990s, consequences correlated with rising temperatures such as heat waves, storms, ice melting, and rising sea level-have been observed. Other human activities such as deforestation and coal burning, the excessive use of gasoline, and emissions from transport vehicles and engines generally contribute to the primary source of carbon emission. However, the increase in greenhouse gas emissions (particularly Carbon Dioxide associated with fossil fuel burning) coupled with deforestation which destroy natural carbon sinks that absorb Carbon Dioxide, increases the amount of heat trapped within the atmosphere and the Earth's temperature[17].

Since the beginning of the industrial revolution there has been an increase in the industrial Chlorofluorocarbons (CFCs) followed by CH_4, Tropospheric Ozone and N_2O resulting in climate change in radioactive forcing of the gases. The observed increase of CO_2 in the atmosphere from about 280 ppmv in the pre-industrial era, to about 364 ppmv in 1997 has come largely from fossil fuel combustion and cement production. Elevation of concentrations *is* predicted to persist in the atmosphere for times ranging from thousand of years. The increased atmospheric level of these gases especially CO_2 increases the IR energy observed by the atmosphere, there by producing a warming influence at the Earth's surface. Changes in the climate system that are confidently predicted in response to increase in the greenhouse gases include increases in mean surface air temperature, increases in the global mean rates of precipitation and evaporation, rising sea level and changes in biosphere. Substantial uncertainties remain in magnitude and about geographical distribution of these changes and in the rates at which they may be expected to occur[18].

Not all scientists agree on the extent of human influence on climate. Studies are generally based on computer models and the Earth's climate is notoriously complicated to predict. However a study by UK researches held in 2001, compared recent satellite readings with data from 27 years ago and found that less radiation is now escaping into space. This suggests that the greenhouse effect has increased, at a rate in line with rising greenhouse gas production. Even if human activities are increasing the greenhouse effect, global climate change might not be entirely their fault. Some scientists suggest that changes in the solar wind (electrically charged particles coming from the sun) might affect the Earth's cloud cover, increasing global temperatures. This would have a stronger effect on global temperatures than greenhouse gas emissions[19]. It is an established fact that human activities are responsible to add more and more gases to the atmosphere. The concentration of CO_2 in the atmosphere increases due to the combustion of fossil fuels, deforestation, desertification and agriculture. Methane (CH_4) is caused by rice paddies, cattle rearing, animal burning, coal mining, ventilation of natural gas landfill, and world fuel use etc. Agriculture, fossil fuel combustion, and use of catalytic converters in the car increase N_2O in the atmosphere. The highly industrialized countries are mainly responsible to add CFCs to the atmosphere used in a wide range of products such as insulations, air conditioning and solvents. These gases are known to deplete the ozone layer in the stratosphere and in addition to acting as a greenhouse gas[20].

The prediction of climate change due to human activities began with a prediction made by the Swedish Chemist, Svante Arrhemins in 1896. Arrhemins took note of the Industrial revolution then getting under way and realized that the amount of Carbon Dioxide being released into the atmosphere was increasing. Moreover he believed Carbon Dioxide concentrations would continue as the world's consumption of fossil fuels particularly coal increased ever more rapidly. His understanding of the role of the Carbon Dioxide in heating Earth, even at that early date led him to predict that if atmospheric Carbon Dioxide doubled, Earth would become several degree warmer. An enhanced greenhouse effect refers to the possible rising of mean temperature of the Earth's surface above that occurring due to natural greenhouse effect. An increase in the concentrations of greenhouse gases in the atmosphere due to human activities has resulted in global warming, which in turn has brought about deleterious changes in climate for example, changes in precipitation, storm patterns, and the level of oceans. Nearly 100 years after the Arrhenins' prediction, Carbon Dioxide in the atmosphere is increasing with the likelihood that it will double by the middle of the next century from the levels at the time of Arrhenins. Post world war -II industrialization has caused a dramatic jump in the amount of Carbon Dioxide in the atmosphere[21]. According to National Academy of Sciences, the Earth's surface temperature has risen by one degree Fahrenheit in the past century with accelerated warming during the past two decades. There is new and strong evidence that most of the warming over the last 50 year is attributable to human activities. Human activities have altered the chemical position of the atmosphere, through the building of greenhouse gases, primarily Carbon Dioxide, Methane and Nitrous Oxide. The heat trapping property of these gases is undisputed although uncertainties exist about exactly how Earth climate responds to them[22].

Table 2.1. A Summary of the key greenhouse Gases Affected by Human Activities

	CO_2	CH_4	N_2O	CFc-12,	HCFc-22	CF_4
Pre-industrial concentration.	280	700	275	0-	0-	0-
Concentration in1992	335	1714	311	503	105	70
Recent rate of concentration change	1.5 ppmv/yr	1.3 ppbv/yr	0.75 ppbv/yr	18.20 pptv/yr	7-8 pptv/yr	11-13 pptv/yr
Per year (over 1980s)	0.4%/yr	0.8%/yr	0.25%/yr	4%/yr	7%/yr	2%/yr
Atmospheric life time (years)	(50-200)	(12-17)	120	102	13.3	50000

The table 2.1 shows that the estimates made by the IPCC in 1994 half indicate that more than life of the increased radiative forces was from CO_2, from the subsequent findings CO_2 has made the largest individual contribution to increased radiative forcing while CH_4 and CFCs have contributed equal but smaller amount[23].

The greenhouse gases, water vapor, Carbon Dioxide and other gases trap some of the out going energy retaining heat some what like the panes of a greenhouse, without this natural greenhouse effect temperature would be much lower then they are now and life as known today would not be possible. Instead, thanks to greenhouse gases, the Earth average temperature is a more hospitable 60°F. However problem may arise when the atmospheric concentration of greenhouse gases increases. However, the increase in greenhouse gas emissions particularly Carbon Dioxide associated with fossil fuel burning, coupled with deforestation which destroys natural carbon sinks that absorb Carbon Dioxide, increases the amount of heat trapped within the atmosphere and the Earth's temperature. After the industrial revolution, the greenhouse effect increased due to anthropogenic activities. Ice cores indicate significant increase in the concentration of radiatively active gases such as Carbon Dioxide (CO_2), Methane (CH_4) and Nitrous Oxide (N_2O). Of these gases it is believed that CO_2 has greatest radiative effect followed by the CFCs, CH_4, tropospheric Ozone and N_2O[24]. Although 96% of the Carbon Dioxide (CO_2) is released by the natural source, rest 4% result from human activities. Still the inputs of CO_2 from human activities affect the balance. The main human activities that affect the sources and sinks of CO_2 are fossil fuel combustion and change in land use such as deforestation. A part of these increases has been due to increased use of fossil fuels namely coal, oil and natural gases, which constitute a major part of the energy base that have fuelled the industrial and post industrial revolution since 1950. The greatest share of fossil fuel emissions is attributed to the industrialized countries with a small portion coming from the developing countries[25].

Enhancement of greenhouse effect resulted in an increasingly high atmospheric concentration of Carbon Dioxide in the atmosphere. Carbon Dioxide is released whenever organic materials (which contains carbon) are burnt but as long as wood was the main fuel, human beings had little impacts on the amount of this gas in the atmosphere. Carbon Dioxide that escapes unto the air when wood and other "fresh fuels" like bio-fuels are burnt, will sooner or latter be absorbed by new vegetation. However, when human beings began to use fossil fuels, they disturbed the natural cycling of carbon between plants and the atmosphere. Over the last century human beings have extracted and burnt a significant portion of the oil, coal and gas stored in the rocks beneath the Earth's surface. These fuels are derived from the remains of the plants and animals that lived a long time ago. The plants living today are unable to bind more than a small fraction of the current surplus Carbon Dioxide. Indeed owing to widespread deforestation and densely populated parts of the world, less Carbon Dioxide is being taken up by vegetation than might otherwise have been the case. Emissions coupled with forest destruction have left the atmosphere with a Carbon Dioxide concentration about 30% higher than that of pre- industrial times (around 200 years ago) and every year the level rises by 0.4%. Virtually the same trend can be observed globally. Since the Carbon Dioxide has a long lifetime in the atmosphere, it spreads all over the world regardless of where it is emitted to the atmosphere[26]

Methane is produced from rice paddies, cattle rearing, bio mass burning, coal mining, ventilation of natural gases, landfill deforestation, wood fuel use. Nitrous Oxide increases from agriculture, fossil fuel combustion, and use of catalytic converters in cars. CFCs - Chlorofluorocarbons are produced from a wide range of products such as insulation, air conditioning and solvents. The phase out of CFCs is regulated by the Montreal protocol and its successive amendments as a result of their calculated role in the destruction of atmospheric ozone[27].

These sources amounted to approximately 6.5PGc/yr. (1pg = 1015g) in 1996. These anthropogenic CO_2 exceed the estimated uptake of CO_2 by the atmosphere and oceans implying a significant but as yet unidentified terrestrial sink. The atmospheric concentration of Methane (CH_4) increased from about 700ppbv in pre-industrial times to about 1721ppbv in 1994. Fossil fuel related sources of CH_4 amount to approximately 70-120 TG. CH_4/Yr.(1Tg=1012). Increases in CH_4 sources resulting from ice cultivation; animal husbandry, biomass burning and landfills contribute about 200-350 TG CH_4/yr. The atmospheric concentration of N_2O has increased from about 275ppbv in pre-industrial times to about 312ppbv in 1994. Estimated anthropogenic emissions of N_2O for the 1980s range from 3 to 8 TGN/Yr. The main anthropogenic sources are from agriculture and industrial sources including adipic and Nitric acid production. Chlorofluorocarbons CFC - 12 and CFC-11 are man made compounds that were appreciably present in the atmosphere before 1950. These compounds have been widely used as refrigerants and in spray propellants and foam blowing. Because of their role in catalyzing decomposition of stratospheric ozone, production of these compounds has plummeted dramatically in response to Montreal protocol and subsequent international agreements. Atmospheric concentrations of these compounds are expected to diminish substantially during the next century. Prediction of future resistance of anthropogenic greenhouse gases in the atmosphere is based on mathematical models that stimulate future additions and removals. The greenhouse gas concentrations predicted by these models are subject to large uncertainties in the effects of both natural process and human activities[28]. Future emissions of greenhouse gases are unknown. Taking many different views of the future into account, it is clear that the range of possibilities for future greenhouse gas emissions is very wide. In fact uncertainties surrounding the future growth of greenhouse gas emission are a major contributor to the uncertainty-surrounding estimate of future levels of greenhouse gases in the atmosphere and hence future global warming. From the point of view of the climate scientist, the emission of greenhouse gases is not as important as the concentrations of the greenhouse gases in the atmosphere. Since greenhouse gases are responsible for keeping the planet warmer than it would be without them, it is reasonable to expect them that any addition to the level of greenhouse gases in the atmosphere would cause the planet to warm[29].

Apart from Carbon Dioxide other greenhouse gases are being emitted in large quantities now than in pre industrial times. The amount of ozone forming in the lower atmosphere has increased as a result of emission of Nitrogen oxides, hydrocarbons and carbon monoxide. Further, intensification of the greenhouse effect is being caused by newly made greenhouse gases entering the atmosphere. These includes in particular a number of substances containing fluorine, among them HFCs (compounds of hydrogen, fluorine and carbons) HFCs are now being used instead of CFCs (Ferons) in refrigerators and other applications and their use is on the increase. Compared with Carbon Dioxide all other greenhouse gases occur in very low concentrations. Per molecule however, these substances are much more effective as greenhouse gases than Carbon Dioxide, which means that they still make an appreciable contribution to the greenhouse effect and its enhancement. What is more, some of the florine compounds have such a long atmospheric lifetime that they will contribute greenhouse effect for ten thousands years to come. Within just a few decades in the levels of the entire greenhouse gases put together is expected a rise in the intensification of the greenhouse effect corresponding to a doubling of the natural concentration of Carbon Dioxide[30].

The Earth climate system has demonstratively changed since the pre industrial era on both global and regional scale, attributing these changes to human activities. Emission of greenhouse gases and aerosols caused by human activities continue to alter the atmosphere in the ways that are expected to affect the climate. During the 20th century concentrations of greenhouse gases and their radioactive forcing have generally increased due to the result of human activities. Almost all greenhouse gases reached their highest recorded levels in 1990s and continue to increase. From the year 1750-2000 the concentration of CO_2 increased by $31\pm 4\%$ and that of CH_4 rose by $15 \pm 25\%$. These rates of increase are unprecedented in climate change. Fossil fuel burning released on average 5.4Gtc yr-1 during the 1980s increased to 6.3Gtc yr-1 during the 1990s. About three quarters of this increase in atmospheric CO_2 during 1990s were caused by fossil fuel burning with land use change including deforestation. During the 19th century and much of the 20th century the terrestrial biosphere has been a net source of atmospheric CO_2, but before the end of 20th century it had become a net sink. The increase in CH_4 is identified with emissions from energy use, livestock, rice agriculture and land fills. Increases in the concentration of other greenhouse gases, particularly tropospheric Ozone, (O_3) the third most important gas are directly attributable to fossil fuel combustion as well as other industrial and agricultural emissions. Future emissions of greenhouse gases and aerosols due to human activities will alter the atmosphere in the ways that are expected to affect the climate[31].

Studies in recent times prove that more than half of the radiative forcing was from the enhanced greenhouse effect resulted from the concentration of CO_2 in the atmosphere. Today, more and more greenhouse effects increased due to anthropogenic activities caused by rapid industrialization, which resulted an increase in the industrial Chlorofluorocarbons (CFCs) followed by CH_4 tropospheric Ozone and Nitrous Oxide (N_2O). The concentration of greenhouse gases resulted in global climate change in radiative forcing of the gases. These changes occur fundamentally due to the imbalance between the sources and sinks of these gases. However the potential cause of global warming depends not only the radiative forces of the gases but also on their residence times, the gases with longer life will have a greater healthy potential, by the fact of being active over a longer period of time. In order to determine the changing composition of the atmosphere, the need is to answer a series of ever more difficult questions, relating to the mechanism known as the greenhouse effect.

(*a*) Will human beings continue to release greenhouse gases and at what rate?

(*b*) How will such emissions affect future levels of greenhouse gases?

(*c*) What are the effects of elevated levels of greenhouse gases on global temperature?

(*d*) If climate were to change what impacts would result?

(*e*) Will other important climatic variables such as rainfall, evaporation, winds be affected if so how?

(*f*) Can anticipate other effects?

Each of these questions has been subjected to intensive investigation. To answer all these questions revolves around largely on the role of the Carbon Dioxide concentration in the atmosphere resulting the climate change[32].

Carbon Dioxide: Carbon Dioxide (CO_2) is probably the most important of the greenhouse gases released by human activity because its greenhouse impacts are large and because human activities generate so much of it. Carbon Dioxide is a very "natural" ingredient in the atmosphere so the natural that only quite recently people began to think of human indeed Carbon Dioxide as a "pollutant". What seems "natural" to humans today can be quite different from what is "natural" from Earth's longer perspective. Some environmentalists fear Carbon Dioxide buildup will bring about catastrophic changes to climate. For a long time Carbon Dioxide was probably the dominant active gas in the early Earth's atmosphere. Today CO_2 makes up only about 0.037% of the atmosphere and the highest estimates are that it could rise to 0.09% by the year 2100 as a result of human activities. Around 4.5 billion years ago, some scientists think it may have made up as much as 80% of Earth's atmosphere, diminishing slowly down to 30% or 20% over the next 2.5 billion years or so. Free oxygen was scarce even non-existent in this early atmosphere and indeed poisonous to most of the anaerobic life forms that existed[33].

In the past century, the concentration of Carbon Dioxide in the atmosphere has increased about 30% while over the same period the average global temperature has increased between 1 to 2F. Climatologists calculate the average of many locations, since have gone up some have gone down. This is much like the stock market - everyday stock go up - and some go down but by watching an appropriate sample the analyst can say the stock has risen or fallen. But still scientists do not consider this slight warming to be proof of a greenhouse warming as there are too many possible causes or fluctuations. There is no evidence that the 1 to 2F temperature rise over the past century is beyond the range of naturally occurring variation. Besides, the temperature rise that has taken place has not been continuous. If the current trends in emissions were to continue, the amount of Carbon Dioxide in the atmosphere would double during the 21st century with further increase there after. Of the several anthropogenic greenhouse gases, CO_2 is the most important agent of potential future climate warming because of its large current of greenhouse forcing, its substantial projected future forcing, and its long persistence in the atmosphere. Understanding climate response to a specified forcing is one of the measure challenges facing the climate research community. In principle empirical inferences of climate sensitivity would be of great value but development of such inferences is confounded by the natural variability of the climate system by local or regional effects that can be different from the global effects and by the simultaneous working of multiple transient forcing and response. Human life as known today, would have been impossible in such a CO_2 rich atmosphere. Fortunately for humans and land animals most of this Carbon Dioxide was removed from the atmosphere later in Earth's history when sea dwelling life, the earliest algae, evolved the process of photosynthesis. In photosynthesis, plants use light energy from the sun to turn Carbon Dioxide and water into sugar and oxygen. Eventually algae-and more highly evolved organisms like plankton, plants, and trees died and locked up most of this carbon in the forms of carbonate minerals, oil shale, coal and petroleum in Earth's crust. What was left in the atmosphere is the oxygen human beings breathe today. Atmospheric Carbon Dioxide comes from many sources - most of them natural - but is usually brought into balance with "sinks" that drain carbon out of atmosphere. The main sources of Carbon Dioxide is the fossil fuel combustion, and production, changes in tropical land use mainly deforestation and exchange of gas between the atmosphere and the ocean surface. The main sources of Carbon Dioxide and the natural processes (sinks), which remove the CO_2 from the atmosphere, are shown in Table 2.2. The difference between the total emissions and the known sinks is described as the inferred sink which is probably partly due to the extra growth of plants stimulated by higher concentrations of CO_2 in the atmosphere.

Table 2.2 Annual average Carbon Budget from human activity for 1980-89

CO_2 Sources	*Amount (Gtc Yr.)*
1. Fossil fuel combustion and cement production.	5.0-6.0
2. Changes in tropical land use mainly deforestation	0.6-2.6
3. Total emission from human activity 1+2	6.0-8.2
CO_2 Sinks.	
4. Storage in the atmosphere	3.1-3.5
5. Ocean uptake	1.2-2.8
6. Northern Hemisphere forest re growth	0.0-1.0
7. Inferred sinks 3 (4+5+6)	-0.2 -2.8

Gtc - 109 tonnes of carbon - Source IPCC 1996.

Carbon Dioxide can be dissolved in water (the process that makes soda water). It cannot also be readily dissolved in the water on the surface of the oceans, and sea surface is constantly releasing Carbon Dioxide back into the atmosphere. These processes are almost entirely physical and chemical. The sea surface releases an estimated 90Gtc/ year to the atmosphere; but a number of studies have estimated that this is offset by the 92Gtc/yr. it takes up. When this activity noted out the sea surface exchange is actually a "sink" for atmospheric Carbon Dioxide taking out more than it puts back. Most important is the magnitude of these carbon flows relative to other processes because small changes in the delicate balance could have a large impact. So the plants take out 102Gtc/yr. from the atmosphere and perfectly balanced by the total 102Gtc/year put back into the atmosphere by respiration and decay. The magnitude of this cyclic flow of carbon is also important to realize, because small disturbances in the balance can have large implications. By comparison, the amount of Carbon Dioxide added directly to the atmosphere as a result of human activities seems at first inconsequential. By burning coal, oil and natural gas withdrawing from nature's bank account, as it were society takes an estimated 5.5Gtc/year out of Earth and puts it into the atmosphere, according to Inter Governmental Panel on climate change. By cutting down and burning forests, humans release perhaps another 2Gtc/year, although there is uncertainty about this amount. But these amounts do matter, because the natural parts of the carbon cycle (the air, sea exchange and biological processes) have long been in good balance, at least on the time scales of immediate relevance to humans. Industrial and unindustrial activities seem to have significantly tipped the balance of the carbon cycle. Many kinds of scientific measurements have shown that the concentration of Carbon Dioxide in the atmosphere has been increasing over the past several centuries. During this time the human population increased geometrically, the steam engine was put to industrial use, the gasoline powered automobile came into use across the globe, and farmer settlers cleared native vegetation from vast expanses of the American, Australia and parts of Asia. During this period the atmospheric concentration of Carbon Dioxide has increased from a pre industrial level (1750) level of about 280 parts per million by volume (ppmv) to about 367 ppmv in 1998, an increase of over 30 percent. That is enough to make a potentially significant difference; if climate is as sensitive to greenhouse gases as may scientists think it is. Precise measurements at the Mauna Loa observatory in Hawaii *far* removed from industrial pollution had charted steady increases from 1958 to 1998 with a brief pause in 1990-92 [34]. The concentration of CO_2 in the atmosphere from human activity has been increasing over longer time. The Carbon Dioxide has long or lifetime in the atmosphere from 50-200 years (depending upon which sink is involved). Human activity is responsible for only a fraction of the CO_2 in the carbon cycle; this is sufficient to alter the concentration of CO_2 in the atmosphere. The greenhouse gas in the atmosphere is increasing by human activity mainly by the burning of fossil fuels. The United States is the world's highest Carbon Dioxide producer on the planet and the former Soviet and Western countries Union and Western countries *are* the second and all the countries in the developing world together producer a fraction of Carbon Dioxide[35].

The greatest share of fossil fuel CO_2 emissions is held by the industrialized countries with a small portion coming from the developing countries. Since CO_2 has made the longest individual contribution, it is useful to look at the estimated shares of different countries or group of countries to global emissions of CO_2. The table 2.3 shows estimates published by German Enquete commission in 1990. Table 2.3. Energy related CO_2 emission shares of global CO_2 emissions and perception for selected countries and the EC in 1986.

Table 2.3

Country	*CO_2 emission from Energy sector Million tonnes*	*Shares of global energy related CO_2 emission(%)*	*Perception emissions from energy sector*
U.S.A.	4766	23-8	19.7
Germany	1067	5.3	13.7
U.K.	676	3.4-	11.9
Italy	365	1.8-	6.4
Norway	31	0.2	7.5
EC	3187	15.9	9.4

Including the former Germany Democratic Republic

Source—Germany Enquete Commission -1990

The table closely shows that emissions of CO_2 from energy sector are quite unevenly distributed. The per capita emissions of the industrial countries listed in the table are substantially higher than global average of 4.1 and of developing countries (i.e. China 1.9, India 0.7, Nigeria 0.3) contribute different amounts of heat trapping gases to the atmosphere. The table below shows data complied by the Oak Ridge National Research Laboratory, which estimates carbon emissions from all sources of fossil fuel burning for a maximum period from 1751 to 1996 (as long a period as is available). Here is listed the 20 countries with the highest carbon emissions (latest data available are for 1996).

The picture emerged from these figures is one where in general developed countries lead in total carbon emissions and carbon emissions per capita, while developing countries lead in the growth rate of carbon emissions. Obviously these uneven contributions to the climate problem are at the core of the challenges the world community faces in finding effective and equitable solutions. Carbon Dioxide is almost indestructible. It can probably continue to circulate between the atmosphere and the ocean for many thousand of years. This means that Carbon Dioxide from fossil fuels could still contribute to the greenhouse effect for several millennia, even if emissions were to cease completely in the near future. If emissions were instead held at their present levels, the concentration of Carbon Dioxide would go on rising in both the atmosphere and the sea gradually strengthening the greenhouse effect[36].

Table 2.4. The Top 20 Carbon Dioxide Emitters

Country	*Total emissions 1000 tonnes of C. tonnes/capita*	*Per capita emissions*	*Total emission rank*	*Growth in %(90-96)*
United States	1446777	5-37	(1)	(9-9)
People Republic of China	917997	0-76	(18)	40-0
Russia Federation	431090	2-91	(6)	-19-2
		Since 1992		
Japan	318686	2-54	(9)	9.1
India	272212	0-29	20	47-7
Germany	235050	2-87	7	-12-2
United Kingdom	152015	2-59	8	-1.1
Canada	111723	3-76	4	-0.1
South Korea	111370	2-46	11	69.2
Italy	110052	1-92	13	1.1
Ukraine	108431	2-10	12	-37.0
		Since 1992		
France since 1992 incl. Manaco)	98750	1-69	(15)	2.4
Poland	97375	2-52	10	2.6
Mexico	95007	1-02	17	18.0
Australia	83688	4-63	(2)	15-3
South Africa	79898	1-88	14	0.6
Brazil	74610	0-46	19	34.9
Saudi Arabia	73098	3-88	3	51.2
Iran	72779	1-04	15	25.6
North Korea.	69412	3-09	(5)	4.0

Source: Mariland G, TA Boden, R.J. Andres 2000 Global Regional and National CO_2. Analysis Centre Oak Ridge National Research Laboratory, U.S. Department of energy Oak Ridge Tenn, U.S.A.

World Carbon Dioxide emissions are expected to increase by 1-9 percent annually between 2001 and 2025. Much of these increases in these emissions are expected to occur in the developing world where emerging economics such as China and India, fuel economic development with fossil energy. Developing countries emissions are expected to grow above the world average at 2-7 percent annually between 2021 and 2025 and surpass emissions of industrialized countries near 2018.[37]

Scientists generally believe that anthropogenic activities are the primary reasons for the increased concentration of Carbon Dioxide in the atmosphere. During the 100 years the additional release of Carbon Dioxide by human activities energy burnt to run cars and trucks, heat homes and business and power factories is responsible for about 80% of the society's Carbon Dioxide emissions. Increased agriculture, deforestation, land fills, industrial production and mining contribute a significant share of CO_2 emissions to the atmosphere.

Methane (CH_4): The next most important greenhouse gas after CO_2 is Methane produced when certain bacteria break down organic anaerobic conditions. It is removed by reaction with hydroxylradical (OH) in the troposphere. Atmospheric concentrations of Methane (CH_4) have increased considerably over the pre industrial levels. The preindustrial concentration of Methane in the atmosphere was about 700 ppbv less than half the 1994 level of 1.720 ppbv. The current growth rate is about 8 ppbv as per IPCC 1996 annual report. As a trace gas in the atmosphere Methane has more warming effect than Carbon Dioxide - 21 times more on a molecule for molecule basis and 58 times more on a pound for pound basis according to the IPCC. Another piece of bad news is that concentrations of Methane in the atmosphere have increased more than two fold since the beginning of the industrial age - about eight times faster than Carbon Dioxide[38].

The main sources and sinks of CH_4 are shown in table 2.5. Of the fossil fuel sources, 40/Mt/yr. comes from natural gas, 30/mt/y from coal mines, 15/mt/y from petroleum industry and a smaller amount from coal combustion. From the difference between emissions and sinks the extent of further emissions is inferred. Sources and sinks and atmospheric increase of Methane are summarized in table 2.5.

Table 2.5 below also summarizes the main sources and sinks for the Methane, It is evident from this table that human related Methane sources account for 66% of the Methane emissions from all sources. It is also clear from the table that there is a large range of uncertainty about the actual release from the each of the major sources of emission. Methane increasing concentration in the atmosphere is considered of importance from the perspective of global warming because it very effective in absorbing infrared radiation.

Table–2.5

CH_4 Sources		
Natural sources	-	160(110-210)
Human sources	-	
Fossil fuel related	-	100(70-120)
Other e.g. Agriculture	-	275(200-350)
Total human sources	-	375 (300-450)
Total identified sources	-	535 (410-660)
CH_4 Sinks		
Sinks of atmospheric CH_4		
Troposphere (OH)	-	490 (405-575)
Stratosphere	-	40 (32-48)
Soils	-	30 (15-45)
Total atmospheric sinks	-	560 (460-660)
Atmospheric increase	-	37 (35-40)
Total of sinks + atmospheric increase	-	597 (495-700)

Sources: IPCC -1996

Table 2.6 Estimated sources and sinks of Methane

CH_4 Sources /sinks	*Annual Release ($TGCH_4$)*	*Range ($TGCH_4$)*	*Percentage of total*
Sources			
Natural wet lands	115	100-200	22
Termites	40	10-100	8
Oceans	10	5-20	2
Enteric fermentation (Wild animals)	5	2-8	-1
Fresh water	5	1-25	-1
CH_4 Hydrate destabilization	5	0-100	-1
TOTAL NATURAL	**180**		**34**
Man made	-75	65-100	-14
Enteric fermentation (Domestic animals)			
Bio mass burning	40	20-80	8

CH_4 Sources /sinks	*Annual Release ($TGCH_4$)*	*Range ($TGCH_4$)*	*Percentage of total*
Rice paddies	110	25-170	21
Land fills	40	20-70	8
Gas drilling venting Transmission	45	25-50	9
Coal mining	35	17-50	7
Total man made	**525**	**400-600**	**100**
Reaction with OH	500	400-600	
Uptake by micro, Organisms in soils	30	15-45	
Atmospheric increase	**44**	**40-45**	**8**

IPCC scientific Report, chapter, 8 page -14

Methane is emitted during production and transport of coal, natural gas, and oil. Methane emission also results from the decomposition of wastes in municipal solid wasteland fills and the raising of livestock. As mentioned above, the most CH_4 is removed from the atmosphere by reaction with the hydroxyl radical to form CO_2 and water vapor. Methane can be regarded as making both a direct and indirect contribution to the greenhouse effect. Methane emissions can be exacerbated by climate change. For example, changes in the temperature and precipitation will influence emissions from Northern Wetland areas of permafrost, and the decomposition of Methane hydrates in continental shelf regions. However, Methane has very short atmospheric lifetime and so the impact of a given amount of emission is relatively short-lived. Each gas differs in its ability to absorb heat in the atmosphere. Methane traps over is times more heat power per molecule than Carbon Dioxide.

Fortunately Methane's atmospheric lifetime is much shorter than that of most other greenhouses - only 8-6 years. Most of it is removed from the atmosphere when it combines with the hydroxyl radical (OH) to form water. Methane is one of the gases formed in the pressure cooker of Earth's interior, and it is vented through volcanoes and other breaks in Earth's crust. The amount of Methane released annually from natural geologic sources has not been measured, forcing scientists to make assumption that Methane sources and sinks closely balance one another in any natural regime that is one undisturbed by humans. Much atmospheric Methane is biological in origin. Another name for Methane is "Swamp gas" (its characteristic order comes mostly from the hydrogen sulfide mix with it). Wetlands are estimated to produce on the order of 115Tg CH_4/yr. about one fifth of the global total natural and human induced Methane emissions of 570 Tg CH_4/year.

Another important source of Methane is intestinal gas - especially from cattle, water buffalo, sheep and other livestock that humans raise in farming. Anaerobic microorganisms in the intestines of these animals make digestion self-possible - but the Methane they produce is vented to the atmosphere. This so called "enteric fermentation from all animals is estimated to produce 80-113Tg CH_4Yr an appreciable amount and probably one that varies with the scale of human agriculture, rice paddies, which in effect are agricultural wet lands and specially created for cultivating rice and are estimated to contribute another 100-110Tg CH_4/ yr.

Other anthropogenic Methane sources include fossil fuel extraction, estimated at 80-100TgCH_4/year, animal wastes 25/TgCH_4/yr, sewage treatment 25TgCH_4/year, land fills 30-40 TgCH_4/year and biomass burning 40 TgCH_4/year. Methane comes from numerous points in fossil fuel infrastructure, venting from coalmines, venting of gas from oil wells, leaky pipelines etc. These estimates have changed significantly in the past few years and remain quite uncertain. Whatever be the uncertainties of the estimates, it seems likely that much of the observed in atmospheric Methane concentrations since the industrial age have been caused by human activity. It follows that without technological change further increase in human population industry and agriculture will probably further increases in atmospheric Methane concentrations[39].

Nitrous Oxide : Nitrous Oxide (N_2O) is commonly known as "Laughing Gas". Its building blocks are the two dominant gases in the atmosphere, Nitrogen and Oxygen, both play important roles in the chemistry of living things (nitrogen gas into amino acids, the "building blocks" of portion and key to act, abolish growth and repair of tissue). Although nitrogen and oxygen make up same 99 percent of the atmosphere, Nitrous Oxide score with a mean concentration of 311 parts per million by volume (ppbv) in 1992, according to IPCC (i.e. less than one thousandth as abundant as Carbon Dioxide). The scarcity of Nitrous Oxide in the atmosphere is countered by its effectiveness as a greenhouse gas: a molecule of Nitrous Oxide is 200 to 300 times more effective than a molecule of Carbon Dioxide in the greenhouse warming it produces. Further more it is longer lived in the atmosphere than Carbon Dioxide and some other radiatively active gases. Nitrous Oxide is eventually broken down by light in the stratosphere into Nitrogen and oxygen, but its atmospheric life times are about 150 years. As a result the cumulative effect of any anthropogenic emissions of Nitrous Oxide will be greater than those of Carbon Dioxide[40]. There are several Nitrogen oxides, which contribute to local pollution and problems such as acid rain, but N_2O is only one that is significant greenhouse gases. There are many small sources of N_2O. The main human activities that emit N_2O are agriculture especialiy the use of Nitrogen based fertilizers and biomass burning and a range of industrial process including production of acidic and Nitric acid. In 1980's human emission of N_2O was about 3 to 8 Mt/ N/y. The main natural sources are the oceans and tropical temperate soils. Emissions from natural sources are probably about twice as those from human activity. The concentrations of N_2O in the atmosphere have increased from a pre industrial period level of about 275 ppbv to 314 ppbv in 1998. The major sink of N_2O is photosynthesis in atmosphere and some is taken by soils. Nitrous Oxide as a greenhouse gas contributes at the rate of 0.2% -0.3% per annum. It is produced from a variety of biological sources in soil and water and its main sink through photosynthesis in the stratosphere[41].

Table 2.6. Estimated sources and sinks of Nitrous Oxide

Sources	*Range TGN/Yr.*
Natural	
Oceans -	1.4 - 2.6
Soils (Tropical forests)	2.2 - 3.7
Temperate forests -	0.7 - 1.5
Total Natural	4.3 - 7.8
Man made	
Fossil fuel combustion	0.1 -0.3
Biomass burning	-0.02 - 0.2
Fertilizer including ground water	0.01 - 2.2
Total Man made	0.3 - 2.7
Total Sources	**4.4 - 10.5**
Sinks	
Removal by soils	?
Photolysis in stratosphere	7-13
Atmospheric increase	3 -4.5

Sources. IPCC, 1990, Page - 26.

Nitrous Oxide is emitted during industrial and agricultural activities as well as during combustion of solid waste and fossil fuels. This gas is known to deplete ozone layer in the stratosphere and in addition to acting as a greenhouse gas. In comparison to other gases these are increasing fastest in the terms of concentrations. The following table estimated sources and sinks of Nitrous Oxide.

The N_2O has a life time of about 120 years in the atmosphere, so even if emissions were held constant it would be many years before the concentration in the atmospheric is stabilized.

At the current rate of increase it is believed that there is an imbalance of about 30% between sources and sinks, which is reflected in table 2.6. It is evident that the sources of Nitrous Oxide are relatively uncertain and dominated by natural sources of the human related activities; it is still unclear which of the activities is the most significant. This trend is to complicate the choice of control options[42].

Scientists estimate that soil deenitrification is the dominant source of Nitrous Oxide going into the atmosphere. Combustion is one source of Nitrous Oxide by burning fossil fuels wood or other biomass. But scientists today think combustion may be less important a source of anthropogenic Nitrous Oxide than the use of fertilizer. Estimates of the amount of Nitrous Oxide put into the atmosphere from fertilizer use vary widely - from as low as 01TgN/yr to as high as 2-2TgN/yr. This kind of uncertainty makes it hard to assess the role of Nitrous Oxide in any human induced greenhouse warming. The estimated range of N_2O going into the atmosphere annually from all sources is 4.4 to 10.5TgN/year. That total includes N_2O from oceans, tropical and temperate forest, soils, fossil fuel combustion bio mass burning, and fertilizer. Nonetheless both combustion, and intensive agriculture are part of human culture. Whatever be the details of possible human induced increases in atmospheric concentrations of the greenhouse gas, Nitrous Oxide they still offer a reminder that human population cannot grow endlessly and still sustain living condition on Earth. Global average abundance in 1998 = 314 ppbv global burden of 1510 TgN N_2O -0.8 ppbv is greater in Northern Hemisphere than in Southern Hemisphere. Almost 60% emissions occur in Northern hemisphere, no vertical gradient in troposphere but decrease in stratosphere.

Chlorofluorocarbons: In recent years the average growth rate of Chlorofluorocarbons (CFCs) has been about five percent per year. The depletion of ozone layer in the stratosphere is caused by these gases which in addition act as greenhouse gases. The concentrations of these gases in the atmosphere are increasing rapidly in comparison to other greenhouse gases. These gases do not have any significant removal mechanisms in the troposphere, but are removed by photo dissociation in the mid and upper stratosphere. There are no natural sources of CFCs and all the sources are made by human activity. The industrial countries are responsible for over 95% of the release of Chlorofluorocarbons (CFCs) to the atmosphere. They have long atmosphere life times in excess of 50 years. Since the beginning of industrial revolution, there have been increases in the industrial Chlorofluorocarbons. Chlorofluorocarbons CFC-12 and CFC-11 are man made compounds that are not found in the atmosphere before 1950. These compounds have been widely used on refrigerators and in spray propellants and foam blowing. It is also used in a wide range of products such as insulations, air conditioning and solvents. Because of their role in catalyzing decomposition of stratospheric ozone layer production of these has been dramatically reduced in response to the implementation of Montreal protocol and subsequent international agreements[43].

Chloroflurocarbons cause destruction of ozone layer. However, there is also destruction of ozone in the lower stratosphere. Atmospheric concentrations of these compounds are expected to diminish dramatically during the next country. The lifetime of CFC-11 and CFC-12 is 50 and 102 years respectively. Hydro fluorocarbons (HCFs), which are being used as substitutes for CFCs, make only a small concentration to total enhancement of greenhouse gases due to human activity. Per fluorocarbons such as CFCs have only made a small contribution since pre industrial time in the atmosphere which is over 1000 years much longer than that of other greenhouse gas. Each greenhouse gase naturally differs in its ability to absorb heat in the atmosphere. HFCs and PFCs are the most heat absorbent than Methane, Carbon Dioxide, and Nitrous Oxide. What intensifies the greenhouse effect in Earth's atmosphere is the Halocarbons. These compounds combine carbon with one or more of the five elements called halogens. Included in the family of Halocarbons are Chlorofluorocarbons (CFCS) and the hydro fluorocarbons (HCFCs), HCFC substitutes and also some others- carbon tetrachloride halons, Methyl / chloride, Methyl / Chloroform and Methyl/ bromide. However, the potential to cause global warming depends not only the radiative forces of the gases but also on their residence times, the gases with longer life will have a greater healthy potential, but by the facts of being active over a longer period of time. The Chlorofluorocarbons and other Halocarbons are strong greenhouse gases but are at present only in low concentrations in the atmosphere.

All other Halocarbons in the atmosphere result from human activities except for Methyl/chloride and Methyl/bromide, which have also important natural sources. The concentrations of Halocarbons in the atmosphere are much lower than those of other greenhouse gases typically between -2 and 16.5 parts per trillion by volume. Halocarbons generally raise some concern because their greenhouse warming effect on a molecule for molecule basis is drastically greater than that of Carbon Dioxide. The five ozone depleting CFCs of most concern have warming effects ranging from 3,000 to 13000 times greater than Carbon Dioxide. The atmospheric lifetimes of CFC-13 and CFC-115, the longest-lived are about 400 years. So whatever harmful effects they may have will continue for centuries after we stop putting them into the atmosphere. Reductions and elimination of CFC production under the Montreal protocol as beneficial side effect help slow the growing concentrations of these greenhouse gases. But some Halocarbons with greenhouse potential are not restricted under the protocol and some of the CFC substitutes whose uses it will encourage are themselves Halocarbons with greenhouse effects.

Tropospheric Ozone: Tropospheric ozone acts as a greenhouse gas in the troposphere and stratosphere by influencing both solar and infrared radiation. Ozone has been cast in the roles of both villain and victim in the media during recent decades. Ozone is an everyday part of the atmosphere that plays a number of complex roles and is constantly being created and destroyed. Its concentration in the troposphere may have doubled in the Northern Hemisphere since pre industrial times, and an increase of around 25 ppbv. Ozone is formed in the troposphere from the reaction of CO No and Non Methane hydrocarbons and from chemical feedbacks involving Methane. Ozone may also move down from the stratosphere. Stratosphere Ozone depletion will have made a small reduction in the greenhouse effect[44]. The ozone around us has an atmosphere with abundant oxygen. In its ordinary form a free element, oxygen usually occurs as a diatomic molecule (consisting of two oxygen atoms) -20. Ozone is a tri atomic molecule consisting of three oxygen atoms and formed when certain kinds of energy, say an electric arc or very intense ultra violet light, are applied to O_2. Ozone is less stable than diatomic oxygen and most other gases in the atmosphere. Every ozone molecule "wants to" give up its extra energy and its extra atom and become oxygen again. Most of the ozone in the atmosphere is created when the high-energy ultraviolet rays of the sun reach the rarified gas molecules of the stratosphere. The ultraviolet energy excites the oxygen atoms and they combine to form O_3. What is fascinating is that ultraviolet rays both create ozone and destroy it. The high-energy ultraviolet rays create it and the lower energy ultraviolet rays break apart the O_3

molecules. Most ultraviolet rays never reach Earth's surface. O_2 absorbs the high-energy rays and the low energy ultraviolet rays are absorbed by ozone. So it is this ozone production and destruction process that absorb excess ultraviolet and protect human and other developers on Earth's surface from sunburn and skin cancer. The role of the ozone in the atmosphere is complex. At ground level it is a pollutant constituent of smog in the "upper atmosphere (stratosphere) it provides an essential barrier to biological damaging, ultraviolet radiation without life on Earth could not survive: Ozone as a greenhouse gas contributes to global warming. Because of increasing concentration at ground level, ozone has grown considerably in the past century. It appears that human activities may have "doubled or tripled the amount of ozone in the lower atmosphere. At ground levels it is the second most important agent of warming after Carbon Dioxide. On the other hand, the loss of atmospheric ozone including the large ozone holes that appears over the poles each year does not cause climate warming. Quite the opposite is the fact that it comes cooling at the Earth's surface. Scientists have estimated that this cooling may have concentrated as much as 30 percent of the global warming that should have occurred due to greenhouse gas since 1979. So far, it appears that the direct warming effect of Halocarbons is very long lived and caused warming for decades or longer. Their effect of destroying ozone compensates for this warming but not completely. Destruction of ozone has reduced their warming effect by about one third so the net effect CFCs is warming. Newer Halocarbons specifically developed to reduce their impact on the ozone layer generally have less of climate effect because they are not around so but they are still greenhouse gases and so not much less effective at warming the climate than the CFCs they" are replacing. The reduction in Halocarbons concentrations resulting from the Montreal protocol helps the ozone layer to recover. Unfortunately, the increasing amount of the greenhouse gases being pumped into the atmosphere appears to be undoing much of this progress. Ozone is not distributed evenly throughout Earth's atmosphere. Concentrations of ozone can be strongly influenced by heating and cooling (expansion and compression) of natural as well as human activities and by winds that move it around from place to place. Ozone in the upper stratosphere and lower stratosphere functions as a greenhouse gas. Just how strong its greenhouse effect compared to Carbon Dioxide, is something scientists have yet to quantify, but it could be much weaker measurement of ozone concentrations, especially because historical trends are few. Some suggest surface ozone may have doubled since pre industrial times. What has been not realized until recently is that global warming by creating conditions that make Halocarbons more effective at destroying ozone, ironically it does this by cooling the stratosphere.

Water Vapor

Water vapor makes a large contribution to the greenhouse effect. Its spatial distribution is controlled mainly by evaporation, condensation and transport process on a global scale it is not thought to be affected by human sources and sinks. Scientists are intensively investigating the interactions of water vapors, clouds, oceans and sea ice with global climate system in order to refine their computer models and to better understand the impacts on these sub- systems and their future role as sources and sinks on heat trapping gas emissions.

A warmer atmosphere will hold more moisture, which as a greenhouse gas will further amplify the warming. About half of this feed back depends on water vapor in the upper atmosphere. The origin of water vapor and its response to an increase on surface temperature is not completely understood. However there is definitely a positive feedback from water vapor in the lower atmosphere and this is probably also true for water vapor in the upper atmosphere. Feedbacks caused by changes in temperature can partially compensate for the water vapor feedback. The feedback effect of water vapor is incorporated in climate models[45]. Paradoxically, the "gas" which is most important to greenhouse warming is one not normally thought of as a gas at all: water (H_2O). Human beings used to think of water in its common liquid form and seldom as a gas (as vapor or steam). The water vapor in the atmosphere is essentially molecules of steam -evaporated water - bouncing around very thinly diluted among the gaseous Nitrogen molecules that make up the atmosphere. This water vapor can be experienced as humidity. Water vapor plays a number of critical roles in affecting both climate and weather. The amount of water vapor in the atmosphere is not at all uniform but changes drastically and abruptly often in a matter of a few hours to cause for example, thunderstorms. It takes a lot of energy to evaporate water. Water vapor is one of the most important "store house" of energy in the atmosphere and in the climate system. The energy does not disappear but instead heat the atmosphere. Thus, energy is redistributed through the process of evaporation and condensation. When water vapor condenses to form clouds it has another important effect: it "shades" Earth's surface and lower atmosphere. In the greenhouse analogy, rolling down a shade over the greenhouse would cool off the interior, just as it cools a sunny room, when clouds shade Earth some of the incoming solar energy is reflected back into space. Some also is absorbed by the clouds and re-radiated upward and down ward.

But water in its vaporous state has an important heat trapping "greenhouse effect". This is explained by water vapor's being relatively transparent to the shorter wavelength at the visible and ultraviolet end of the light spectrum (the form which much incoming solar energy takes). But after this energy has warmed Earth's surface and been re-radiated upward in the infrared bands of the spectrum, water vapor readily absorbs the trapping heat in the lower atmospheric sphere (Troposphere). Thus water vapor is like the heat trapping "glass" in the greenhouse analogy. Eventually this trapped heat finds its way upward and outward and is reradiated into space. But first its works its way through various parts of the atmosphere. Because incoming solar radiation (now out going heat radiation) is thus delayed in returning to space, the temperature of the lower atmosphere is greater than it would be without the water vapor. Human activities add and subtract water vapor to and from the atmosphere. But these amounts are insignificant compared to the amounts added and subtracted by the natural processes. Water vapor is nevertheless important because its atmosphere warming effects are huge and because they are hard to quantify, model and predict. In fact the amount of water vapor in the atmosphere affects the climate - a classic "feedback loop." As there is scientific uncertainty about the water's role as vapor or clouds, it has both warming and cooling effects, water is a "wild card". Water vapor in the lower atmosphere is very effective greenhouse gas. Base line values controlled by temperature of tropic tropo pause, which in turn changes with climate - It reacts very quickly with CH_4 Co and varies greatly with atmospheric chemistry intensity of solar UV, time of day, season, and geography. This is very fast photochemistry and major sinks for CH_4.

Aerosols

Aerosols (particles of diameter 0.001 -10um) suspended in the atmosphere reflect sunlight and so tend to cool the Earth. The main sources of aerosols are fossil fuel combustion, which emits SO_2 (converted to sulphates in the atmosphere) and bio mass burning which releases organic and elemental carbon. Aerosols influence the radiative balance by absorbing and scattering solar radiation back to space and by acting as nuclei for condensation and so influencing the properties of clouds. Aerosols have a short lifetime and vary regionally, so their overall impact on the global climate is hard to assess, but it has been concluded that the increase in sulphate aerosols since 1850 has a cooling effect. IPCC scientists have suspected for a decade that aerosols of smoke and other particles from burning, rain forest, crops, plants and fossil fuels are blocking sunlight and counteracting the warming effect of Carbon

Dioxide emissions. Until now they reckon that aerosols reduce greenhouse warming by perhaps a quarter cutting increase by 0.2Yc: So the 0.6Yc of warming over the past century would have been 0.8Yc without aerosols[46]. But Berlin workshop concluded that the real figure is even higher aerosols may have reduced global warming cutting increases by 1.8Yc. If so, the good news is that aerosols have prevented the world from getting utmost two degrees warmer than it is now. But the bad news is that the climate system is much more sensitive to greenhouse gases than previously guessed. As those gases are expected to continue accumulating in the atmosphere, the role of aerosols to stabilize or fall that means dramatic consequences for estimate of future "climate change. Past calculations of the cooling effect of aerosols have been inferred from 'missing global warming predicted by climate models. But direct measurement as reported in Science (Vol.300 p 1103) in May by Theodore Anderson of the University of Washington in satellite, shows a much greater parasol effect. The Berlin Meeting also had evidence that past warming areas had higher temperatures - than they ought to if estimates of atmospheric composition at the time and greenhouse models are correct. Again this suggests greater sensitivity. "It looks like the warming today may be only about a quarter of what would have got without aerosols".

But the health effects of many aerosols in smog are so great that even in the poor world, they are already cutting emissions for good reasons aerosols levels look set to fall. Moreover, most aerosols emissions only stay in the atmosphere for a few days. Most greenhouse gases on aerosol will protect less and less from global warming. They are giving a false sense of security right now. One tentative estimate put warming two or even three times higher than current middle range forecasts of 3 to 4 Yc based on a doubling of greenhouse gases in the atmosphere, which is likely by late this century. That suggests global warming will remain above the IPCC forecast of 5.8Yc. Back of the envelop calculations now suggest a "worst case" warming of 7 to 10Yc. Steffen of the Swedish Academy of Sciences says the message for the policy makers is "clear". They need not to get on top of the greenhouse gas emissions problem sooner rather than latter[47]. The greenhouse effect is neither new nor necessarily bad. In fact without the greenhouse effect life as well know it would probably not exist on the Earth. The combined warming effect (positive radiative forcing) from the other trace gases is approximately equal to that of CO_2. In addition, there are small particles (aerosols) that can directly or indirectly help cool the atmosphere (Negative radiative forcing). Examples include, sulphates (e.g. produced by burning coal, volcanic dust) some of these gases and aerosols which are very effective in trapping heat or blocking incoming radiation, but are relatively removed from the atmosphere. Others can trap heat but stay in the atmosphere longer[48].

Effect of greenhouse gases on Climate change

The atmospheric concentrations of the principal anthropogenic greenhouse gases, CO_2, CH_4, N_2O, CFC-11 and CFC-12 have increased significantly during the industrial period. Elevated concentrations are predicted to persist in the atmosphere for times ranging to thousand of years. The increased atmospheric levels of these gases, especially CO_2, increases the IR energy absorbed by the atmosphere, there by producing a warming influence at the Earth's surface. Global mean temperature has increased between 0.3 to 0.6 during the last 150 years. This change has not been monotonic, but it is unusual in the context of the last few centuries. On the time scale of the last few thousand years, there has been relatively low. It is clear that atmospheric CO_2 this not only influences global climate. However, there have been large natural variations of CO_2 in the geologic past, and their changes are correlated with general features of climate change. There is no known geologic precedent for large increases of atmospheric CO_2 without simultaneous changes in other components of the carbon cycle and climate system. Changes in climate system that are confidently predicted in response to increases in the greenhouse gases include increases in the mean surface air temperature, increases in global rates of precipitation and evaporation, rising sea level, and changes in the biosphere. Substantial uncertainties remain in the magnitude and geographical distribution of these changes and in the rates at which they may be expected to occur[49]. Within just a few decades changes in all levels of the greenhouse gases put together are expected to have resulted in an intensification of the greenhouse effect corresponding to a doubling of the natural concentration of Carbon Dioxide. An enhanced greenhouse effect should result in higher temperature on Earth. According to theoretical calculation, the increases in greenhouse gas concentrations that have occurred so far should have raised the global annual mean temperature by at least 0.5c: warming on the scale has in fact been observed in the course of 20th century. The majority of glaciers have receded partly as a result of their melting, sea level has risen by at least 10cm. According to latest IPCC report, we can expect a further global rise in temperature of 1.4 to 4.5.8 c by the 2100. The Earth would thus end up warmer than it has been at any time in the last 150,000 years. Even if atmospheric concentration of greenhouse gases is stabilized in a hundred years of time, warming is likely to continue even further into the future[50].

There is strong scientific consensus that there has been an increase in the atmospheric concentration of greenhouse gases and especially of Carbon Dioxide over recent decades and centuries. There is steady upward trend in CO_2 concentration since1958 when measurements began. It increased about 16.53 percent according to the recent research. All these increases have resulted from human actions. The increase is much larger than the natural variability. Isotope analysis of the carbon in the atmospheric CO_2 suggests that much of these increases did come from fossil fuel burning. Some greenhouse gases for example like CFCs result entirely from human activities. Human beings developed them and human actions have led to their release into the atmosphere. Without humans there would be no CFCs. The explanations for increased Methane and Nitrous Oxide concentrations above background levels may be a little more uncertain. Finally, the amount of Carbon Dioxide exchanged with the atmosphere annually by the oceans at land plants is so big that it drafts that overshadows emanate from human activities. Variations in these processes may account for some of the increase. Scientists are the first to admit they have yet to arrive at any final or precise quantification of Earth's carbon budget[51].

Emissions of Carbon Dioxide, Methane and certain other gases intensity the greenhouse effect of the atmosphere and can thus cause long term climate change - primarily a rise in temperature. Further, intensification of the greenhouse effect is being caused by entirely new man made greenhouse gases that are entering the atmosphere. The concentration of Carbon Dioxide would be rising even faster if it were not for the fact that some of the surplus is absorbed by the oceans. After a number of centuries, less than a fifth of the Carbon Dioxide that has been emitted so far will remain in the atmosphere. Unfortunately though Carbon Dioxide is utmost indestructible it can probably to circulate between the atmosphere and the oceans for many thousands of years. This means that Carbon Dioxide from fossil fuels could still contribute to the greenhouse effect several millennia hence, even if were to cease completely in the near future. If emissions were instead held at their present levels, the concentrations of Carbon Dioxide would go on rising in both the atmosphere and the sea gradually strengthening the greenhouse effect[52]. Scientists believe that increased emissions of greenhouse gases are causing too much energy to be trapped and increasing global temperature. However, a study by UK researchers held in 2001 compared recent satellite readings with data from 27 years ago and found that less radiation now escaping into space. This suggests that greenhouse effect has increased at a rate in line with rising greenhouse gas production. Even if there is increasing greenhouse effect, global climate change might not be entirely a fault. Some scientists suggest that changes in the solar wind (electrically charged particles coming from the sun) might affect the Earth's cloud cover increasing global temperatures. This would have a far stronger effect on global temperatures than greenhouse gas emissions. greenhouse gases such as Carbon Dioxide, Methane, Nitrous Oxide, Hydro fluorocarbons and Chlorofluorocarbons heat the Earth and occurs naturally (with the exception of Chlorofluorocarbons), creating a habitable environment. However, the increasing greenhouse gas emissions (particularly Carbon Dioxide associated with fossil fuel burning, deforestation which destroys natural carbon sinks that absorb Carbon Dioxide), increase the amount of heat trapped within the atmosphere and the Earth's temperature[53].

Human activities are increasingly altering the Earth's climate. These effects add to natural influences that have been present over Earth's history. Scientific evidence strongly indicates that natural influence cannot explain the rapid increase in global near surface temperature observed during the second half of the 20th century. Human impacts on climate system include increasing concentrations of atmospheric greenhouse gases (i.e. Carbon Dioxide, Chlorofluorocarbons and their substitutes Methane, Nitrous Oxide etc.), air pollution, increasing concentrations of airborne particles, and land alternation. A particular concern is that atmospheric levels of Carbon Dioxide may be rising faster that any time in Earth's history, except possibly following rare events like impacts from large extraterrestrial objects. Atmospheric Carbon Dioxide concentrations have increased since the mid 1700s through fossil fuel burning and changes in land use with more than 80% of this increase, occurring since 1900. Moreover, research indicates that increasing level of Carbon Dioxide will remain in the atmosphere for hundred to thousands of years. It is virtually certain that atmospheric concentrations of Carbon Dioxide and other greenhouse gases will cause global surface climate to be wetter. The global climate is changing and human activities are contributing to that change[54]. Future emissions of greenhouse gases are unknown. However by predicting population growth, economic activity, rates of technological changes and the energy likely to be used by different nations, it is possible to develop scenarios for the future greenhouse emissions. Taking emissions many different views of the future into account, it is clear that the ranges of possibilities for future greenhouse gases emissions is very wide. In fact uncertainties surrounding the future growth of greenhouse gas emissions are a major contributor to the uncertainty-surrounding estimate of future levels greenhouse gases in the atmosphere, and hence future warming[55].

The increase in greenhouse gas concentrations is well documented but the results of the enhanced greenhouse effect are less certain. The most optimistic observer claims that the Earth will compensate for the increases in GHGs by unforeseen natural mechanisms, and hence no action is necessary to maintain the current global climate. The pessimistic observers claim that the temperature rise is already well under way, and some time next century will result in unpredictable and catastrophic climate change through out the world. The realistically expectable effects of global warming are some where between those two extremes. The primary greenhouse gases are CO_2, CH_4, N_2O CFCs and O_3, each of three gases has a different "greenhouse warming potential (GWP), so that their effects on atmospheric temperature are not in direct proportion to their quantity of emissions. One ton of N_2O has the same warming effect as 14 tons of CH_4, which has the same effect as 290 tons of CO_2, the most potent GTTG are the CFCs some of which achieve the same effect with only 54 kilograms of emissions[56].

Although CO_2 is weakest in terms of relative warming effect it is estimated in the largest quantity by far, so it accounts for 61% of the total GWP[57]. N_2O and CH_4 are not as reality monitored, as CO_2 and their sources are not known quantively[58]. The CFCs are already controlled under the Montreal protocol (the Ozone treaty) and their emissions are being phased out now. Human beings emit CO_2 at a current rate of 21.8 billion metric tons per year, some of which is reabsorbed into the oceans, biomass and soil, the rest accumulate in the atmosphere[59]. That emission rate causes a current atmospheric CO_2 concentration of 353ppm (parts per million) compared to a pre industrial level of 280 ppmv[60]. The atmospheric concentration is increasing at a rate of 1.6ppm per year and because energy usage is increasing, the rate of increase of atmospheric CO_2 concentrations is increasing as well [61]. The rate of increase 0.5% per year, represents a doubling of CO_2 concentration in 140 years which is translated into a temperature increase of between 1.9c and 5.2c. To limit the temperature increase to the tolerable rate a decrease in CO_2 emissions by 20% from their projected levels for the year 2005 should be adhered to[62].

It is now widely believed that the increase atmospheric concentration of greenhouse gases (GHGs) is contributing to the process of climate change and global warming. Most OECD countries under the 1994 United Nations Frame work Convention on Climate Change committed themselves to stabilize emissions of GHGs at 1990 levels by 2000 and further agreed to implement the 1997 Kyoto Protocol, which specified the levels of emissions for the target period 2008 to 2012. Changes in the Climate system that confidently predicted to increase in greenhouse gases include increases in mean surface air, temperature, increase in global mean rate of precipitation and evaporation, rising sea level and changes in biosphere. Substantial uncertainties remain in the magnitude and geographical distribution of these changes and in the rates at which they may be expected to occur.

As the Earth gets warmer there is a serious risk the climate will change in ways that will seriously disrupt life on Earth. Among the several consequences, a rise in sea level, more heat waves and drought, more extreme weather events, producing flood and property destruction, and tropical diseases spreading to areas where they have never been known before. If we do not take action, global warming will threaten health, cities, farmers, forests, wet lands, other natural habitats and what not will occur in future. Under all scenarios, the world will warm even faster in this century than the last, rising by 1.4 to 5.90c by 2100 as compared with 1990. Most land areas will warm faster than this, especially Northern North America and Northern and central Asia. Glaciers and ice caps will continue to shrink though the Antarctic ice sheet will grow due to increased snowfall. Mean sea level will rise by anything between 9 and 88 cm, due to expansion of seawater and run off from melted glaciers and ice sheets. The higher temperature will evaporate more water, which will lead to increased and more variable precipitation. If that were not bad enough, the report concludes that if the concentration of greenhouse gases were stabilized, global temperature would continue to rise for centuries and the sea level would go on rising for thousands of years.[63]

IPCC fourth assessment report in 2007[64] notes that the rates of warming accelerated in the 20th century. Most of the observes increase in globally averages temperatures since the mid-20th century is very likely [greater than 90 per cent probability] due to the observed increase in anthropogenic greenhouse gas concentrations. The reort also concludes, on the basis of climate models, that it is very unlikely (less than 20 per cent probability) that climate changes of at least seven centuries prior to 1950 were due to variability generated within the climate system alone, such as aerosol from volcanic eruptions, and changes in solar irradiance, and not due to anthropogenic forcing which becae evident in only in the early 20th century. The reort adds that the impact human activities now extends to other aspects of climate, including ocean warming and sea level rise, continental average temperature extremes and wind patterns. On the basis of analyses of ice cores spanning thousands of years, the report concludes that anthropogenic emissions have resulted in a marked increase in atmospheric concentrations of Carbon Dioxide, Methane and Nitrous Oxide since 1750 and now far exceed preindustrial values. The global in crease in Carbon dioxide concentrations, points out the report, is primarily because of fossil fuel and land use change, while the increase in methane and nitrous oxide concentrations from 280 parts per million(ppm) to 379 ppm in 2005 is far greater than the natural increase from 180 ppm to 300 ppm over the last 650,000 years. The 1.9 ppm growth rate of CO_2 concentration during 1995-2005 was notwithstanding inter-annual varability, larger than the 1.4 ppm recorded from 1960, when continuous direct atmosheric measurement began, up to 205.

The report notes that eleven of the last 12 warmest years since the global surface temperature began to be recorded in 1895. The 0.76 increase in temperature over the past 100 years is higher than the Third Assessment Report (TAR) figure of 0.6C for the period 1901-2000. The warming trend over the past 50 years has ben twice that for the past 100 years. Observations show that since 1961 the ocean has warmed to a depth of at least 3,000 meters and has been absorbing more than 80 per cent of the heat added to the climate system. Such warming causes water to expand, resulting in a rise in sea level.

References

1. Environment Protection Agency EPA, "greenhouse Gas and Climate Change", Sweden 1983, www. internet. Naturvardsvercet.se/2k
2. Sieve Meyer - Ken Hubbard; "A Discussion of greenhouse Gases", Stockholm, Nebraska Cooperative extension, NF-91-27 May, 1991, p. 2.
3. Renewing India Organization, "greenhouse Gas an Overview". www.wisegreek.com.
4. Sleve Meyer- Ken Hubbard, *op.cit,* p. 2.
5. Regional Study on greenhouse Effect and its impact on the region; Kathamandu, SAARC, Secretariat, December 1992, p. 1.
6. Jill Jagar Tim 'O' Riordan; "History of Climate Change Science and Politics", Problem of Anthropogenic climate change; London, New York, Routledge, 1996, p.5.
7. "greenhouse Threat Looms Large", Hindustan Times, No. 29, Date 9.5.1990.
8. Tamaras S. Ledley, Eric T. Sundquist Stephen E. Schwartz, Dorothy K. Hall, Jack D. fellows and Timothy L. Killen; "Climate Change and greenhouse Gases", Massachusetts Ave, Cambridge; Vol. No.-80, No.-39 28th September 1999 P-453. http:/cdiac/esd.ornl.gov/pns/current.ghg html;(visited in the line).
9. BBC Science and Nature Hot Topic Climate change - The greenhouse effect, www.bbc.co.uk/science/hottopics/36k.
10. Sturges, W.T. et. al 2000; "Extension of Heat Trapping Gases and Aerosols" A potent greenhouse gases identified in the atmosphere; SF 5 CF 3-Science – 289, 611-613.
11. R.N. Trivedi; "A Text book of Environmental Science", Chapter-32, greenhouse effect a continuing catastrophe, New Delhi, Anmol, 1997; pp. 204-05.

12. SEAP, "Climate Change and greenhouse Effect," http/ www. globalchange, com./berry.html, 27.3.2004, p. 1.
13. Sieve Meyer and Ken Hubbard, "A Discussion of greenhouse Gases" published by Cooperative Extension of Agricultural and Natural Resources, Linclon University of Nebraska, NF-91-27, May 1991, p. 2.
14. R.N. Trivedi, *op.cit,* pp. 204-05.
15. Sieve Meyer and Ken-Hubbard, *op. cit,* p. 2.
16. Jill Jagar Tim 'O Riordan, *op. cit,* p-6.
17. BBC-Science and Nature-Hot Topics, *op.cit,* p. 1.
18. Tamoras S. lendley, *op.cit.,* p-453.
19. BBC-Science and Nature-Hot Topics, *op.cit,* p. 1.
20. Jill Jagar Tim 'O' Riordan, *op.cit,* p. 7.
21. Svante Arrhenius-Swedish Chemist "A Discussion of greenhouse Gases", Stockholm: Nebraska Cooperative Extension, NF91-27, 1991.
22. "Global Climate Change", CRS Report 98-235, US greenhouse Emission Status, EPA-Global Warming Climate, Washington DC., p. 1.
23. Jill Jagar Tim 'O' Riordan, *op.cit.,* p. 7.
24. SAARC Secretariat, Kathamandu, op.cit., chapter -I, p. 2.
25. *Ibid.,* p. 3.
26. EPA, Swedish,1983, *op.cit.*
27. Jill Jagar Tim 'O' Riordan, *op.cit.,* p. 7.
28. Tamras S. Ledley, *op.cit.,* p. 453.
29. Chris Mitchell, "greenhouse and Science of Uncertainty." Australian Broadcasting Corporation, 1997, pp. 3-4.
30. Swedish EPA, *op.cit,* p. 2.
31. Third Assessment Report of IPCC, Question No-2, WGL-TAR-Chapter-3-4 and SRAGA, 2001.
32. Chris Mitchel, *op.cit.,* p. 3-4.
33. Flavim Christopher, Odil Tunali, "Reporting on Climate Change", June 1996.
34. C.D. Keeling, T.P. Whorf. "Reporting on Climate Change", Scripps Institution of Oceanography, Lajolla: California, 1998.
35. Carl Segan's viewpoint of a global phenomena, Feeling the Heat, US, SEN/26.5.1990, p. 6.
36. Swedish EPA, *op.cit.*
37. Energy Information Administration, Washington D.C., 2003.
38. greenhouse Gases, Envirotools, org.factsheets, Australia, 1990, p. 2.
39. IPCC Report - 1990, "Understanding the Science".
40. "Reporting on Climate Change", Climate Research Unit, University of East: Anglia.
41. SAARC, Secretariat, Kathamandu, *op.cit,* p. 5.

42. *Ibid.*, p. 5.
43. *Ibid.*, p. 5.
44. Wuebbles. D.J. C.N.Hewitt, W.T. Sturages Elsevier; "Global Atmospheric Climate Change", 1993.
45. IPCC (1996 A) Climate change - 1995. The Science of Climate Change, Summary for Policy Makers and Technical Summary of the Working Group-I Report, University Press: Cambridge, UK, p. 56.
46. Theodore Anderson, "New Scientist Environment Report/Climate Change", Washington, Vol. 300, 1.5 1999, p. 1103.
47. *Ibid.*, p. 2.
48. Source of Global Warming, "Why The Climate Change", Emission of heat trapping gases and aerosols. visited in line - http/www/ucsusat.org/ global. environment/global warming page frame page ID=963.
49. Tamara S. Ledley; *op cit.*, p. 453.
50. Swedish EPA, *op.cit.*, p. 3.
51. C.D. Kelling, *op.cit.*
52. Swedish EPA, *op.cit.*, p. 2.
53. BBC Science and Nature, *op.cit.*
54. "Human Impacts on Climate Change" Adopted by Council December - 2003. www. agu.org/sci_soc/policy/climatechange position.html.
55. Holper P.N., "greenhouse Gas and Science of Uncertainty", London/New York: Cambridge University Press, 1994, p. 81.
56. (PIGW) 1991, adopted from the economics of long-term climate change, US Department of Energy; 1990, p. 140.
57. IPCC 1989, p-XXI, Table-5.
58. (PIGW) 1991, 1985 Estimate from US Doe. p. 104.
59. (PIGW) 1991, Current estimate are 1990, pre industrial estimates is for 1950 and is ±10ppm. p. 1.
60. OTA. 1991, Management Exploitation from Mauna Loa observing data cited from GGMCC 1990.
61. PIGW, 1991, *op. cit.* p. 18.
62. Mathews, final report citing IPCC recommendations which also assume that CFCs are eliminated entirely by 2005 per the Montreal protocol. 1991, p. 332.
63. Climate Change Information Sheets; UN Environment Programme: Chatainina, July 1999.
64. Summary of the IPCC Fourth Assessment Report, 2007, quoted in Frontline, Vol. 24, No. 4, February 24—March 9, 2007, pp. 4-9.

3

Global Warming : Causes and Consequences

Climate change involves the systematic change of the global atmosphere, which is inseparably linked to the oceans, the biosphere and the world water cycle including its ice sheets and glaciers. Climate change science has come a long way in understanding the fundamentals of global warming. Historical records show that climate has changed in the last one hundred years. Not only are long-term averages changing, but the shorter-term variability in climate, from year to year and decade-to-decade is also beginning to display changing patterns.

Global warming refers to the increase in the Earth's surface temperature due to the accumulation gases some times referred to as "greenhouse gases" that trap heat in the Earth's atmosphere. The Intergovernmental Panel on Climate Change (IPCC), the Academy of science and the union of concerned scientists document on increase in the Earth's average surface temperature of 0.6 degree over the last hundred years. According to this research even a 1degree change over time can result in extreme weather changes such as droughts, flooding and more severe storms. As of 2000, studies document on the erosion of ecosystems and bio-diversity and property damage. A recent study predicts the extinction of much of species by 2050, due to vast rise in average global temperatures, which researchers say could increase from 2.5 to 10.4 degrees Fahrenheit by the year 2100[1]. The atmosphere around the Earth is made up gases. Some of these gases function like the panes of a greenhouse, they let some radiation from the sun in but also retain heat in the atmosphere that is they do not let all radiation back out. As a result of this natural effect it is warmer on Earth than it would be without these trapping gases. Human contributions of certain gases to the atmosphere have increased this greenhouse effect. According to IPCC, the possible warming effect on the surface of stratosphere system arises from the emission of greenhouse gases[2].

Global mean surface temperature has increased about I.I.F.(0.6°C) since the beginning of the 20th country with night time minimum increasing more than day time maximums. The warming record shows the significance of spatial and temporal variability, and the global upward trend is unambiguous. Most of the warning in the 20th century occurred from about 1910 to 1945 and since 1976. Twentieth century warming is likely to be the longest during any century over the past 1,000 years for the northern Hemisphere, with the 1990 the warmest decade and 1998 the warmest year. The tenth warmest years since 1860 have all been recorded since 1980[3].

Scientists expect that the average global surface temperature could rise 1-4.5°F (0.6-2.5°C) in the next 50 years and 2-2-10°F (1.4-5.8°C) in the next century with significant regional variations. Evaporation will increase as the climate warms, which will increase the average global precipitation. Soil moisture is likely to decline in many regions, and intense rainstorms are likely to become most frequent. Sea level is likely to rise two feet along most of the US coast[4]. IPCC concluded that the balance of evidence suggests a discernible influence on the global climate about 10-25cm over the last 100 years Increased temperatures will have caused some expansion of sea water and retreat of the glacier and ice caps. Using the emissions scenarios, the IPCC project that the global mean temperature will increase by 0.9 to 3.5°C by the year 2100, relative to 1990. The average rate of warming from these emission scenarios would probably greater than any seen in the last 10,000 years. The temperature would continue to increase even after stabilization of greenhouse gas concentrations in the atmosphere, because of the thermal inertia of the oceans. By 2100 sea level is projected to rise by between 13 and 94 cm. There is also the possibility that unusual weather events such as severe storms may become more frequent.

Ecosystems, agriculture and forestry and human health are sensitive to the climate change. Ecosystems provide many essentials including food, materials, energy and water resources. Some ecosystems may be unable to adapt to climate change at an adequate rate. Agriculture and fisheries may also be disrupted with the consequence of food shortages. This may be exacerbated by sea level rise causing widespread flooding. At a more mundane level, demand for heating and cooling will be changed. Secondary impacts of climate change may include increasing numbers of environmental refugees, altered patterns of tourism and large claims being made on the insurance Industry[5].

An international UN group of experts has concluded that the world wide temperatures will rise 2 degree within 35 years and more by 6 degrees by the end of the next century if nothing is done to combat global warming. The panel predicts that the temperature will be far greater than experienced in the last 10,000 years raising the spectre of 'withered crops', spread of dustbowls, melting of polar ice caps, and flooding of coastal areas of the world and other disasters[6].

According to the state of world population 1990 report by the middle of 21st century the world will become hotter place to live in than it is now due to the bourgeoning population. The report published earlier this year says global population will reach at least 6.25 year billion by the turn of the century and by the year of 2025 it will touch an astounding 8.5 billion. This fastest growth in human numbers in all history will leave an adverse effect on the environment of the many countries of the world including India, the report predicts[7]. The present estimate suggests that the global temperature will rise from 0.1 to 0.2°C per decade. In the scenario of highest emission of greenhouse gases it is estimated that by 2020 global mean temperature will increase by 1.8°C over the pre industrial temperature. In other words, the temperature will increase between 1.3 to 2.5°C by 2050[8].

It is generally believed that the increasing concentrations of Carbon Dioxide (CO_2) Methane (CH_4) and water vapor and other trace gases cause the Earth's atmosphere to trap more of the sun's heat and raise the world's temperatures. Scientific studies estimate that greenhouse effect caused by increasing accumulation of gases such as Carbon Dioxide, Methane, Chlorofluorocarbons (CFCs), which forms a blanket that traps the sun rays reflected from the Earth, warm the globe and may raise its average temperature by a few decades in the next 40 years. Most studies of the scientists and environmentalists into the phenomena so far have recommended measures to reduce consumption level of these gases so that a catastrophe could be averted. Various climate models have predicted a rise of 4 to 5 degrees in the average global temperature[9]. The quantities of gases emitted into the atmosphere exceed the ability of the atmosphere to absorb them. This relentless and continuous emission of gases causes global warming. The global warming is a reality and not a myth, it is difficult to predict the long term impacts of global warming and they are likely to be serious in future. During the last 100 years global mean temperature has gone up by 0.4 degree centigrade and in the last 50 years the ocean level raised by 10 centimeters. The fear now is that the burning of large quantities of fossil fuels, which pours Carbon Dioxide and other gases into the atmosphere will raise the Earth's temperature further by 2 degrees, when atmospheric content of Carbon Dioxide doubles. The consequence is rise in sea levels which could be disastrous to coastlines around the world[10]. According to the report prepared by the United Nations Funds for the Population Activities (UNFPA) as the world population starts going up the temperature of the world is already warmer by 0.6 degree centigrade than it was just a century ago that will begin to increase[11].

The greenhouse effect promotes global warming and threatens mankind. Now the concentration of Carbon Dioxide with Methane and Nitrous oxide has led to an increase in global temperature by 0.8 to 2.5°C. The earth is going to get hotter by 3 to 5°C within the next century. However without this shield, the Earth would be a frozen lifeless planet with an estimated surface temperature of 20°C[12]. It is predicted that the rise of global temperature to 2 degrees warming would be uniform throughout the globe. These would be 10 degree increase in polar temperature, two or three degree increases in the middle latitude and almost imperceptible rise in the tropics[13]. According to the middle range of projections, the temperature by the middle of the next century will rise by 1.5 degree centigrade to 2-8 degree centigrade much more than any time during past 12,000 year and the consequences of the global warming will be alarming. As the global warming proceeds by the middle of the next century, due to melting of ice and thermal expansion, the sea level may rise to 7 to 67 centimeters. If the higher projections come true many countries of the world may face disastrous consequences[14]. Scientists say that the planet will become warmer as Carbon Dioxide and other gases are increasing in the atmosphere, where they act as a blanket to trap heat from the sun and warm the Earth. Carbon Dioxide is a by-product of industrial age produced by all forms of burning including combustion of gasoline, coal and oil and destruction of forests. The UN panel says that global temperature will on current trends increase by about half a degree per decade on average resulting in an average global increase of two degree by 2005 and 6 degree by the end of the 21st century. According to them land would be warmed more rapidly than the oceans and temperature in southern and central North America will be higher than global average[15].

The problem of environmental pollution in the seas as on lands has outstripped men's preparedness for assessing it in ecological terms, and the dangers presented to animals and plants could in the many cases be more serious than garnered from the available data. The seas cover 70.8 percent of the surface of the planet Earth with an area of 36,105,7872 ac-km and hold 1445 million cubic km of water. So the deterioration of the environment of the seas will have far reaching adverse effects on the Earth's atmosphere. As the oceans greatly influence the formation of weather, deterioration of marine environment will result in catastrophic changes[16]. A warming and cooling of the Earth's climate by 2.5-100F is not uncommon, it has occurred many times in the past. The difference between previous climate changes and the anticipated "greenhouse" warming is only one of time. The climate changes of the past have occurred over many millennia while the present "greenhouse" warming is envisioned to occur over a couple of centuries. However, the observed warming trend is not entirely consistent in the Carbon Dioxide change. Most of the temperature increase occurred before 1940, after which the Earth started to cool until the early seventies, when warming resumed. Carbon Dioxide on the other hand has been increasing steadily throughout the past century. Some of the effects like volcanic aerosols, sulpher dioxide and other pollutants might affect the amount of solar radiation that reflected back to space, which causes a cooling that could counteract the warming due to Carbon Dioxide and other greenhouse gases. Taking into consideration all these effects prediction can be expected on climate changes in the next century. As the gases are expected to continue accumulating in the atmosphere resulting in dramatic consequences for climate changes. One tentative estimate put warming two or even three times higher than current middle range forecasts of 3 to 4YC based on a doubling of greenhouse gases in the atmosphere, which is likely by late this century. That suggests global warming will remain above the IPCC maximum forecast of 5.8YC. Back of the envelope calculations now suggest a "worst case" warming of 7 to 10YC. The reason why this menance has been assuming serious proportion is that global climate change has started showing its various impacts and adverse consequences i.e. too much of heat or cold or extreme type of summer and winter drought or territorial rain, frequency of flood or drought, formation of circles high or low pressures of air amidst the seas or oceans, land slides or land erosion, extension of deserts, and appearance. Asthma and so many unpredicted neurological orthopedic, pediatric, respiratory and cardiac diseases[17].

According to Geoff Jenkins, Head of the Hadley centre for climate prediction and research in the UK, Planet Earth is warming up faster than experts expected. The consequences of dying forests, expanding deserts and rising sea levels will wreak havoc on human and animal lives sooner than anticipated as global warming accelerates. A 2001 United Nations report forecasts a climate change that global temperature would rise two to five degrees Celsius by the end of the century. But recent data suggest temperature could rise even higher as a worst case scenario shows four times as much CO_2 emitted into the atmosphere from today's levels, which Jenkins said is significantly higher than previously expected. The warmer weather will generate more droughts, floods and rising sea levels, which many fear will create millions of refugees from drowning island nations and possible war over increasing scare fresh water. Economics is also likely to take a blow as farming, fishing and business will be affected by the change in climate[18].

According to U.S. climate expert, Robert Dickinson of Georgia Institute of Technology's School of Earth and Atmospheric Sciences- "If the world cut back drastically thirst for fossil fuels, the gases they have already produced will continue to trap extra heat in the Earth's atmosphere for at least another century. But the effects of Carbon Dioxide (CO_2) that have been released into the atmosphere from the burning of fossil fuels will last for at least 100 years. That means, any reduction of CO_2 that is expected to be possible over this period will not result in a cleaner atmosphere and less global warming that we see today for at least a century". David Phillips, a senior Climatologist of Canada, "Warming is relentless and it will continue". It can slow down (with population controls) but it can not be reversed". Another climate and global warming expert, Henery Hengeveld of Canada, says the Earth climate reacts gradually to the pollutants we produce. "The Earth has inertia. The pressures putting on the system will take decades to reach equilibrium (i.e. neither warming nor cooling) after stop more emission". That is primarily because the oceans take a long time to warm up. There is a tremendous volume of water, the process is similar to living beside a lake that warms up in spring and summer more slowly than the air. The concentrations of CO_2 into the atmosphere contribute to global warming, and the temperature increase expands the oceans and causes ice sheets to melt, in turn increases gas level. World famous physicist Stephen Hawking says he is worried that global warming could destroy human life on Earth. The planet was warming rapidly. Huge changes threatened to overwhelm our civilization. Oceans were swelling with heat and continuing to rise for at least a century. Despite the ceaseless accumulation of evidence in the science that has become unassailably robust and the impact that have become undesiably visible – the world had a done nothing of consequences to address this issue.[19]

Impacts of Global Warming

The rise of temperature in the atmosphere will have far reaching consequences of physical, chemical, ecological, environmental, socio, economic, political and institutional at the global, regional and country level. It is expected that global mean temperature will rise by 0.5 degree Celsius to 3 degree Celsius. The Inter Governmental Panel on Climate Change (IPCC) report comes out about horrible consequences that the global warming will be having on the Earth.

Impacts on Agriculture and Food Supply

Temperature variations can affect the agricultural production, environment and resource base of the agriculture sector. The consequences of changes in the farming systems for the economy such as food system, trade, employment, income, etc., are the third order impacts[20]. The extent of impacts on agriculture and food system will depend very much on situation already prevailing. For example, in the semiarid Tropical regions, which comprises large areas of geographical region of the SARRC countries, the vulnerability of agriculture to change derives not only from high levels of dependence on a number of range of rainfall levels and patterns but also on the characteristic conditions of poverty, high population growth and environmental stress including erosion and desertification. These conditions make adjustment to different agricultural practices difficult[21]. According to U.S. climate expert, Robert Dickinson-the world can expect large shifts in agricultural productivity. Some region will become more productive and others will be become less so because of changing patterns in temperature and rainfall. Overall there will be more rainfall but also more evaporation leading to more floods and more droughts. It seems obvious that any significant change in climate on a global scale, impacts local agriculture and therefore affects world food supply. Climate change presents crop production with prospects for both benefits and drawbacks.

IPCC in its report (1995) has summarized the potential international effects of climate change over the next several decades. Within developing countries, especially in arid and semi arid regions where available water is already a limiting resource, the potential impacts of climate change on agriculture are quite large. The potential for disruptions of food production appears real, and closer in time than many might appreciate. A major challenge of climate change for agricultural production involves the capacity of nations to adapt to the changes that might be expected to occur. Farmer around the world are, after all, familiar with the vagaries of the weather and understand that regardless of long term trends there are wet and dry years to which they must adapt. However, the ability of farmers to adapt varies considerably with respect to their current economic conditions, their access to accurate current information, their access to knowledge about potential future conditions and their access to knowledge and technology to improve agricultural practices in ways that might enhance future productivity without suffering additional environmental damage. In developing world, the changes could be far reaching, from reduction in overall national productivity at a time when countries can least afford it, to an increasing dependence on imports for meeting the demands of growing populations, to a reduction of control over food production because of increased foreign ownership. One cannot predict with certainty which scenarios, might become reality, but it is clear that the changes in the climate system that are projected for the next several decades provides major challenges for continuing to meet basic human needs that exacerbate today's problems[22].

Greater atmospheric concentrations of CO_2 tends to increase crop growth, as a result more CO_2 is absorbed and converted to carbohydrates. Under CO_2 enrichment, crops may use less water even while they produce more carbohydrates. In middle and higher latitudes global warming will extend the length of potential growing session allowing earlier planting of crops in the spring, earlier maturation and harvesting and the possibility of complexity of two or more cropping cycle during the same session. The effect of high temperature resulting in growth as well as reducing yields is another aspect of climate change. Agriculture of any kind is strongly influenced by the availability of water. Climate change will modify rainfall evaporation, run off, and soil moisture storage. Changes in total seasonal precipitation on its pattern of variability are both important. The occurrence of moisture stress during flowering pollination and grain filling is harmful to most crops and particularly so to corn, soybeans, and wheat. Increased evaporation from the soil and accelerated transpiration in the plants themselves will cause moisture stress, as a result there will be a need to develop crop varieties with greater drought tolerance. Finally, intensified evaporation will increase the hazard of the soil accumulation in the soil. Extreme metrological events such as spells of high temperature, heavy storms, or droughts, disrupt crop production[23]. Higher air temperatures are likely to speed the natural decomposition of organic matter and increase the rates of other soil processes that affect fertility. Additional application of fertilizer to counteract these processes enhances crop growth resulting in increased atmospheric CO_2. Additional use of chemicals may impact water and air quality at the cost of environmental risk. There will be continual cycling of plant nutrients like. Carbon, Nitrogen, Phosphorus, Potassium and Sulphur in the soil plant. Atmosphere system is also likely to accelerate in warmer conditions accelerate CO_2 and NO_2 and other greenhouse gas emissions. An expected increase in convective rainfall caused by stronger gradients of temperature and pressure and more atmospheric moisture may result in heavier rainfall. When and where it does occur, such extreme precipitation events can cause increased soil erosion. Conditions are more favourable for the proliferation of insect and pests in warmer climates. Grasshoppers and larvae may cause infestation during the crop season. Altered wind patterns may change the spread of both wind borne pests and of the bacteria and fungi that are agents of crop disease. Livestock disease may be similarly affected. The possible increases in pest infestations may bring about greater use of pesticides to control them.

Global warming is predicted to lead to thermal expansion of sea water along with partial melting of land based glaciers and sea ice resulting in a rise of sea level which may range from 0.1 to 0.5 meters (4 to 20 inches) by the middle of the next century, according to present estimates of the Inter Governmental Panel on Climate Change (IPCC). Such a rise could pose a threat to agriculture in low lying coastal areas where impeded drainage of surface water and of ground water, as well as intrusion of sea water into estuaries and aquifers might take place. In parts of Egypt, Bangladesh, Indonesia, China, the Netherlands, Florida and other low lying coastal areas already suffering from poor drainage, agriculture is likely to become increasingly difficult to sustain. Some island states are particularly vulnerable to risk. Agriculture is not a wholly benign actor on the environment, as it causes accelerated soil erosion by water and wind through cultivation and often introduces nitrates and other chemicals into water supplies through the application of chemical fertilizers and pesticides[24]. The steady increasing human population has already led to a rise in the demand for food. As more land comes under agricultural cultivation, there will be more pressure on natural ecosystem. Climate change will affect agriculture yield directly because of alternations in temperature and rainfall and indirectly through changes in soil quality, pests, diseases; in particular the yields of cereals is expected to decline in India, Africa and middle East. As temperature rises, conditions will become more favourable for pests such as grasshoppers to complete a number of reproduction cycles thereby increasing their population. In the higher latitude (in Northern countries) agriculture will benefit with rise in temperature as the winter season will be shorter and the growing season longer. This will also mean that pests will move towards the higher latitudes as the temperature rises. Extreme weather conditions such as high temperature, heavy rainfall, floods and drought etc. will also adversely affect the agricultural productions.

Agriculture as a Green House Gas Contributor

The role of climate as a determinant of agriculture has long been recognized. The role of agriculture as a potential contributor to climate change has come to light in the last decade. Clearing forests for fields, burning crops, and raising large herd of cattle and other ruminants and fertilizing with Nitrogen release greenhouse gases to the atmosphere. The clearing of Northern Hemisphere forests for agriculture was the largest agent of change in the Carbon cycle. Emissions from agriculture sources are believed to account for some 15 per cent of today's anthropogenic greenhouse gas emissions. Land use changes, often made for agriculture purposes contribute another 8 per cent or so to the total. As a result, agriculture ranks third after energy consumption (which is also in part agricultural) and chlorofluoro-carbons production as a contributor to the enhanced greenhouse effect. Emission of greenhouse gases from agricultural sources are likely to increase in the years ahead, given the necessity to expand food production in order to provide for world's growing population. Thus agriculture produces greater consequences on climate change resulting in global warming. New study finds rising levels of atmospheric Carbon Dioxide interfering with plant's ability to incorporate certain forms of Nitrogen, leading to dramatic changes in plant's life and forcing significant changes in agricultural fertilizer use. According to Boom study, plant and tree species in natural ecosystem that depend on nitrate conversion into amino acids in their leaves, are likely to be at competitive disadvantage to those species that are either able to convert nitrate into amino acids in their roots or use ammonium as their predominant nitrogen source. This may result in significant changes in the distribution of plants in the world as atmospheric Carbon Dioxide levels continue to rise[25]. North American farmers found their wheat withering under the unusually fierce summer of 1988. Europeans mired in last year's unseasonally warm winter, even rural Africans who suffered as their continent faced drought for twentieth consecutive year, may have had the phrase "greenhouse effects on their lips". If the weather is bad the fashionable thing today is to blame it on the greenhouse gas or as it is less imaginatively called global warming[26].

Impacts of Climate Change on Human Settlements

Impacts of climate change on human settlement have far reaching consequences on (1) housing and shelter (2) the surrounding community (3) physical infrastructure (4) social and cultural services.

The consequences of global warming could be serious for many countries of the world especially for developing countries in several important areas as noted below :

- **Housing and land resources :** Densely populated costal villages and island countries of the world may be affected seriously due to sea level rise depriving many people of their housing shelter and land resources causing major problems for human settlements.
- **Tropical cyclones :** As sea surface temperature rises due to thermal temperature expansion, the ocean areas which can spawn

tropical cyclones (typhoons, hurricanes etc.) are expected to increase in the coming century as the globe warms, resulting in innumerable hazards to coastal areas. The intensity of these storms may increase in future and will have major implications for livelihoods.

- **Flood :** The greenhouse gas effect will enhance the hydrologic cycle, producing more instances of heavy rainfalls causing high floods affecting shelters and crops of the developing countries very often.
- **Drought or water shortages :** As global warming occurs, drought and shortage of drinking water may become a much greater problem in the coming years. Global warming may be expected in some region to lower the ground water, increase the salinity due to evaporation, decrease in surface of many lakes, or inland waterways and drop in the water coral of such bodies. It resulted in food crisis, decline in food production in tropics and subtropics, despite steady global production.
- **Loss of Biomass :** Among other climate change, global warming will accelerate loss of biomass as a result of increased drought and shortages of rainfalls.
- **Rapid Thawing of permafrost :** As global temperature rises rapidly it adversely affects existing structures and constructions of building, roads and bridges. Migration and resettlement may occur as a result of climate change causing loss of housing (due to river or sea flooding or mudslides) loss of living resources, like water energy, food supply, or employment and loss of social and cultural resources in the case of devastating flood or super cyclones.
- **Bio diversity :** The environment of all inhabitants of the globe would be altered significantly by the magnitude of climate change changing the location, size and character of wildlife habitants at unprecedented rate. It is apprehended by the scientists that worldwide climate changes will result in the extinction that would be wide spread because habitants would have shifted, shrunk or disappeared all together. The consequences of greenhouse effect for wildlife hinge on whether, a given habit will become warmer or drier or warmer or wetter[27]. It is expected that global warming will cause far-reaching implications for the very survivals of human beings on Earth. Global climate is relentless and could destroy the entire human civilization one day or other. If the

environmental degradation continues at the current rate the next two decades will witness desertification of Himalayan region forcing people to leave their villages in search of greater areas elsewhere[28].

Impacts of Climate Change on Marine and Coastal Resources

The IPCC has identified coastal zone and marine ecosystems as highly vulnerable to climate impacts such as the sea level rise and increased intensity of extreme weather events, particularly in coastal nations throughout the Caribbean, the Pacific and Sub Sahara Africa. Among others, climate change might result in shifting migration patterns for major pelagic fisheries such as the western pacific tuna fisheries. Such shifts will have major implications for local fishermen whose livelihoods are based on catch levels in certain waters. While it remains to be seen exactly how rising temperature will affect off shore fisheries, it is fairly clear that coral reefs and the inshore fisheries dependent on them are extremely vulnerable to rising temperatures. Increasing sea surface temperatures associated with the recent ENSO have led to mass coral bleaching events worldwide in the last few years. Perhaps few ecosystems are as vulnerable to the projected temperature increase as coral reef systems. The greatest impacts on coastal and marine resources may result from their vulnerability to the 0.9 to 0.88 meter sea level rise projected to result from climate change. Sea level rise quite obviously results in shoreline displacement through inundation and storm surge as well as exacerbated coastal erosion. Higher sea levels provide a higher base for waves and floods during storms and can greatly exacerbate damages to coastal areas and commuhities as a result. If coral reef acceleration cannot keep pace with sea level rise, reefs will lose potentially further decreasing sediment supply to the shoreline and increasing erosion. Finally, coastal and marine resources are particularly vulnerable to any increase in extreme whether events such as cyclones. Data is still inconclusive as to whether or not hurricane and cyclone wind speeds will increase under climate change condition. But the IPCC predicts, increased peak and mean precipitation during such extreme events will result in increased flooding and damages to coastal areas. The physical and biological impacts have direct development impacts. Specific impacts include those on food security as a result of declining fisheries and the degradation of coral reefs and other critical marine habitants and on public works infrastructure. Transportation systems, protective dams, etc. are at risk due to sea level rise and extreme weather events; likewise tourism will be severely affected[29].

Marine ecosystems especially tropical coral, which grows at a slow rate, would be affected by climate change. This would affect the diverse marine life forms that need support. According to Inter Governmental Panel on Climate Change assessment report, the developing countries are twice as vulnerable as developed countries and small island nations at three times as vulnerable, "Recent regional changes in climate particularly increases in temperatures have already affected hydrological systems and terrestrial and marine ecosystems in many parts of the world[30]. Populations that inhabit small islands and or low lying coastal areas are at risk of severe social and economic effects from sea level rise and storm surges. Many human settlements will face increased risk of coastal flooding and erosion and breaches with tens of millions of people living in deltas in low lying coastal areas and small islands searching for homes. Fresh water, fisheries, coral reefs and atolls and wildlife habitat would also be at risk[31]. As estimated 50 to 70 percent of the glcbal human population lives in coastal communities and coastal populations are growing at a faster rate than most other settled areas. The IPCC report states that "In large measure, human social and economic well being depends directly or indirectly on the availability of environmental goods and coastal systems. Coastal and marine environments are intrinsically linked to the prevailing climate in many ways. Heat given off by the oceans warms the land during the winter, and ocean waters help to keep coastal regions cooler during the summer. Moisture evaporated from the oceans is the ultimate source of precipitation and the run off from the precipitation carries nutrients, pollutant and other materials from the land to the ocean. Sea level exerts a major influence on coastal zone, shaping barrier islands and pushing salt water up estuaries and into aquifers. During the 1982-83 and 97-98 EL Nifio events, erosion damage was wide spread along the pacific coastline. Climate change will affect interactions among conditions on the land and sea and in the atmosphere. Warming is likely to alter coastal weather and could affect the intensity, frequency and extent of severe storms, melting of glaciers and ice sheets and thermal expansion of ocean waters will cause sea level rise, which is likely to intensity erosion and endanger coastal structures. Rising sea levels and higher temperatures are also likely to affect the ecology of estuaries and coastal weathers. Higher temperatures coupled with increasing CO_2 concentrations are likely to severely stress coral reefs, and the changing temperature patterns are likely to cause fisheries to relocate and alter fish migration patterns[32].

Estuaries, wetlands and shorelines along the Atlantic and Gulf coasts are especially vulnerable. Impacts on fixed structure will intensify even in the absence of an increase in storminess. However, because the slope of these areas is so gentle even a small rise in sea level can produce a large inland shift of the shoreline. The rise will be particularly important if the frequency or intensity of storm surges or hurricanes increases. Coastal erosion increases the threat to coastal development, transportation, infrastructure, tourism, fresh water aquifers, fisheries and coastal ecosystems, coastal cities and towns. Especially, those in storm prone regions such as the South East, are particularly vulnerable. Intensive residential and commercial development in these regions is placing more and more lives and property at risk. Climate change and sea levels rise could present significant threats to valuable productive coastal ecosystems, Changes in run off are also likely to adversely affect estuaries. Decreased run off is likely to reduce fishing, decrease the size of estuarine nursery zones and increase the range of estuarine habitat susceptible to predators and pathogens of selfish. The projected increase in the current rate of sea level rise is very likely to exacerbate the current rate of loss of existing coastal wetlands. Coral reefs are one of the longest global storehouses of marine biodiversity sheltering one quarter of marine life and containing extensive untapped genetic resources. The demise or continued deterioration of reefs could have profound implications for the environment and economies of the coastal areas of the world. The last few years have seen unprecedented declines in the health of coral reef. Climate change is very likely to substantially alter the distribution and abundance of major fish stocks, many of which are shared international resources. Along the Pacific coast, impacts to fisheries related to the EL Nifio Southern Oscillation, illustrate how climate directly affects marine fisheries on short time scale. The changes in fish stocks resulting from climate change area also likely to have important implications for marine populations and ecosystems. Changes over the long term that will affect all nations are likely to include pole ward shifts in distribution of marine populations and changes in the timing, locations and perhaps viability of migrations and nesting and feeding areas for marine mammals and other species[33].

Impacts on Human Health

Global warming is predicted to have large effects on temperatures and weather patterns. It will therefore also greatly impact human health through a number of direct and indirect measures-one important being global warming which is to have a significant increase of the heat waves in both number and severity. This will create a greater amount of heat stress in cities leading to a large number of deaths. This will pose the biggest problems for the young and the old. It will also present obstacles for the poor people, who face greater heat exposure due to inadequate living conditions and lack of air conditioning. Although global warming will lead to fewer cold related deaths due to an overall increase in average temperature, this decline will be more than balanced out by increase at other end of the climate spectrum[34]. Throughout the world the prevalence of particular diseases and other threats to human health depend largely on local climate. Extreme temperature can directly cause the loss of life. Moreover, several serious diseases only appear in warm areas. Finally, warm temperatures can increase air and water pollutions, which in turn harm human health. Extremely hot temperatures increase the number of people who die on a given day for many reasons :

- **Increased Risk of heat related morbidity or mortality :** Extreme heat associated with cramps fainting, heat exhaustion and heat stroke and lengthy or repeated heat waves likely to induce mortality increase during heat waves in the summer may not allow people to recover. The ill health effects may also be compounded by other problems such as high humidity and poor air quantity. People with heart problems are vulnerable because one's cardiovascular system must work harder to keep body cool during hot weather. Heat exhaustion and some respiratory problems increase. Most research on heat mortality indicates that high temperature alone has a very dramatic effect. Statistics on mortality and hospital admissions show that death rate increases during extremely hot days, particularly among very old and young people living in the cities. The impacts of weather on human well-being go beyond mortality even birth rates and sperm counts appear to be affected by climatological phenomena. Continued warming could have significant implications for human health. Coping with extreme heat waves will be just one of human concerns[35].
- **Air Polluted diseases :** Global warming and increased UV-radiation would both accelerate the photochemical reaction rates among chemical pollutants and increase ozone concentration in urban areas. The natural layer of ozone in upper atmosphere blocks harmful ultraviolet radiation from reaching the Earth surface but in the lower atmosphere ozone is a harmful pollutant. Ozone and other photochemical oxidants may be associated with many respiratory diseases and cancer. Increased UVB radiation causes a number of disease of the eye and skin such as cataract, non melanoma and melanoma, skin cancer. Ozone damages lung tissue, and causes particular problem for people with asthma and

other lung diseases. Even modest exposure to ozone can cause healthy individuals to experience chest pains, nausea and pulmonary congestion. In many nations, a warming of 4°F could increase ozone concentrations by about 5 percent. Ground level ozone is produced by a complex series of chemical reactions involving sunlight, oxygen, water vapor, volatile organic compounds and oxide of nitrogen. The rate of these reactions increases higher temperatures resulting in hazardous impacts on human health.

- **Chemical Pollution :** Global warming may result in an increase of pesticide use in agriculture, and accelerate the volatilization and atmospheric transport of much organic pollution in global ecosystems causing adverse effects on human health.
- **Water borne diseases :** As global warming could alter precipitation, water quality may be affected greatly. High salt concentrations and less water supply threatens the dry lands. Through impaired drinking water and food production extreme rain storms can swamp municipalities sewage and store water capacities increasing the risks of water pollution and water borne infectious diseases:- As a result, out breaks of water borne diseases such as Crypto Sporidiosis or Giardiasis may become more frequent or widespread if extreme rain storms occur more often. As projected under climate change, particularly in areas with polluted waters diseases such as cholera that tend to accompany algal blooms could become more frequent, when flooding causes the contamination of drinking water by sewerage systems. There will be increases in disease transmission due to breakdown in sewerage and garbage services. Food and water borne diseases are also suspectable to climate change. Scientists speculate that if temperature rises under global warming, the incidence of diseases caused by food poisoning and by contamination of drinking (and swimming) water could increase dramatically. While there are indications that global warming trend may increase the risks of certain water borne and animal carried diseases. Sanitation and public health systems in many developing countries lack the resources and public health systems needed to prevent such out breaks.
- **Vector borne diseases:** since global warming changes rainfall and temperature some infections diseases including parasitic and viral diseases such as Malaria Schistosomiasis dengue fever and yellow fever have the potential to increase in many countries

especially tropical and subtropical areas. The occurrence of many infectious diseases is strongly seasonal, suggesting that climate plays a role in influencing transmission. Some vector borne diseases such as lyme disease or more recently, west Nile incephalitis, have expanded widely across the region. While this spread is attributed largely to land use changes, future changes in rainfall or temperatures could encourage greater reproduction or survival of the disease carrying insects, which include ticks and mosquitoes respectively. Many infectious diseases are dependent on vector organisms which are sensitive to environmental factors and therefore will be affected by global warming. Biological modeling under various climate scenarios suggests a widening of the potential transmission zone of some disease pathogens and their vectors such as mosquitoes.

- **Decreased risk of cold related morbidity or mortality :** Cold related health risks are likely to decline over time as the frequency of extreme cold water periods during winter decreases. In countries that currently experience extremely cold weather in winter an increase in mortality rate in summer might be offset by a decrease in winter mortality. Northern countries with severe winters have a higher mortality rate in winter because more sick and elderly people succumb in cold weather and because blizzards and extreme cold create dangerous conditions in which deaths are more likely. Winters will tend to be milder under global warming with the likely effect that winter death rates will decline. Warmer temperatures many decrease the number of people who die each year from cold weather. For the most part cold related deaths occur during occasional cold spells in areas with mild winters where people prepare less for the cold or during extreme events like the severe snowstorm. Finally deaths due to the heat are more sensitive to temperature changes than deaths due to the cold. The difference between 20F and 15F for example has a much smaller impact than an increase from 950F to 1000F. Although global warming will lead to fewer cold related deaths due to an overall increase in average temperature, this decline will be more than balanced out by increase at the other end of the climate spectrum.

It is expected that global warming causes innumerable hazards to human health, death and diseases. Heat stress, vector and water borne diseases could claim more lives as the tropical habits of insects expand northwards. The effects of climate change on human health in small islands countries and coastal areas are likely to be serious. In case of human health particularly in lower income poor population predominately in tropical and subtropical countries the effects are projected to increase. Perhaps the most significant impacts of climate change would be low availability of water. Projected climate change would execrable water shortage and quality problems in many areas of world, but it would also alleviate these in some other areas. As it happens, climate change will fall disproportionately on developing countries and poor persons within all countries, accentuate inequalities in health status, adequate food, clean water and other resources. The exposure of populations in the developing countries to relatively high rates of adverse impacts from climate change and their diminishing capacity to adapt to impacts combine to make populations in developing countries generally more vulnerable on health than the populations of developed countries.

Overall climate change is projected to increase threats to human health directly. Taking into account tolerance limits of humans large number of deaths during heat waves are found among poor inner city residents who have little access to cooler environments. The mortality of infants and elders' variations in response among sex and races is higher during heat waves. However from recent studies it is found that white mortality rates are higher than black's almost in all examined conditions. The environmental protection agency of the United States reported to the Congress that it is expected that a seven-fold increase in heat related death by the middle of the 21st century, if acclimatization does not occur. This would render heat related deaths as a major killer relating the present number of death from Leukemia. Global warming and climate change will result in various human health disasters with increasing cases of heat stress. During the current century extreme heat periods are likely to be more common increased risk of heat related morbidity or mortality. The climate change associated with global warming is likely to be hardest on the elderly, the infirm and poor particularly in developing countries. Climate change largely caused by greenhouse gas emissions from human sources raises the possibility that elevated temperatures are contaminated and changes in precipitation patterns could pose increased health risks. Global warming trend may increase the risk of certain water borne and animal carried diseases often leading to an increase in the number of human deaths.

It is difficult to predict the future effect on mortality levels because as heat waves become more frequent, increases in psychological stress, depression and feeling of isolation amongst people affected by natural health disasters are evident. Scientists predict from the rate at which global temperature rises, extreme heat waves will enhance the heat related morality and directly cause the loss of life with the appearance of serious diseases in warmer areas of the world. Warm temperatures can increase air and water pollution which ultimately increase the risk of certain water borne and vector borne infectious diseases among poor communities of the developing countries. Global warming is a threat to mankind throughout the world in the face inevitable disasters directly affecting the human health. If the present trend of global warming will continue, it will lead to the end of complex human civilization.

Impacts of Sea Level Rise

While the scientists and environmentalists in developed and developing countries differ in the causes of global warming, steady rise in sea level rise cannot be denied. It is argued that an increase in the global atmospheric temperatures would have two consequences. The melting of ice from high latitude and latitudes will add to the total volume of the ocean. The volume of seawater will increase due to thermal expansion. Some studies suggest that cyclone will be more frequent and destructive as the greenhouse effect gets more prominent. It has been estimated that during the last century the global sea level has risen by 10 to 15 cm. A rise of 5 cm can be linked to thermal expansion. Because of global warming and deglacierization with existing approximations the estimates of global sea rise for the year 2060 vary from 23.8 to 116.7 cm and for the year 2100 from 56.2 to 345.9 cm[36]. According to some academicians, global warming will lead to melting and drowning of millions of people due to a rise in the sea level. Others say that the change in the atmosphere will lead not to warming but to a freeze and millions will perish in the cold[37]. Scientists say world wise impacts of global warming will increase temperature of 3-100′ F over the next 100 years. Rising sea levels, volatile climate changes with increased EL Nino, flooding and droughts and shifts in crop productivity are now unstoppable even if greenhouse gas emissions are dramatically cut now. Scientists say, global warming will continue for the next hundred years even if the use of fossil fuel is dramatically reduced. Climate models indicate temperature increases of three to more than 10 degrees Fahrenheit this century. Meanwhile, a rise in sea levels of six inches to nearly three feet is also being observed. And now experts attending the US biggest science meeting have told so much greenhouse gases are in the atmosphere already that nothing can stop the world from continuing to heat up over the next 100 years.

The 20th century witnessed the greatest increase in temperature of any century during the last thousand years, and the 1990's were the warmest decade. As the temperature rises, so does the sea level with profound consequences all over the world. In its 2001 assessment of global warming, the Inter Governmental Panel on Climate Change (IPCC) projected that global mean sea level is expected to rise between 9 and 88 centimeter by 2100, with a best estimate of 50 centimeters. Higher temperatures lead to higher sea levels- A warmer world will have a higher sea level because as the land and lower atmosphere of the world warm, heat is transformed into the oceans. When materials are heated they expand thermal expansion. So the heat that is transferred causes seawater to expand, which then results in a rise in sea level. In addition, water from land based ice such as glaciers and ice sheets may enter the oceans, thus adding to the rise. A point to remember is that no extra water is added to the oceans when ice floating in the ocean melts. As floating ice melts, it only replaces the volume of water that it originally displaced. Warmer temperatures could lead to the melting ice or thermal expansion of water, which contribute the most to the sea level rise.

- **Non polar glaciers :** If non polar glaciers such as those in New Zealand and Norway melted they would release water that may enter the ocean and contribute to a sea level rise Glaciers are rather sensitive to climate change and they could melt rapidly.
- **Green land ice sheet :** In Greenland ice increase from snowfall is balanced by ice loss from melting and the discharge of glaciers. Projections indicate that increased melting from higher temperatures would exceed any increase in precipitation. This change in the ice balance would add water to the ocean.
- **Antarctic ice sheet :** Nearly all of Antarctica is covered by an ice sheet that is an average 2.5 Kilometers thick. If all land ice covering Antarctica were to melt-that around 30 million cubic kilometers of ice, the seas would rise by over 60 meters. However in Antarctica it is so cold that even with increases of a few degrees, temperatures would remain below the melting point of ice. In fact warmer temperatures could lead to more snow, which would increase the amount of ice in Antarctica.
- **Thermal Expansion :** While thermal expansion is an less obvious process than melting ice, the IPCC projects that thermal expansion will be the main component of expected sea level rise over the 21st century.

On average it is expected that by 2100 sea levels will have risen in most places by around half a meter. In many places 50 centimeter would see entire beaches being washed away together with a significant chunk of the coastline. For people living on low lying islands such as Tuvalu,

Kiribati or the Maldives where the highest point is only 2-3 meters above current sea levels, an extra 50 centimeters could see significant portions of their islands being washed away by erosion or covered by water. Even if they remain above the sea, many island nations will have their supplies of drinking water reduced because seawater will invade their freshwater aquifers. While these islands have sizable populations, they are insignificant compared to the tens of millions of people living in the low level costal areas of South Asia. These include the coastlines of Pakistan. India, Sri Lanka, Bangladesh and Burma[38]. Sea level is rising more rapidly along the US coast than worldwide. EPA and others have estimated that along the Gulf and Atlantic coasts, a one-foot (30 cm) rise in sea level by 2050 may be seen. In the next century a two foot rise is most likely, but a one foot rise is possible, and sea level will probably continue to rise for several centuries, even if global temperatures were to stop rising a few decades. Rising sea levels inundates wetlands and other low lying lands, erodes breaches, intensifies flooding and increases the salinity of rivers, bays ground water tables. Some of these effects may be further compounded by other effects of changing climate. Coastal marshes and swamps are particularly vulnerable to rising sea level because they are mostly within a few feet of sea level. As the sea rises, the outer boundary of these wetlands will erode, and new wetlands will form inlands as previously dry areas are flooded by higher water levels. The amount of newly created wetlands, however will be much smaller than the area of wetlands that are lost. The amount of dry land within a few feet above the wetlands is much less than the area of wetlands that would be lost if sea level rises a few feet[39].

Nationwide impacts of sea level rise estimates the areas of dry and wetlands that would erode or to be inundated from a 50, 100, or 200 cm. rise in global sea level. A study by the Federal Emergency Management Agency (FEMA) estimated potential increases in flood damages and the areas of the coastal flood plain resulting from a one or 3 foot rise in sea level IPCC response strategies point out sea level rise threatens ground water supplies of the Nile, Ganges, Niger, Mekang, Yellow and other major five deltas. Global warming has adverse implications and hazards to the very survival of mankind on the Earth. The gradual rise of temperature is likely to be serious causing steady rise in the sea levels due to melting of ice caps, and resulting in drowning of millions of people. The consequence is rise in sea levels which could be disastrous to coastlines around the world[40].

Sea level rise due to global warming is likely to cause major problems to densely populated coastal villages depriving many people of their land

and resources. It may badly affect the island countries of the world.[41] Warmer Earth would see melting of ice and rise of ocean, which may wipe out Holland, Jamaica, Maldives, Bahamans etc. The highest natural calamity of the century according to some estimates has claimed five lakh lives in Bangladesh that seems to be only indicator of the of the disastrous implications of impending climate change like global warming and rise in sea level[42]. Addressing to the Ninth conference of the parties to the United Nations Framework Convention on climate change, Dr. R.K. Pachuri, Chairman of IPCC on 10th December 2003 highlighted that the climate change level is projected to rise by 0.09 to 88 meters between the year 1990-2100 for the full range of SRES set by the IPCC. This would happen primarily due to thermal expansion of seawater and loss of mass from the caps. These glaciers and ice caps are projected to continue their wide spread retreat during 21st century. Rise sea levels inundate low lying areas, drown coastal Marshes and wetlands, erode breaches, exacerbate flooding and increase salinity of rivers, bays and aquifers. Increased global temperatures would also mean an increase in the intensity and number of storm surges[43]. 20th Century warming has contributed significantly to the observed sea level rise through thermal expansion of seawater and wide spread loss of land ice. Within present uncertainties, observations and models are both consistent with a lack of significant acceleration of sea level rise during the 20th century. There is no demonstratable change in overall Antarctic sea extent from the year 1978-2000. In addition there are conflicting analyses and insufficient data to assess changes in intensities of tropical and extra tropical cyclone and local storms in the mid latitudes[44].

In contrast to the Antarctic ice sheet, the Greenland ice sheet is likely to lose mass during the 21st century and contribute a few cm. to sea level rise. Ice sheet will continue to react to climate warming and contribute to sea level rise for thousands of year after climate has been stabilized. Climate models indicate that the local warming over the Greenland is likely to be one to three times the global average. Ice sheet models project that a local warming of larger than 3°C if sustained from all millennia would lead to a complete melting of the green land ice sheet with a resulting sea level rise of about 7 cm. A local warming of 5.5C if sustained to 1000 years, would likely result in a contribution from Greenland about 3cm. to sea level rise. Continued warming would increase melting of permafrost in polar, sub polar, and mountain regions, and would make much of this terrain vulnerable to subsidence and landslides which affect infrastructure, watercourse and wet land ecosystems[45].

As the Earth gets warmer, there is a serious risk of climate change in ways that will seriously disrupt life on Earth. Globally glaciers are melting and sea ice is declining resulting in sea level rise as much as 50 cm by 2100. Millions of people living in low lying coastal nations such as Bangladesh could be displaced by rising sea levels. Many studies agree that in the 21st century sea level rise is not likely to exceed .8 m, which is enough to cause serious environment problems in many Coastal Zones[46]. The IPCC Third Assessment Reports finds that in the last 40 years, the global average sea level has risen, ocean heat content has increased and snow cover and ice extent have decreased, which threaten to inundate low lying Island nations and coastal regions through out the world. As a result of global warming, sea level rise trend is still continuing and will continue for many more years after heat trapping gases are stabilized. Scientists predict, sea level could rise 3.5 to 34.6 inches between 1990 and 2100 making coastal ground water saltier, endangering wetlands and inundating valuable land and coastal communities. Coastal areas and small islands are among the most densely populated parts of the world. They are also the most threatened because of rises in sea level that global warming may cause. The heating of oceans and melting of glaciers and polar ice sheets, is predicted to raise the average sea level about half a meter over the next century. Sea level rise could have a number of physical impacts on coastal areas, including loss of land due to inundation and erosion, increased flooding and salt-water intrusion. These could adversely effect coastal agriculture, tourism, fresh water resources, fisheries and aquaculture, human settlements and health. There could be large decreases in the availability of water in many rivers because of rainfall and snow. The volume in other would increase due to glaciers melting for example the rivers originating in the Himalayas, shifts in water availability could also affecte hydropower generation, and industries, such as paper, pharmaceutical and chemical manufacturing that use large quantity of water. Building and other infrastructure would be vulnerable to any increase in the frequency of storms and other extreme events, which could also disrupt transport routes.

Global sea level rise is caused by delivery of water to the ocean as the land ice melts such as mountain glaciers and polar ice caps. Current evidence of global warming includes widespread retreat of glaciers on 5 continents. As the temperatures rise, ocean spread occupying more surface area on the planet. The 20th century has seen a dramatic rise in sea levels. A one meter rise in sea level would inundate half of Bangladesh rice lands. Bangladesh would be forced to migrate by millions to other rice growing low lands, which include those of Vietnam, China, India and Thailand. Millions of climate refugees could be created by sea level rise in the Philippines, Indonesia and Egypt[47]. According to IPCC findings, the impacts of higher average sea level on coastal areas may be increased greatly during high tides and storms. Higher average sea level means high tides will be higher and coastal storm, flooding and storm surges high, and water driven ashore by strong winds-will cover more area, potentially flooding and damaging larger stretches of coastal lands. This includes both buffer areas, such as wetlands, breaches and barrier islands and developed coastal cities, towns and resort areas. The projected impacts of increased sea levels and sea temperature rise on already vulnerable coastal areas will include increased flooding and storm damage, increased erosion of shore lines, decreased marine and coastal biodiversity, and contamination of drinking and irrigation water with salt water. The situation will be much more worse in future. The tides come and go like clockwork, and coastal regions will face more erosion damage than the seas and the gentle image might be changed in the eyes of those affected[48].

Worldwide measurements from tidal gauges indicate that global mean sea level has risen between 10 to 25 cm. (18 cm. average) during the last 100 years. This rate is greater than the average of the last few thousand years estimated from geological and archaeological records. Sea level rise in a given location will vary depending on factors, such as vertical land movement, wind and pressure patterns, ocean circulation and rates of warming. Coastal wetlands and lowlands breaches, barrier islands and ocean islands and soils are especially vulnerable to rising seas. As rising seas threaten property structures and natural resources, the problems afflicting much of the world will likely to be horrible if predictions of future climate change and sea level rise are accurate. In the next century a two foot rise is most likely but a four foot rise is possible and sea level will probably continue to rise for several centuries even if greenhouse gas emissions could be stabilized by the end of the 21st century. Sea level rise from ocean thermal expansion may only have reached half its eventual level by the year 2500. As the sea level rises at faster rates causing more intensive storm damages and erosion of many breaches, and coastal property may become more vulnerable to the effects of climate change.

Impact on Ecosystems

IPCC projections based on its greenhouse forcing scenarios are that sea levels rise of 18 cm. by 2030 as the best estimate and 8 cm. as the lowest estimate with 29 cm. as the highest estimate. The primary effects of a sea level rise will be increased coastal flooding, erosion, storm surges and wave activity. Ecosystems being affected by climate change have been placed in three categories to reflect the relative vulnerabilities.

- "Front line" ecosystems, which include coral reefs, mangrove ecosystems, and the arctic marine ecosystem, may be affected by global warming.
- Highly vulnerable ecosystems are those where there is evidence of a significant climate threat.
- "High risk" ecosystems are those which appear in jeopardy but for which the precise impacts of a climate change yet not clear[49]. The deterioration of ecosystems will have far reaching adverse effects on the Earth's atmosphere. Two ecologists Dr. Jay Malcom of the university of Toronto and Dr. Louis Pitelka of the university of Maryland, Centre for Eenvironmental science reviewed evidence of potential ecosystems being affected by global warming.

Their report describes the "very real possibility" that global warming will disrupt the integrity of many of the land based ecosystems on which human beings depend. Ecosystems provide humans such valuable goods and services such as food, raw materials, recreational opportunities, clean air and water and erosion control. The importance of ecosystems extends beyond economics and tangible benefits with many people placing a high value on the spiritual and aesthetic role nature plays in their lives the report notes. Despite the crucial roles of terrestrial ecosystems, they are increasingly threatened by the impacts of a growing human population, through habitat destruction and air and water pollution and now as a result of global climate change.

This report describes how climate change is likely to profoundly alter the natural environment. As the Earth warms, the distribution of land based ecosystems will change as plants and animals follow the shifting climate. Both the amount and rate of anticipated warming poses threats to the nation's biological diversity. The rate of anticipated climate change is estimated to be ten times than seen in the last ice age. As a result, certain species may face dwindling number and even extinction if they are unable to migrate fast enough to keep up with changing climate.

Climate change is likely to alter the quantity and quality of the various goods and services that ecosystems provide. For example, climate change is likely to affect the ability of ecosystems to filter air and water pollutants and to control soil erosion. The effects of climate change on ecosystems must be considered in the context of a range of human caused impacts on ecosystems. Climate change is likely to be particularly damaging for ecological communities and species that have suffered the greatest disruption from human development. Natural ecosystems already under stress because of air and water pollution will have diminished capacity to adapt to climate change. Likewise habitat destruction and fragmentation will lessen the chances that species will able to migrate to more suitable climate and habitats. Because ecosystems are inherently complex it is hard to predict how ecosystems will adapt to climate change[50]. Scientists are also continuing to work to pin down the likely impacts of global warming on natural and managed ecosystems, since higher Carbon Dioxide levels, higher temperatures and changed precipitation patterns exert interactive effect on those systems be they natural wetlands, cultivated crops or forest communities. Today global warming causes creeping environmental change due to the atmospheric concentrations of GHGs. Creeping which means an incremental change, will have added up to major environmental change. The environmental change will have turned into an environmental crisis. In this regard global warming is similar to other creeping environmental changes such as air pollution, acid rain, ozone depletion, soil erosion, deforestation and so forth. There is convincing and mounting evidence that human activities related to industrial processes and deforestation are altering the global ecosystems. Warming trends will change the distribution of trees and other native plants, altering animal habitat. Normal associations of plants and animals may be disrupted. Climate extremes kill plants and wildlife plants may be killed if the temperature falls below freezing for even a few hours; like wise birds and insects may die if temperatures get too warm. Quick change may cause drastic consequences on ecosystems.

Impacts on Weather System

Today climate change appears to be a potent danger affecting the weather systems. This trend is likely to be intensive in future. The reason why this menance has been assuming serious proportion is that global warming has started showing its various impacts and adverse consequences i.e. too much of heat or cold or extreme type of summer and winter, drought or territorial rain, frequency of flood or drought, formation of circles high or low pressures of air amidst the seas and oceans, land slides and land erosion, extension of deserts.[51]. The duration, location, frequency and intensity of extreme weather and climate events are very likely to change and would result in mostly adverse impacts on biophysical systems[52]. More hot days and heat waves and fewer cold and frost days are very likely over nearly all land areas. Increases in mean temperatures will lead to increases in hot weather and record hot weather with fewer frost days and cold waves. A number of models shows a generally decreased daily variability in summer in Northern hemisphere land areas. The changes in temperature extremes are likely to result in increased crop and livestock losses, higher energy use for cooling and lowering heating and increased human morbidity and heat stress.

Recent regional climate increases in temperature have already affected hydrological systems and terrestrial and marine ecosystems in many parts of the world. The rising socio-economic costs related to weather damages and to regional variations in climate suggest increasing vulnerability to climate change. Preliminary indications suggest that some social and economic systems have been affected by recent increases in floods and droughts with increases in economic losses for catastrophic weather events[53]. Models project that atmospheric concentrations of greenhouse gases will result in charges in daily, seasonal, inter annual and decadal variability. There is projected to be a decrease in diurnal temperature range in many areas with right time lows increasing more than daytime highs. A number of models show a general decrease of daily variability in summer in Northern hemisphere land areas. Current projection shows little change or a small increase in amplitude for EL Nino events over the next 100 years. Many models show a more EL Nino like mean response in the tropical pacific, with the central and eastern equatorial pacific sea surface temperatures projected to warm more than the western equatorial pacific and with a corresponding mean eastward shift of precipitation. Even with little or no change in EL Nino strength global warming is likely to lead to greater extremes of drying and heavy rainfall, and increase the risk of droughts and floods that occur with EL Nino events in many different regions[54].

Two new studies find increase in number of extreme rainfall and flooding events during last few decades which was due to global warming, and predict further increase in "100 year" floods across Northern Europe and Asia, Canada and Alaska, as well as in equatorial tropics and South east Asia. Two separate teams of scientists predict more extreme rainfall and greater flooding in this century. Although people may adapt to gradual climate change, the effects of extreme rain and flooding are often broad, devastating and costly to society. Landslides, avalanches and flooding damage of infrastructure such as roads, bridges and buildings and hurt agricultural productivity because of lost crops, soil erosion and land covered by sands. Disaster relief often requires enormous funding and the loss of human life and livestock animals may also be high[55].

Christopher Milly, atmospheric scientist of the U.S. Geological Survey - said it is reasonable to assume that increased flooding over the past century was related to global warming and the increase is likely to continue. The model suggests that instead of the chances of a 100 year flood occurring once every 100 years which is what you expect, the risk will increase in the 21st century to some what between 3 to 6 chances in 100 which is a manifold increase. The increase in temperature sparks an increase in evaporation. "Warm air can hold more water" clouds tends to suck more water up out of the ocean and it has to drop some time". Major international insurance companies warm global warming will cause a massive increase in weather related disasters whose already insured losses due to weather disasters during the 1990s were 11 times greater than those of the 1960s. Global warming will cause a massive increase in weather related disasters such as hurricanes in coming decades. The UN top scientists have warned such extreme weather events could become more common because of global warming. A UN panel of climate change scientists has said the "greenhouse effect" caused by pollution of trapping heat in the atmosphere could raise the average global temperature six degree celsius this century. The higher temperatures could disrupt weather patterns and raise sea levels leading to more frequent natural disasters. Greenhouse effects promote global warming and threaten mankind. The problem of cloud formation and acid rain and river pollution is likely to increase. Sulphur dioxide coming out of steel mills and coal fired thermal stations reacts with moisture and produces acid rains, resulting in massive damages of crops.

The amplitude and frequency of extreme precipitation events is very likely to increase over many areas and the return period for extreme precipitation events are projected to decrease. This would lead to more frequent floods and landslides with attendant loss of life health impacts i.e. epidemics, infectious diseases, food poisoning, property damage, loss to infrastructure and settlements, soil erosion, pollution, heavy loss to insurance and agriculture losses amongst others. A general drying of the arid continental areas during summer is likely to lead to increase in summer droughts and could increase the risk of wild fires. This general drying is due to a combination of increased temperature and potential evaporation that is not balanced by increase in precipitation. It is likely that global warming will lead to an increase in the variability of Asian summer monsoon precipitation[56]. Nearly all land areas will very likely warm more than global averages, particularly those at Northern latitude in winter. Globally averaged precipitation is projected to increase during the 21st century, though at regional scale both increases and decreases are projected to be typically 5 to 20%. It is likely that precipitation will increase over high latitude region in both summer and winter. Increases are also projected over Northern mid latitudes, Tropical Africa and Antarctica in winter and in Southern and Eastern Asia in Summer. Africa shows consistent decreases in winter rainfall[57].

IPCC models project that increasing atmospheric concentrations of greenhouse gases result in changes in frequency, intensity and duration of extreme weather events such as, more hot days, heat waves, heavy precipitation events and fewer cold days. Many of these projected changes would lead to increased risks of high floods, and droughts in many regions and predominantly adverse impacts on ecological systems, socio economic sectors and human health. High-resolution modeling studies suggest that peak wind and precipitation intensity of tropical cyclones are likely to increase over some areas. There is insufficient information on how very small scale extreme weather phenomena (i.e. thunder storm, Tornadoes, hails storms and lightening) may change. In recent past on 26th December 2004, due to the impacts of climate change high level sea waves approximately soared 100 meters high and flooded many parts of the South Asian countries, like, Indonesia, Philippines, Malaysia, Maldives and India. The so-called Tsunami killed millions of people and washed out their settlements and other resources. By the creation of earthquake in the seas, the high thunders of the oceans destroyed the lives and infrastructures that cannot be compensated within long spans of time. The impacts of Tsunami continued for months together creating havoc and dread among the people of that regions. The fear of re-occurrences of such event is yet not subsided. More hot days and heat waves are likely to occur over nearly all land areas. Frost days and cold waves are very likely to become fewer. Frequency of extreme precipitation events is projected to increase. According to the most recent projections of the Intergovernmental Panel on Climate Change (IPCC) the global mean temperature could increase by 1.40C to 5.80C between 1990 and 2100. The climatic effects of such a temperature might include:

- More frequent extreme high maximum temperatures and less frequent extreme low minimum temperatures.
- An increase in the variability of climate with changes to both the frequency and severity of extreme weather events perhaps the most obvious impact of global warming will be direct effects a warmer planet will experience more extreme heat waves. As seen in Europe in 2003, heat waves often lead to an increase in the number of human deaths, particularly temperate countries where people are often not accustomed to very hot weather and where houses and other infrastructure are not designed to Cope with it. The sick and elderly are most vulnerable because their bodies are less able to increase cardiac output and sweat function for cooling purpose, they are often less able to afford cooling technologies.

It is difficult to predict future effect on mortality levels, because as heat waves become more frequent can societies be expected to adjust technologically, behaviourally and physiologically? So heat waves are likely to have disproportionate effect in less developed countries and in the poor segments of rich societies. In countries that currently experience extreme cold weather in winter, an increase in the mortality rate in summer might be off set by a decrease in winter mortality. Northern countries with severe winters have higher mortality rate in winter because more sick and elderly people succumb in cold weather and because blizzards and extreme cold create dangerous conditions in which accidental deaths are more likely. Winters will tend to be milder under global warming with the likely effect that winter death rate will decline.

Most computer models generated by scientists indicate that future climate will be more variable than in the past, and that droughts and floods will be more severe. Some of the health effects of weather related disasters, in addition to immediate death and injury to people and damage to property include :

- Increases in psychological stress, depression and feelings of isolation amongst people affected by natural disaster.
- Decreases in nutrition due to poor agricultural yields caused for example by prolonged drought and problems of food distribution.
- Increases in disease transmission due to break down in sewerage and garbage services. For example, cholera is one disease that thrives in such situations, particularly when flooding causes contamination of drinking water by sewerage systems[58].

That climate change is a stress will be superimposed over expected population and other environmental stresses, said G.O.P. Obasi, Secretary General of the World Meteorological Organization (WMO), which together with United Nations Environment Programme (UNEP) launched the IPCC in 1988. “Life as known today on the planet will be forced to respond to the shift to a warmer world. Every natural and socio-economic system appears to be vulnerable to climate change. However it is the least developed countries that are the most vulnerable”. No country can afford to ignore the coming transformation of its natural and human environment “said Michael Zammit Cutajar, Executive Secretary of the UN Framework convention On Climate Change”. The poor and vulnerable are at great risk”. Projecting trends that could continue through the 21st century and beyond, UN report cites impacts of global warming. Desertification is expected to worsen in response to reduced rainfall in parts of Africa. Declines in agricultural productivity will diminish food security in many

Asian countries and floods and droughts will become more frequent in Latin America. The Earth has been experiencing the 10 warmest year since 1983 and the 7 warmest years on record have been since 1990 intensifying the weather patterns contributing to global warming. As we continue to pump gasified carbon and other greenhouse gases into the atmosphere, nature is beginning to respond with a furious energy. Storms are becoming more violent- droughts more prolonged, downpours more torrential and heat waves more intense. As we humans heat the far North and melt the polar ice, nature repays us – at least in the short term with cruler, more severe winter, as the melting ice chills the South flowing current from the Arctic Circle and the northeasters whip the cold air into bitter and seemingly interminable winters.

The coming changes that will make the biggest headlines will not be the increasing extinctions of species, changes in timing of seasons, or the gradual transformation of forest into grasslands, what will grab attention will be increasing of upheavals from natural disasters. Death from disease and starvation, wars over diminishing resources and refugees from homeland submerged by rising sea level will be horrifying. Rather than making end of nature as far more threatening and hostile force, global warming will not destroy nature but it does promise to destroy our highly organized complex civilization unless we quickly develop a newfound respect for her mother's arsenal of retaliatory responses. [59]

Impacts on Water Resources

The impacts of global warming on water resources are likely to be serious in coming decades. Perhaps, the most significant impacts of climate change would low availability of water in the world. Projected climate change would exacerbate water shortages and quality problems in mass areas of the world, but it would also alleviate these in some other areas. As it hapens, climate change will fall disproportionately on developing countries and poor persons in all countries with access to clean water generally more vulnerable. Climate change exacerbates water shortage in many water scare areas of the world. Demand for water is generally increasing due to population growth and economic development, but it is falling in some countries because of increased efficiency of use. Climate change is projected to substantially reduce availability of water (as reflected by projected run off) in many of the water scares areas of the world, but to increase it in some other areas. Fresh water quality would be degraded by higher water temperature but this may be offset in some regions by increased flows[60].

Impacts of climate change on water resources throughout the world are already under stress with demand approaching or exceeding supply.

The continuation of this trend would exacerbate water shortage that is already apparent in many areas with increasing demand for water resources. The global warming and climate change that is happening will adversely reduce the supplies of drinking water because sea level rise will invade the fresh water aquifers. A more severe impact is the seaward migration of salt water/fresh water under face, which will cause billions of cubic meters of fresh ground water to substitute salt water in the areas between former and new interfaces positions. Warmer temperatures and drier conditions would further increase the demand for water resources, which are very essential for the survival of the people and for future generations. Projected trend that could continue throughout the 21st century is expected to worsen the water supply and demand directly from the changes in run off and the levels of water of river lakes and aquifers. It appears that the trends of global warming on water resources will be horrible in future. As flow patterns and water levels respond to the changing climate, water supplies will be affected. Diminishing surface water and ground water supplies, coupled with increased demands for these resources would challenge all aspects of water resource management. The consequences of climate change for water resources depend not only on possible change in the resource base (supply) but also on changes in the demand of both human and environmental for that resource[61].

Future water demand will be affected by many factors, including population growth, wealth and distribution. Globally it is estimated that almost two billion people are already under high water stress and this number is expected to increase significantly by 2025, due primarily to population growth and increasing wealth. Warmer temperatures and drier conditions due to climate change would further increase future water demand in many regions. Where climate change is associated with increased aridity, it would directly affect water demand with respect to agricultural and domestic uses. Warming of surface waters would have direct impact on industrial operations by decreasing the efficiency of cooling systems, which could in turn reduce plant outputs. Adequate supply of fresh and clean drinking water is a basic need for all human beings on the Earth. Fresh water resources all over the world are threatened not only by over exploitation and poor management but also by ecological degradation. Polluted water like chemicals in drinking water causes problem to health and leads to water borne diseases.

Changing climate is expected to increase both evaporation and precipitation where evaporation increases more than precipitation, soil will become drier water levels will drop, and rivers will carry less water.

Lower river flows and lower lake levels could impair navigation, hydroelectric power generation and water quality, and reduce the supplies of water available for agricultural, residential and industrial uses. Some areas may experience both increased flooding during winter and spring as well as lower supplies during summer. Climate change could impair navigation by changing average water levels in rivers and lakes, increasing the frequency of both floods during which navigation is hazardous, and droughts during which passage is difficult, and necessitating changes in navigational infrastructure on the other hand. Changes in the flows of rivers would have a direct impact on the amount of hydropower generated, because hydropower production decreases with lower flows. Because of the ambiguous projections of changes in future river flow, studies of climate change show ambiguous effects on hydropower production.

The potential changes in water supplies would result directly from the changes in runoff and the levels of rivers, lakes and aquifers. Decreased river flows and higher temperatures could harm the water quality of the nation's river, bays and lakes. In areas where river flows decreases, pollution concentrations will rise because there will be less water to dilute the pollutants. Increased frequency of severe rainstorms could increase the amount of chemicals that run off from farms, lawns and streets into the seas, rivers, lakes and bays[62].

It is expected that global warming coupled with changing climate and growth of population at unprecedented rate will face the problems of shortage of water resources for drinking water and food production by the year 2050. Thus, global warming exerts drastic consequences over the water resources, which is key to survival of mankind on Earth. The continuation of this trend would exacerbate water shortage diminishing surface water and ground water supplies throughout the world in the mid of the present century. An overall assessment of the impacts of the global warming presents a wide range of severe implications and catastrophic effect on agriculture and food production, which in turn seriously affect the economy, trade and commerce, employment and income of the ever-growing populations of the world. Extreme weather conditions cause heavy rainfall, floods and droughts, which ultimately act as a deterrent to agriculture and food production, environment and resource base in future. The consequences of global warming could be serious for many countries of the world affecting the housing and land resources causing major problems for human settlements due to sea level rise. tropical cyclones, hurricanes, floods and storms. As the global temperature rises rapidly it will adversely affect the existing structures, constructions of building, roads and bridges. Problems of migration and resettlement may exacerbate as a result of frequent natural calamities of devastating flood, super cyclones and earthquakes.

Increased temperatures, rising sea levels and more intense extreme weather events, affect the coastal zone and marine ecosystems in many parts of the world. Higher sea levels provide a higher base for waves and floods during low pressures, which greatly exacerbate damages to coastal resources and marine ecosystems. Marine ecosystems are highly vulnerable as result of declining fisheries, degradation of coral reefs, breaches, freshwater, marine habitats, public work infrastructures and coastal erosion through inundation and storm surges. The global warming is considered as one of greatest threats on human health causing serious diseases and leading to an increase in the number deaths throughout the world. Global warming coupled with extreme temperatures, increases heat related morbidity, waterborne and vector borne infectious diseases and directly causes the loss of life. In the present century heat waves increase the hospital admissions, and deaths causing catastrophic threats to the human health. It is expected that impact of global warming would be severe on human health in future if no preventive measures are taken to combat the global warming. The present century experienced the greatest increase in temperature rises contributing significantly to the rise of sea level due to melting glaciers and polar ice-sheets, and thermal expansion could adversely affect coastal agriculture, tourism, fresh water resources, land fisheries, aquaculture, human settlements, infrastructures, roads and bridges and many low lying island Nations seriously disrupting life on Earth. The 20th century has witnessed a dramatic rise in sea levels with increased coastal flooding, breach erosion, storm surges and wave activity, threatening the survival of life and species extinction with changing climate. An increase in number of cyclones and hurricanes over the last few years has been a testimony to global warming.

Today climate change experiences more hot days and heat waves and fewer cold and frost days affecting the weather systems, intensifying too much of heat and cold, for extreme type of summer and winter, drought and torrential rain, extreme rainfall and flooding events resulting in weather related disasters. The increasing atmospheric concentrations of greenhouse gases result in changes in frequency, intensity and duration of extreme weather events leading to unusual changes in weather patterns causing innumerable hazards and damages to human beings. The rapid changes in weather patterns could become more common leading to frequent natural disasters in future. Global warming caused by weather related devastating effects is likely to increase in number and magnitude in the form of high floods, droughts, super cyclones, thunder storms, hurricanes, tornadoes creating an atmosphere of "panic" in many parts of the world. In countries that currently experience extreme heat and cold waves is found an increase of deaths for catastrophic weather events. It is difficult to predict weather related disasters for the future generations in the next century. The impacts of global warming appear to be serious to meet the challenges created for the water resources in many mass areas of the world. The present trend of global warming would exacerbate availability of fresh water, diminishing surface water and ground water supplies. The impact of climate change on water resources throughout the world is under stress relating to domestic uses and agricultural purposes to meet the ever-expanding needs of the growing population of highly industrialized societies.

Fresh water resources all over the world thus threatened are expected to cause problems to human health and ecological degradation. The problems of water supply will be acute as rapid changes occurred in the resource base and water levels to respond the changing climate. No country can afford to ignore the catastrophic effects of global warming. Many of the physical changes that scientists have assessed as being consistent with global warming can already be witnessed today. These trends are expected to continue through the 21st century and beyond. In parts of Africa, desertification is expected to worsen in response to reduced rainfalls, run off and solid moisture. In many Asian countries declines in agricultural productively will diminish food security, while sea level rise and an increase in the intensity of tropical cyclones could displace tens of millions of people in low lying coastal areas. In Australia and New Zealand water is likely to become key issue due to projected drying trends over much of the region. The risk of flooding will increase across much of Europe. In Latin America floods and droughts will be more frequent and vector borne infectious diseases will expand pole ward. In North America sea level rise is expected to enhance coastal erosion and flooding and the risk of storm surges, particularly in Florida and along much of the Atlantic coast. Small island states are likely to be among the countries most seriously affected by climate change. In all regions developing countries will have difficulties adapting to climate change[63].

Highlighting the impacts of global warming a new UN report says increases in global temperatures are bringing changes in weather patterns, water resources and extreme climate events that will affect Africa, Asia, Europe, North America and other regions of the world over coming decades. Extreme weather events, droughts and rising sea levels threaten the lives and livelihood of millions of people around the world. Analysis of air bubbles trapped in an ice core from Antarctica shows that atmospheric Carbon Dioxide concentration is 27% higher than the highest recorded label during the last 650000 years, say scientists.[64]

During the naturally fluctuating cycle of 2005, climate related events of scientific observation given as follows:

- January 05: WWF warns that total area of Arctic ice cap covered by summer sea ice is decreasing by 9.2% each decade, threatening world's population of 22,000 polar bears with extinction.
- February: British Antarctic Survey reports that Larsen B Antarctic ice sheet, previously assumed to be stable, is starting to collapse. At least 300 of 400 mountain glaciers on peninsula are in retreat.
- March: Satellite images confirm that six successive years of poor rain have left sub-Saharan Africa in severe drought.
- April: Scientists from Cambridge University find large-scale ozone losses above Arctic over past year. They report that about 30% of ozone layer has been destroyed.
- May: Satellite images of Siberian Arctic lakes show that permafrost is thawing and lakes are disappearing. Scientists at UCLA discover that since 1973 total number of large Arctic lakes has decreased from 10,882 to 9,712. One hundred and twenty five lakes have vanished completely while rests have decreased in surface area by six percent.
- June. Scientists at MIT warn that tropical cyclones have grown more powerful and destructive over past three decades due in part to global warming. Highest wind speeds have increased by about 50%.
- July. Western India suffers worst floods in a century. Large parts of Maharashtra inundated. State Capital Mumbai is deluged with 940mm of rain in 24 hours. Monsoon rains kill 1,039 people.
- August. U.S hurricane centres warn residents and government officials in risk areas to have hurricane preparedness plans in place.
- September. Study of effects of 2003 heat wave in Europe shows biggest fall in agricultural output for 100 years. Researchers at Laboratories des Sciences du Climate de I' Environment say extreme temperatures which claimed 35,000 lives- cut plant growth by nearly a third.
- Atlantic hurricane season is most violent on record with 25 named storms and 13 hurricanes. Previous record was 21 storms (1933) and 12 hurricanes (1969)

- November: Scientists at Rutgers University find ocean levels worldwide are rising twice as fast today as they were before the industrial revolution. Drill core samples and satellite images show 2 mm a year rises in sea level. 980 people are to leave South Pacific Carterets before atolls are swallowed by sea[65].

Reflecting on the genesis of the book MC. Kibben . B (1999) The End of Nature, recently wrote "The sadness that drove me to write this book in the first place has not really lifted ... We did not create this world but we are busy decreating it ... This buzzing, blooming, mysterious, cruel, lovely globe of mountain, sea, city, forest: of fish and wolf and bug and man : of carbon and hydrogen and nitrogen – it has come unbalanced in our short moment on it. It's mostly us now.[66]

References

1. BBC Science and Nature "Hot Topics Climate Change greenhouse Effect", Visited in the line, www.bbc.co.uk/sciencehottopics/36k.
2. IPCC, Science of Climate Change; "Relative Forcing of Climate Change." New York : Cambridge University, 1995, p. 1.
3. IPCC, Climate change -2001, Scientific basis working group-I contribution to the Third Assessment Report.
4. CRS Report 98-235-congressional library, "Global Climate Change US greenhouse Gas Emissions- status, URI Yosemite-EPA, Global Warming Climate, Jan 7, 2000. www.faic.stategov/c4763/htm-33k.
5. IPCC (1996 A) Climate Change 1995. Science of Climate Change, London : Cambridge University Press, UK, p. 56.
6. World to be hotter by 2 degrees; Washington, May 27, 1990 (PTI) Indian Express Daily/28.5.1990, p. 7.
7. The World's Turning Hot, New York, May 20, 1990, UNI & Indian Express Daily/21.5.1990, p. 5.
8. "Climate Change Who is Responsible for the Present State", New Delhi-IED/21.5.90.
9. N. Suresh; "Live with Global Warming", Times of India /1.5.1991, p. 16.
10. "Global Warming", Indian Express Daily/21.8.1990, p. 19.
11. UNI/Indian Express Daily/21.5.1990,op.cit, p. 5.
12. R.N. Trivedi; "A Text Book of Environmental Science", chapter-32 greenhouse effect a coming catastrophe, New Delhi; Anmol; 1997, p. 2004-05.
13. Indian Express Daily/21.8.90, *op.cit,* p. 19.
14. UNI/Indian Express Daily/21.5.90, *op.cit,* p. 5.
15. Indian Express Daily/28.5.90, *op.cit,* p. 7.
16. "Are They Oceans or Dumping Ground", Hindustan Times /10.5.1991, p. 93.
17. R.N. Trivedi, *op.cit,* pp. 101-102.

18. "Experts Warm World Warming Faster Than Expected," Yahoo; Reuters, 13.5.2002.
19. Ross Glebspan, "Global Warming and Political Power : The End of Nature and Beyond", London, New Delhi, Sage Publication (S), Thousand Oaks, Organization and Environment, Vol.18, no. 2, June 2005, p. 186.
20. N.S. Jodha, "Potential Strategy for Adopting greenhouse Warming Perspective from the Developing World", USNAS: Washington, 15 June, 1998, p. 12.
21. "Climate Change Meeting", a report by common wealth group of experts, London: Common Wealth Secretariat, 1989, p. 12.
22. Janetos Anthray; c.et.al.2000; "The Impacts of Climate Change on Agriculture" Synergies of Rio convention, 2000.
23. Cynthia Rosenzwing and Daniel Hillel; "Potential of Climate Change on Agriculture and Food Supply," National Geographic Research and Exploration, Vol. I; No. 2; p: 5-12.
24. *Ibid.,* p. 5 & 12.
25. Bloom, NASA; High CO_2 levels hamper Nitrate in corporation by plants. 2.4.2002. Visited in the line www.spacedaily.com/news/life-04228.html.
26. Pramitpal Choudhuri; Global Warming is Earth to hot to handle; States Man/ 5.8.90, p. 16.
27. Regional Study of the greenhouse Effects and its Impacts on the Region, SAARC Secretariat: Kathamandu, Dec.1992, p. 18.
28 R.S. Bhandari, "Denudation may Turn Himalaya into Desert", BPO/ 26.9.1991, p. 77.
29 Biagini Boni and John Virdin; "Proposal on Climate Change Impacts on Coastal and Marine Resources", World Resource Institute, Washington DC.(2001).
30. Climate Change 2001, Question No.2, approved by the IPCC at its fifth session; (Sanjose Coasta Rica) 15-18 April 1999.
31. Ibid., Question No. 3, p. 23.
32. Climate Action Report-2002. Chapter-6 "Potential Interaction with Coastal areas and Marine Resources", The United States America's Third National Communication under UNFCCC.
33. *Ibid.*
34. "Global Warming Health Concerns" Environment Agency United States, 2000. yesmit/epa.gov/ocr/globalwarming.nsf/content/impactshealth.html
35. Wallmer and Sicker, "Global Warming and Health", Australian Academy of Science, May 2004.
36. Getting into hot water; "Global Warming and Rising Sea Levels" Nova science in the news published by Australian Academy of science, March 2004, p. 1-3.
37. Bangla Cyclone a pointer to Global warming, BPO 16.5.91, p-105
38. "Global Warming may Benefit US Farmer", Washington, May 23, 1990; BS/24.5.1990, p. 5.

39. "Global Warming Impacts Coastal Zones", Environment Protection Agency: US, January 2000.
40. "Global Warming" Indian Express Daily/21-8-1990, p. 19.
41. UNI/Indian Express Daily, *op.cit,* p. 5.
42. "Bangladesh, Cyclone a Pointer to Global Warming" op.cit.
43. *Ibid.,* p. 105.
44. *Ibid.,* p. 105.
45. "An Assessment of IPCC Synthesis Report 2001".
46. IPCC Report , Climate Change 2001, Question No-4,89, p. 16.
47. Prof. Oteg Anistmoy; "Impacts of Global Warming on High Latitudes", Deputy Head of Climatological Department State Hydrological Institute: St. Petersburg, Russia.
48. Jeffrey Chanton Phd, "Global Warming and Rising Oceans", American Institute of Biological Sciences, 2002.
49. July Spyres, "A Global Warming and Coastal Land Forester Communications": US, 1999-2001, p. 1.
50. "World Wild Life can Nature Survive", Global Warming, Awwf. International Discussion Paper, chapter – 2, Feb-May1992.
51. Cat Lazaroff; "Global could Threaten Human Ecosystem", Washington D.C. Health Environment New Service, Dec. 13, 2000.
52. R.N. Trivedi, *op. cit.,* p. 101-102.
53. WGI - TAR Sections synthesis Report, IPCC, 1996.
54. Climate Change – 2001, Question No. 2, Synthesis Report of IPCC.
55. WGI TAR Sections, 9.3.5.6 & WGI TAR Section 14, 13.
56. Christopher Milly, Atmospheric Scientist of the US Geological Survey; "National Geographic Climate Studies Point more Floods in this Century", 30.1.2002.
57. WGI, *op.cit.,* Question 4, (4.6)
58. IPCC Synthesis Report, *op.cit.,* Question No.3, p. 12.
59. Australian Academy of Science, *op.cit.,* May 2004.
60. Mc Kibben B., "The End of Nature", 1989.
61. IPCC Synthesis Report *op.cit.;* p. 22.
62. "Water Resources and Water Demand", Public works and govt. services Canada publishing and depository services Ottawa: Albert Street, Ontario, Canada; p-1, http:/www.nrcan.gc.ca/notice.e.html.
63. Climate Change -2001 "Impacts Adaptation and Vulnerability", UN Intergovernmental Panel on Climate Change, (IPCC) Feb. 20, 2001.
64. Carbon Dioxide level now at the highest in 6 lakh years say scientists, Visakhapatnam, The Hindu, November 30, 2005.
65. Science Nature, AAAS Hadley Centre: wwf National Academy of Science, U.K., 2005.
66. MC. Kibben. B. (1999), "The End of Nature: 10th Anniversary Ed.", New York, Anchor.

4

Major International Conferences on Climate Change

History of global climate change is closely associated with the magnitude of potential threat of global warming and depletion of ozone layer resulted from climate change and greenhouse effects which is considered one of the serious problem for the very survival of mankind on Earth. Realizing the gravity of these changes in global climate system, climate scientists and experts in related fields continue their research to refine our understanding of Earth's complex atmospheric system. Ultimately, advances to improve appropriate action to address the threat of global warming develop consciousness in international level for the in-depth analysis of the environmental phenomena. International response to climate change was created since 1950s, which began the process of connecting the scientists and different disciplines and nationalities into the network of collaboration in the International Geographical year 1957-58. The U.S. Department of Defence starting in 1958 in at Maonaloa, Hawaii Charles keeling of the Scripps Institute of Oceanography at Lagolla, California, kept accurate observation of the concentration of the atmospheric Carbon Dioxide that was rising steadily. In the year 1960-65 atmosphere scientists intensified their efforts to estimate climate and its variability with increasing concentration of Carbon Dioxide impacts in different parts of the world. By the mid of 1970s, from the available data it was evident that concentration of greenhouse gases was steadily increasing. By the end of 1970s from general circulation models of the atmospheric estimates it reveals doubling of CO_2 concentrations from its pre-industrial value[1]. However, since the beginning of 1970s scientific concerns over the possibility of human activities in changing the global climate received increasing attention in national and international institutions. A series of meeting mostly technical often held under the auspicious of various United Nations agencies began exploring the enormous implications of these findings for the world climate.[2]

The Stockholm conference of 1972 marked the beginning of modern era of International Environmental Law with its associated political regime towards trans-boundary environmental deterioration in creating political awareness of nations' responsibility. The Stockholm conference was determined to raise consciousness about the potential of humans to cause environmental damages. The tone of the conference was divisive. Differences surfaced among developed and developing nations. One area of agreement was the founding of the United Nations Environmental Programme (UNEP). UNEP began to provide leadership and encourage partnerships in caring for the environment by inspiring, informing and enabling nations and people to improve their gravity of life without compromising that of future generations. In 1973 a full-fledged environmental conference was held in Stockholm called the Conference on Human Environment, the attendees talked about from the beginning common efforts on international environment issue. In 1973 the governing council of UNEP called for a global environmental monitoring system (GEMS) to begin collecting data of Earth sciences and technology. It proposed to have new efforts and other international monitoring programmes.

In 1974 a second environmental conference was held in Nairobi, Kenya called the International Meeting on Monitoring. It approved the GEMS to track environmental changes affecting the ocean and world agricultural supply. Nairobi became the Head quarters of UN Environmental programme[3]. Around 1977 gleaned from lecture halls and scientific conferences attended by international experts, new insights and findings about global climate change—the continued result of greenhouse gas emissions seemed to be thrown upon the negotiating tabes for finding solutions and embarking upon new policy decisions. Gradually during late 1970s early 1980s environmental consciousness was created to cooperate internationally for climate change negotiations. At that time the third world was aware of the perilous effects of the large-scale industrialization, modernization and high technology fixation.[4]

Scientific concern over the possibility that human activities could change the global climate has been expressed at the various intervals over past 100 years. The enhanced green house effects, which cause global warming required an international treaty to address the international nature of the problem. Unilateral action or action by a group of countries would be insufficient to solve the problem. The negotiation for the climate change was greatly influenced by the historical emissions of Carbon Dioxide by the Northern industrialized countries and the European nations. The developing countries have modelled their developmental process as per the structure determined by the Western world. Since the pattern of development is based on combustion of fossil fuel technology being ubiquitously imitated by the developing countries, their contribution to carbon dioxide emission into the atmosphere will also be dangerously aggravating the situation[5]. The global community realized the possibility that human activities are mainly responsible to change the global climate, and stated showing its various impacts and adverse consequences in the form of extremely climate conditions as expressed at various international conventions, prior to first World Climate Conference.

First World Climate Conference

The first World Climate Conference was one of the major international meetings on climate change held on 12-23 February 1979 in Geneva, Switzerland. The conference was sponsored by the World Meteorological Organization (WMO), the United Nations Environmental Programme (UNEP) and the International Council of Scientific Unions (ICSU). It was a scientific conference attended by many scientists from a wide range of discipline and at the same time commanded little political attention. The Conference organized four working groups to look into climate data, the identification of climate topics, integrated impact studies and research on climate variability and change. The main focus of the conference was on how climate change might impact human activities.

It considered the possible impacts on agriculture, fishing, forestry and hydrology. The world climate conference draws its conclusion in highlighting the international community's emerging as perception of the climate as a vital natural resource. The climate change was recognized as a serious problem and adverse to the well being of humanity. Further, it recognized survival of humanity requires to live in harmony with nature, and it is urged Government's "to see and prevent potential man made change in climate. The declaration of the conference identified the leading causes of global warming as increased atmospheric concentrations of Carbon Dioxide resulting from the burning of fossil fuels deforestation change in land use. The conference decided for the establishment of World Climate Programme (WCP) emphasizing the need for more scientific research into the causes and effects of climate change. The world climate programme was set up under the joint responsibility of world Metrological Organization (WMO), the United Nations Environment Programme (UNEP) and the International Council for Scientific Unions (ICSU). It is composed of the World Climate Data Programme, World Climate Application Programme, the World Climate Research Programme and the World Climate impact Programme[6]. In 1979, the first official world climate conference was held, largely a scientific meeting. It considered the impact of climate change world impact human civilization and what the Nation of the world could to do to avoid climate disruptions. It called for world climate programme to handle such issues. A number of Inter Governmental Conference were held to study the scientific findings and discuss possible political action[7].

The first world climate change conference of 1979 took steps to limit Carbon Dioxide emissions through energy economic modelling and ozone depletion research. In 1979 a report published by the U.S. National Academy of Science stated the doubling of CO_2 concentration would lead to an increase of the average temperature of the Earth's surface of between 1.5 to 4.5C°, which called for global action. The climate change conference identifies the monitoring of changes in the climate system as an important component of the commitments of its signatories. It encourages systematic observation of phenomena, analysis of development of data, activities with the objective of further understanding or reducing the uncertainties associated with the climate system. The multitude of climate change further impinged upon states and parties to cooperate internationally in such efforts. The impact of enhanced greenhouse gases was felt in the 1970's and 1980's. The first world climate conference was a concrete effort to address the climate change. Though it commanded little political attention, this scientific gathering explored how climate change might affect the human activities. However, after First World climate change conference, by the mid 1980's further concrete attempt was made to assess the state of knowledge[8]. A series of international conferences were held until mid 1980's. However policy implications of these conferences' findings slowly realized and the issue of anthropogenic climate change was still framed as a "CO_2 problem. Further, a number of international conferences were held following the International Meteorological organization 1980, United Nations environment Programme 1983 and the International Council for Scientific Unions 1985 which have enormous implications for the policy and joint implications of climate change.[9]

The first joint UNEP/ICSU/WMO meeting of the experts was held in Villach Austria in November 1980 to assess the role of the Carbon Dioxide (CO_2) variations and its impacts upon the Earth. This conference investigated how increasing green house gas concentrations could affect various region of the Earth during coming up century. Participants discussed various questions relating to technical, financial and institutional options for limiting or adapting to climatic change. Together with increasing scientific evidence, the conference helped to raise international concern about the issue. The representatives of the three organizations of the WCP /WMO / UNEP/ICSU met in October 1982 in Geneva

Switzerland, and after deliberation recommended that the continuing assessment of Carbon Dioxide believed to be responsible for global warming. Following the first meeting of 1980, for the assessment, the next meeting was held every five years, and called for global action. In 1982, the convention on law of the sea spelled out guidelines for conservation of maritime resources and protection of ocean environments[10].

Villach Conference 1985

The third Villach conference was organized by the World Meteorological Organization (WMO), the United Nations Environment Programme (UNEP) and the International Council of Scientific Unions (ICSU) in 1985. It was a major international review of the issue of the scenarios for the future emission of all the significant greenhouse gases and not just carbon Dioxide alone. After deliberation about potential seriousness of the green house gases, international scientific consensus was achieved. The problem of anthropogenic climate change was considered seriously and moved into the political agenda for further deliberation[11]. The issue of climate change gained increasing attention in order how to reduce greenhouse gas emissions. As the greenhouse gas issue persists through out the entire century and beyond, so further time should not be wasted to approach the issue in a collaborative way.

In Villach Conference 1985, the invited scientists expressed their consensus about the seriousness of the problem of the enhanced greenhouse effect. After deliberation over the issue, they suggested that it was the time to talk with the policy makers. The conference also recommended to set up an advisory group to provide regularly up dated evaluations of the greenhouse issues to the Heads of the World Meteorological Organization, the United Nations Environment Programme and the International Council of Scientific Unions[12]. The Advisory Group on Green House Gas (AGGG) consisting of six experts was established and met for the first time in July'1986. Among the members of the AGGG, Gardon Goodman, then of the Beiger institute in Stockholm was very interested in pursuing the goal of the Villach Conference. The advisory group suggested establishing a dialogue between the scientists and the policy makers over the issue of global climate change. It was also decided and agreed at the meeting of the Advisory group in July 1986, that Goodman with the help of the International steering Committee should organize two workshops under the auspices of the Advisory group on green house group in 1987. As per the decisions of the AGGG, two workshops were held in Villach, from 28 September to 2nd October and a workshop was held in Bellagio from

9 November to 13 November 1987, to assess the potential impacts of greenhouse gases. The two workshops produced a joint report recommending that a prioritized list of steps to be taken to the issue of climate change[13]. The Villach Conference, despite major remaining uncertainties, was evident of sufficient scientific understanding to undertake long-term interpretation of causes and effects of climate change phenomenon to justify further research for new policies. Research into impacts of climate change should start immediately in the pilot project form in selected regions of the world. The governments and funding agencies should come forward to support and assist the climate research. It is further recommended that the conclusions of the Villach Conference be made widely available to create awareness and public understanding of the global climate change issue. To continue the work started at the Villach conference follow of meeting should be held to conclude the possibility of a climate treaty. The recommendation of the two workshops stressed on immediate steps to limit greenhouse gas emissions, implementation of Montreal protocol, adoption of new energy and deforestation policies to combat global warming. Further it included to limit the impact of sea level rise by elaborating river and coastal zone policies based on the studies of vulnerability of particular areas, and to promote under standing through the use of management tools and monitoring and research programmes on green house gases effect. At the Bellagio workshop of 1987, the scientific community offered an early estimate of how much the Earth surface may warm, was based on a doubling of the atmospheric concentration of Carbon Dioxide[14]. The Villach Conference on climate change thus contributed a significant role in creating awareness in international sphere on the issue of climate change. The issue of climate change gained increasing support of participants and scientists to the potential impacts of global climate change. Thus it paved the way in stimulating efforts in international sphere to combat the impacts of global warming into the network of collaboration. In 1987 Common Future report on environmental issues was presented to the United Nations. General Assembly.

Toronto Conference, 1988

The Toronto Conference was held in June 1988 on the basis of Villach and Bellagio workshop of 1987 in response to climate change politics. The Government of Canada had offered to host a conference on "the changing atmosphere during a hearing for the Brundtland commission. The Conference had played an important role in stimulating action in a number of countries, and developing awareness in international sphere on the issue of global climate change. The participants and scientists came to the conclusion after hearing about the drought in US mid West that this was the evidence of global warming. Thus, Toronto conference became the source of media attention by highlighting the headline news relating to the climate change issue. The major outcome of Toronto conference was to secure the support of a pro active group of representatives of environmental non government organizations and the increasing attention of the large media to the potential consequences of climate change. The conference highlighted the threat of anthropogenic climate change, which was not less than the threat of nuclear war. All the developed countries were required to cut their CO_2 emissions by 20% from the 1987 levels by the year 2005. This Toronto goal was discussed in many countries of the world and implemented in some countries like Austria. A study team was asked to investigate the achievement of Toronto goal in Germany. It concluded that in spite of 30% reductions of the Enquete commission's recommendation, cabinet agreed to full fill more ambitious reduction of 25-30 percent of the Toronto goal[15]. Thus, Toronto conference seems to be increasing the attention to the new findings to deal with the stabilization of greenhouse gases concentration in the atmosphere. Thus, it was felt that dangerous anthropogenic interference required a consideration in a global context by the positive participation of governments and not just by the group of interested scientists alone. The Toronto conference of 1988 was a turning point to open the eyes of the world governments about the threat posed by global warming and which resulted in the growth of United Nations Inter Governmental Panel on Climate Change in 1988.

United Nations Inter Governmental Panel on Climate Change

The Inter governmental Panel on Climate Change (IPCC) was established in 1988 in response to international concern about threat posed by global warming organized by United Nations Environment Programme and World Meteorological Organization. The discussion about the character and role of the panel began in mid 1987. The Inter Governmental Panel on Climate Change was formed in close association with United Nations Framework Convention on Climate Change (UNFCCC) with the following specific objectives:

- Assessment of scientific information relating to the various issues of global warming.
- Evaluation of potential and socio economic impacts on climate change.
- Formulation of realistic possible response strategies to combat global climate change[16].

The IPCC was charged with the performing the first world government sponsored assessment of global climate change and its members were requested to consider issues associated with the science, impacts and possible response strategies to prepare for the possible onset of a green house warming[17]. The first meeting of the newly created U.N. Inter governmental Panel on Climate Change (IPCC) was convened in Geneva on November 9-11, 1988. The plenary meeting of the IPCC included representatives of some 35 nations, including the United States, former the USSR and several other foreign governments and inter governmental and non-governmental organizations. The Non-governmental organizations served as observers and functioned as advisory bodies in the proceedings. As a result of this meeting, the IPCC was charged by the U.N. General Assembly to prepare an integrated state of the art report on the science and responses to global climate change by September 1990[18].

Following up the Toronto Conference in 1988, a "meeting of legal and policy experts" was held in Ottawa on February 20-22, 1989. Participants in this meeting discussed the feasibility of climate change convention and after deliberation issued a statement that among other things addressed considerations and elements for a specific convention on climate change, which would govern emissions of Carbon Dioxide implicated in global warming and a target of 20% reduction there of[19]. The fourth international conference on environment held at Budapest on last May 1990 identified five major problems confronting world community today as stated by Dr. G.M. Oza, General Secretary of the International Society and Naturalist (INSONA). In participating in five days conference at Budapest, Dr. Oza identified five issues, which are, population explosion, and ever increasing consumption of renewable and non renewable environmental resources, the progressive degradation of environment at all levels, the loss of biological diversity, the increasing disparities of wealth among nations and grinding poverty in many developing countries, and the growing impediments to social advancement resulting from hunger, disease, ignorance and strife[20]. The conference attended by 130 scientists and scholars from the different parts of the world, discussed the issues and suggested to reduce the disparities between rich and poor nations, to achieve population control, system of education for women and improved economic conditions, there by permitting attainment of sound environment and development. In Budapest conference, these participants put emphasis on basic issues, which were responsible for steming the tide of environmental degradations.

Scientists' responses to potential global climate change as well as policy makers' summary of the special committee on the participation of developing countries were organized by the World Meteorological Organization and United Nations Environment Programme on 31st August 1990. The views clinched from the policy makers' summaries, present conclusions, and proposes, line of action including suggestions, which form the basis for negotiations and outlines the coordinated work that required for a more complete understanding of the problem of climate change resulting from human activities. This document was intended to be prepared in conjunction with the three field reports of working groups. Each task was assigned to a working group. Working group-I chaired by United Kingdom was to consider the scientific basis of concern, working group-II chaired by former Soviet Union was to stdy the renewed likely impacts and working group-III chaired by United States covered realistic response strategies. While concentrating on control and adaptive strategies, the United States the Third working group also considered financial and industrial means of assisting the Third World in its response. The three working groups published their findings in the summer of 1990, and their reports acted as a basis for international negotiation on climate change convention. The executive summary of the report clearly pointed out that there is national greenhouse effect and the group was certainly sure about the increasing concentration greenhouse gases resulting from human activities. The report of 1990, introduced the idea of "Global Warming Potential" (GWP) as a tool for translating scientific information into policy relevant material. The GWP provides basis to compare the relative warming effect of different gases. Alternatively, it could be used to calculate the effect of reducing Carbon Dioxide emissions to a certain amount for a specific time horizon compared with reducing CH_4 emissions[21].

Three consensus documents on science, impacts and responses of the working groups were viewed throughout by the international scientific and global diplomatic community as the definite statement of the state of the knowledge about global climate change. A majority of participants and independently polled scientists highly commended the reports of each working group as a relative success and major accomplishment for multidisciplinary scientific and social research bodies participating within a potential policy making milieu. The report of the Third working group was severely criticized that it offered concrete recommendation as to what government should do either to mitigate or adapt to potential climate change. Further more, a group of dissenting scientific groups claimed that their opinions were neither considered nor presented in the final IPCC documents. Again, IPCC review process was criticized as because no comments and reaction to comments were ever exchanged between the IPCC and the independent policy reviewers[22]. The formation of IPCC working groups intensified their efforts to estimate climate change and its variability with increasing concentration of Carbon Dioxide resulting from anthropogenic activities. Gradually, it tries to develop consciousness among the world community with the objective of further understanding of reducing uncertainties associated with the climate change. The Three working groups submitted their findings to the full IPCC in June 1990 on climate change. The IPCC in a plenary session in August 1990, submitted its first interim assessment report to the 45th session of the UN General Assembly. The second world climate conference was held in Geneva in 1990 under the auspices of WMO, UNEP and ICSU. The so called integrated assessment report of the IPCC, consequently adopted by the UN General assembly, would form the basis for International negotiations toward a framework convention on climate change. In the following year, the integrated report of the IPCC consisting of interim assessment, a fourth working paper prepared by the Adhoc IPCC working group on financial and technical assistance and an IPCC assessment overview document prepared by the IPCC secretariat was subject to a short period review during adjunct General Assembly scientific and technical sessions[23].

The scientific consensus reflected over the IPCC assessment that there was no reason to widen or narrow this range. The issue of climate change was given more priority on the political agenda and the negotiations for the climate change began as the basis of strong statements as made by the working group-I. After presentation of the IPCC integrated interim assessment of the global climate change and the second world climate conference and subsequent adoption by the UN General Assembly beyond expectation of some countries the SWCC was split into two parts- a scientific and a ministerial conference. The negotiating session for regulatory mechanism to address potential global climate change would begin during ministerial session that immediately followed the scientific and technical sessions. The conference statement of the scientific part called for serious policy responses to the issue of climate change while the ministerial declaration was much less committed to action. The difference of opinion was clearly expressed when the United States and the former Soviet Union among others, however were firmly opposed to making any commitment at that time, especially legally binding and the conference called for a framework to develop an international treaty on climate change. A framework would allow a continuing series of talks to assess the changing needs of such a treaty[24].

The United States strongly opposing this, argued that such matter should be placed before United Nations General Assembly for appropriate consideration and not by the World Meteorological Organization, with further suggestion to the interested nations to reconvene negotiations for specific regulatory action that would address global climate change. The consensus of the report was that the global temperature had been increasing during the last century. Shortly after the second world climate conference, the UN General Assembly on December 21, 1990 recalling its resolution 43153, December 6, 1988 and 441207 of December 22, 1989, in which it recognized that climate change is a common concern of mankind, called for policy actions to be taken by world leaders to address potential impacts of climate change caused by increasing concentrations of CO_2 and other greenhouse gases. The UN General Assembly being supported by the WMO and UNEP, called for the establishment of Inter-governmental Negotiating Committee (INC), which was charged with preparing an effective frame work convention on climate change, containing appropriate commitments and any related legal instruments as might be agreed upon. This resolution A/RES/45/212 called for the framework convention on negotiations to be completed and opened for signature during that conference prior to the United Nations Conference on Environment and Development (UNCED) in June 1992 in Rio de Janerio[25].

The Inter Governmental Negotiating Committee and Frame work convention on Climate Change session for the first time met in Chantilly, Verginia in February of 1991 under the host offered by the United States of America. The meeting was titled "Protection of Global Climate for Present and Future Generations of Mankind". The aim was to negotiate relating framework convention on climatic change on basic questions. The negotiation began slowly with a series of procedural questions. The basic questions relating to trans-boundary pollution and stratospheric ozone depletion were discussed. The European community and small Island states favoured the establishment of a target and time table for limiting the emission of greenhouse gases, while the United States and oil producing states were against the procedure[26].

The atmosphere of bitter debate and dissension marred the progress in the negotiations of the international negotiating committee. The outcome of the first meeting of the INC was criticized by some as unproductive, because no protocols, memorandum of understanding or term of reference relating to Frame work Convention on Climate Change were achieved. The United States delegations insisted that INC focus at its first meeting primarily on organizational business and the administrative requirements. Shortly before the closing session of the INC in April 1992, the US and UK brought in the compromise formulation, which is now in Article 4 of the FCCC with non-binding call for an attempt to return to 1990 emissions of CO_2 and other greenhouse gases not controlled by Montreal protocol. The issue of climate change at the FCCC took another turn with the action taken by the United States. It acted as stumbling block in the way of further progress of the work of the INC. It highlighted the intention of the US administration in monitoring the global climate change. Shortly after the first session of the INC, the second session of the INC met in Geneva, on June 19-20, 1991. The third session was convened in Nairobi, on September 9-20 and fourth session in Geneva on December 20, 1991. These meetings of the INC called for a framework to develop an international treaty on climate change. It provided as opportunity of continuing a series of talks to assess the changing needs of such a treaty and to devise plans for stabilizing concentrations of greenhouse gas in the atmosphere by the year 2000. The fifth and last session of the INC took place in New York City between April 29 and May 8, 1992. This session was the last opportunity for the party to meet as a whole and agree upon a final text for a so called framework convention on climate change that would open for signature by June at the United Nations Conference on Economic Development (UNCED) in Rio de Janerio in June of 1992. At the conclusion of this last session on May 8, 1992, voluntary response by nations to reduce net atmospheric concentration of greenhouse gases would be the backbone of the climate convention that would open for signature at (UNCED)[27].

Out of 15 months of talks, 150 nations finalized the draft of the convention, which contained "non binding aim". It is in the nature of voluntary commitments for industrialized countries to begin to return their net emissions 'greenhouse' gases to 1990 levels, and to devise plans for stabilizing concentration of gases in the atmosphere by the year both by controlling sources of emissions and enhancing sinks for greenhouse gases. It was adopted on May 9, 1992, at UN Headquarters in New York City. The IPCC also declared a need to reassess the indirect global warming potential of other greenhouse gases and their concentrations and efforts over different time horizons, that would mitigate climate change. The Unites State of America in its "Statement on Commitments" submitted on 27th Feb 1992, at the further session of INC, outlined a new course of measures to be set forth in the text of future climate change agreement by the UN framework convention. Some analysts estimated that the action of United States could enable it to realize reduction in CO_2 about 14% below 1990 levels by the year 2000 where as other environmentalists criticized these new measures as simply a delineation of what United States was prepared to do at all. A study of Bush Administration released in April 1992, showing a picture US view on climate change was not far from the goal of reducing its net emissions of CO_2 to 1990 levels by 2000 by undertaking INC sponsored mitigation and adaption strategies for climate change that were already under way in existing federal and state programmes. The global efforts towards achieving climate change protection reached a significant milestone with the adoption of UN Framework Convention on Climate Change (UNFCCC) in 1992, under which the United States along with 152 other nations agreed to achieve the ultimate objective of stabilization of greenhouse gas concentrations in the atmosphere at a level that would prevent dangerous anthropogenic interference with the climate system. The United States and some other industrialized developed countries also agreed to pursue various voluntary measures to limit their emission targets of greenhouse gases to 1990 levels by the year 2000. Since the US ratification of FCCC in 1992, there have been a sound of caution by Congress that if United States is to become a party to any future international regulatory agreement, the decision to do so should be well informed and sufficiently sound and that all nations, parties should have proportional responsibilities for global climate protection. Accordingly, Congress sought to acquire information about possible climate change for the formulation of appropriate policy responses. Being aware of the global implications of this problem, Congress took keen interest internationally through direct communication with world leaders, meeting in International conferences, exchange of views and information with international organizations within and outside the United Nation system for passage of resolutions and legislations[28].

The United Nations General Assembly established the intergovernmental Negotiating committee INC for a framework convention on climate change (UNFCCC) in 1990. The convention drafted by the INC was adopted on 9th May 1992. It was signed in June 1992 at the United Nations conference on Environment and Development (UNCED) or the Earth Summit in Rio de Janerio by 154 states and European Union (EU). The convention entered into force on 21st March 1994. By November 1999, 161 states and the EU ratified the convention, which committed signatories to make voluntary efforts to cut their GHG emissions[29].

The UNFCCC contained an action framework that would commit the world's industrialized countries to voluntary reduction of greenhouse gases and such other action as necessary to enhance green house sinks stabilizing atmospheric concentrations of greenhouse gases at 1990 levels by 2000. The convention also contained other binding agreement for all signatories including developing countries for the establishment of support administration. Further more it divided to continue the negotiations by means of a Conference of the Parties to pursue subsequent actions to counter the global warming similar to the 1985 Viena convention that preceded the Montreal protocol on protection of the ozone layer. The objective of the convention was to achieve stabilization of greenhouse gas concentration in the atmosphere at a level that will prevent dangerous anthropogenic interference with the climate system (UNFCCC Article 2). The convention further states "such a level should be achieved within time frame sufficient to allow ecosystems to adjust naturally to climate change to ensure that food production is not threatened and to enable economic development to proceed in a sustainable manner. Considering the global nature of climate change the convention calls for appropriate international response in accordance with each country's "common but differentiated responsibilities" and assigns the lead in combating global climate change to industrialized countries. Thus, Framework Convention on climate change significantly influenced the attitudes of the industrialized countries for involvement in international negotiation Process on the issue of Climate Change and was intended to implement measures to address potential global climate change. Under the convention industrialized countries (members of the organization for economic development) OECD and the states of Central and Eastern Europe collectively called Annex-I Countries made voluntary commitments to limit their emissions of green house gases, so that by 2000 they were emitting no more than they were in 1990[30].

The sixth meeting of the INC was convened in Geneva, Switzerland on December 7-10, 1992, to discuss the future of the INC including its organizational structure and to revaluate the urgency measures of moving forward on measures to combat potential impacts of global climate change. The INC was requested to act as the interim coordinating body on business matters relating to global climate change for the UN Secretary General until the first meeting of the Conference of the Parties would be established.

After the signing of Rio Earth Summit in June 1992, several steps were undertaken to bind the signatories. Ratification by fifty signatories or similar approval was required which was completed with the deposit of ratification by required minimum numbers after three months. The first Conference of the Parties was to be held within a year. After Rio conference, the first Conference of the Parties was held in Germany with the deposit of 50 ratification on December 1993, and the convention came into force on March 1994. The UNFCCC has more extensive commitments than the other conventions. It set up a number of new institutions and provision for providing financial assistance and technology transfer for the developing countries. The institutions established by UNFCCC include, the Conference of the Parties (CoP), Subsidiary Body on Science and Implementation (SBSI) for reporting and review procedure. The convention also stated that the parties should take precautionary measures to anticipate or minimize the courses of climate change and mitigate its adverse effects, thus establishing the precautionary principle as a guiding principle in international response to climate change[31].

In February 1995 the INC was dissolved and the Conference of the Parties (CoP) comprising all members who have ratified the convention, became the decision making body of the convention. The CoP is responsible for promoting and reviewing the implementation of the convention and keeping the entire process on track[32]. Prior to the first meeting of the Conference of the Parties the United Nations Framework Convention on Climate Change collected, scientific data on global warming that have gradually accumulated. Research institutions and political leaders around the world have recognized that effective measures to prevent global warming must be developed through international co-operation. Since the creation of the IPCC, it was the first intergovernmental scientific research institution to focus its energies primarily on the question of global warming. Since its inception, the IPCC has played a leading role in the world in the compilation and analysis of scientific data to support its stand for control of global warming[33]. Gradually, the international community and world leaders grew concerned with the issue of global environment. Scientific basis for concern about the potential worldwide warming trend has become increasingly cloudy in the past decade. In contrast, the considerable sacrifices that would be required of the industrialized countries to counter the alleged danger of global warming remained significant. Nevertheless, vested interests in Europe and the United States relentlessly pressed for a global treaty to reduce emissions of green house gases[34].

Climate change is considered one of the most serious threats to sustainable developments with natural resources and physical infrastructure being degraded. Global climate varies naturally but scientists agree that rising concentration of anthropogenically emitted green house gases in the Earth's atmosphere is leading to changes in the global climate.

Conference of the Parties First Session Berlin : 28th March -7th April 1995

Since Rio, there have been several follow up negotiating session to the UNFCCC, concerning climate change. The first meeting of the Conference of the Parties on climate change (CoP-I) took place in Berlin, Germany from 28th March to 7th April 1995. It was attended by delegates from 117 parties and 53 observer states including 2000 observers and journalists to address a number of important issues relating to global climate change. Delegates reached an agreement, about the adequacy of the commitments made in the UN FCCC. The "Berlin Mandate" was the central issue before CoP-I. Since the grouping of group-II chaired by Russia and working group-III of the IPCC chaired by United States was politically dictated, it was guaranteed that both groups would be effecting all important negotiation process [35].

To begin a process towards appropriate action an open ended Adhoc Group on the Berlin Mandate (AGBM) was established. This led to a general discussion of the necessary next steps ranging from strengthening of the commitments contained in Annex -1 parties, through the adoption of a protocol or another legal instrument with commitments for Annex-1 parties, with targets and time tables for emission reductions.[36]

(1) Appropriate policies and measures regarding energy, transport, industry agriculture, foresting, waste management, economic instruments, institution and mechanisms should be implemented.

(2) Quantification of legally binding objectives for emission limitations within specified time tables such as 2005, 2010 and 2020 with respect to their anthropogenic emissions by sources and removed by sinks of green house gases not controlled by Montreal protocol.

(3) All the parties were required to continue in advance the implementation of the existing commitments agreed to in Article 4(1) of the convention.

(4) Further, a mechanism to allow the regular review and strengthening of the commitments embodied in a protocol or other legal instruments.

(5) Further, concrete action should be undertaken to strengthen global efforts to speed up the development, application, diffusion and transfer of climate friendly technologies, practices and processes to commitments.

CoP-1 also requested the secretariat to make necessary arrangements for the session of the Subsiding Body for Scientific and Technological

Advice (SBSTA) and the Subsiding Body for Implementation (SBI).The information provided by competent international bodies and the policy oriented heads of the conference of the parties SBSTA would serve as the link to coordinate between scientific and technology assessments during the process of AGDM.SBSTA addressed several issues including the treatment of the IPCC Soon Assessment Report (SAR). SBI was created with a view to develop recommendations to assist the CoP in the preparation and implementation of its decisions and the review of assessment of the implementation of the convention. SBI also addressed several key issues such as the national communications, activities and implementation jointly during the AGBM process. The Adhoc group on Article 13 (ag-13) was set up to consider the establishment of a multilateral consultative process available to parties to resolve questions on implementation. They also reviewed first round of national communication and finalized much of the institutional and financial machinery needed to support the action under the convention in the coming year. The work of the IPCC has been criticized for representing the rich industrialized world's agenda and interests and limiting the extent to which industrialized countries need reexamination and reconstruction of their own deep commitments in order adequately to address the contemporary debate. The UN Conference on Environment and Development in Rio avoided a number of contentious issues to reach an agreement and to be dealt by the CoP. After lengthy discussion in Berlin in 1995 some parts of the 1995 Assessment Report were published. The executive of the Summary of the reports were discussed "line by line" in plenary sessions and politics continued to dominate some of the discussions. The industrialized world regularly entered these scientific debates in order to protect their vested interests and issues to reach an agreement[37].

The IPCC Second Assessment Report written and reviewed by 2000 scientists and experts world wide in December 1995 was published in April 1996. It was widely acknowledged for concluding that the balance of evidence suggests there is a discernible human influence on global climate. However, the report did much more, for example, confirm the availability of so-called non-regret options and other cost effective strategy for combating climate change. At CoP-1 in Berlin, in March 1995, the participating nations issued the so called Berlin Mandate that the voluntary approach had failed and agreed that there would have to be binding commitments by the industrialized countries to reduce their emissions of heat trapping gases some time after the year 2000[38]. In CoP-I, Berlin, three issues dominated the proceedings: the need to clearly define adequate commitments, elaborate on financial mechanisms and set the criteria for joint implementation projects[39]. The EU proposed to stabilize its emissions by 2000, the G-77 countries including India and China agreed to negotiate for a mandate that would ask for legally binding commitments from Annex-I signatories. The Organization of Petroleum Exporting countries (OPEC) was particularly concerned that global efforts to reduce emissions from use of fossil fuel may have serious impacts on its economics. It wanted protection from any stronger convention and even sought compensation for the economic losses they may have to face as a consequence of these abatement initiatives[40].

Intergovernmental consultations continued within the UNFCCC frame work and at its first full scale member party conference (CoP-I) held in Berlin 1995, the Berlin Mandate was adopted as a basic guideline document for drafting of an international agreement aimed at specifically the prevention of global warming[41]. The G77 countries also agreed to participate in experimental abatement projects with developed countries, which was called Activities Implemented Jointly (AIJ) pilot phase. On final day, Ministers from the 117 national parties adopted Berlin Mandate which called for new talks containing stronger commitments. It concluded that 60% to 80% reduction in Carbon Dioxide emissions would be necessary to stabilize atmospheric concentrations of greenhouse gases[42]. The Conference of the Parties in its first meeting develop the process of co-operation and mutual understanding between developed and developing countries. They intensified their efforts to implement the adequacy of the commitments under the Berlin Mandate. The Conference of the Parties serving as the meeting of the parties to the protocol, at its first session or as soon as practicable, considered ways to facilitate such co-operation taking into account all relevant information. Although the rich industrialized world, particularly United States and European Union dominated the negotiations and discussions to protect their own interests, the issue of enhanced green house gases was recognized as a serious problem. It is widely acknowledged that human activities are mainly responsible for the present day global warming, which have been due to the increase of greenhouse gas concentrations in the atmosphere.

The conference commits it members to take actions to stabilize the atmospheric concentration of greenhouse gases at a level "that would prevent another dangerous anthropogenic interference with the climate system". It also asserted 'the precautionary principle" that action should not wait for scientific certainty and the industrial nations should take the lead in combating climate change. The attitude of the developed countries changed towards developing countries when it was decided at the CoP-I meeting that developing countries should be exempted from legal obligations to regulate the emissions of greenhouse gases. Admitting many uncertainties and controversies hovering on global warming, CoP-1 succeeded in creating awareness of the gravity of the global warming, CoP-1 succeeded in creating awareness of the gravity of the global environment. After all the first Conference of the Parties (CoP.-I) represented the consensus of the world community in different context taking into account the interface between scientific findings and political or economic interest. Nevertheless, the initiatives and steps formed the basis for winning the support of the international community to combat the potential danger of the climate change. The political and economic interest reflected the differences amongst various parties with respect to levels of development, the relative priority attached to environmental and development concerns, the anticipated impacts of climate change and the equitable apportionment of responsibility for the costs and courses of climate change. After much wrangling, the North, headed by US finally agreed to commit itself to a legally binding schedule for reduction of Carbon Dioxide and blazed the trail for further negotiation with a minor victory for the developing world.

Conference of the Parties - 2

CoP.-2 : The second Conference of the Parties was opened at Geneva, on 8th July 1996 by the Mrs. Angela, Federal minister for the environment, Nature conservation and Nuclear Safety of the Federal Republic of Germany as the President of the conference at its first session. Welcoming all participants, she indicated to carry out an interim evaluation of the implementation of the United Nations Frame Work Convention on Climate initiated at the first session with the adoption of the Berlin mandate and progress made in the negotiation process. In response to Berlin mandate, the parties were called upon *inter alia* to negotiate a protocol or another legal instrument in order to strengthen the commitments of Annex.-I parties in Article 4.2(a) and (b) for adoption at the third session of the conference. The Second Assessment Report of the IPCC contained the scientific findings confirming that global climate was undergoing changes as a result of human activities, which requires urgent precautionary action. The first National Communication of Annex.-I parties reveals that some of them expected to be unable to meet the emission reduction targets of the convention to 1990 levels by the year 2000. Further, Berlin mandate introduced no legal binding new commitments for the developing countries. For successful protection of global climate, action was to be taken on a worldwide level. The conference should therefore consider what joint action could be taken to advance the implementation of the existing commitments. As a necessary first step there was the need to decide on the guidelines for the National Communication of Annex.-I parties. Among other practical approaches included particularly the co-operation of all parties in the field, climate protection technologies, the pilot phase for activities implemented jointly and stronger involvement of the private sector. In concluding statement, she expressed the hope that the conference realizing the urgency of the findings of IPCC to fresh out the Berlin Mandate stressed on further efforts regarding the implementation of the existing convention commitments, and action for the intensification of negotiations. A ministerial declaration in that vein would be an important signal of the parties' joint willingness for action. Progress had been made, but shared commitment, trust and close co-operation were still indispensable in face of the global challenges of climate protection and sustainable development[43].

In seeking solutions to the problems, what needed to be addressed is the importance of equity considerations. Limited financial and technological resources of the developed countries with limited human and institutional capacities could not be over emphasized. Many developing countries, especially in Africa remained dependent on agro based industry that was climate sensitive and were hit hard by miserable economic conditions and a huge external debt burden. Their associated problems like poverty alleviation, the improvement of social services and job creation through industrial expansion, remained therefore, the most vulnerable to the impacts of climate change and variability. More over, the low-lying countries and small Island states were beyond their national capacities to implement the cost adoption measures. In conclusion, all parties urged to render their full support and co-operation to implement the Berlin mandate and their combined efforts will strengthen them to combat the climate change. The second session of the Conference of the Parties held on 8-19 July 1996,adopted the following draft decisions. Statements were made by 50 parties including one on behalf of the European Community (EU) and its member states, another on behalf of the group of 77 and China and another on behalf of the alliance for small island states, and representatives of two states not parties to the convention also made their statement with a representative of one non governmental organization making a statement for consideration. The Second Assessment Report of the IPCC, contains the most comprehensive and authoritative assessment of scientific and technological information relating to global climate change and its impacts and policy implications.

To fully assess the ultimate objective of the convention, more information will be required on regional scenarios of climate change and more efforts should be directed in current knowledge of climate change to reduce uncertainties associated with the problem. There are large differences among countries relating to economic development, infrastructure choices and natural resource base, the costs of reducing green house gas emissions and enhancing skills. "No regrets" policies and measures available for immediate use in many countries at little or no cost should taken into consideration. The developing countries' relying on production of fossil fuels, and the economic impacts of potential policies or measures to limit or reduce green house gases causing vulnerability must be addressed. There is need for all parties in order to meet their commitments, the need of equity and differentiated responsibilities must be taken into account. The Second Assessment Report expresses divergent views on implication to address the climate change. Thus it required careful consideration by the Conference of the Parties and particularly by the Adhoc Group on the Berlin Mandate (AGBM) in their future activities as a basis for urgent action. The participants expressed their views that as the Second Assessment Report does provide sufficient information in determining what constitute dangerous levels of greenhouse gas concentrations, and due to the scientific uncertainties and lack of sufficient economic analysis, it would be premature to take action beyond what is appropriate with no targets policies and measures to mitigate at climate change, which requires more and more research for achieving the objectives of the convention[44].

GENERAL DESCRIPTION OF STEPS : In accordance with Article 12.1 each party not included in Annex.-1 should communicate a general description of steps taken or envisaged by the party to implement the convention. Taking into account the chapter of Article 4.(1) the initial communication should seek to include as appropriate:

(*a*) Programme related to sustainable development, research and systematic observation, education and public awareness training etc.

(*b*) Policy options for adequate monitoring systems and response strategies for climate change impacts on terrestrial and marine ecosystems.

(*c*) Policy framework for implementing adoption measures and response strategies in context of coastal zone management, disaster preparedness, agriculture, fisheries and forestry with a view to integrating climate change impact information as appropriate into national planning process.

(*d*) It undertook to hold National Communications and/or sub-regional capacity as appropriate to integrate climate change concerns in medium and long term planning.

(*e*) Programmes containing measures by party are concerned with addressing climate change and its adverse impacts, including the abatement of increase in greenhouse gas emissions and enhancement of removal by sinks[45]. Parties not included in Annex-I may provide any other information relevant to the achievement of the objective of the convention including feasible material relevant for calculation of global emission trends, consensus and obstacles etc.

At the CoP-2 in Geneva in 1996 US stated that it was examining stabilization schedules for periods only beyond the year 2000. It proposed a framework of broad abatement goals achievable over larger time frames. The EU however reiterated its commitment to work towards the year 2000 goal. The Alliance of Small Island States (AOSIS) was particularly happy with the EU Commitments since they saw a ray of hope against the potential acceleration of global warming, which could lead to their submergence[46]. The representatives were instructed to accelerate negotiations on the text of a legally binding protocol or other legal instrument to be completed in due time for the adoption at the third session of the Conference of the Parties. It is hoped that the outcome should fully encompass the text of Berlin mandate. Welcoming the efforts of developing countries to implement the convention to address the climate change and its adverse impacts in making their initial natural communications in accordance with the guidelines adopted by the Conference of the Parties at its second session it called on the GEF to provide necessary expeditious and timely support to these parties and initiate work towards a full replenishment in 1997. Thanks to the government of the Swiss confederations for its contribution to the work of second session of the Conference of the Parties in Geneva and look forward to meeting again at the third session in Kyoto in 1997, thanks to the generous offer of the government of Japan[47].

There was large difference among the participant countries relating to economic development to meet the costs reducing green house gas emissions and enhanced sinks. The developing countries relying on production of fossil fuels expressed divergent views to meet their commitments causing vulnerability to their sustainable development. The developed countries like United States and European Union supported legally binding targets to be completed in due timetable to achieve stabilization of greenhouse gas concentration in the atmosphere. The conference calls for appropriate international response in accordance with each country's common but differentiated responsibilities and assign the lead to the industrialized countries in combating global climate change. The industrialized countries while accepting the responsibility to set and meet emissions reduction targets imposed no burdens on developing countries to impede their economic development. The Berlin Mandate was adopted as a basic guideline document for the drafting of an international agreement to further the negotiation process to address the potential impacts of climate change. In the Conference of the Parties in Geneva, all the member states agreed that reduction of greenhouse gas emissions was a legal obligation of the international community to achieve the objectives of the framework convention. Although the Second Assessment Report of the IPCC does not specify what constitutes dangerous anthropogenic interference, it had played a leading role in evolving international response to combat global climate change. The attitude shown by the developed countries towards the developing countries encouraged the negotiation process for the third session of the parties and generated signs of the hope for combating the threat of climate change.

KYOTO PROTOCOL

Conference of the Parties (CoP-3)

The Conference of the Parties to the convention continued to meet on a regular basis at a fixed interval to monitor climate change and review the implementation of commitments in response to changes in "Scientific understanding and political will". The United Nations Framework Convention on Climate (UNFCCC) called for international action to help slow global warming trend that has the potential to disrupt the Earth's climate system and destabilize human society[48]. As per the decision of the CoP-2, the third session of the conference of the parties was held in Kyoto, Japan on Dec-1-12, 1997. The convention set the overall framework for intergovernmental efforts to address climate change. It established an objective, principles and commitments for different group of countries and a set of institutions to enable governments to monitor the conventions and implementation and continue their talks on how best to tackle the problem[49]. The ultimate objective of the convention is "to achieve stabilization of atmospheric concentration of greenhouse gases at levels that would prevent dangerous anthropogenic (human induced) interference with climate system." Addressing climate change is clearly not an easy task raising different dilemmas such as how to distribute the burden of reducing emissions among different countries and dealing with scientific uncertainty. The conventions embodied the common understanding of governments on how to deal with these dilemmas.

The principles of "equity" and "common but differentiated responsibilities," are based on the fact that, are based on the industrialized countries have contributed the most to the problem and have more resources to address it. The developing countries are more vulnerable to the adverse effects and their capacity is generally lower from technological economic and institutional point of view to combat it. Thus, the convention defines a global framework for addressing climate change. So the industrialized countries take the lead by modifying their long-term emission trends and to help the developing countries by providing financial and technological help to tackle the problem and adapt to its adverse effects. The convention responds to dilemmas like "precautionary measures" and development problem to achieve sustainable development while addressing climate change. In addition to these problems, the convention calls for policies and measures to deal with climate change to be cost effective, so as to ensure global benefit at the lowest possible cost[50]. After intense negotiation and deliberations more than 150 participant nations signed the Kyoto protocol on Dec.11, 1997 in Kyoto, Japan. The framework convention on climate change and the Kyoto protocol have established a structure for global action to mitigate the threat of climate change. Proponents of the Kyoto protocol widely acknowledge that it is only a first step in the international effort to reduce emissions. This unprecedented treaty committed industrialized nations to legally binding reductions of emissions of sick gases - Carbon Dioxide, Methane, Nitrous oxide, Hydrofluorocarbons (HFCs) Perflurocarbons (PFCs) and Sulferhexafluride (SF_6). The called for reductions vary from country to country, but would cut emissions an average of about 5% below 1990 levels by the first commitment period 2008-2012. The United States agreed reductions of 7%, Japan to reductions of 6 percent and members of European Unions to joint reductions of 8%. Key to such relatively ambitious agreement by the U.S was a concurrent agreement among industrialized countries that established a system of emission trading by which nations with binding limits could buy and sell among themselves the right to release greenhouse gases.

The convention divides countries into two main groups. A total of 41, industrialized countries are currently listed in the convention's Annex-I including the wealthy industrialized countries that were the member of the Organization for the Economic Co-operation and Development (OECD) in 1992, plus countries with Economies in Transition (the EITs) including the Russian Federation, Balatic states and several central and eastern European states. The OECD members of Annex-I not the EITs are also listed in the convention's Annex-II They are currently 24 such

Annex-II parties. All other countries not listed in the convention's Annexes mostly, the developing countries are known as Non Annex-I parties, they currently number 145. All parties to the convention- those countries that have ratified, accepted, approved, or acceded to the treaty are subject to an important set of general commitments, which places a fundamental obligation on both industrialized and developing countries to respond to climate change. Under these commitments, all parties must prepare and regularly up date national climate change mitigation and adaptation programmes, including members to address sources of greenhouse gas emissions and to protect and enhance the so called Carbon "sinks" "reservoirs" (forest and other natural systems that remove carbon from the atmosphere). All parties must also promote the development application and transfer of climate friendly technologies and practices as well as the sustainable management of carbon sinks. Parties are required to make preparations to adapt to climate change and submit reports known as "National communications" on the action they are taking to implement the convention.

The Annex-I parties in order to demonstrate their leadership in addressing climate change, should adopt policy and measures to ful fill their commitment in reduction of greenhouse gases to 1990 levels by the year 2000. Due to the recent economic and political upheavals experienced in EITs, the convention grants "a certain degree of flexibility to implement their commitments. The Annex-Ii parties are also required to provide financial resources to the developing countries to meet their obligations and to help them adapt to the adverse effects of climate change. The Annex-II parties must "take all practicable steps" to promote the development and transfer of environmentally friendly technologies to both EITs and developing countries.

The convention recognizes vulnerability of developing countries, such as countries with low lying coastal areas and those prone to drought and desertification face particularly high risks from the adverse impacts of climate change, and others such as countries that are highly dependent on income generated from the fossil fuel, production, processing or export, feel more vulnerable to the potential economic impacts of climate change. The convention calls for full consideration to be given to possible funding, insurance and technology transfer that could help meet the specific needs and concerns of these vulnerable countries. The U.N. classified 48 countries as Least Developing Countries (LDCs) that are given special consideration on account of their low capacity to respond to climate change and adapt to its adverse effects. Parties were urged to take full accounts of special situations of LDCs with regards to funding and technology transfer. The supreme decision-making body of the convention is its Conference of the Parties (CoP). It meets every year to review implementation of the convention and adopt decisions to further develop the convention's rulebook, and negotiate substantive new commitments.

The convention's two subsidiary bodies - The Subsidiary Body for Scientific and Technological Advice (SBSTA) and the Subsidiary Body for Implementation (SBI) meet at least twice a year to carryout preparatory work for the CoP. The SBSTA is responsible for providing advice to the CoP on scientific, technological and methodological issues as well as co-operation with IPCC and other relevant international organizations. The SBI helps in the assessment and review of the convention's implementation, including the analysis of national communications submitted by parties, liaison with GEF and financial and administrative issues.

The climate change secretariat provides support to the CoP and the subsidiary bodies performing such functions as preparing book ground documents, organizing negotiation sessions compiling emission data and giving advice on technical matters, as compiling by the parties. The secretariat composed of some 150 staff and consultants is currently based in Bonn, Germany. The global environment facility and governmental panel climate change are not formally part of the convention's institution but provide important service to it. The GEF operates the convention's financial mechanism, which channels funds to developing countries as a grant on concessional basis. The CoP provides regular policy guidance to the GEF on its climate change policies, programme priorities and eligibility criteria for funding, while the GEF reports on its climate change work to the CoP every year. The IPCC is now one of the most important sources of information for climate change regime playing an important role in publishing Assessment Report on the state of climate change science roughly every five years. The Third Assessment Report of the IPCC came out in 2001. The Kyoto protocol is a successful legal document produced by the international community specifying legal binding emission targets for the industrialized countries and voluntary reduction commitment for all countries to reduce emissions of greenhouse gases to combat the dangerous consequences of the global climate change. The Kyoto Treaty as a meaningful starting point took many years of hard work and complicated negotiation to achieve through globally coordinated action in providing a powerful solution to the issue pressing challenges to the future generations. Thus, the ongoing negotiation progress gave a new dimension to the collective regulation of global warming with strong determination and confidence.

Fourth meeting of the Conference of the Parties to the UN Framework Convention on Climate Change-took place November 2nd - 13th 1998.

The fourth meeting of the Conference of the Parties to the UN framework convention on climate change was held from November 2-13, 1998 in Buenos Aires, Argentina. Delegates to the convention debated the agenda of CoP-4 at length and focusing attention on items concerning voluntary commitments for Non Annex-I parties, deleted from the consideration. Hiroshi Ohki, President of CoP-3 recalled the important role of the Berlin Mandate and CoP-4 is going to face the political momentum and challenges created in Kyoto, and noted the need to review existing economic structure and re-examine life styles. Maria Julia Alsogaray, Secretary of Natural resources and Sustainable Development of Argentina was elected president of CoP-4. Analyzing the historic responsibilities of Argentina and other groups for commitments leading to a solution, wanted CoP-4 signal a new momentum in the process of climate change. She urged for an action plan for future work should be established here, while the developing countries share the burden of responsibility in responding to this issue, they have an ethical duty to ensure sustainable development. Michael Zammit Cutajar, Executive Secretary of the FCCC observed that this was the first CoP to be held in a developing country. He anticipated an action plan with ambition and free from political decline would be created as a result of this meeting. He noted that CoP-4 presents an opportunity to revitalize the FCCC itself through strengthening the transfer of technology, financial support and marks the occasion in which the role played by business community, through efficient programme conducted in an equitable way in combating climate change was commendable.

A number of participant countries presented general statements that outlined the idea of voluntary commitments, financial assistance, and transfer of technology with domestic and international programmes and elaborated their expectations from the CoP-4 and future negotiations. Delegates opposed the initiative of voluntary commitment of the host country and the compromising proposal of the CoP President for informal consultations. They were deadly against the proposal to ensure that the issue does not reenter the formal deliberations over the remaining sessions. One concern is whether and how the issue might reemerge under the guise of other agenda item 4(d) as the second review of Adequacy of Convention commitments. Delegates noted a great number of outstanding issues and several protocol elements to be elaborated and resolved under the convention. These issues should take precedence at this point in the negotiation[51].

UN FCCC Fourth Conference of the Parties on 3rd November 1998

The Subsidiary Body for Scientific and Technological Advice and Subsidiary Body for Advice discussed matters relating to land use change and forestry, organizational matter and the flexibility mechanisms to the Kyoto protocol. Several key issues raised by the parties, after an extensive debate indicated that informal negotiation would be held on this matter. Some NGO observers reported "hints" of a "hostile negotiating climate", when a number of developing countries resisted an immediate review of the (AIJ) pilot phase and called for an extension. Some developing countries in order to allow more countries to gain experience prior to the implementation of clean development mechanisms explained that they were determined to hold out for extension of the pilot phase. One NGO observer suggested, however that the U.S. may pay a high price for its position on voluntary commitments, if the flexibility mechanisms are delayed. This could result in uncertainty about Annex-B parties' commitments to the protocol and their preparedness to tackle GHG emissions. Ironically, it could difer the conditions for developing countries to assume voluntary commitments[52].

Highlights - CoP-4-on Nov. 4, 1998

The SBSTA and SBI in a joint plenary and contact group considered the Kyoto protocol's flexibility mechanisms. The SBSTA debated the issue relating to Development and transfer of technology and research and systematic observation. SBI considered national communications, the financial mechanisms and amendments to the FCCC Annexes. The participant countries highlighted problems with quality and frequency of observations and spatial groups over some critical important areas. The joint contact group discussed the preparation of a comprehensive work programme on flexibility mechanism. The EU and umbrella groups" distributed draft decisions and discussion documents. Other parties including G-77 and China called for more time to consider the volume of documentation. Several developing countries supported addressing a wide range of issues related to flexibility mechanisms including technology transfer, adverse impacts, methodologies, reporting and compliance. Two small island states supported a package of 11 themes for the work programme. The chairs distributed a "dummy" draft work programme on mechanism and conducted informal consultations[53].

UN FCCC-CoP-on 4th - 5th November 1998

The delegates considered preparation for the first session of the Conference of the Parties serving as the Meeting of the Parties (CoP/MoP) in a joint plenary session. The SBSTA and SBI discussed research and systematic observation and other matters. In the afternoon and evening, the contact groups discussed on communications, technology transfer under Art-4-8 and Art 4-9 and adverse effects on developing countries, the financial mechanisms under Art-4 (2)(a) and (b) for review of commitments. Official negotiations at CoP-4 have mellowed considerably since Monday's confrontational but cathartic exchanges. Some observers suggested however that politically sensitive talks were underway behind the scene. One delegate noted that technology transfer threatened to become a linchpin issue for those meeting. He expressed concern that some developed countries have underestimated the degree of significance, the G-77/China places on the issue perhaps to halt the point of negotiation, unless the CoP takes a decision. Some observers suggested that the consultation by the host party be initiated and continue over the week end[54].

CoP - on 4th -6th November 1998 -Report

CoP-4 President Maria Julia Alsogaray, Argentina offered condolences to the Caribbean and Latin America countries recently devastated by hurricane Mitch. She noted that over the past, floods, fires, droughts and hurricanes profoundly affected countries around the world and suggested that "Mother Nature" remind the delegates that urgent action was needed. EL SALAVADOR for the CENTRAL AMERICAN group said these events should remind all participants of their vulnerability requiring immediate discussion and prompt action.

SBI chairman, Bakray Kante reported that all items referred to SBI had been considered. Contact groups were considering budgetary issues, national communications from Annex-I parties, internal communication from Non-Annex-I parties and second review of the adequacy of the commitments. On implementation of FCCC Article-4-8 and 4-9 contact group would base its discussion on those that began at last session. The President of the CoP initiated comments on the review of implementation of commitments and other provisions of the convention (FCCC/cp/1998/L-2). The meeting ended without clear resolution about the report the co chairs should present to the SBI[55]. Delegates debated on references to atmospheric observing systems and measurement of green house gas concentrations and agreed to the text that "urges practices to actively support, national, meteorological and atmosphere observing systems including measurement of green house gases." Delegates also debated on issues-requesting parties to submit information on their participation in global climate observing systems and requesting SBSTA to report to CoP-5 on developments regarding observational net works. On land use change, and forestry, FCCC/SBSTA invited parties to provide submission on issues to be covered at the workshop. At the request of the former Russian federation and other parties, the title of the draft conclusion was amended to read, "Land use, Land use change and Forestry". The draft conclusions were amended and adopted accordingly. The SBSTA considered a recommendation on the relationship between efforts to protect the stratospheric Ozone layer and efforts to safeguard the global climate systems (FCCC/SBSTA/1998/CR-P.8). The contact group met in a closed session under the chairmanship of Bokjellon (Sweden) and Mohammad Salamat (Iran) prior to the meeting on the implementation of FCCC Article 4-8 and 4-9 (decision 3/CP-3 and protocol Article 2.3 and 3.14 (adverse effects). The chair circulated a draft decision, which decided that the basic elements for further analysis include the identification of adverse effects, determination of impacts of implementation measures in developing countries, the identification of the specific needs and concerns of developing country parties to get protection from such adverse effects and impacts, and identification of further necessary actions related to funding insurance and the transfer of technology. A programme workshop of experts met on April 1999 for further discussion on subsidiary bodies, SBSTA and SBI on 10, June 1999 in order to meet the needs of the developing countries for identification of needs for further information needed for CoP-5 on October 1999 and decisions to be made at CoP-6, on October 2000). Delegates were unable to reach agreement and continued discussion.[56]

Highlights from the 4th Conference of Parties on 11th November-1998

The fourth plenary of the CoP- met to hear statements from the Under Secretary General of the U.N., the President of Argentina and representatives from intergovernmental agencies and Non Governmental Organization's (N.G.O's). Speaking on behalf of the U.N. Secretary General Kofi Annan, Nitin Desai, Under Secretary for U.N. Commission for Sustainable Development, said, the Kyoto protocol offered a sustainable path for industrialized countries and demonstrated shared stewardship for the planet. He understood the need for early ratification of the protocol and action on issue relating to technology transfer, domestic measures and scientific research. He called for a new dead line to maintain momentum and pledged for UN support.

The World Meteorological Organization (WMO) highlighted 1998 as the warmer year in recorded history and emphasized attention on sinks, elaboration of protocol mechanisms and adaptation issues. He called for improved co-operation in addressing concerns common to Montreal and Kyoto protocol. United Nations Development Programme (UNDP) called for early ratification of Kyoto protocol to combat environmental degradation and poverty. As the developing countries were responding in a meaningful way, he highlighted the linkages between development of poor communities, poverty eradication and climate change initiatives. United Nations Environmental Programme (UNEP) called for the establishment of Buerus Aires Plan to develop coordinated action to be enacted at CoP-6. The World Bank committed to promotion of sustainable development, showed concern for the vulnerability of developing countries to climate change. After consideration, SBSTA chair, Kok Kee Chow provided a report on the activities of agreed draft decisions on research and systematic observation, scientific and methodological aspects, land use change and forestry, impacts of single projects on emissions in the commitment period, and the relationship between efforts to protect the stratospheric Ozone layer and efforts to safeguard the global climate system. The draft decisions were later adopted by the CoP without amendment. No decision on flexibility mechanism was reached and two-draft texts were forwarded to the CoP for decision on AIJ and Transfer of Technology. The issues relating to National Communications from Annex-I parties, review of information communicated under Article-12, second review on Adequacy of Article 4-2(a) and (b) and implementation of Articles 4-8 and 4-9 and decision of 3/CoP-3 and Articles 2-3 and 3.14 of the Kyoto protocol were forwarded to the CoP, since agreement on their adoption had not been reached. The SBI recommendation of draft decision on administrative and financial matter was adopted by the CoP-4. The CoP-4, President proposed to convene a group of friends of the President at the Ministerial level to address the outstanding issues from the SBI and SBSTA[57].

The goal of the CoP-4 of the Buenos Aires, Argentina, was to negotiate rules for key elements of the Kyoto protocol, including emission-trading compliance, carbon sinks and clean development mechanisms. By the end of the meeting, negotiation did manage to set a deadline of November 2000 for deciding on these issues. Seeing the potential environmental and financial advantages in opting unto an international trading system, Argentina and Kazakhstan announced their intention to adopt voluntary commitments to limit their emissions, whereby their economies might benefit from increased foreign investment in clean energy. Some powerful members of the developing block opposed the steps that instead of engaging in International emission trading and pushing for limits on developing countries, they consider it as the moral duty of the industrialized nations to begin by reducing their emissions at home. It was seen that U.S. had failed to live up to the Berlin Mandate, having done little to restrict greenhouse gas emissions so far. The United

States announced to affix its signature to the Kyoto protocol during second week of the Buenous Aires conference. Yet the current U.S. Senate is unlikely to ratify the treaty until more and more developing countries agree to binding reductions, on the ostensible ground that the agreement would stifle the U.S. economy and lead to the flight of many energy intensive industries abroad. On the last night of the meeting in Buenous Aires, a group of developing countries - China, India, Saudi Arabia, Kuwait, Venezuela and Nigeria formed a rejectionist block and walked out of the negotiations at 3.00 A.M. They were met out side the door by delegates from small Island states, which are the most to loose from rising sea levels caused by climate change and few members of other developing nations as well as members from Argentina recognized that the entire framework of the climate treaty was in danger of collapsing. These delegates forced the rejectionist block inside by threatening to take their place at the bargaining table[58].

Several delegates stated that they were disappointed with the meeting as a result of the often bitter and "bracket calculation", during the length of the Thursday night session. They hoped that this experience would not thwart the progress of the negotiations, but rather inspire a reassessment of the deliberations and aspirations of the CoP. CoP-4 at Buenos Aires in 1998 saw Argentina a non Annex-1 country taking a voluntary commitments with financial gains to be derived from emission trading. Argentina also supported U.S. demand for meaningful participation in GHG emission abatement by developing countries. Honduras, several Latin American and African countries and the U.S. called for rapid creation of CDM opportunities. India and China said that the CDM without emission entitlements for all countries as a per capita basis was not likely to support the sustainable development imperatives of developing countiries[59]. Executive Secretary, Michel ZammitunitaJar informed delegates that Jordan had offered to host CoP-5 in the coming year 1999. After Kyoto protocol, intergovernmental efforts to mitigate climate change talks continued in the summer of 1998 in Bonn by the representatives of 150 nations to set the agenda for the fourth conference of the parties CoP-4. With the proposed three major plans and mandated emission cut backs, the agenda for CoP-4 lacked the expected consensus plan that was needed to guide the CoP-4 meeting at Buenos Aires, Argentina. One of the historical facts was that the conference of the parties meeting was held in a developing country in Argentina for the first time to encourage the developing countries to achieve agreed global environmental benefits. From the very beginning the negotiations concluded in a atmosphere of friendliness and good will, the delegates put forth their statements on various issues relating to climates change and its adverse impacts. The debate continued in an orderly and peaceful atmosphere, with special reference to the implementation of Montreal and Kyoto protocol. The Argentina's declaration of ratification of Kyoto protocol and voluntary support for emission reductions did not exert any influence over the developing countries. Many substantial issues were discussed and failed to reach unanimous decisions. The United States of America tried to shift the yoke of responsibility to the less polluting countries. The hollowness of US claims of its commitments to sign the Kyoto protocol to protect global environmental and its hidden desire to unleash ecological imperialism becomes obvious. Global action that needs to be taken for saving the planet from an environment catastrophe, without vulnerability to the sustainable development of the developing countries. Thus, the rich industrialized countries should come forward to bear the responsibility of emission reduction commitments within a targeted timetable. Instead of ratifying as well as implementing the so called reduction targets, they are imposing voluntary commitments over the developing countries, which hinder the negotiation processes to meet the objectives of the frame work convention.

The industrialized world was trying to impose mandatory restrictions on developing countries to meet voluntary emissions. Any such attempts at fixing the rate of increasing emission reductions in poor nations could certainly jeopardize the process of their development. Looking at the attitude of the developed countries China, India and several developing countries formed a separate block to counter the negotiations involving political questions as well as social and economic considerations of the adverse effects of climate change treaty. One after another international meets on the subjects designed to evolve positive action plans for retarding global warming process seemed to be less meaningful as expected by the international community. The conflicting interests were identified over many issues to safeguard world climate systems. The rich industrialized world tried to impose technological bondage over the developing countries. Hot exchanges and much wrangling marked the conference lack of consensus among the participant countries to reach agreement for draft decisions.

The conferences raised many different dilemmas and dealt with many scientific uncertainties to the problems to be addressed. The developed world were not at all ready to pay adequate attention to the needs of the developing countries who for their part are more vulnerable to its adverse effects, and their technological, economic and institutional capacity to respond was generally lower. Instead of providing financial and technological help to developing countries to tackle their problems and to adapt to its adverse effects the developed countries avoided effective actions to improve the process of negotiations. The CoP-4 aimed to demonstrate co-operation on environment and development problems and focus on many obstacles to effective international solutions to mitigate the threat of climate change. The CoP-4 received a little response from the developing countries to take measures to facilitate eventual implementation of Kyoto protocol's flexibility mechanisms. It failed to concretize the founding structures laid down at Montreal and Kyoto protocol, and to secure collaboration from the nations of the world to combat the global climate change. Still remained much issues to be determined at the CoP-5, which required mutual understanding and combined efforts keeping in view rapid changes in climatic conditions to accomplish the desired objectives of the framework convention.

U.N. Frame Work Convention on Climate Change

Fifth Conference of the Parties (CoP-5)

As per the declaration made at Bunos Aires, the fifth conference of the parties to the United Nations Framework Convention on Climate Change met from October 25 to November 5, 1999 in Bonn, Germany. Gerhard Schroeder, Germany Chancellor when opened the conference probably the biggest splash occurred right way, with a dramatic challenge to the developed nations to ratify the Kyoto protocol by 2002. Up till now only 14 countries; primarily small island nations have done so for, though New Zealand was expected to ratify the treaty later this year. Many called for a goal "Rio+10" which would bring the treaty into force by 2002, the 10th anniversary of the Earth submit in Rio. Responding to the call to meet this deadline, the European union and Japan expressed their ready willingness to ratify the protocol. Canada and the United States called for the treaty to enter into force "at the earliest possible date."

The Clinton administration already hesitant to set a firm date for ratification was especially cautious because of the Senate's rejection of the Comprehensive Test Ban Treaty just weeks before. Some participants put emphasis on apparent easing of the three-way deadlock between the United States and its allies, the European Union and the developing countries. The European Union was less insistent about limiting the extent to which emissions trading can be used to meet Kyoto commitments. Even the developing countries began to act as though they might more seriously consider agreeing to limitations on their green house gas emissions in the future. Part of this new constructive dynamic might also have been the result of divisions in the internal ranks of each of these groups. Within the EU, several countries, most notably the Netherlands pushed for a less restrictive emission-trading regime. Within G-77 group, which includes the developing nations, the Latin American countries seemed to realize that agreeing to emission limitations might work to their advantages by bringing in additional revenue and increased investments to their economies as an active market in emissions trading would be established[60].

Another contentious issue that divides the developing nations was the question of "adverse effects", despite though the UNFCCC consideration of negative impacts on developing countries arising either from climate change or from the implementation of measures to address climate change. This section of the treaty seems to be controversial, which involves the possibility of actual reparations because it puts the small Island states which may loose much of their land areas to rising sea levels, against OPEC countries, which fear losing oil revenues as a result of efforts to control climate change. Looking at the attitude of the OPEC countries, which appeared to work at every opportunity to block progress on the treaty, the developing nations as a whole at CoP-5 seemed increasingly ready to break away from those countries. To help the developing countries in their capacity building to respond to climate change has long been recognized in the climate change process. It was considered a separate item at CoP-5, 1999 in the context of such issues as the development and transfer of technology, the preparation of national communications and the financial mechanisms.

The framework called on developing countries and EITs to continue providing information on their specific needs and priorities while promoting co-operation among themselves and stake holder participation. Annex-II parties, for their part should provide additional financial and technical resources for capacity building through GEF and other channels; while all parties would improve the co-ordination and effectiveness of existing activities. In order to improve the preparation of national communications from developing countries, Consultative Group of Experts (CGE) on national communication from Annex-I parties was established by CoP-5 in 1999. Its mandate was to analyze problems encountered by Non Annex-I parties in preparing their national communications (e.g. concerning financial or technical support of data quality or availability) and provide a forum for these parties to exchange information on their experiences with the national communication process. The CGE composed of 24 members met twice a year and also held workshops to gather information on national experiences[61]. COP-5 at Bonn in 1999 witnessed deliberations on the limits to tradability of credits. EU demanded that all credits generated through a statement task should not be accounted for compliances to commitments nor should all the credits be traded. This demand was to ensure that industrialized countries also carry out domestic action in order to account for compliance with commitments[62].

Under the convention most developing countries believe it is unfair of developed countries to ask them to make voluntary commitments to reduce emissions. Keeping in view the need for development, no commitments are required on part of the developing countries. The U.S. has been however unwilling to make binding emission reduction commitments unless developing countries with large rapidly growing economies such as India and China make voluntary commitments to reduce their emissions. Most developing countries are unwilling to comply with the demand of the United States. They argue that commitments that are in any way "required" cannot be called voluntary. Even without making binding or voluntary commitments countries such as India claim that they are already involved in activities aimed at climate change mitigation. CoP-5 also took note of the need to integrate Indian's call for ensuring that the parameters of flexibility mechanisms adequately integrate the equity concerns of the developing countries, and the need to achieve clearer perspectives on the equity issue has been placed on the agenda for CoP-6 to be held at Hague, Netherlands in November 2000. The next and more difficult deadline will be CoP-6 to be held in Hague, Netherlands in the fall of 2000. At this meeting, agreement reached on a whole host of difficult issues, including how much trading in emission allowances would be permitted, how carbon sinks such as forests would be enforced. If any of these issues was not resolved major player like U.S. might simply not make concerted efforts to cut their emissions. In recognition of this fact, negotiations agreed on a new set of interim workshops to hammer out the details separately on each of these issues.[63]

The 5th Conference of the Parties took into consideration many delicate issues, which were not resolved in Buenos Aires conference. The Chancellor of Germany considering the rapid changes in the climatic conditions, called for appropriate international response to ratify the Kyoto protocol. The Montreal and Kyoto protocol constituted the basic framework to further negotiations to address the potential threats of climate change. The developed countries while accepting the responsibility to set and meet emission reduction targets within stipulated timetable, in turn insisted that the developing countries should voluntarily implement their emission reductions. The attitude of the industrialized countries towards developing countries goes against their development in mitigating climate change. It created bitter and hostile attitude among the developing world to accept specific actions. In accordance with each country's "common but differentiated responsibility", the United States of America avoids to ratify the Kyoto protocol and comply the burden of cutting emissions. The conflicting and hostile relationship developed between the developed and developing countries to collectively address the emerging concern about the impacts of global warming. It was hard to motivate countries to act when no one knows whether the problem big or small is imminent or distant. The industrialized countries are also expected to provide new and additional financial resources to help greenhouse gas reduction projects as well as promote and finance transfer of environmentally sound technologies to non-annex-I parties. Moreover, the developing countries have the most to loose from global warming. They have fewer resources to adapt to climate change, and their economies rely more on agriculture, and they are potentially more vulnerable to changes in the weather.

Diplomacy and bargaining dominated the deliberation over substantial issues. No commitments are required of the developing countries (referred to as Non Annex-I parties) in recognition of their capacity building and sustainable development. However, the issue of emission reductions for the developing countries went to the extent of such a stage the activities of OPEC seemed to be stumbling block in the way of progress in negotiations. The issues like development, transfer of technology, national communications and financial mechanisms were considered separately in CoP-5, which faced conflicting opinion of the parties to arrive at any consensus in scientific understanding and political will. The EU, small Island states and G-77 countries including China and India took interest to make the negotiation meaningful to adopt draft decisions. From the overall assessment, it is found that with the United States not taking concerted effort to cut their emissions, disagreement continued among the parties to make any progress to coordinate and improve the situation and to take any effective decisions. Due to the prevalence of hot atmosphere, major issues relating to global climate change remained unsolved. However, agreed direction is more important than an agreed target. The more immediate task should be developing some degree of international consensus about framework conventions that are needed for future action. The CoP-5 key policy issues favoured a more flexible approach and it insisted that a massive response was urgently needed to provide high profile in climate change mitigation efforts. The CoP-5 at Bonn considered many things to address the climate change but achieved a very insignificant outcome to settle certain problems. Participants expressed a desire to wait how did situation develop, what would happen next to be seen in Hague conference.

The Hague Conference : CoP-6

The Conference of the Parties CoP-6 to the United Nations Framework Convention on Climate Change was held in the Hague, the Netherlands on November 13-25, 2000. Jan Pronk, the President of Netherlands attempted by convening high-level informal plenary session to facilitate negotiations on many political and technical issues, where nations met to evaluate the accords and compliance with meeting on reduction targets. This was intended to warp up three years negotiations on the implementation of Kyoto protocol.

The Buenos Aires Plan of Action (BAPA) set CoP-6 as the deadline for reaching agreement on the operational details of the protocol and on strengthening implementation of the UNFCCC. In CoP-6, issues the addressed included rule relating to mechanism regimes for assessing parties' compliance, accounting methods for national emissions and emission reductions and rules on crediting countries for carbon sinks. Issues under UNFCC requiring resolution included question of capacity building, the development of transfer of technology, and assistance to those developing countries particularly vulnerable to the adverse effects of climate change and action taken by industrialized countries to combat climate change[64]. After almost 36 hours of intense deliberations in the final two days of the CoP-6 on Saturday afternoon on 25 November 2000 president Prank announced that delegates had failed on a range of topics particularly financial issues, the use of the mechanisms, compliance and LULUCF to reach agreement. The Hague conference was collapsed due to the US wanting carbon sinks as a part of agreement (as well as other provisions like nuclear energy etc.), which receives enormous criticism from all the delegates.

The United States with about 4 per cent of the world's population and emitting about 24 per cent present the world's Carbon Dioxide, is pivotal in this process but with president Bush coming into power and declaring that he opposes Kyoto protocol, and responsible for hindering progress. In another issue, the Europeans were not swaying in their insistence that US should be given exception and should be allowed to meet much of its greenhouse gas reduction targets without actual emission while Britain and John Prescott attempted to find that the US should not get special treatment. It was this that was largely responsible for the collapse of CoP-6 at the Hague conference. This caused some rifts between European and United States, climate and environment group for example, the Washington based National Environment Trust blames the European union for passing up a U.S policy that was a major progress towards reducing global population as attempting to weaken the outcomes and any trade offs could be regarded as "major progress". The developing countries at the Hague were side linked with the consideration of Kyoto protocol. The G-77 and South developing countries were not consulted with regard to tradeoffs issues. The umbrella group then consisting of the U.S., Japan, Australia and New Zealand had huge differences on many issues with European Union and developing countries. The umbrella group, led by United States had direct business and economic interests, directing the type of issues to be debated. As a result, fears developing that it could lead to either save situations on many issues or watered down agreements to tackle climate change issues have unfortunately come true[65]. It is not surprising in the same way, while in other it is profoundly absurd at how their "extremely sparse" media coverage in United State mainstream. It was not surprising in that the mainstream media is corporate owned and share similar views to the business living groups that have been hostile to climate change negotiations. Again, it is profoundly absurd in the sense that how once again the media of most powerful nations does not provide much information to its population. The business interests of U.S. were blamed largely for the collapse of talks at the Hague. Hence, the delegates then agreed to suspend Part-II meeting of the CoP-6.

The US administration repudiated the agreement reached in Kyoto protocol in March 2001, stating that it considered the protocol to be "fatally flawed" as it would damage its economy and exempt key developing countries like China and India from emission reduction targets. Parties reconvened at CoP-6 Part-II and SB-14 from 16-27 July 2001 in Bonn, Germany[66]. President Pronk presented his proposal for a draft political decision after protracted consultations with participants. Despite the support from the several parties, disagreement surfaced over the nature of the compliance regime. After several days of high-level consultations, Ministers agreed to adopt president Pronk's political decision or "Bonn Agreement", which needed to be operationalized through CoP decisions. These decisions were considered a "Package" and since no agreements was reached on the mechanisms of compliance and LULUCF, all draft decisions were forwarded to CoP-7[67]. The Hague conference negotiations indeed was more a less a sparing session between the United States and the European Union, which left out developing countries. The outcome of sixth Conference of the Parties CoP-6 held in the Hague 2000 and the more recent declaration of President George. W. Bush of the United States have caused serious dilemmas to the outstanding decisions. The President Bush's declaration made things worse, leading to a deadlock for the whole negotiation process. What can be done to move ahead and stimulate a new impetus in the climate challange[68]? The existence of so many unsolved issues signals the importance of the upcoming sixth Conference of the Parties CoP-6 in the Netherlands in November 2000. Many observers saw progress on CDM rules as a particularly important outcome of CoP-6. The lack of clear rules currently acts as a disincentive to undertake otherwise environmentally beneficial projects that would qualify for crediting under the CDM. Timing is important to the economic value of the CDM, the sooner CDM is operational, the larger the role it may play on the global GHG market[69].

CoP-6 could have been a turning point for all outstanding decisions concerning the negotiations on particularly the flexible mechanisms. However, it only brought to light the differences between the EU, and the United States. CoP-6, finally brought the negotiations to a standstill instead of making things move forward.

Comments

The adoption of the United Nations Framework Convention on Climate Change (UNFCCC) in 1992 and the Kyoto protocol in 1997 have established a structure for global action generating signs of hope to mitigate the threat of climate change. Scientists across the world concede that global temperatures have increased over the past century and continue to increase as a threat to mankind and a new burden for the whole humanity. Thus, the objective of the climate convention and related legal instruments call for stabilization of greenhouse gas concentration in the atmosphere at a level that would prevent dangerous anthropogenic interference with the climate system. Such a level should be achieved within a time frame sufficient to allow ecosystems to adapt naturally to climate change, to ensure that food production is not threatened and to enable economic development to proceed in a sustainable manner.[70] In order to combat the catastrophic effects of the climate change, international efforts were in the form of Conference of the Parties from time to time in different parts of the world to discuss related problems and take effective measures to meet climate challenge. To begin with was the first conference of the parties at Berlin, followed by other 5 conferences concerning climate change issues. But the outcome of the sixth conference of the parties (CoP-6) held in Hague considered many important issues, which were not resolved in previous conferences. But the actions taken by the industrialized countries led to a deadlock for the process. However, it brought into light the differences of opinion between developed and developing countries. Moreover, the recent declaration by President, George. W. Bush of United States has seriously affected the negotiations. Indeed, the negotiation in the Hague was disturbed with the stand taken by the United States without turning the progress into a global agreement.

The search for co-operation among world community turned into confrontation for all outstanding issues to be discussed at the CoP-6. The communication process instead of bringing the parties closer they are driven farther from taking steps to put the world more firmly on the path seriously to combat global warming. The approach taken by individual countries to address the problem and the extent of their involvement in the decision making process to promote co-operation aimed at making things move forward. The existence of so many unsolved issues aggravating the situation with differences of opinions expressed by the parties, resulted in the collapse of negotiation process. Subsequent repudiation of Kyoto protocol by the US administration widens the rifts between European Union and the developing countries. The umbrella group led by the United States having direct business and economic interest faces strong resistance and huge differences from European Union and developing countries on many political and technical issues. The industrialized countries with huge resources imposed their will to those developing countries particularly vulnerable to the adverse effects of climate change. The very purpose of the conference is going to be defeated due to lack cooperative efforts on parts of the participant countries. The United States of America was ultimately responsible for creation of division and discord in the negotiation to achieve consensus. The meaningful achievements of combined efforts made in CoP-1, 2,3 gradually declined from CoP-4 and it reached its final stage of collapse at CoP-6.

CoP-6 could have been a turning point for all outstanding decisions concerning negotiations and particularly the flexible mechanisms. However, it brought in the picture of confrontation and difference between the European Union and the United States of America. The Clean Development Mechanism and other measures of the Kyoto protocol, making out from the diplomatic deadlock achieved consensus for their implementation. CoP-6 finally, brought the negotiations to a stand still instead of moving forward to continue its operation. It was expected that the issue would be taken up again at the second round of the CoP-6 to be held in Bonn in July 2001 but the chances of reaching a comprehensive agreement were bleak after the recent retreat of the US President. With or without United States the process of climate change negotiations should continue. It is not a matter of "doing something, that will harm the economy" of a particular country or a particular region. It is rather a question of being responsible and being concerned about the future of all humankind. The real issue is to develop a long-term climate change strategy as soon as possible. The disparities between North and South were responsible for stabilizing the climate futures through international co-operation and mutual assistance. North-South co-operation is an essential ingredient for the success of such climate change strategies over the long term. Europe is well positioned to promote such co-operation if strong political will prevails in decision-making. Europe in co-operation and partnership with the south must break the diplomatic deadlock and stimulate new impetus in the climate challenge[71]. In order to lead in this direction, the agreement of the EU, Canada, Japan, Russia and developing countries can only be achieved with a major diplomatic initiative from the EU, who will need to champion such a path of going ahead without US. Alternatively, it is most likely the U.S. which is given a chance to come back with some proposals to accommodate those views or what they might look like let alone or what would be a suitable response from the rest of the world. It was yet not clear what action would be taken by the United States at the next meeting of the CoP-6 in Bonn, Germany in July 2001.

Seventh Conference of the Parties – CoP –7 : 29th October to 10th November 2001

The seventh Conference of the Parties to the United Nations Framework Convention on Climate Change was held at the Palisades congress, Marrakech, Morocco on 29th October 2001. Ur-Jan Pronk, Minister of Housing, Spatial planning and Environment of the Netherlands, the then President of the sixth Conference of the Parties opened conference and said that the adoption of the Bonn agreement on the implementation of the Buenous Aires Plan of Action had proved that international community was capable of reaching agreement on global climate problems. Moreover, they now made Kyoto protocol rectifiable, so that it could enter into force before the world summit on sustainable development in 2002. The development in international Sphere made the role of the United Nations and international relations more important than ever. The events of 11 September 2001 attack over the world trade center in United States had reverberated the world and placed international relations in a new light showing the relevance of international co-operation to solve the world problems. The main aim at the sixth Conference of the Parties in its 2nd meeting in July 2001 was to reach an agreement on the implementation of the Buenos Aires Plan of Action. The Third Assessment Report of the IPCC showed that the Kyoto protocol represented only a small step, much remained to be done and the conference must not shy away from further debate on the adequacy of commitments while respecting the principle of "common but differentiated responsibilities".

In Bonn all parties had reaffirmed their intention to complete the work on the outstanding issues, for making the Bonn session of the conference a grand success. The President expressed his deep appreciation to all participants for their co-operation. At its first plenary meeting on 29th October on the proposal of the outgoing President, Mr. Mohamed Elyazhgi, Minister of Terrestrial Planning, Urban Management, Housing and Environment of Morocco was elected as its President of the Conference of the Parties-CoP-7. On assuming office, the President welcomed all participants to the seventh Conference of the Parties. Morocco was indeed proved to be the host of the conference to be held in Africa continent, which greatly suffered from the negative effects of climate change. A country rendered its support to international efforts to counter act those effects. Moreover, Morocco was particularly vulnerable to impacts of climate change whether through flood or through droughts every year. It was thus a firm supporter of process initiated at Rio de Janerio in 1992, and would complete the legislative procedures for accession to the Kyoto protocol very soon. He highlighted the outstanding contribution of his predecessor, Jon Pronk, whose perseverance, wealth of ideas and velocity of solutions had left indelible mark on the success of Bonn agreement. The present session of the conference had but one aim to give effect to Bonn agreement, to lay the foundation for the entry into force of the Kyoto protocol and present a strengthened convention to the Johannesburg summit.

The Third Assessment Report of the IPCC, "Climate Change 2001," suggests that role of the conference was not only to devise response and solutions to address global climate change, but to do so in a manner that would be comprehensible to the people in their daily lives. The convention should undertake its rightful place along side the instruments of biodiversity, and desertification, in the fight against poverty, hunger and the problems of water supply. Hence, the present session should demonstrate multilateral negotiation within the framework of United Nations and was capable of concrete decisions and commitments. The seventh Conference of the Parties called upon parties to consider the problems of global warming, drought, the depletion of Ozone layer and greenhouse gas emissions in order to avert a worldwide disaster. As a signatory to the framework convention in 1992 at Rio, Morocco had taken early measures to deal with the problems of environmental degradation. Marrakech being tourist center of Morocco was undertaking measures to protect the green heritage of the beautiful city, as well as taking steps to reduce greenhouse gas emissions in the waste treatment and transportation sectors. Mr. Michael Zammit Cutajar, the executive Secretary highlighted Bonn Agreement 2001 as a major step forward in combating climate change, as well as breakthrough for multilateral co-operation and impinged on all to maintain the political momentum generated at the Bonn and transform it into substantial decisions which would guarantee the progress of the conference and the implementation of its Kyoto protocol. The withdrawal of the United States of America does not affect the implementation of Kyoto protocol. The remaining Annex.-II parties must ensure that the implementation of protocol would lead to genuine reductions in their greenhouse gas emissions, despite the flexibility permitted by Bonn agreement. The actions of those countries would change the long-term trends of their emissions, which the convention sought to attain with regard to climate change.

The Conference of Parties gathering for the first time in the African continent, to give special consideration to the situation faced by the African countries to the potential threats of climate change. The release of Third Assessment Report of the IPCC included in the Agenda to guide the future work of the convention. At the first plenary meeting on 29th October 2001, the participant parties made their statements for consideration. All those who spoke, reiterated their commitment to maintaining the political integrity of the Bonn agreement (decision 5/CP-6) and indicated that the task of the present session was to translate those agreements into legal language in order to complete the implementation of the Buenous Aires Plan of Action (BAPA). The seventh Conference of the Parties and concurrent session of the subsidiary bodies were attended by representatives of 170 parties to the United Nations Framework Convention on Climate change. At its first plenary meeting on 29th October 2001, on organizational matters was adopted the status of ratification of the United Nations Framework Convention on Climate Change and its Kyoto protocol. Ratification accorded by 42 parties were appreciated and invited others to take necessary measures to do so. The Conference of the Parties on the proposal of the President decided to refer certain items to the subsidiary bodies for consideration and the presentation of appropriate draft decision or conclusion as follows:

(*a*) Date and venue of the eighth session of the conference of the parties.

(*b*) Calendar of meeting of convention bodies 2005-2007.

(*c*) Report of the Global Environmental Facility (GEF) to the Conference of the Parties.

(*d*) Proposal to amend the lists in Annex.-I and Annex.-II to the convention by removing the name of Turkey. Review of information and possible decisions under Article 4, paragraph 2 (f).

(*e*) Amendment proposed by Kazakhstan to add Kazakhstan to the list in Annex.-I.

(*f*) Third Assessment Report of the IPCC for consideration and report by Subsidiary Body for Scientific and Technical Advice, (SBSTA).

The Conference of the Parties decided to implement the Buenos Aires Plan of Action and adoption of decision giving effect to Bonn Agreement 2001. At the 2nd plenary meeting on 2nd November 2001, the conference heard reports from the Chairman of the Subsidiary Bodies and Co-chairman of Negotiating groups on the progress of work in their various consultations. Statements were made by the representatives of five parties including one speaking on behalf of the umbrella group and one speaking on behalf of the European community and its member states. At the third plenary meeting on 6th November 2001, the conference heard further reports by the Chairman and Co-chairman on the progress made in their various consultations. In this connection, the conference was informed that the negotiation group considering "Procedures and Mechanism relating to Kyoto Protocol had been able to agree on a consensus text on this issue.

At the 8th plenary meeting on 10th November 2001, the President announced that consensus now had been reached on the texts of the decisions on all different issues relating to the implementation of Buenos Aires Plan of Action, which would constitute "The Marrakech Accord". The President extended his appreciation to all who had contributed and tendered their valuable services to these major achievements on outstanding issues, on mechanisms of Kyoto protocol, sustainable development and land use, land use change and forestry.

The actions taken by the Conference of the Parties in relation to different texts and incomplete decisions were presented to the seventh session for adoption.

1. Capacity building in developing countries non-Annex.-I parties.
2. Capacity building in countries with economies in transition.

3. Development and transfer of technologies decision (4/CP-4 and 9/CP-5).
4. Implementation of Article 4 paragraph 8 and 9 of the convention decision (CP-3) and Article 2 paragraph 3 and article 3 paragraphs 14 of the Kyoto protocol.
5. Additional guidance to an operating entity of the financial mechanism.
6. Funding system under the convention.
7. Activities implemented jointly under the pilot phase decision (6/ CP-4 and 13/CP-5)
8. Matter relating to article 3 paragraph 14 of the Kyoto protocol.
9. Funding under the Kyoto protocol.
10. Impacts of the single project on emission in the commitment period (decision 16/CP-4)
11. Matter relating to land use, land use change and forestry.
12. Principles, nature and scope of mechanisms pursuant to Article 6, 12 and 17 of the Kyoto protocol.
13. "Good Practices" in policies and measures among parties included in Annex.-I to the convention.

At the 8th plenary meeting on 9th November 2001, the Conference of the Parties adopted decision 36/CP-7 entitled improving the participation of women in the representation of parties in bodies under UNFCCC or the Kyoto protocol, acting upon the proposal of the president FCCC/CP-2001/L-22. At the 8th plenary meeting on 10th November 2001, the representatives on behalf of the group of G-77, China, European community, the control group, African group and on behalf of the least developed countries, expressed appreciation and paying tribute to the work of President, Co-facilitators, chairman of different groups, subsidiary bodies and executive secretary of the seventh conference of the parties[72]. In his closing remarks, President expressed his deep gratitude to all participants for the success of the conference for the first time held in one Islamic country on African soil. Highlighting the Third Assessment Report of the IPCC, be made it clear that the threat of the climate change was genuine, and the increasing trends towards global warming had direct impact upon the whole of humankind owing to the vulnerability of the ecosystems and the fragility of the economic and social systems. He urges therefore for adoption of programmes where new technologies could be a useful tool in minimizing the effects of climate change, with promotion of sustainable development based on the synergy between economic growth, social equity and the preservation of natural resources. He highlighted the multiple negative impacts of the climate change including aggravation of poverty, hunger, food security, the problem of fresh-water, sea levels, making it difficult to combat climate change effectively by the world community.

In conclusion, he highly appreciated the achievements of the 7th Conference of the Parties, which represented a milestone in the process to combat the climate change, and would ensure the ratification of Kyoto protocol before the Earth summit 2002, a prompt start to the CDM and step forward in the participation of women in climate change discussions. In order to contribute efficiently to the world wide efforts for the protection of climate change in terms of commitments arising form the frame work convention on climate change and form the RIO summit, the African countries and developing nations in general are very in need of strong international support for the effective development and transfer of environmentally friendly technologies to pursue their sustainable development and capacity building. More over these efforts require new additional and financial resources as well as reduction of burden of the external debt of these countries. This extra effort would enable them to allocate more sustainable resources to pursue their sustainable development capacity building as well as to fight against poverty, which is still a major factor in the deterioration of the environment in the southern part of the planet.

It is a remarkable achievement to note that the three decade long process, which was initiated in the heart of the North Europe, Scandinavia for the protection of environment, has ultimately reached its turning point and concluded in Morocco, a country of the South with a long history of support for the just cause of this very South. This occasionally confirms that if there should be one single issue, one common source of concern which has turned citizens, bound by the duty of solidarity towards the same Earth and the same humanity, notwithstanding occasional tragedies and drifts, this issue certainly concerns the protection of environment, an environment whose strength or weakness knows neither North nor South, it is limited by no boundaries.

Accordingly, what the world needs today is a new approach to ecology based on concentration the crisis on the search for solutions of among all the parties involved. It is an approach which makes good the provision of the Rio declaration according to which the sovereignty of a state stops when it starts affecting the environment of other states or areas located beyond the boundaries of its national jurisdiction and it is an approach which takes into account the legitimate national and strategic interests of all countries and which guarantee, fairness and transparency in such a way that we feel encouraged each at each level to manage the planet as the common heritage of mankind. With the closure of the seventh session of the Conference of the Parties, the President announced that the venue of CoP-8 will be convened in New Delhi, India in December 2002.

The diplomatic crisis created in CoP-6 first session was averted by outstanding contribution of Jan Pronk with adoption of Bonn Agreement 2001 and the implementation of the Buenos Aires Plan of Action in July 2001. After withdrawal of the United States from the ratification of Kyoto protocol, creation of deadlock situation at CoP-6 conference, was tried to be removed by Europeans union and developing countries to tackle climate change issues. Realizing the magnitude and potential threat of the climate change, the world community was capable of reaching an agreement to ratify Kyoto protocol so that it could enter into force to meet the adequacy of commitments with common but differentiated responsibilities. The political momentum generated at the Bonn, despite U.S. opposition continued in the seventh Conference of the Parties showing international co-operation to adopt important decisions. On the basis of Buenos Aires Plan of Action, decisions on all different issues were arrived at by consensus, constituting the Marrakech Accord that was one of the major success in the history of climate change politics. Another important achievement of the conference was adoption of decision on women participation in the representation of parties. The Conference of the parties to the seventh session of the United Nations Framework Convention on Climate Change considering the Third Assessment Report of the IPCC, felt the greater need for adoption of programmes with new technologies to combat the threat of climate change vulnerable to ecosystems and sustainable development. The role of the seventh Conference of the Parties was a milestone in the process of climate change negotiations. The parties in the conference rendered their full support without any difference of opinion in order to contribute to worldwide efforts to counter the adverse effects of climate change. The outcome of this conference would undoubtedly make a key contribution to finding lasting solutions to the complexities created in the past.

Under the circumstances, the other developed countries will have to work on their own without being able to depend upon the return of the United States to the Kyoto protocol. In order to lead in this direction, Europe can take lead with other developed and developing countries to take the process forward. The negotiations in CoP-7 at Morocco were conducted in a favourable atmosphere without any split, division, discord or hot exchanges in air. The ratification by 42 countries of Kyoto protocol influenced others to adopt the line of action to improve the climate change measures. The Marrakech Accord has launched a new implementation phase for the both the convention and Kyoto protocol based on architecture of institutions, rules, procedures and mechanisms and without any doubt it was among the most elaborate of any international environmental agreement. A focus on implementation however does not mean the end of negotiations in the climate change process. Talks will resume on further developing both the convention and the Kyoto protocol rulebook. New rounds of negotiations would also be launched to strengthen and extend commitments in order to move closer to achieving the ultimate objectives of the convention. The stage is thus set for continuous development of the climate change process with implementation and negotiations going hand in hand to meet unfinished business and challenges. After the isolation of United States from the meeting of the Conference of the Parties, rapid progress made and consensus over substantial issues was a mark of dramatic changes in climate change politics. The Conference of parties in Morocco developed positive out look, with greater fellow feeling, which paved the way for greater intergovernmental co-operation to help improve the effectiveness of climate policy. The CoP-7 successfully resolved the deadlock of the past and contributed toward continuing the process by overcoming the breakdown in negotiations. Admitting the challenges posed by United States how far world communities meet the eventualities of climate change in coming days is yet to be seen.

Conference of the Parties -8 (CoP-8): October 23-November 1, 2002

The United Nations Framework Convention on Climate Change the eighth session of the conference of the parties (CoP-8) in conjunction with seventeenth session of the SBSTA and SBI was held in New Delhi from October 23 to 1st November 2002.

Although most of the issues were relatively minor compared to those in the Bonn Agreement and Marrakech Accords reached at CoP-5 and CoP-7 respectively, parties struck to entrenched position and overall made little significant progress. Many of the issues were diferred for further consideration at future meetings.

The outcome of CoP-8 remains as follows:

1. Adopted the Delhi Ministerial Declaration on climate change and sustainable development.
2. Adopted rules of procedures for the executive board of the clean development mechanism.

3. Completed the work on reporting, required of developed countries to assess their compliance under the Kyoto protocol.
4. Adopted guidance to Global Environment Facility. (GEF) for managing two new funds established at CoP-7 to assist developing countries.
5. Adopted new guidelines for national communications to be submitted by the developing countries on their emissions and steps they are taking to meet their commitments under the framework convention.
6. Requested the Intergovernmental Panel on Climate Change (IPCC) and Montreal Protocol's technological and Assessment Panel to conduct a regular report on the question of HFCs and PFCs compounds that have replaced Ozone depleting substances but contributed to climate change.

Delhi Declaration

As the host of CoP-8, the India government with adoption of a Delhi declaration issued a broad political statement to signify the meeting's success. An initial draft circulated by the Indian chair of the conference reflected a strong developing country perspective emphasizing on the issue of sustainable development, adoption and implementation by the developing countries of their commitments under the framework convention. The draft was silent on the question of steps beyond Kyoto's first commitment period 2008-2012, prompting strong objections from the European Union and some other developing countries. The United States was largely content with the Indian draft as it concurred with by the umbrella group calling for acknowledgement of the need for "global participation" in addressing climate change. The G-77, representing the developing countries, called for a stronger emphasis on financial assistance and the adverse economic effects on developing countries of measures taken to reduce greenhouse gas emissions. The adoption of Delhi Ministerial Declaration on climate change made no reference to future steps to further elaborate the climate regime. It largely underscored the principles established in the framework convention and the themes adopted at the world summit on sustainable development earlier this year in Johannesburg. The Declaration states that:

1. Parties that had ratified Kyoto protocol strongly urge others to do so in a timely manner. (As nations declared in Johannesburg)
2. The Third Assessment Report of the IPCC clearly spells out that significant cuts in global emissions will be necessary to meet the convention's ultimate objective.

3. All parties should continue to advance the implementation of their convention commitments and developed countries should demonstrate that they are taking the lead in modifying long-term emission trends.
4. Overriding priorities on economic and social development and poverty eradication of developing countries.
5. Urgent action needed to enable countries and in particular the least developed and small Island countries to adapt to the impacts of climate change.
6. Early actions are required to develop cleaner, more efficient and affordable energy technologies including fossil fuel and renewable energy technologies.

The declaration was adopted by consensus in statements in the closing plenary session of the CoP-8. The European Union, Japan and Canada expressed their disappointment as it did not offer a clear long-term vision. The European Union said that it would submit its own statement for record. Developing countries and the United States expressed strong support for the declaration. Nigeria thanked the United States for serving as a "constructive force" in the negotiations. Sri Atala Bihari Vajpayee, Prime Minister of India in his address strongly rejected "misplaced" calls for a process leading to developing country commitments. He argued that as the per capita incomes and emissions are much lower in developing countries, and that the developing country's contribution to atmospheric concentration of greenhouse gases will remain small compared to that of industrialized nations "for several decades to come".

Future Commitments

The looming of future commitments heavily shaped the political dynamics of CoP -8 and dominated much of the political dialogue, although as a matter of negotiation developing countries continued to publicly oppose any suggestion that they had to take some form of emission targets. There was a strong reversal of roles between the European Union and the United States, with the former pressing the question of future steps and latter declaring such discussion premature following Kyoto's entry into force and on the question of what action should be taken after 2012. The EU in its response to the draft of Delhi declaration called for the establishment of "forward looking process" should be conducted with a view to" have a more inclusive and long term global co-operation based on broader and balanced participation". In a statement to plenary meeting, Denmark which holds the presidency of EU made it clear that EU, is not talking about and in favour of imposing any emission reduction targets on developing countries. The views of EU were echoed by some other developed countries particularly Australia and Canada. In the past, the United States demand for stronger action relating to commitment of emission reduction by the developing countries remarkably changed. In Delhi however, the United States declared that" it would be unfair - indeed counter productive to condemn to slow growth by insisting that they take impractical and unrealistic greenhouse gas targets".

The CDM, one of the Kyoto protocol's flexibility mechanisms allows developing countries to meet their emission targets in part with Certified Emission Reductions (CERs) generated through emission reductions and sinks projects in developing countries. The Conference of the Parties at Morocco adopted general rules for the CDM and established an interim Executive Board to get the CDM underway pending Kyoto's entry into force. The CoP/MoP-1C, the first meeting of the Kyoto parties following the protocol's entry into force will ratify the decision of the interim executive Board and the CoP, and that the interim Board will become permanent. The Conference of the parties adopted the report of the Executive Board, which outlined its activities during the past year with few modification. One of the most contentious issues relating to attendance by observers that the meeting of the Executive Board pressed on the United States. The United States, which having rejected Kyoto protocol is considered an observer and insists that "attendance" means access to the meeting room. The annual reports of the Executive Board decided to inform the CoP how it was addressing the attendance issue.

Reporting Requirements under the Kyoto Protocol

The Conference of the Parties determines a set of detailed guidelines for the developed country parties to the Kyoto protocol, which accounts for several types of emission units established by the protocol and deals with how to transfer these units through Kyoto's flexibility mechanisms-emission trading, joint implementation and the CDM. In order to allow linkage of national emission target, the guidelines requires trickling and reporting of emission units on transfer in a uniform format. To assess the compliance with the protocol, procedure for expert review of registries was established, including the requirement that parties keep a portion of their emission units off the market in a "commitment period reserve" to ensure that they do not sell units needed to meet their reduction targets. Parties which failed to comply with reporting requirements under the Kyoto protocol can be deemed ineligible to participate in the trading mechanism.

Funding

Funding to assist developing countries in meeting their commitments under the convention and in Coping with climate charge adverse impacts continued to be divisive issue in CoP-8.

At CoP-7, the parties decided to establish three new funds to assist developing countries to mitigate the climate changes and a group of developed countries pledged a total of approximately $400 million. At the CoP-8, developing countries pressed for funding to implement adoption projects, detailed guide lines to the GEF for managing the new funds and regular contribution to funds. The parties requested that the UNFCCC and GEF secretaries, keeping in view the needs of the developing countries, should submit a comprehensive assessment report at SB 20 in summer 2004. The GEF also requested to review its projects cycle with a view to make it simpler and more efficient.

HFCs and PFCs

The Kyoto protocol established that the emission targets apply to "Baskets" of six greenhouse gases including HFCs and PFCs-two classes of substitutes for ozone depleting substances. The protocol gives flexibility to the parties as to which of the six gases to control. Since Kyoto, the EU has confined to focus special attention on HFCs and PFCs and several EU states have imposed phase out schedules for HFCs and PFCs as part of their domestic climate change policies, thus the EU pressed other countries to implement it. To address the issue raised by the EU, CoP-8 invited the IPCC and Montreal protocol's Technological and Economic Assessment Panel (TEAP) to prepare a special report to develop balanced scientific technical and policy relevant information. The parties also decided to remove HFCs and PFCs as separate issue as the SBSTA agenda at CoP-7, the parties decided that reforestation and afforestation project would be eligible under the CDM, but not other land use activities such as avoided deforestation and forest management. At CoP-8, the SBSTA identified two options: insurance against the destruction or degradation of forestation and creation of a different type of CER unit for sink projects that would be temporary in nature (so called TCERs) The SBSTA did not resolve the issue and adopted only a procedural conclusion calling for early work shop next year for further consideration. The framework convention requires developing countries to summit national communications detailing funding support from the developed countries with steps they are taking to meet their emission targets commitments under the convention. Many developing countries have yet to submit their initiated reports, which was to be considered at CoP-9.

Brazil Proposal

Following the withdrawal of the United States from Kyoto protocol, Brazil has proposed a formula for the developing countries to establish emission targets as their historical responsibility for climate change (as measured by the contribution to increased temperature). Since SBSTA, consideration of the issue has broadened to include 1- all source and sinks of all regions, not simply carbon emissions from the industrialized countries and, indicator of climates change other than increased temperature, such as relating to forcing and increased atmospheric concentrations. As a result of broadening the focus to all countries, some developing countries became concerned with the possible future developing country's commitments. At CoP-8, the SBSTA agreed that work, as per the Brazilian proposal should continue in the scientific community. The SBSTA encouraged research institutions and invited experts to research programmes to continue their work and report to the SBSTA 20 in summer 2004.

After the withdrawal of the United States from the Kyoto protocol, Canada has proposed that it would be allowed emission credit for seiling natural gas and hydroelectricity to the United States, stating that these clean energy exports reduce US global emissions. Canada proposal carries two dimensions - establishing the principles that Kyoto parties are entitled credit for emission reductions resulting from their exports of clean energy (defined as natural gas and hydroelectricity) to non- Kyoto parties and granting up to 70 million tons of credit a year in the first commitment period. the latter proposal received little support but the broader idea of credits for clean energy exports received support from the countries like Russia, New Zealand and Poland. As the proposal strongly opposed by the EU and to the surprise of many delegates by the United States, the SBSTA simply decided to continue its consideration of the matter at its next session. This issue became linked to the policies and measures and adverse effect issues. The Kyoto protocol allows each developed country flexibility to pursue policies and measures to reduce gas emissions and enhance sinks of its own. Since Kyoto, the EU has put pressure for development of methodologies to assess the effects of PAMs (policy and measures) on greenhouse emissions and to elaborate "best practices". At CoP-8, the issue was derailed by Saudi Arabia's insistence that the assessment of PAMs focus not only on their effectiveness but on adverse economic effects on developing countries, particularly on oil producing states. The SBSTA was unable to adopt any substantial conclusions and decided to continue its considerations of this issue at its next sessions.

Adverse Effects of Responsive Measures

The framework convention requires "full consideration of what actions are necessary" to meet the specific needs and concern of developing country parties arising from the impacts of the implementation of response measures. The Kyoto protocol includes a similar provision. The oil producing states led by Saudi Arabia continued to press on the issue of the adverse effects of mitigation measures not only under the agenda items that explicitly address them but also in the discussion of the PAMs and the Canadian clean energy proposal. But these issues failed to achieve substantial conclusions by the SBSTA and SBI and decided to continue considerations of these issues at the next session. The EU highlighted the Third Assessment Report of the IPCC based on scientific consensus that human activity being the principal cause of climate change provides new challenges to the international community to decide actions to combat climate change beyond 2012. As it is strongly resisted by the other countries, the SBSTA called for further consideration of the TAR at its next session. The parties considered a new agenda item for an effective participation in the convention process at the insistence of the United States. The SBI called for notification to access to proceedings for participation in work shops and expert bodies including notification of meeting on the UNFCCC website and a default rule allowing participation by any NGO or party observer accepting complains from United States and other industry representatives.

Following the Kyoto protocol's entry into force, the Conference of the Parties will serve also as the Meeting of the Parties (MOP) to Kyoto. However, the Kyoto protocol does not clear, whether the meeting should be held sequentially or concurrently, and what the arrangements should be regarding agenda, offices and so forth with Kyoto's possible entry into force next year SBI considers the arrangements for CoP/MoP-1 and in particular its relationship to the Conference of the parties. The Secretariat had proposed a concurrent meeting of the CoP and the CoP/Mop with separate agenda items identifying which items are CoP items and which are CoP/Mop items and which are common issues to be considered in the joint meeting of the CoP and the CoP/Mop. The SBI considering the issue fails to reach conclusions on how joint meeting would be organized and how decision would be adopted regarding issues of common concern to both the convention and the protocol. The SBI referred the matter to its next session for more consideration on mechanics and implications of joint meetings. The Conference of the Parties at New Delhi considered many issues like future commitments, CDM, Executive Board, Reporting requirement under the Kyoto protocol, funding HFCs/PFCs, sinks in

CDM, Non Annex-I communications, Brazilian proposal, Canadian proposal, Clean energy exports, policies and measures, adverse effects of response measures, TAR of IPCC and effective participation and arrangements for CoP/Mop-I but all the issues were referred by the SBSTA and SBI for further consideration at its next session. Parties accepted an offer from Italy to host CoP-9 set for early December' 2003, with location to be determined. Following the withdrawal of United States from the ratification of Kyoto protocol by the Senate it became a challenge to other countries of the world to increase their combined efforts to secure international co-operation to address the climates change. This was considered for discussion on many substantial issues for the adoption of new guidelines to meet the commitments under the Kyoto protocol.

The adoption of Delhi declaration at CoP-8 was one of the major achievements relating to sustainable development and implementation of commitments by the developing countries under the convention. Active participation of the United States in the CoP-8 calling for umbrella groups to acknowledge the Delhi declaration for global participation in combating climate change, demonstrates its changing attitude to adopt decisions on important environmental issues, though the draft declaration evoked strong protest from the EU and other developing countries. From the very beginning, American policy over the climate change has been dominating, more becoming self-oriented policy directed against the collaborative ventures by rejecting the Kyoto protocol. In CoP-8, the actions seemed to be very constructive for the strong support to the decisions of the Delhi conference by relaxing commitments of emission reduction for the developing countries. In the Conference of the Parties meeting, several issues were taken for consideration but failed to achieve consensus of opinion due to lack of mutual understanding and compromising attitude to make the negotiation process meaningful. While adopting draft decisions, major issues remained unsolved and left to be considered in the meeting of next session. The magnitude of accumulation of greenhouse gases resulting in global warming in comparison to the mitigation efforts taken by the world community in conference of parties meeting seemed to have drawn very low response to combat the ever-growing trends of climatic conditions. The conflicting and hostile attitudes of the developed and developing countries and their responsibility to protect the ecosystems from the threat of the climate change could not make significant progress. After Kyoto, five successive meetings of the parties were held in different parts of the world, but uncertainty and deadlock continued affecting the implementations of the Kyoto protocol's mechanisms to ensure compliance. Despite the support of the several countries, the actions of the United States made things worse to find an acceptable compromise to identify new and stronger initiatives to combat climate change. Climate change being the global phenomenon ongoing negotiations aimed at strengthening the original treaty and bringing the Kyoto protocol to fruition. In the initial stage, it secured the response from all but gradually generated apparent reluctance due to the repudiation by United States to make significant progress and vigorous efforts to address the adverse effects of climate change in future. In spite of several hurdles, results achieved in the 8th conference of the parties are a clear manifestation of good relationships among negotiators to understand each other's problems that would constitute friendly atmosphere to move ahead to adopt new strategies and policies for effective mitigation of climate change problems. Keeping in view the rapid changing trends of the climate conditions efforts were made to make the treaties more certain and permanent, which are so vital for the purpose of rapid, effective, sustained and safe management of global warming.

Ninth Conference of The Parties (CoP-9): December - 1 to 12, 2003

The Ninth Conference of the Parties to the United Nations Framework Convention on Climate Change was held at Fiera Milan Congress centre in Milan, Italy from 1st December to 12th December 2003. Over 500 participants from 166 governments, four observer states, 312 intergovernmental and Non-governmental and other observer organizations and 191 media outlets attended the conference. Throughout the meeting, parties convened in several contact groups and informal consultations as well as plenary sessions of the SBSTA and SBI and CoP. On behalf of the CoP-8 President T.R. Baalu, India's Joint Secretary for Environment and Forest, C. Viswanath called on Annex-I parties to take the lead in addressing the impacts of climate change and to provide developing countries with financial and technological assistance. He rejected the introduction of commitments for the developing countries. Hungary was elected as CoP-9 President by acclamation. In his opening statement, President Persanyi highlighted the need for efforts in developing countries to implement climate friendly production patterns. He stressed that although the protocol has yet not been entered into force, it has not lost its importance and needed ratification by numerous parties. Altero Matteoli, Italy's Minister for Environment and Territory said, CoP-9 provided an opportunity to identify new and stronger initiatives for combating climate change. Roberto Formigoni, President of the Region of Lombardy stressed the importance of regional action to combat climate change, while Gabriel Albertini, Mayor of Milan said, delegates must take long term views of climate change, its impacts and the well being of the future generations. Luigi Cocchiaro, for the President of the province of Milan called for increased implementation in the areas of transport and renewable energy. UNFCCC executive secretary, Joke Waller Hunter said that while the date of protocol's entry into force remained uncertain, it was encouraging that this had not slowed the momentum for action. She emphasized the need to ensure that adequate resources were provided to meet programme delivery and implementations of CoP decisions.

Morocco speaking for G-77/China called on the Russian federation to ratify the protocol and the U.S to "comeback" and expressed concern about the low level of parties' contributions to the secretariat. Zimbabwe, on behalf of the African group said Annex -1 parties have failed to assume emissions and lacked political will to do so. Italy speaking for the EU urged the U.S. to take actions in comparison to those that would have been expected from them under the protocol. Tuvalu, for the Alliance of Small Island States (AOSIS) said, the discussion on sinks in the CDM must maintain the social environmental and economic integrity of the mechanism. Pakistan said, work at CoP-9 must focus on capacity building, technology transfer, and the special climate change fund. Highlighting the vulnerability of LDCs Tanzania for the LDCs, stressed the need for entry into force of the protocol and constructive work on matters relating to technology transfer, capacity building and LDCs[72]. After discussions at CoP-9, parties adopted numerous decisions and conclusions on various issues including definition and modalities for afforestation and reforestation activities under the clean development mechanism, good practice guidance on land use, Land Use Change and Forestry (LULUCF), the Special Committee Change Fund (SCCF) and the Least Development Countries (LDC) fund. The Ministerial High level round table discussions were held on Wednesday and Thursday on 10-11 December[73].

The official negotiations while remaining deadlock on several issues, reached consensus on some decisions. Two sides of the UNFCCC, two "faces" were clearly visible at CoP-9. The first face was that of the ongoing negotiations aimed at strengthening and building original treaty and bringing the Kyoto protocol to fruition. While the official negotiations enjoyed some progress at CoP-9 including an agreement on the use of sinks in the Clean Development Mechanism (CDM), this side of meeting could hardly be seen as an overwhelming success. The official intergovernmental negotiations seemed to be set by inertia and lack of leadership.

The CoP-9 corridors were buzzing with what some saw as the second "face" of the meeting, the "implementing face". This side of CoP-9 was reflected in the workshops and other side events that shared the vision and enthusiasm demonstrated for the convention by its observer constituencies, environmental NGOS, business and industry groups, local governments, indigenous peoples organizations and research and independent NGOS (RINGOS). It is there constituencies who continue to prove that regardless of some parties' apparent reluctance to make significant progress, vigorous efforts to address the adverse effects of climate change are already under way and are gaining momentum. While CoP-8 was referred to be as the "adaptation CoP" due to the progress made on adoption issues, for similar reasons negotiators may one day reminisce that CoP-9 was the "forest CoP". Even since CoP-4 in 1998, the issue of sinks in CDM has been plugged by complex and time consuming discussions and often diametrically opposed negotiating positions. The long period of sessional and inter-sessional consultations, which forged good relationships among negotiations and allowed parties to understand each other's problems, was the basis for a much more cordial atmosphere at CoP-9[74].

Essentially, the debate could be viewed as one between buyers and sellers of carbon sequestration credits among the EU, Norway, Switzerland, Bolivia, Colombia and other Latin American countries respectively. While the buyer countries were mostly concerned about the quality of the product and sought conditions that would protect their investments, the seller countries strove for favourable "crippling" transaction costs. They sought more flexible crediting periods on insurance approach to credits.

Irrespective of results achieved in the discussions, there was limited progress in TAR Negotiations as was evident under the new agenda item on adoption and mitigation. The G-77/China's strong resistance to adopting a CoP decision on the TAR and in fact discussing anything beyond procedure for further consideration of this issue is a clear reflection of groups' determination not to allow negotiations to head any where closer to the issue of developing countries future commitments. With frustration over Annex-I parties failures to fulfill their commitments, limited transfer of technologies and insufficient financial support, developing countries held firmly to preventing negotiations from turning towards mitigation activities by Non Annex-I parties in the future[75]. On Non Annex National communications it would be surprising to say that great advances have been made. The parties were encouraged to submit their National communications as soon as possible. But G-77/China's unwillingness to move ahead on anything other than the obligations of the developed countries was indicative of its decision to avoid future National communications on their part. Despite many EU member states' emphasis on the issue, it remained unclear to observers why this was given up by the EU without any resistance.

On the other hand, in spite of strong opposition marked in Negotiations, the high-level round table discussions among ministers provided a refreshing change of pace allowing an opportunity to step back and take a wider perspective on the UNFCCC process and the issue of climate change itself. The ministers were strictly confined to the point and presented the issue which they believed are most pertinent in the broader context of climate change, such as sustainable development adoption and transfer of technologies, Kyoto targets etc. and which are not new remains, the non negotiated out comes of the CoP-9[76]. While the official negotiations were taking place, the UNFCC's "second face" was also highly visible at CoP-9. The Milan CoP demonstrated that climate change issue remain high on the political agenda of many NGOs, business group and Academic community regardless of what was taking place in the last round of intergovernmental negotiations while diplomats were often left agreeing on the lowest common denominator, more than one hundred side events also took place at Milan almost all of which were focused on the highest common denominator achieving the concrete and necessary steps to meet the UNFCCC's ultimate objective To many attending the CoP-9, the attention and interests generated in these debates overshadowed the impasse and unwillingness of some parties to engage in substantive negotiations on progress or lack thereof. The side events often stressed on the various paths on which negotiations seemed "afraid to travel" again highlighting the somewhat contradictory nature of two faces of the UNFCCC mostly visible at CoP-9. First, a large majority of side events stressed on future actions" and "post first commitment period thinking". This contrasted sharply with the official negotiations, where the issue of the second review of the Adequacy commitment was held in abeyance for the fifth CoP running. The last day of CoP-9 saw an informal discussion between environmental NGOs and some Annex-I and Non Annex-I parties to discuss the urgency of defining future actions.

Secondly, negotiations on National Communications were continuously "blocked" over concerns that the submission of information on inventions and P & Ms would lead to "New obligations". The constituencies active in the side events have already built and solidified the foundations for the successful sharing of experiences, capacity and lessons learned, clearly demonstrating the value and contribution of such information in shaping debates on mainstreaming climate change, adoption, local action and innovative projects. CoP-9 also saw the official recognition of the RINGOS constituency, first created in CoP-8, who took its place along side other recognized observer constituencies. RINGOS formed an important new constituency of organizations engaged in independent research and analysis and their inclusion as a key constituency would inevitably strengthen the research elements of the climate change process[77]. While CoP-9 had a rocky start it ended on a positive note, calling the protocol "an unrealistic and ever increasing regulatory strait jacket. U.S Under Secretary of State for Global Affairs, Pawa Dobriansky had written in a major financial news paper that the "only acceptable cost effective option" to reduce greenhouse gas emission was the American way. This viewpoint was argued vigorously by the 60 strong delegations in Milan. Days later, an advisor to Russia Presidency throughout sounded that Russian ratification was unlikely. Nevertheless, these statements did not detract parties from keeping the process on track. In fact, the overwhelming message from the high level segment was that the protocol is the "only show in town". CoP-9 not only highlighted the division between the developed and developing countries, but also the leadership and initiative gap between negotiations and constituency groups. While resolving the differences on a paragraph by paragraph basis the significant number of side events signalled a change towards a more positive outlook for the future CoP sessions. In that sense, the major outcome of the CoP-9 was a renewed emphasis on the role of the UNFCCC's constituencies as an important component of the process to deliver an equitable global climate change regime—a point clearly made by their demands for strong climate action, dedicated leadership, information sharing and free thinking. The tenth conference of the parties to the UNFCCC (CoP-10) was held from 29 November to 10 December 2004, in Buenos Aires, Argentina.

The international political response to climate change continued by the Conference of the Parties, which aimed at stabilizing atmospheric concentrations of greenhouse gases in order to avoid "dangerous anthropogenic interference with the climate system. The effects of climate change have already been observed by the IPCC in its successive reports and majority of scientists believe that precautionary and prompt action is necessary to combat climate change.

At subsequent meetings, parties negotiated most of the rules and operational details determining how countries will cut emissions and assess emission reductions. Passing through ups and downs for reaching an agreement on the operational details of Kyoto protocol and on strengthening the implementation of issues to address adverse effects of climate change. Many disputed political and technical issues remain yet to be determined. From the beginning, the attitude of the developed countries towards developing countries marked no significant changes to facilitate negotiations. The CoP-9 at Milan provided an opportunity to identify new and stronger initiatives among the developed and developing countries to implement decisions of the CoP for combating climate change. Keeping in view the well being of future generations, parties should render their full support to advance work without creating obstacles to increase common understanding in the spirit of compromise to accomplish the objective of the convention. The parties at the CoP-9 meeting discussed many substantial issues and adopted draft decisions that demonstrated the presence of commitment and political will to establish institutional framework for action. Parties adopted numerous decisions and conclusions on various issues, but at the same time negotiators faced deadlocks on several issues to combat climate change. Three high level round table discussions on climate change, adoption, mitigation, sustainable development and transfer of technologies, focused on the some what contradictory nature of two faces of the UNFCCC's most visible at CoP-9, which had demonstrated the unwillingness of the parties for future actions. The conference of the parties at Milan started negotiations with greater aspirations and strong determination to promote action calling for global collaboration, political will, creative thinking and avoidance of political rhetoric. But throughout the session, CoP-9 highlighted the division, discord and challenging atmosphere between the developed and developing countries, which was mainly responsible to defeat the essence of the conference. Nevertheless, CoP-9 provided the opportunity to the negotiators to understand each other's concerns in a cordial atmosphere, building and reinforcing co-operation to the development of concrete measures and strategies for the future. This CoP has an important role in encouraging effective approaches to international co-operation to suit different interests and different national circumstances of a global response to climate change. Integrating climate change and sustainable development, new avenues for international co-operation were opened.

Tenth Conference of the Parties to The UN Framework Convention on Climate Change - 6-18 December, 2004

The tenth Conference of the Parties (CoP-10) to the United Nations Framework Convention on Climate Change (UNFCCC) and the twenty first session of the CoPs Subsidiary Body for Scientific and Technological Advice (SBSTA) and subsidiary Body for implementation (SBI) were held at La Rural exhibition center in Buenos Aires, Argentina from 6-18 December 2004. Over 6100 participants from 167 governments, two observer states, 272 intergovernmental and non-governmental and other observer organizations and 240 media outlets attended the conference. The year 2004 was a significant one for the UN Framework Convention on Climate Change and its Kyoto protocol. The year marked the tenth anniversary of the entry into force of the UNFCCC and as such, many have been looking back with a sense of accomplishment at the progress achieved over the past decade. In addition, to the delight of the world the Russian federation ratified the Kyoto protocol, ensuring the continuity of mitigation efforts into the next decade as the protocol enters into force from 16th February 2005. To make sure that the "house" is in order for the protocol's imminent entry into force, parties gathered at CoP-10 to complete the unfinished business from the Marrakech Accord and reassess the building blocks of the process and discuss the framing of a new dialogue on the future of climate change policy. UNFCCC Executive, Secretary, Joke Waller Hunter highlighted the tenth anniversary of the UNFCCC and presented a report of the UNFCCC first decade, underlining the challenges that lie beyond 2012. She suggested that parties consider an equitable and effective future strategy to ensure that all countries contribute fairly to achieving the UNFCCC's objectives[78].

Numerous speakers welcomed the Russian federations ratification of the Kyoto protocol and expressed the hope that the US would also follow and ratify the protocol. Qatar on behalf of the G-77/China noted the impacts of recent climate related disasters on developing countries and emphasized on Annex-I parties responsibility for financial resource mobilization for adaptation, stressing on the principle of common but differentiated responsibilities. During the CoP-10 meeting, parties met in CoP plenary sessions on Monday, 6 December Wednesday 8 December, Friday 17, December and closed on Saturday 18 December. A high level segment took place on Wednesday and Thursday 15-16 December and included four panel discussions. During the conference, parties addressed and adopted numerous decisions and conclusions on various issues including Technology Transfer, issues relating to land use, land use change and forestry, the UNFCCC financial Mechanisms, Annex-I National Communications, capacity building and adverse effects and adaptation and UN FCCC. CoP-10 provided an opportunity for delegates to reinforce the two main building blocks: climate change architecture of the policy response to climate mitigation and adaptation. In fact, for the first time adoption featured equally to mitigation to the extent that CoP-10 was nicknamed "the adoption CoP". Many are delegates however noted that this was the third consecutive CoP to have received this undeserved nickname, suggesting that a more fitting name for CoP-10 would be Adaptation fiasco."

With several developed and developing countries providing testimony to the rise in extreme weather events in their regions and other recent scientific assessments, such as the Arctic climate impact assessment and also drawing attention to climate change impacts, it was becoming increasingly apparent that adaptation is crucial and countries will need to spend considerable amounts of money to adapt to climate change and recover from extreme weather events. Nevertheless, others expressed concern asserting that there is no proof of connections between extreme weather events and climate change. Reaching an agreement on the "adaptation package" was therefore as arduous struggle as the urging to respond to the impacts of climate change, which was not evident during the negotiations[79].

The Netherland on behalf of the EU, Bulgaria, Rumania and Turkey expressed continued commitment to addressing climate change and highlighted the launch of the EU emissions trading scheme in January 2005.He supported limiting global temperature rise to 2 degree Celsius, noting that a greater increase would result in irreversible damages. Tuvulu on behalf of the Alliance of Small Island States (AOSIS) highlighted the need for strong linkages with the 10 years review of the implementation of the Barbodus Programme of Action for Sustainable Development of Small Island Developing States while many delegates were agreeable to providing support for Small Island Developing States (SIDS) and the LDCs to adapt to the devastating impacts of climate change. A deadlock resulted due to the demands of some states to address impacts from response measures as the world moves away from fossil fuels. During a long Friday night, which extended into Saturday morning at the and of the CoP, there were several moments when delegates doubted that a suitable arrangement could be found that balanced the demands for support for addressing impacts of response measures and support for adaptation to the adverse effects of climate change, In the end, an adaptation package was adopted that facilitated inter alia the further implementation of measures for adaptation to the adverse effects of climate change and facilitated further activities on modeling and economic diversification regarding the impacts of response measures. In a climate in which some saw little chance for agreement, this compromise text was likely to be a success since no one was particularly happy. Least developed countries, most vulnerable to the impacts of climates change failed for the second consecutive year to secure a decision for full cost funding of adaptation through the Global Environment Facility (GEF). All financial resources for the LDC fund were channeled through the GEF. The problem encountered by the LDC fund shed light on the core problem of addressing adaptation in the context of the UNFCCC.

context of the UNFCCC. Adaptation is an integral part of development and as such, no project directed at adaptation would fall squarely within the scope of the UNFCCC but would rather have components that included other aspects of the development such as disaster preparedness, water management, desertification prevention or biodiversity protection. The GEF would only be able to finance a portion proportional to the additional harm that floods have caused or will cause as a result of climates change.

The question to be asked is whether UNFCCC parties are willing to provide the institutional flexibility needed to complex urgent issues that deny traditional approaches to development aid. Fundamentally, some say the transfer of financial resources to LDCs is not directly a climate change issue, but is in fact a development issue that should be dealt with elsewhere. Others do not seem to be in any hurry and are willing to allow the financial mechanism all the time it needs to find a suitable solution for the opertionalization of these funds including the creation of funding criteria. Those most vulnerable have a different view on the urgency of the matter, but it is evident from the CoP-10 outcomes that LDCs lacked the bargaining power of oil producing countries within the negotiations and presented feasible proposals that fitted however loosely into the existing financial architecture developed countries as the other land will need to spend up the analysis of this issue within the GEF and come up with creative solutions that given the GEF the will and flexibility it needs to address the problem.

The recently released report of the UN High level panel on threats, challenges, and change underlined that countries must take action and commence negotiations for long-term strategy to address climate change. Moreover, the Kyoto protocol requires that parties initiate considerations of post 2012 commitments by 2005. The challenges presented to delegates at CoP -10 were how to engage non-parties to the protocol in this process and how to ease concerns of many developing countries regarding imposition of new commitments. Delegates struggled behind closed doors over the possibility of exactly when and how to discuss future commitments, and opinions varied widely. Some wanted a series of informal meetings or seminars to openly discuss the future of the climate change regime. But few countries felt it was inappropriate to discuss future commitments altogether, and some countries appeared to try to limit the discussion of climate change issues to the UNFCCC process and not show links to other processes, such as the international meeting to the 10 year review of the Barbados programme of action for the sustainable development of small island developing states (BPOA+10), the World

Conference on Disaster Reductions (WCDR) or the UN Commission on sustainable development (CSD)[80].

Several NGOs urged delegates to move ahead without non-parties to the protocol in the hope of raising the lowest common denominator of consensus and promoting more progressive future commitments. After a full night of intensive consultations on the last day of the COP, delegates agreed to have one seminar in 2005 that would not open negotiations leading to new commitments.

The outcome of the seminar according to one expert, will ultimately depend on the skills of the organizers to bring to gather parties in an environment that enhances both trust and frank exchange of views and perhaps moves beyond the technical foci of recent CoP meetings. Some NGOs and scientists have already voiced concern that the process may lack transparency and called for Wider Civil Society access. These seminar will also fall amidst a number of other very important processes taking place in 2005, such as the review of the progress in the implementation of the millennium declaration, initiation of review by the C&D of the implementation of existing climate change commitments.

Until the 11th hour, many remained pessimistic about the potential for a deal at CoP-10. The agreement on seminars was not only a victory for Argentina but was also an important internal policy maker for some parties with the agreement on seminars and adaptation and completion of land use, land use change and forestry issues. It is safe to say that although many issues remained unsolved much was achieved in the past ten years. However, what became crystal clear at CoP-10 is that some parties were not ready to embark on post 2012 negotiations. For now the best that can be hoped for is that Annex.-1, parties will begin to comply with their emission reduction commitments and implementation of protocol mechanisms to prove that emission reduction is possible and compatible with development, if carbon market and/or other tools and incentives are in place so other parties can see the benefits of participating, and if costs of the climate change impacts start to accrue significantly, the international community may be ready to take further steps in the coordinated global response to climate change[81].

The tenth Conference of the Parties to the United Nations Framework Convention on Climate Change was significant one to complete the unfinished work with effective strategy to combat the climate change. Climate change is a global problem requiring action from the entire world community. Countries from around the world are working together in the conference of the parties from time to time in different parts of the world, to share continuity of mitigation efforts, technologies, experience, resources and talent to lower net greenhouse gas emissions and reduce the threat of global climate change. The CoP-10 marks the tenth anniversary of the entry into force of the UNFECC designed to help countries to address climate change. The Kyoto protocol constitutes the basic legal frame work to meet the challenge of climate change ratified by most of the countries of the world including Russian Federation. The CoP-10 continues to grow and develop international co-operation relating to mitigation and adaptation, policies, measures and appropriate response to climate change. The CoP-10 provided an opportunity for the delegates to construct architecture of policy and co-operation among countries to reduce greenhouse gas emissions to tackle the global warming problem. Major countries of the world except United States continue to render their supports and research for ways to meet the climate change challenge efficiently and effectively. In fact, for the first time participants reached consensus on adaptation policy on climate change and for which the CoP-10 was known as "Adoption CoP". During the negotiations, several issues were discussed resulting arduous struggle and hot exchanges among developed and developing countries, showing little chance for agreement regarding the impacts of response measures.

The delegates faced the challenges in finding suitable measures as to how to engage non parties to the protocol in this process and how to ease concerns of many developing countries regarding imposition of new commitments to address climate change. The global challenge of climate change impacts imposes an unprecedented requirement for international co-operation obviously a global dimension of the climate change problem requires equally global solutions. The choosen way the international community has pursued to agree upon was how and possibly jointly to respond to the expected future common threats in the negotiations of a cost effective international agreement. It has become clear that industrialized countries have responded politically in different ways ranging from ardent calls to take the lead in cutting emissions to equivocation in the face of lingering scientific and economic uncertainties. Developing countries did not respond politically in the same way to climate change. Without the United States, the big developing countries have become more receptive to the idea that their participation in the global effort would result in favourable outcomes for them. By abandoning the negotiating process without offering an alternative to the Kyoto protocol, the United States endangered the progress that was achieved. It remains to be seen what can be done to bring United States back to the negotiating table but strategies to do this are clearly needed over the near term. It is safe to say that although many issues remain multiple of countries on future climate change policy. The importance of focusing more an adaptation issue in the international negotiation was generally agreed upon. It was also considered an important issue to take further actions on mitigation and adaptation activities in a more comprehensive way "recognizing the lack of consensus on the definition of adaptation among the parties. Many participants pointed out the necessity for further accumulation of scientific knowledge and enhancement of information sharing.

It is necessary for all countries to further strengthen their actions against climate change. Several countries expressed their views that both Annnex.-1 and non Annex.-1 countries will need to take prudent actions against climate change. Developing countries also showed their willingness to take further actions based on their country's specific conditions in line with "Sustainable Development Policies". Various opinions were expressed to reactivate the formal CoP process to discuss future climate change actions. To combat climate change the United Nations Framework Convention on Climate Change (UNFCCC) in the past ten years remarkably progressed has been made on fashioning a global response to climate change given the complexity of the politics of climate. Thus, CoP-10 prepared the ground for CoP-II: the key to successful co-operation in finding activities that will help all countries achieve their economic, environmental and developmental goals in a climate friendly manner.

The Eleventh Conference of the Parties (COP-II) to the UN Framework Convention on Climate Change (UNFCCC) and the first conference of the parties serving as the meeting of the parties to the Kyoto protocol (COP/MOP) took place in Montreal, Canada, from 28 November to 10 December 2005. The event drew 9500 participants, including 2800 government officials, over 5800 representatives of the UN bodies and agencies, intergovernmental organizations and Non-governmental organizations and 817 accredited members of the media[82].

After an intense two weeks of negotiations in Montreal, the global community moved ahead with plans for the future action on climate change. Numerous important decisions were agreed upon forming the components of the "Montreal plan of Action". One of the key decision is that 40 industrialized nations that are already bound by emission reduction targets and time tables in the Kyoto protocol have established a process to negotiate further for deeper cuts after the 2012, the expiry of first commitment period of the Kyoto protocol. Not participating in its decision are the United States and Australia, which have not ratified the Kyoto protocol. This is a disappointment but does not mean that the majority of the industrialized countries are not going to let those two countries distract. The rest continued supporting the move being bolstered by the increasing rigorous scientific evidence of human induced climate change. A second important decision acquiesced in by the U.S. and Australia, is that all countries will begin a "dialogue" about any and all possible measures to cut emissions. This is a non-building process and has neither deadlines nor specific objectives as a result of a watering down of the initial plan in order to meet American objectives. It does mean that there is still a table around which all nations will gather to address climate change[83].

COP-II addressed issues such as capacity building technology, development and transfer, the adverse effects of climate change on developing and lease developed countries and several financial and budget related issues, including guidelines to the Global Environment Facility (GEF), which serves as the convention's financial mechanism. After lengthy negotiations the COP also agreed on a process for considering future action beyond 2012 under the UNFCCC.

The "Marrakesh Accords" the rule for the Kyoto protocol, were adopted early on in the conference representing an initial success and meaning that the protocol is in full implementation mode. The United Nations climate change conference closed with the adoption of more than forty decisions that will strengthen the global efforts to fight climate change. Reflecting on the success of the Montreal 2005, the conference president Canadian Environment minister, Stephane Dion said; "Key decisions have been made in several areas. The Kyoto protocol has been switched on a dialogue about the future action and parties have moved forward working on adaptation and advancing the implementation of the regular work programme of the convention and the protocol. Richard Kenlay, acting Head of the United Nation's climate change secretariat said. "This has been one of the most productive UN climate change conferences ever. Its success was in implementing the Kyoto protocol, improving the convention and Kyoto and innovating for tomorrow which led to an agreement on a variety of issues. This plan sets the course for future action on climate change".

Key decisions were made that outlined the path to future international action on climate change. Under the Kyoto protocol, the process for future commitments beyond 2012 got under way. A new working group was established to discuss future commitments for developed countries for the period after 2012. It would start work in May next year. Under the convention, a dialogue on strategic approaches for long-term global cooperative action to address climate change was also launched. A series of workshops were planned to develop the broad range of actions needed to respond to the climate change challenges[84].

In his closing comments early in the morning on 10 December, COP, President Stephane Dion declared the meeting a success, expressing satisfaction that they have avoided so many potential pitfalls and achieved a consensual outcome. Most participants agreed that COP-II and COP/MOP-I was an important milestone in moving the process forward. He thanked delegates and participants for making this meeting a success. Congratulating parties on completing the "Montreal Marathon", he added that there still remained a long race to run. Twelfth conference of the parties to the UNFCCC and second meeting of the parties to the Kyoto protocol would take place from 6-17 November 2006 in Kenya.

References

1. Jill Jagar Tim 'O' Riordan; "History of Climate Change Science and Politics", Development of Scientific Understanding, New York, London, Routledge, 1996, p. 12.
2. J.W. Anderson; "History of Climate Change as a Political Issue", Journalist US Newspaper, 1.1.1999, p. 1.
3. Kathy Finberg, "Expanded History of UN Ecological Summits", From Stockholm to Buenos Aires, Facsnet Section Editor posted No.-4, 1997. Revised Jan 28, 2000. p visited in the line www. facsnet. org/issues / specials/ gcc/ politics/ expand.php3.
4. Rupak Dasgupta, "Consciousness of Environment", Indian Express Daily/21.5.1991, p. 18.
5. Jill Jagar Tim 'O' Riordan, *op.cit,* p. 11.
6. Climate Change fact sheet-213, "Environment Policy and Law", No. 5, 1979,and No.6,1980, p-103,www.climatechangeeducation. org.
7. Kathy Finberg, *op.cit,* p. 2.
8. *Ibid,* p. 2.
9. Jill Jagar Tim 'O' Riordan, *op.cit,* p-16.
10. Kathy Finberg, *op.cit,* p. 26.
11. Jill Jagar Tim 'O' Riordan, *op.cit,* p. 17.
12. *Ibid,* p-17.
13. Summary of workshop held in Villach 28 September to 20 October 1987 and Bellagio 9, 13 November 1987 under the auspices of Beijer Institute Stockholm: Report written by Jill Jagar, Beijer Institute, April 1988.
14. World Climate Programme Impacts Studies, Developing Policies for Responding to Climate Change Document. WMO, TD No.-225.www.aciavaf.edu/pdfs/acia-policy-documents.pol.

15. J. Jillgar Tim 'O' Riordan, *op.cit,* p. 18.
16. Regional Study on Green House Effects its Impacts on the Region: Kathamandu, SAARC Secretariat, Dec. 1992.
17. Congressional Research Service, Report guide to Federal programme in Appropriation Bills, National Library for Environment: Washington 20006-202-530-5810.
18. Department of Commerce, National Oceanic and Atmospheric Administration National Climate Programme Office, US, (IPCC News No.-1. March 1989.
19. CRS Report, op.cit, www.fpc.stategov/c4763htm-33k.
20. "Problem of Ecology Identified" Times of India, News Service Baroda. No.-29. May 5, 1990.
21. J.J. Tim 'O' Riordan, *op.cit,* p-15.
22. CRS Report, *op.cit,* p-6.
23. *Ibid., op.cit.*
24. Kathy Finberg, *op.cit.*
25. CRS Report, *op.cit.*
26. J.J. Tim 'O' Riordan, *op.cit,* p-19.
27. CRS Report, *op.cit,* p-7.
28. *Ibid, op.cit,* p-3.
29. UNEP-1999, Convention of Climate Change : UNEP information unit for the conventions xsxdxx for the Climate Change: Geneva, Secretariat, FCCC/CP/1999, INF-2. Status Ratification of the United Nations Framework convention on climate change and Kyoto Protocol. www.unFCCC; de.
30. P. Bhandari, "Historical Perspective on Negotiation in Climate Change" Post Kyoto Perspective from the South, New Delhi, Tata Energy Resource Institute, 1998, pp. 45-60.
31. J.J. Tim 'O' Riordan, *op.cit,* p. 19.
32. Climate Change Information Kit, UNEP's Inf. Unit: Geneva. 1999.
33. Hiroshi Ohki, "Combating Global Warming, a common task for Mankind : Chairman Special Committee on Global Environment Issues (L.D.P) and Chairman to Special Committee for Okinawa and Northern Hemisphere (H.R). Visited in the line www. mansfieldfdn. org/ pubs/ pub_pdfs/ohki.pdf.
34. Jeremy Robkin, "Green House Politics on the Issues American Enterprise Institute(AEI)", on line Washington, November 1997, p. 1.
35. J.J. Tim 'O' Riordan, *op.cit,* p. 19.
36. "Earth Negotiation Bulletin", New York : International Institute for Sustainable Development (IISD), Monday 12 November 1998.
37. J.J. Tim 'O' Riordan, *op.cit,* p-16.

38. Leonine Haimson; "A History of Climate Change Negotiations", 1.1.99, p. 1.
39. FCCC/1995/Report of CoP-1 held in Berlin. www.unFCCC.de.
40. A. Agrawal, S. Narain and A.Sharma, "Boiling Point in Green Politics" Global Environmental Negotiations. New Delhi, Centre for Science and Environment Vol-1, 1999, p-16-121.
41. Hiroshi Ohki, *op.cit,* p. 13.
42. Fathy Finberg, *op.cit*, p. 2.
43. FCCC/CP-1/1996/L-10, p. 5.
44. FCCC/CP-1/1996/L-11, p. 4
45. FCCC/CP-1/1996/L-12, p. 2
46. A. Agrawàl, *op.cit,* p. 16-121.
47. FCCC/CP-1/1996/L-17, p. 4.
48. K.Finberg, *op.cit,* p. 1.
49. "A Guide to Climate Change Convention and its Kyoto Climate Change, Bonn UNFCCC, Secretariat, 20 June 2003, p-9.
50. Framework Action, Bonn, Germany UNFCCC Secretariat, 20 June 2003 p-9. visited in the line www.unFCCC.int.
51. *Ibid.,* 4 Nov. 1998
52. *Ibid.,* no. 901/5 Nov, p. 2.
53. *Ibid.,* No. 92, p-2.
54. *Ibid.,* No. 93, 9 Nov, p. 2.
55. *Ibid.*
56. *Ibid.,* No. 95, 12 Nov., 1998, p. 2.
57. Leonie Haimson, *op.cit.*
58. A Agrawal, *op. cit,* p. 16-121.
59. L.Haimson, *op.cit,* p-5.
60. A. Sharma, "Another Crawl for Mankind"- New Delhi, Down to Earth. 15th December 1999.
61. FCCC/CP/1/1999/6. Report of the CoP its Fifth Session held at Bonn, Germany.
62. L. Haimson, *op.cit,* p. 3.
63. Earth Negotiation Bulletin, New York, IISD/Vol. No.12/No.231, p. 2.
64. Anup Shah, Hague Conference, 4th September 2001, p. 2.
65. *Ibid,* p-3.
66. IISD, No. 231, *op.cit,* p. 3.

67. Safemul Haq Youha Sokana, Climate Change, view point from South, p. 1.
68. International efforts at Combating Climate Change, preparing the Protocol Flexibility Mechanism for Implementation : Netherlands, 20th October 2001, p. 6.
69. S. H. Y. Sokana, *op.cit,* p-1
70. *Ibid,* p-2.
71. Earth Negotiation Bulletin, *op.cit.*
72. *Ibid.*
73. *Ibid.*
74. *Ibid.*
75. *Ibid.*
76. *Ibid.*
77. Earth Negotiation Bulletin, New York, IISD, Vol-12, No.260, 20th Dec 2004.
78. *Ibid.,* p. 14
79. *Ibid.,* p. 14-15.
80. *Ibid.,* p. 15.
81. CoP 11/mop 1 Report, IISD Vol.12, No.291, 12 December 2005, p. 1.
82. David H. Hallman. wccc. Climate Change Programme Coordinator: COP 11/ mop-1 Report 2005. An overview UNFCCC Press, 9th December 2005.
83. CoP-11/Mop-1 Report, *op.cit,* p. 1.
84. UNFCCC- CoP- 11/Mop-1, Report Secretariat Press, 10 Dec. 2005, p-2.

5

Kyoto Protocol : Limitations and Constraints

Climate change expected to result in global warming is probably the most serious environmental problem that the world faces today. While the threat is long term, the magnitude and rate of these impacts on ecosystems, livelihood, human health and food security, will pose a major challenge for humanity. The threat of global climate change has been described as the biggest environmental challenge of the 21st century. The latest projections of the IPCC are for global average surface temperatures to rise by between 1.4° and 5.8°C over the course of the next century. The IPCC concluded "The Earth's climate system has demonstrably changed on both global and regional scale since the pre industrial era". Human influence will continue to change atmospheric composition throughout the 21st century. The National Academy of Sciences 2001, commissioned by the White House stating that "Green house gases are accumulating in the Earth's atmosphere as a result of human activities, causing surface air temperatures and sub-surface ocean temperatures to rise" but we cannot rule out that some of the significant part of these changes are also a reflection of natural variability, while the biggest contributor to global warming due to increases in greenhouse gas emissions are the rich industrialized countries, it appears likely that the countries that will be most adversely affected by climate change in the next 100 years are the developing and poorest countries that can least afford to take measures to combat it.

The threat of global climate change and the challenge of how to respond to it is therefore a problem of considerable complexity. It is a global issue, as ultimately it will require global collective action of all countries to lessen the threat to be successful. It is an intergenerational issue, as the decisions and life style choices of today's generation will affect the decisions and lifestyle choices of future generations. It is an environmental issue, but it is also a social, economic, political and ethical issue.[1]

Global efforts towards achieving climate change protection reached a significant milestone with the adoption of the UN Framework

Convention on Climate Change (FCCC) in 1992 under which the United States along with 152 other nations agreed to an ultimate objective of stabilization of greenhouse gas concentrations in the atmosphere, at a level that would prevent dangerous anthropogenic interference with the climate system. The United States and certain other industrialized countries also agreed to pursue various voluntary measures to limit their emissions of greenhouse gases to 1990 levels by the year 2000. In October 1993, President Clinton outlined a voluntary Climate Change Action Plan (CCAP) designed to limit U.S. emission of greenhouse gases. Since the US ratification of FCCC in 1992, there have been bipartisan expressions of the sense of Congress that, if United States is to become party to any future international regulatory agreement, the decision to do so should be well informed and that all nations party to the FCCC should have proportional responsibilities for global climate protection.[2]

The international efforts at climate change are continuing. The convention was opened for signature on 4 June 1992, at the UN Conference on Environment and Development (UNCED), the so called "Earth Summit" which came into force on 21 March 1994. Since the convention's entry into force, parties have met annually in the Conference of the Parties (CoP) to monitor its implementation and continue talks on how best to tackle the climate change.

Many decisions taken at the CoP at its annual sessions now make up a detailed rulebook for the effective implementation of the convention. When they adopted the convention, however governments knew that its commitments would not be sufficient to seriously tackle climate change. At the first CoP Berlin in March/April 1995, in a decision known as the Berlin Mandate, parties therefore launched a new round of talks and more detailed commitments for industrialized countries.

The FCCC established a negotiating body to consider the more stringent measures for climate change protection and proposed to draft a protocol or some other legal instrument that would be more regulatory in nature. The FCCC after two and a half years of intense negotiations formulated the Kyoto protocol, which was adopted at CoP-3 in Kyoto Japan on 11 December 1997. Kyoto protocol on climate change, if it enters into force, would implement the first legally binding reduction of greenhouse gas emissions with the aim of stabilizing (if not reducing) atmospheric concentrations of these pollutants a some point in future.[3]

At the time of negotiating the Kyoto protocol it was described as a first step in the international effort to curb emissions of greenhouse gases and limit the effects of global climate change. Since then, the countries have been negotiating the details of this protocol with the aim of having it enter into force by September 2002 when the World Summit on Sustainable Development (WSSD) is convened in Johannesburg. These negotiations which lasted for three years were completed in Marrakesh in last November 2001 following a successful political agreement in Bonn in July 2001 (arrived at even with the United States the biggest GHG emitter, abandoning the process). Consequently, there is high expectation that Kyoto protocol will come into force by late 2002.

The FCCC specified that developed countries should bear the primary responsibility for reducing greenhouse gases and setout a system of voluntary reduction commitments for these countries with common monitoring and reporting requirements for all countries. The Kyoto Protocol encompassed many key decisions but of most importance was the decision for developed countries to accept reduction commitments that would become legally binding when the protocol was ratified.

Subsequent to 1997, negotiations on the rules for implementing the protocol have continued. The layout protocol and its rulebook set out in Marrkesh accord consists of five main elements:

1. Commitments- At the heart of the Kyoto protocol lies its set of legally binding emission targets for the industrialized countries. The annex-1 parties must at least on average aim at reduction of 5 percent from 1990 levels by the year 2008-12. The total reduction is shared so that each Annex -1 parties has to meet its own individual emission target. These individual targets listed in Protocol's Annex -B were decided upon in Kyoto protocol through intense negotiation. The 15 member states of the European union will take advantages of a scheme under the protocol "bubble" to redistribute their joint 8% reduction targets among themselves. The protocols emission targets cover the six main greenhouse gases such as, CO_2, N_2O, HCFs, PFCs and SF_6.

Parties may offset their emissions by increasing the amount of greenhouse gases removed from the atmosphere by carbon sinks in the Land Use Change and Forestry, (LULUCF) sector from 1990 levels to the baseline, parties must reduce or limit their emissions. Parties must achieve the emission targets by the so-called commitment period 2008-2012. In meeting their targets "demonstrate progress" by 2005, must be submitted in a report showing evidence of that progress by 1st January 2006. A five-year commitment period was chosen rather than a single target year keeping in view smooth and annual fluctuation in emissions assignment. If a party achieves more substantial units in its emissions than is required by its targets, it may carry over the difference to the next commitment period with certain limits.[4] Delegates approved the Kyoto protocol, which set terms for legally binding commitments for the industrialized countries. It also proposed mechanisms to enable countries to move towards cleaner technology.[5]

In addition to emission targets for Annex -1 parties the Kyoto protocol also contains a set of more general commitments that reinforce the fundamental obligation of all parties both industrialized and developing nations to tackle climates change.

These commitments includes preparing natural climate change, mitigation, and adaptation programmes taking steps to improve the quality emission data, promoting friendly technology transfer cooperating in scientific research and integrated climate observation networks, and supporting climate change education, training, public awareness and capacity building initiatives.

Annex-II parties (the OECD countries) are committed to providing financial resources to help non annex -I parties to meet their general commitment under the protocol through the GEF as the financial mechanism, supplementary parties included in Annex-B may transfer Emission Reduction Units (ERUs) among themselves, or acquired Certified Emission Reductions (CERs) from non Annex-B countries from projects, which are aimed at reducing greenhouse gases reduction thus achieved have to be in addition to any that would have acquired or been achieved even otherwise.[6]

Policies and Measures

To achieve the protocol's targets, Annex -1, parties will implement climate policies and measures that might help mitigation of climate change and promotion of sustainable development priorities in their emission reduction efforts through activities such as enhancement of emerging efficiency, protecting and enhancing greenhouse gas sinks, promotion of sustainable agriculture, promotion of reasonable energy, carbon sequestration and other environmentally friendly technologies, removal of subsidies and other market imperfections for environmentally damaging activities, encouraging reforms in relevant sector to promote emission reductions taking transport sector emission and controlling methane emission through recovery and use in waste management.

Thus the protocol calling the parties to improve the effectiveness of climate policy work on "good practices" in policy and measure by exchange of information and experience on their mitigation measures for greater intergovernmental co-operation, for the protocols to entry into force by the SBSTA. The IPCC in its Third Assessment report highly commended the recent technical progress in greenhouse gas emission reduction targets, which has been faster than anticipated, and that "no regrets."

Kyoto Flexibility Mechanism

Further negotiations led to defining three innovative mechanism for emissions abatement. They are: First, Joint Implementation (JI) of projects that generates credits among industrialized countries. Second, a Clean Development Mechanism (CDM) in which industrialized countries make investments in developing countries to both reduce emission and promote sustainable development in returning credit for emission reduction, and third, International Emission Trading (IET) among Annex-1 countries. These mechanisms aim to maximize the cost effectiveness of climate change mitigation by allowing parties to pursue opportunities to cut emissions or enhance carbon sinks more cheaply abroad than at home.

Joint Implementation :- Art -6

Joint implementation allows to annex-1 parties in the territories of other Annex-1 parties to implement projects that reduce emissions or increase removals by sinks generation of Emission Reduction Units (ERUS) by such projects that can be best used by investing annex-1 parties to help to meet their emission targets. A joint implementation project might involve, for example replacing a coal fire power plant with a more efficient combined heat and power plant or reforesting land. In practice joint implementation projects are most likely to find favour in EIRS, where these tend to make sCoPes for cutting emissions at low cost. Joint implementation projects must have the approval of all parties involved and must lead to emission reduction or removals that are additional to any that would have occurred without the projects.

There are two possible procedures for carrying out a joint implementation project. The first procedure (track one) applies when the host party fully meets all the eligibility requirements related to the protocol's methodological and routine obligations. In this situation, the host party may apply its own procedure to projects, issue ERUS and transfer them to the investing party. The second procedure (track two) applies if the host does not meet all the requirements. The 10 member supervising committee set up by CoP/Mop at its first meeting, must verify and supervise the amount of ERUS generated by a project. The project designs documents after evaluation to make sure that the baseline and monitoring plan must be devised according to standard criteria with assessment of the project's environmental impacts. Based on its evaluation the independent entity will determine whether the project should proceed, unless the project participant or three supervisory committee members request a review and that after 45 days a report must be submitted to the independent entity on the estimated emission reduction or removal generated by the project.

After review and determination by independent entity, the emission reduction or removals(ERUs) by the host party is determined. In case no request by project participant or at least three supervisory committee members for review will be treated as valid after 15 days. The host party may then issue the ERUS and transfer them to the investing party, subject to meet the necessary eligibility requirements.[7]

Clean Development Mechanism: - Art-12. The CDM allows Annex-I parties to implement projects that reduce emission in the territories of Non Annex-I parties. The certified emission reductions- CERS- generated by such projects can be used by Annex-I parties to help meet their emission targets, while the project also help Non Annex-I parties to achieve sustainable development and contribute to the ultimate objective of the convention.[8]

Like JI the CDM is based on the premise that the countries with high emission reduction costs will have an incentive to pursue projects in lower cost countries. Both mechanisms seek to increase the cost effectiveness of achieving global emission reduction targets with project level emission trading. The implementing framework of both mechanisms may encourage private sector companies to structure most transactions with governments to play an active role. In principle the governments could package internal projects and then arrange the sale of the CDM credits. In either case, government approval of the project transactions will be required before a transaction is finalized. However, CDM transactions will occur between Annex-B and Non Annex-B countries, while JI trading will occur between Annex-B countries. [9]

The Kyoto protocol establishes the following key differences between JI and the CDM. The CDM projects aim at playing a leading role to advance the sustainable development goals of developing countries. The CDM project developers must allocate a portion of the project funds to support climate change mitigation activities in developing countries. This support could include helping the small island states, for example which could suffer substantial damage from rising ocean levels. This "Adaptation tax" may be extended to the other flexibility mechanisms "Currently" however, it applies only to the CDM. Because CDM projects occur in Non Annex-B countries (i.e. countries with no emission allocation, or reduction commitments), the CDM could "print credits" and potentially undercut the aims of the protocol. For this reason, Art-12 requires that the projects "additional" to reductions that otherwise would have occurred is to be taken note of. Implementing this "additional" standard is proving technically and politically difficult. The scope of CDM trading is not yet fully defined. Negotiations are currently hovering on for example, whether forestry and land use change projects will be eligible for CDM status.

From the stand point of developing greenhouse gas markets- a key attribute of CDM- is that CDM based Certified Emission Reductions (CERS), can be banked starting in the year 2000. Banked CERS can be used against Annex-B Emission Reduction Mandates in the first Kyoto protocol commitment period (2008-2012). The CDM is the only protocol mechanism that can generate reductions in the near term future that will count against the countries falling in Kyoto commitments.

At the same time the CDM has been a continuous subject of discussion, on the one hand, Annex-B countries and private sector in those countries perceive the CDM to be crucial to the cost effectiveness of global emission reduction efforts. Development of CDM probably is key, for example to potential ratification of the protocol by the United States. Many observers also argue that the CDM could be a powerful tool for funding sustainable development activities in and transferring new technologies to the developing countries. On the other hand, the CDM is some times characterized as an industrialized country's ploy to avoid the onus of carrying out real emissions reductions at home, and strip developing countries of low cost mitigation opportunity, they eventually will need, and take advantage of the inferior negotiating position of developing countries and their private sectors.[10]

International Emission Trading(IET)

Art.17. IET provides the means for Annex-B countries to sell "surplus" portions of their emission allocations under the Kyoto protocol. Like JI and CDM emission trading, it is not a project-based mechanism. Moreover, IET applies only to the countries with emission reduction obligations, since without an agreed upon target, the countries have nothing to trade. During the Kyoto protocol's first commitment period from 2008-2012, most Annex-B countries are expected to have emissions above their Kyoto protocol targets. Thus they will be in the market to buy emission reductions through the protocol's flexibility mechanism. Several Annex-B countries (e.g. Russia and Ukraine) are expected to have emissions below their Kyoto protocol targets, and thus, these countries will be in the market to sell their "surplus" reduction credits.

The sale of these reductions remains politically controversial. The controversy stems from the fact that at least the initial transactions under the IET are unlikely to result from specific emission reduction policies or measures. Instead, these transactions will be based on emission reductions that occurred when the economies of these countries almost collapsed in the early 1990s. Some observers argue that these so called "hot air" reductions serve no environmental purpose and undercut the goal of the protocol. However, Article-17 with it implied transfer of wealth from "net purchaser" Annex-B countries to "net seller" Annex-B countries such as Russia was another important compromise reached in Kyoto,[11] preparing the protocol's flexibility mechanism for implementation in the global greenhouse gas market. The flexibility mechanisms are expected to be important mitigation devices under the Kyoto protocol. However, specific rules governing operation of JI, CDM and IET are not very clear. The rules have the potential to significantly affect the operation, environmental effectiveness and economic values of the three mechanisms. Key questions that need to be resolved before the CDM will be ready for implementation. Minimizing the impacts on the developing countries, the protocol pays special attention towards the developing countries, those who were vulnerable to the adverse impacts of climate change and to the implementation of responsible measures to the specific needs of the least developed countries. The protocol therefore, commits the Annex-I parties to take utmost care to implement policies to meet their emission targets by minimizing adverse impacts on developing countries. The parties will furnish information on emissions over the commitment period and the action they have taken to implement the protocol and transactions under the mechanisms to assess the compliance with protocol. The Annex-I parties must also submit regular national communications that will include information on the actions they are taking to implement the protocol. The flexibility mechanisms are expected to be an important mitigation tool under the Kyoto protocol. However, specific rules governing operation of JI, CDM and IET are not resolved to acquire consistency. Establishing the CDM's Executive Board and operational entities and defining their duties and responsibilities remain nebulous. Specifying many rules for CDM projects will be an international responsibility. If these countries are overtly bureaucratic, the CDM could come to a stand still. Managing project transaction cost by developing transparent and not by overtly bureaucratic control, national and international procedures for project evaluation approval and monitoring and verification, would be highly sought for mechanisms to meet the Kyoto targets. High transaction costs could undercut the CDM's competitiveness.

Developing additional, baseline, development leakage, and other project's screening and qualification standards will determine the environment effectiveness of the CDM, the sectors pursed for CDM projects and the likely value of CDM and CERs. Standards that are to loose could flood the market with questionable credits, standards that are too strict could restrict trading and advancement of the CDMs sustainable development objectives. Most of these rules will need to be set at the international level to ensure consistency across countries. Interpreting the CDMs sustainable development mandate, it has not yet been determined whether countries will be free to identify their own sustainable development criteria or whether there will be common standards. Implementing the CDM's supplementary Mandate, Article 12 mandates that the CDM be "supplemental" to Annex -B countries' domestic emissions reduction efforts. Negotiations are currently being broached on whether this requirement should result in a quantitative limitation on the CDM. A limitation potentially could create multiple GHG markets and market prices. Developing countries might compete for CDM "Quota" for example, setting one price for CDM credits. Domestic emission reduction projects in Annex-B countries might have a different B, and significantly a higher B market-clearing price.

Implementing the CDMs Adaptation Finding Mandate

The share of CDM finding that will go to adaptation finding as required by article 12 has not been determined.[12] The Framework Convention on Climate Change and the Kyoto protocol have established a structure for global action to mitigate the threat of climate change. Proponents of the Kyoto protocol widely acknowledge that it is only a first step in the international efforts to reduce greenhouse gases emissions and limit the effects of global climate change. The protocol stipulates emission reduction commitments for the period 2008-2012. It was foreseen that this would be followed by subsequent commitment periods in encompassing a wide range of countries with commitments (of same kind) to reduce emissions. Concerns about cost and fairness dominated the negotiations over the Kyoto protocol signed in December 1997. The treaty embodies two key decisions. First: the United States and 37 other countries pledged to cut their emissions of Carbon Dioxide and five other heat trapping gases between 2008 and 2012 to an average of 5 percent below that they had been in 1990. Individual targets varied. The United States pledged to cut its emissions to 7 percent below 1990 level. Second: Kyoto left it upto developing countries to decide whether to reduce their greenhouse gas emissions. The Clinton administration had wanted a change in the language requiring developing countries to curb emissions.

This American position reflected political reality as much as any thing in July 1997, the Senate voted 95-0 to oppose any agreement exempting developing countries from emission reductions. Despite this warning, developing countries successfully fought off that urged voluntary compliance. China led this fight even though it apparently reduced its emission in the late 1990s overhauling its energy infrastructure to reduce urban air pollution. Beijing worried that any limit would constrain its future economic growth.

The developing countries' exemption was just one of the problems plaguing the Kyoto protocol. The treaty did not solve global warming. With developing countries unrestrained, world wide emissions of heat trapping gases will rise albeit some what more slowly, even if the treaty terms are fully implemented. Moreover, the negotiators reached an agreement by postponing decisions about the most controversial issues. The protocol for example, omitted the operational details of its proposed emissions trading programme, which in theory would hold down to cost of compliance by lifting firms and countries that cannot meet their emission targets, and buy credits from those that can. The treaty was similarly vague in its provisions allowing countries to claim credits for "carbon sinks"- the ability of trees and soil to absorb carbon dioxide. Such a provision could encourage countries to preserve and extend forests, it could also be used to let countries hit their emission targets without changing their behaviour.[13] The Kyoto protocol has come in for its fair share of criticism from all hues of political spectrum. As is to be expected with any global agreement such as this, there are parties who think it does too little in forms of trying to prevent climate change, and others who believe it tries to do too much.[14] The complexity of the negotiations, however, meant that considerable "unfinished business" remained even after the Kyoto protocol itself was adopted. The protocol sketched out the basic features of its "mechanisms" and compliance system, for example, but did not flesh out the all-important rules of how they would operate. At first, 84 countries signed the protocol indicating that they intended to ratify, many were reluctant to actually to do so and bring the protocol into force before having a clear picture of the treaty's rulebook.[15] While the flexibility mechanisms seek to provide the greatest economic efficiency in GHG abatement efforts, they may in fact overlook ecological efficiency and effectiveness, which would lead to achieving the ultimate objective of the convention- namely the climate change mitigation.

The most notable criticisms of the Kyoto structure in recent time have stemmed from the U.S administration who in 2001 decided to withdraw from the Kyoto agreement. The main reason put forward by the U.S.

cabinet review of the Kyoto protocol states that the agreement is "fundamentally flawed" because firstly, it fails to establish a long term goal based on science", secondly, " it poses serious and unnecessary risks to the U.S. and world economies" and thirdly, it is an ineffective mechanism in addressing climate change because it excludes major parts of the world.[16] World leaders were stunned when President Bush announced in March that the U.S. would not be bound by the emission targets agreed in Kyoto protocol to climate change convention. Since U.S. emissions are estimated to amount 23% of the world total, the repudiation of the protocol negotiated in 1997, is seen as a major setback to global efforts to nullify the devastating effects of global warming.[17] President Bush on 13th March 2001 in a statement said "I oppose the Kyoto protocol because it exempts 80 percent of the world, including major population center such as China and India from compliance, and would cause serious harm to U.S. economy". It is relevant to draw attention to the part 1 in the context of the discussion on long term targets in section 2. However, the two points of concern raised by US that are most relevant to this section are points (2) and (3). The U.S. is not only Annex-B country to express concern about these issues.[18] The Kyoto protocol represents a vast investment of intellectual and negotiating effort. Since the protocol was launched in 1997, these has been much negotiation and refinement. As noted, much has been agreed by over 180 countries that have a huge diversity of views, interests and understanding. "Such achievements far from being perfect are not to be highly discarded".

The Kyoto protocol in its current form (based on quantitative targets and on emission trading regime) has the strong advantages of providing some certainty as to the environmental outcome. The main disadvantage of Kyoto agreement is that there is uncertainty as to the costs countries will eventually face in fulfilling these commitments. Proponents of non-binding targets and dynamic targets consistently return to two key arguments. Firstly, such measures are the best way of bringing developing countries into a global agreement. Secondly, if there is less uncertainty as to costs, it is possible that countries will adopt more ambitious targets. To this extent, there may be in the choice of policy instrument between the certainty of environmental outcome, the potential stringency of the targets and wide global participation.[19] At present, Kyoto protocol divides countries into two groups, those with quantified binding targets and those without any commitments. In the future, it appears likely that parties to the protocol could be split into firstly, a fixed, binding emission reduction targets for developed countries secondly, binding dynamic targets for the wealthier developing countries and thirdly, voluntary targets for the least developing group of poorest countries. So far, the time frame is fixed for the developed and developing countries to reduce emissions in stipulated first commitment period (2008-2012), second commitment period (2016-2028) and the third commitment period (2024-2028) to achieve the targets.

The CoP-3 was the product of long and serious discussions and the drafting of voluminous documents in which thousands of experts, government officials and cabinet ministers had participated for several years. The conference itself was attended by nearly 10,000 men and women including the official representatives of no fewer than 150 countries and approximately 4,000 journalists who had gathered from all over the world. It is therefore not an exaggeration to say that the recent pronouncement by the Bush administration to discard the Kyoto protocol constitutes a serious repudiation of cooperative efforts made by the world community over the course of many years to create an effective system for combating global warming.[20] Much to the Bush administration's surprise, its opposition did not kill Kyoto, the European Union fought to keep the treaty alive, and in Bonn in July it reached an agreement with Japan, Australia and Canada, on the issue that had derailed the talks at the Hague. Ironically, the Bonn agreement incorporated many of the changes the Clinton administration had sought, including allowing credits for carbon sinks. These changes make it easier for countries to hit their emissions targets; initial assessments indicate that if Kyoto is fully enacted, it will reduce emissions 2 percent below 1990 levels for the participating countries. But for the moment, at least Bonn clearly leaves the United States isolated. Kyoto's supporters hope that this isolation will eventually force Washington to rejoin the treaty, which would substantially improve its chances for success. The phenomenon of climate change and the international response to it present a mass of equity issues. "The impacts of climate change are likely to fall disproportionately upon the poorest countries and the poorest persons within countries, and thereby exacerbate inequalities in health status and access to food, clean water and resources. How should the efforts needed to prevent or minimize climate change be distributed amongst the various nations of the world, rich and poor? The IPCC second assessment report (IPCC, 1996) summarized the equity issue thus: "The challenge of climate change mitigation from an equity perspectives is to ensure that neither the impact of climate change nor that of the mitigation policies exacerbate existing inequities both within and across nations".

The equity is a prominent theme in the UNFCCC. The first principle of the UNFCCC (Article 3.1) states. "The parties should protect the climate system for the benefit of the present and future generations on the basis of equity and in accordance with their common but differentiated responsibilities and respective capabilities. Accordingly, the developed country parties should take the lead in combating the climate change and the adverse impacts thereof." Further, the equity issue includes "the share of global emissions originating in developing countries with growth to meet their social and developmental needs. Industrialized countries are required to assist developing countries in Coping and adapting with the impacts climate change (various paragraph in Article 4). Further more, under the Kyoto protocol currently non annex-I countries are exempted from mitigation obligations. National commitments to reduce or limit are differentiated between the Annex-I countries. The Clean Development Mechanism (CDM) was established to assist developing countries in achieving sustainable development while contributing to the ultimate objectives of the UN FCCC. However, it is generally acknowledged that when looking beyond the first commitment period (2008-12) and need to involve all countries in a cooperative strategy to reduce global GHG emissions, equity issue has a key role to play[21] in achieving reductions in global concentrations in both developed and developing countries. The major issue facing all countries is how the task of reaching this goal should be distributed. At present, in the context of FCCC there is a political agreement that developed countries will act first when and how developing countries would play a part has not yet been determined. The fact that the Kyoto protocol excludes developing countries from reduction commitments in the first commitment period was one of the key reasons cited by US for their withdrawal from the protocol in 2001.

The question of how to distribute the responsibility for reducing global emissions of greenhouse gases amongst different countries often referred to as "burden sharing", underpins international negotiations on climate change. The quantified emission reductions agreed to in Kyoto protocol were a first agreement on burden sharing. The differentiated targets were not founded on any specific method but rather were the result of negotiations taking into considerations various interests and the national circumstances of the parties.[22] The only attempt so far made to achieve the globally coordinated action urgently needed to fight climate change has been the Kyoto Treaty, which took many years of hard work and complicated negotiations to achieve. Though the Kyoto Treaty is nothing like as strong as it needs to be, it makes some kind of a start to putting the breaks on the slide towards catastrophe, and embodies the principle that there must be mandatory limits to the greenhouse gas emissions of all the nations round the world. The Kyoto protocol was an agreement reached in 1997 in Kyoto by which industrialized nations would initially cut their "greenhouse gas" emissions by 5%. The climate talks in the Hague in November 2000 were supposed to finalize the treaty and put it into action, but the U.S. - then under the Democrat Clinton administration tried to find excuses and loopholes essentially to avoid doing their share and as a result the talks broke down without making any progress. In March 2001, the then the New Republican President of US George W. Bush dumped the Kyoto treaty, which was an act of arrogance and highhanded irresponsibility that shocked the world saying that the Kyoto agreement was of "no interest" to his administration. The rest of the world agreed to go ahead with the Kyoto in Bonn in July 2001, in defiance of the US but the action of the U.S. strengthened the hand of those who wanted to weaken the treaty and thereby caused it to be even weaker than it would otherwise have been.

US Opposition Exploiting Scientific Uncertainties

The U.S. is now the greatest obstruction to the world battle against climate change. Climate change urgently requires globally coordinated action to effectively bring it under control, so far the United States of America, the most powerful nation in the world, has proved the greatest force acting against any such globally coordinated action. The United States all along opposed to the idea of strong climate treaty setting a very higher target on the ground that it will impact its economy. But recent studies show with a very minimal impact on the economy. Greenhouse gas can be reduced though sensible policies and international co-operation. On the best-case scenario it predicted stimulated economic growth. The US is responsible for about one quarter of the world's greenhouse gas emissions with only 4% of world population. Since 1990, emissions in the U.S. have increased by 20%, while experts warn the industrialized nations must reduce their CO_2 emissions by 60% by the middle of this century. Further more, while other countries are working to reduce their emissions, Bush's energy plan ensures that US emissions will continue to rise. The answer to this lies in the fact that the Bush administration is more transparently and overwhelming controlled by special interest- wealthy corporations that fund the Republican Party and wield immense power in the US political system than any before it. These wealthy corporations include many from the fossil fuel industry, which has especially strong and close links with the current administration. Those who control fossil fuel industry fear that their profit will be cut if action is taken to reduce the CO_2 emissions created by the burning of fossil fuels-oil coal and gas that cause global warming. Exxon Mobil ("ESSO" in the UK) and many environmental organizations like the friends of the Earth and Green Peace now urging a boycott of this company on the basis that it has done more than any other corporation to sabotage progress in tackling climate change.

Since 2001, each effort to get a final energy bill to the President's desk has been held up in the Senate and some Senators are pushing some questionable additions to the current version. Accommodating their wishes could turn a bill once intended to expand energy supplies into anti energy bill that would impose costs often billions of dollars or more per year. In particular, expensive measures to combat global warming do not belong in the energy bill. Carbon dioxide- the ubiquitous byproduct of all fossil fuel energy combustion has been implicated as a greenhouse gas that contributes to global warming. But reducing carbon dioxide emissions requires costly constraints on the use of coal, oil and natural gas. Those fossil fuels provide most of our energy. Thus, dealing with global warming in any serious way means unprecedented levels of energy and central planning. Congress has previously considered measures to regulate Carbon Dioxide emissions but rejected then as too expensive. These costs loom even larger now that there are growing doubts about the extent of man made warming and the seriousness of its consequences. The United States continues to refuse to ratify the Kyoto protocol and has indeed dragged another major developed country Australia along with it, which has huge coal industry and at the behest of the U.S. administration, its premier John Howard has also refused to ratify the Kyoto protocol. These are the only two major developed countries not to ratify, but their shortsighted intransigence is blocking any really effective progress towards dealing with climate threat by the world community.

The treaty requires developed nations to reduce greenhouse gas emissions below 1990 levels by 2008 to 2012. The Department of Energy's Energy Information Administration (EIA) forecast that the cost of US compliance with Kyoto at as much as $397 billion dollars annually, depending on initial assumptions.[23] Much of the cost would come from the need to move rapidly away from coal which has high carbon emissions but currently provides half of America's electricity needs. Kyoto would also place constraints on gasoline supplies and increase prices at the pump. Proponents of the Kyoto protocols have criticized this cost estimate as too high, but the early experience with Kyoto reaffirms that compliance is expensive. Most of the 15 Western European nations that ratified the treaty are not quick to meet their emission reduction targets due to the unacceptably high impact of compliance on energy cost.[24] This is particularly true of those European nations with an energy mix and emission history similar to that of US. For example, Spain's environment minister recently conceded that compliance is very unlikely, citing costs that are proving to be "astronomical".[25] These initial difficulties provide the first world confirmation that compliance with Kyoto protocol will be very expensive that America's decision to stay out is based on a solid rationale.

According to a study made by WHO and WRI on the impact on human health, by the end of the second decade of the next century more than eight million avoidable deaths will have occurred because of air pollution associated with burning of fossil fuels. In U.S. nearly a half a million lives overall would be saved by 2020 if climate protection measures are implemented. Such a goal though expensive can be achievable without insurmountable social disruptions. The kind of response and address needed to combat the crisis, the Kyoto failed to winnow from the rich industrialized North particularly the United States who are being the biggest polluters expected to set the targets.

From the very beginning, American policy debate on Kyoto protocol has been dominated by persistent accusations of unfairness to the United States and its citizens. In his opening statement of a hearing by the US House of Representatives sub-committee on National Economic Growth, National Resources and Regulatory Affairs- The Kyoto protocol. Is the Clinton- Gore Administration selling out Americans? Part III, 20 May 1998 - Chairman David M. Mc Intosh, for example, declared that Kyoto protocol is also presently unfair because it exempts 77 percent of all countries from any obligations. China, India, Mexico and Brazil just to name a few, are completely unfettered by the treaty. These countries already have the competitive advantages of cheap labour, lower production costs and lower environmental, health and safety standards. If president Clinton has his way, now these countries will be free to develop and pollute all they want, while the U.S. economy goes into a deep freeze. Exactly a year later before the same body a fellow Michigan Republican House member - Rep. Joe Knollenberg by then well known in climate change circles for "the amendments", reiterated this statement. This fatally flawed agreement (the Kyoto protocol) is blatantly unfair because it exempts developing nations from making any commitments to reduce their emissions of greenhouse gases. As a result, nations like, Chine, India, Mexico and Brazil will be given a free pass while the United States is forced to struggle with the Kyoto treaty's stringent mandates.

There is a clear consensus that the Kyoto protocol is an unfair and ineffective means of addressing global climate change concerns. These charges of inequity have to be taken seriously, for there is arguably nothing more discrediting to any piece of legislation than to be perceived as being unfair. Indeed, the President's remarks heralded the anti treaty attitude of the US towards the Kyoto protocol. To keep up anti treaty rumblings alive in the U.S., the Denver based Western fuels Association has been financing paper by some scientists who propose that having more Carbon dioxide in the atmosphere will be good not bad. This attitude has been reflected in American Congress. Debate over a long term equitable sharing of the burden has continued since the negotiation of the Kyoto protocol, while the details of the protocol's implementation are still being negotiated. Several developing country representatives continue to press the claim that the Annex-I countries should do even more to reduce GHG emissions given their historical responsibility for GHG emission. Developed countries accept the concept of differentiated responsibilities but want greater assurance as when and how developing countries would start industrial emitters in the future. This concern was underscored in the Byrd-Hagel resolution passed by 95-0 by the U.S. Senate. That resolution opposed ratification of Kyoto treaty until developing countries committed to binding emissions limits in the some time frame as the United States decides not to ratify the Kyoto protocol exploiting scientific uncertainties. The United States branded the Kyoto protocol as unfair, as because of the lack of meaningful participation of developing countries and their not being subject to emission reduction targets. In advancing these arguments, it claimed that in the near future developing countries are going to be worse emitters than the United States of America. Under the protocol, the US will be ruined while developing countries get away scot-free if not buffer off.

The injustice is taken to arise from the lack of meaningful participation because America is being punished while others, who it is claimed will be much more offenders are not - indeed - may even benefit, or as paraphrased from the US perspective, "We are going to be punished for becoming more virtuous". The inequity felt will be particularly strong if and as implied by the second claim, the punishment seems to be disproportionately large. Keeping in view the two premises, the United States took stands for the rejection of Kyoto protocol. Internationally, this is not a widely accepted view, however, if we disregard the past, comparing current and projected US and developing countries' behaviour as carbon emitters. Much of the projected increase in Carbon Dioxide emission is expected to occur in developing world, where emerging economies are expected to produce the largest increases in energy consumption. Developing countries alone account for 81 percent of the projected increment in Carbon Dioxide emissions between 1990 and 2000 and 76 percent between 1990 and 2020. Continued heavy reliance on coal and other fossil fuels as projected for developing countries, would ensure that even the industrialized world undertook efforts to reduce Carbon Dioxide emissions and world wide Carbon Dioxide responsibility. For 81% of anything would indeed seem to be substantial, if one infers not unreasonably that developed countries would therefore have to be responsible for remaining 19%.

The United States of America exploiting scientific uncertainties for the implementation of Kyoto protocol, as because making developing countries "twice as responsible than industrialized one would seem to recommend this increment measures" as ideal for justifying the claim not to ratify the Kyoto protocol. The projected emission behaviour of the U.S. and the key developing countries does not significantly change over the time horizon but more importantly that the U.S. continues to behave, as it were, more than twice as badly 'than its nearest developing country competitor namely China.[26]

US Withdrawal from Kyoto Protocol

The Kyoto agreement was only over meaningful participation as a "starting point". It proposes reduction of 5% though the many loopholes in the agreement mean that it is not likely to be achieved. Meanwhile, experts warn that reduction of 60% is needed by mid century, or around 90% for developed countries, which have a higher target since they are responsible for the bulk of emissions to date.

Soon after assuming office, US President, George W. Bush reneged on a campaign pledge to curb emissions from coal power generating plants. He then unveiled on February 14 proposals that administration claims, are aimed at reducing greenhouse gas emission. This plan is being promoted as an alternative to the Kyoto protocol on global warming from which the U.S. withdrew last spring. However, the administrations new policy particularly as it affects Carbon Dioxide, will be entirely voluntary. It is essentially an abandonment of any attempt to curb such emissions, which are viewed by most scientists as the primary cause of global warming. As seen recently, in the Hague and Bonn Conference of Parties to the climate change convention, U.S. withdrew from the rest of the world community working desperately to begin to address the climate crisis. Stabilizing the climate requires global emission reduction of 60% to 80%, this will require a far more radical approach than is embodied in the current draft protocol. A recent study published in the journal, Nature found that unless the world gets half its energy from non-carbon sources by 2018, the planet will experience an inevitable quadrupling of the heat trapping atmospheric carbon concentration near the end of the century. Against this background, the Kyoto protocol falls far short of its goal of climate stabilization. U.S. emissions are projected to grow rapidly, they would increase farther, if the National Energy Policy proposals for the power sector are implemented, and the domestic climate change programmes are put forward in this, and the proposed NCCTI would curtail this by less than 0.5% during this decade. Domestic programmes so far proposed, would not stabilize U.S. emission, let alone return them to 1990 levels, an aim established for industrialized countries under the 1992 Framework Convention on Climate Change (FCCC).

Prominent and long standing American objections to the Kyoto protocol are that it is ineffective and unfair to the U.S. due to the lack of 'meaningful participation' by key developing countries and that any agreement should also include current commitments from these countries. Neither the past, present, nor projected (business as usual) emissions warrant these claims. No developing country is projected to surpass total U.S. carbon emissions in the next 20 years. Furthermore, equity considerations have to be assessed in terms of "average" inhabitants' emissions. The average of U.S. citizens is many times higher than, and is projected to continue growing faster than, the global average, while those of the average Chinese and Indian are below the average and will grow at the world average rate if not substantially below it. In addition, U.S. analysts have tended to amplify the likely costs of Kyoto and mostly suggest that the developing countries neglect commonly held principles concerning the equity implications of large international income disparities as well as agreed principles of industrialized country leadership under the FCCC.

President, George W. Bush announces new global warming plan: A Valentine Day gift for energy corporations.[27] The announcement by President Bush rejected the Kyoto protocol shortly afterwards the U.S. administration announced it would come forward for alternative approach to climate change problem indicating that these could be expected before the next major global negotiating session, which had already been deferred until mid July 2001 to accommodate the original request from the new administration to give them more time to propose. The U.S. Cabinet Review published on 13 June 2001 gives no indication of what alternatives might be proposed and at the international consultation on 27 June, the U.S. representative stated that the U.S. would not after all be proposing any alternative before the next negotiating session. This has left much of the rest of the world uncertain about whether (when they convene in Bonn) to press ahead with completing negotiations on the rules for implementing or whether to wait longer to see what the U.S. might propose.[28] The net result arrived at the Hague and Bonn conferences with U.S. shadow falling large on Japan and EU who acted as its proxies, is that the Kyoto protocol is now even more or rather less of a paper victory than earlier. But more than that, it represented a wasted opportunity given that the longest polluter is no longer part of the signatories and the provision of more loopholes for use of sinks and hot air trades, the protocol will now do even less than it was originally going to do in terms of emissions or concentrations.

However, the Bush plan has provoked opposition both at home and abroad, Jennifer L. Morgan of the World Wildlife Fund noted, "They are trying to set up mechanisms to allow indefinite increase in emissions".[29] The withdrawal of the United States from the Kyoto agreement, which was signed last year by most of the world, excepting the U.S. and includes mandatory emissions reductions - provoked considerable anger over the America's unilateral policy. The new global warming plan has only confirmed Europeans' suspicions that the US avows to prevent strict emissions regulations. While it is important that Kyoto treaty and all it stands for is kept going and kept alive and it cannot form the basis for effective globally coordinated measures against climate change without the participation of the U.S. By refusing to cooperate with the international community on this, the U.S. has effectively put a stranglehold on all progress towards dealing with the climate change threat at a global level. It is often said that the U.S. will have to come on board the treaty eventually but in the mean time we are loosing precious time in the race against escalating climate change. We simply do not know how much irreparable damage we have done already, and the consequences of further delay in taking effective action, in terms of suffering and loss of life of future generations, are quite incalculable.

The preoccupation of the U.S. with its own selfish short term interests to the exclusion of any concern about this potential catastrophe of quite unparalleled scale for all the people of the world; may come, in due course, to rank as the most staggeringly criminal folly of all time.[30] Olivier Deleuze, Belgium's Green party energy minister, declared Bush's plan to be "immoral commenting," its really shocking in its ambit like saying: wealth is for US today in 2002 and we will leave the problem for our children or for people in Africa or Asia. French environment minister, Yves Cochet called in the European Union to oppose the plan and urge Bush to ratify protocols instead. The American's proposal has also been meet with a cool response from Japan, which has been one of the strongest supporters of Kyoto.

Weakness of Kyoto Protocol

Concern about accumulation of greenhouse gases in the atmosphere and possible effects on global temperatures have led to a series of international initiatives for collective action.[31] Under the protocol, thirty eight developed countries are to reduce greenhouse Gas (GHG) emissions by approximately 95 percent of 1990 levels by 2008-2012. The United States is to lower its discharge of Carbon Dioxide (CO_2) to 93 percent of 1990 emissions. These actions will not be without costs, although neither the costs, nor the benefits of emission controls are known with certainty.

Uncertainty arises because of lack of conclusive information about (*a*) the human sources and pace of temperature change; (*b*) the costs and benefits of global warming and their distribution across countries; (*c*) the costs, benefits and effectiveness of different forms of regulations and; (*d*) the extent of treaty compliance by sovereign countries. We argue that uncertainty seriously affects the ability of political constituencies within countries and hence, politicians and their agents to calculate the net gains of taking and complying with international agreements to address global warming. Under these circumstances, international collective action will be more difficult to mobilize and sustain.[32] The strategy outlined in Kyoto Protocol enjoins upon the Annex-I parties to meet their commitments without shouldering the area of reducing greenhouse gases at home. It may therefore, not be reduced to stabilization of greenhouse gas concentration at a level that would prevent dangerous anthropogenic interference with the climate system.

Except through Clean Development Mechanism and emissions trading introduced into the strategy outlined in the protocol, it does not insist on the developing countries' participation. It means, it does not recognize the atmospheric rights of the current and future generations of the developing countries while bestowing the same on the current generations of industrialized countries. Greenhouse gas emission is not based on equity on the basis of current emissions. Even a strict interpretation of the Kyoto protocol, which calls for industrial nations' emissions to 1990 levels after the year 2000, and then enforcing the freeze, is inadequate to control global warming. Stabilization of the Earth's atmosphere "will require short cuts in industrial country's emissions and a rapid slow down in emissions growth in developing nations".[33] Such meager progress toward an effective and meaningful international policy can hardly leave the participating Kyoto Protocol nations content regardless of the difficulty of implementing global climate change policies.

Ironically, the weakness of Kyoto treaty is actually used as an argument against it by those who would like to weaken it yet further. But in terms of internationally coordinated action - with agreed mandatory limits on greenhouse gas emissions - the Kyoto treaty is "the only shown in town"... or " a fragile talisman of hope."

Another complaint made about the Kyoto Protocol is that it only obliges industrialized countries to reduce their emissions. Developing countries like China and India do not have to. But this is only fair because by far greater part of the greenhouse gases in the atmosphere now, has been put more by the industrialized countries not to mention the fact that it is naturally much easier for richer nations to take actions and make sacrifices, than poor ones. It is entirely right that they should take the first step and lead the way. However, the rapid increase of greenhouse gas emissions from the rapidly developing countries like China and India poses a huge threat to the stability of global climate. That it makes it all the more urgent that the long industrialized countries set a good example, points the way to a low carbon model for development and takes the first step towards the coordinated international action to fight climate change that we need.[34] The world is stressing on the percentage of reduction being targeted by a country in the Kyoto Protocol, numbers game, anything that help increase the emissions in the base year, especially because of activities that have since ceased or reduced immediately gives the country a head start. Emission Trading, Joint Implementation and Clean Development Mechanism further provide opportunities to borrow emissions reduction from other countries where emission reduction is already taking place because of a slowing down of the economy. Countries, which promise a higher percentage reduction are seen as good players and those arguing for a lower percentage are seen as difficult ones. For example, if a developing country were to achieve energy efficiency in a big way, then it would already have an energy efficient economy by the time its base year is set and then high percentage reductions on that base year would not only be difficult to achieve but also too much expensive. On the contrary, if that country were to persist in the use of high percentage technologies and fossil fuels, then by the time its base year is set, it could easily agree to stick to higher percentage reduction and look good in front of the world. Whereas, those have already taken advance action and contributed proportionately less to the atmospheric greenhouse gas concentration would look bad. Thus, the strategy spelt out in the protocol provides non Annex-I countries with a perverse incentive to perpetuate on their current rate greenhouse emissions and make it even worst, if possible.

However, the emissions of greenhouse gases of US are still increasing obviously. Kyoto protocol becomes less effective for reducing greenhouse gases without U.S.' involvement. The other countries, which have ratified the Kyoto Protocol are working at bringing back U.S. to Kyoto protocol. Obliviously, U.S. stress on the technology innovation and market power and questions about the uncertainty of climate change. Clearly, there is still considerable uncertainty of effects of global warming. Global climate is a risk issue characterized by considerable uncertainty as regards the chances of negative outcomes. Waiting or delaying for deep cutting greenhouse gas emissions may cost humanity more in the future for global sustainable development.[35]

The issue of climate change associated with disappointments and problems as because the "common but differentiated responsibility" could not be implemented within a relatively homogeneous manner, that is manifested in a lack of coordinated action under the Kyoto protocol. The contention of the countries of North that unless developing countries participate in addressing the problem of climate change, their own effort would bear little fruit, arises from inevitability of higher GHG emissions from the countries of South. Higher population growth and expanding economics, it is expected would increase emissions from developing countries to nearby half a global emissions by 2015.[36] Under the Byrd resolution, the U.S. Senate categorically stated that it would not support a treaty that excludes developing nations from building commitments and emission reduction targets. A proposal to coordinate policies and measures amongst different countries was debated at length early in the Kyoto negotiation process. The argument at the time was led by the EU and strongly resisted by the U.S. and other countries. Their arguments were that coordinating policies and measures would be insufficient because it would not adequately reflect national diversities and would infringe upon national sovereignty regarding the appropriate choice of instrument. Further more, it was generally accepted that such an approach would be insufficient to provide countries with any real incentive to reduce emissions.

President Bush formally disavowed the 1997 accord negotiated by the United States and 158 countries in Kyoto to limit the greenhouse gas emissions, and is not planning to put forward a different international agreement to halt climate change. The failure of Kyoto protocol was the confrontation between the United States and the European Union and the developing countries relating to the question of flexible measures to combat the climate change.

Kyoto protocol is one of the greatest landmarks in the history of climate change science and politics. It is emerging as the first international document widely acknowledged by the international community to combat the forces of climate change. After a long and intense negotiation, the efforts and steps manifested in the form of a historical legal instrument to respond to the effects of global climate change. However, the outcome of the Conference of the Parties, the so-called Kyoto protocol was a timely and realistic agreement to materialize the process of co-operation amongst different countries of the world.

As the developed industrialized countries were solely responsible for emitting more and more heat trapping gases to the atmosphere, causing global warming they should take the lead to accept the legally binding obligations for the reduction of greenhouse gases within a targeted timetable under the protocol. The protocol gathered wide support from developed and developing world through establishment of a structure to mitigate the potential danger of climate change. The Kyoto framework with its clean development mechanisms assured full compliance in the face of issues and challenges of climate protection and sustainable development. The developing countries were exempted from the legally binding commitments to reduce emissions.

After 1950s a series of international conferences on climate change were held to protect the environmental degradation and depletion of Ozone layer from the increasing concentration of heat trapping gases in the atmosphere. With the conclusion of Kyoto protocol, it appears a unique international agreement ever produced as a mark of meaningful co-operation of the nations of the world to address the potential threat of the climate change. Realizing the ever increasing tendency of the climate change thereby causing innumerable hazards to the mankind and ecosystems, the Kyoto protocol's mechanisms bear the testimony to measures to combat effectively the eventualities of global climate change. The aim of the protocol is to follow the underlying principles of equity and common but differentiated responsibilities on the basis of "convergence as per capita emissions of industrialized and developing countries in the long run within the corridor of sustainability. However, in promoting co-operation and consensus to tackle global warming as a global problem included improving monitoring networks and technological assistance to the developing countries, to advance the science of climate change and focus attention on the many key areas of uncertainty. In spite of many inconsistencies and uncertainties with varied problems, parties call for immediate action and combined efforts to proceed further galvanizing scientific and technical knowledge forging an effective response to climate change.

The action of United States' President to discard Kyoto protocol, taking stand for voluntary action to regulate emissions and 'flexible measures' to be included as part of the obligation in the abatement of GHG emissions for meaningful participation of developing countries adversely affects the combined efforts to combat global climate change processes. The attitude developed by the United States shifting the world into 3 groups, directly or indirectly hampers the essence of the conference to finalize rules and regulations concerning the scope of the flexible measures to reduce emissions. Unfortunately the problem remained unsolved throughout the conference. New rounds of talks and negotiations will also be launched to strengthen and extend support to international efforts to solve environmental challenges.

Art 12 defines the Clean Development Mechanism (CDM), which has been identified as a mechanism for North-South cooperation in combating climate change. The Kyoto Protocol says that the purpose of CDM is to allow developing countries to assist parties in Annex I in achieving compliance with their quantified emission limitation and reduction commitments. There has been no other role left for the developing countries expect helping the Annex I countries in combating climate change. The only rationale for joint implementation is the one that was outlined by the Government of Norway in the early 1990s. The argument by the Norwegian government was that cutting future carbon dioxide emissions in developing countries is less expensive and cheaper than cutting those in industrialized countries. This means the industrialized countries need not be bound by any kind of commitment to reduction of greenhouse gas emission at their home front and yet meet their carbon dioxide emission reduction targets by investing in joint implementation projects in developing countries.

Many experts and countries are of the view that it is not really very expensive to reduce emission in developed countries. What is at stake is the political cost, as people may not relish higher energy prices and also a change in their life pattern and style. Democratic governments will not risk the discontentment of people by recoursing to such unpalatable measures. Once the developing countries attain high levels of energy efficiency with the investment and assistance from developed countries, the latter will no longer feel any economic incentive to continue investment in the developing countries. Since the developed countries have not taken any step to reduce emissions on their domestic front, the threats of global warming will loom large thrusting pressures on the developing countries to cut down emissions on their own. This will prove very expensive for these developing countries. The CDM does not answer the question: what will be the form of North-South cooperation then? In other wards, it allow the current generation of the developing countries to sell off cheaper emissions-control options today leaving the future generation gripped with high-cost options.

The worst aspect of the Kyoto protocol is that barring the small amounts that the industrialized and heaviest emitters of greenhouse gases are expected to reduce as a percentage of their current emission, these countries are bestowed with full entitlements to their heavy current emission without taking into account their past emissions and differential responsibilities. The final level of emissions that industrialized countries are expected to reach in their first commitment period from 2008 to 2012, is described as their assigned amount. But in the Kyoto protocol this assigned amount has gone well beyond being a mere target to be reached. It has been turned into a right by giving developed countries several property rights over these assigned amounts the right of a nation to trade any part of the assigned amount it is not going to use in the first commitment period for use in future commitment periods.

This provision of rights over the assigned amounts of industrialized countries which takes them well beyond being mere targets to be reached, has not only opened up opportunities for hot air to be traded but also left developing countries without any entitlements of their own. Even though, their per capita emissions are both currently and have historically been low, they cannot back any emissions for use by their future generations. Measures to combat climate change must be based on two key elements as identified in Art. 3 of the Framework Convention on Climate Change (FCCC). These should bring benefits to both the current and future generations, and they should be built on the basis of equity. Pathetically, there is nothing in the Kyoto protocol that comes as a testament to these two key elements being adhered to Entitlements built around current emissions have been created on the basis of a most unjust principle and there is spectacular absence of protection given to the rights of the future generations living in the developing countries.[37]

Going Beyond Kyoto to Stabilize CO_2

The cut down in the emission of Carbon Dioxide to the atmosphere as agreed to by the industrialized rich in the Kyoto treaty is like a drop in the ocean. It shows their lukewarm response to the magnitude of the crisis and the threats that global warming will pose to humanity in future. They seem to have ignored the wake up warning given by IPCC. Even if global annual emission of Carbon Dioxide, iron fossil fuel burning air stabilized at present levels, a near doubling of pre-industrial atmospheric concentrations would still occur by 2100, which would probably result in the onset of climate change. To avert this threat, it further suggested that global emissions be reduced by 60% by 2050 and stabilized thereafter. But the current government policies and business practices are driving emissions in exactly opposite direction. It also predicated a 70% increase in global emissions by 2025. This increase will likely trigger climate catastrophe for millions of people in low-lying coastal regions around the world. [38]

In order to have a safe atmosphere permitting a fair share of access to the global atmosphere as a waste dump to all the nations, Westing suggested a more radical step. According to him, "to achieve the goal of safe atmospheric carbon dioxide levels will require overall reductions of the order of 50% present world wide emission levels, that is, to the levels of about the year 1965. [39]

The level of CO_2 emissions to which the rich industrialized countries agreed to climb down, is far below the suggested the levels and appears to be too inadequate to combat the spectre of global warming.

The United States all along opposed the idea of a strong climate treaty setting a very high target, on the ground that it would impact its economy.[40] But studies show that with a very minimal impact on the economy, greenhouse gases can be reduced through sensible policies and international cooperation. On the best case scenario they predict stimulated economic growth.[41]

Such a goal, through expensive is achievable without insurmountable social disruptions. [42] The kind of response and address needed to combat the crisis, the Kyoto meet failed to win- now from the rich industrialized North, who are, being the biggest polluters, expected to set the target. This means, to achieve the goal, a gradual through not immediate overhaul of its pattern of economy and development has to take place simultaneously with digging out alternatives to Cope with the situation. The core position peremptorily occupied by the U.S. and its allies in the world economic structure with the developing world plummeting to the periphery coupled with its paradigm of development based on combustion of fossil fuel technology and industrialization, being accepted as a universal model of development, hence increasingly redounded to the economic bonanza of the North. The predominant role that the U.S. and its allies play in the world economy may remain fundamentally central to the success of any climate treaty in future, which poses a very high target for these countries for reduction of CO_2 emissions. This remains the million-dollar question whether the U.S. and its allies are in a position to overcome this kind of limitation and impact that the treaty will be having on their economy.

A study by Electric Power Research Institute, an industry R & D organization, estimates that after discounting to present value, the cost to U.S. economy of cutting CO_2 emissions by 20% would be US $800 billion to US $3.6 million.[43] Attainment of a higher target than this would add much more to this. The industrial lobby often used to rely on those scientific predictions, which say that global warming is uncertain.

This is the kind of pressure tactics put on the government, to which as it is alleged, the U.S. government caves in. Industry supporters of the U.S. policy point out that if the uncertainties are great, so too are the consequences of misjudgment. If it transpires that the planet is not experiencing a significant climate change, they argue, the money wasted will run into billions of dollars. The U.S. based Global Climate Coalition (GCC), founded in 1989 with American Petroleum Institute, Shell Oil, Exxon, General Motors and more than 40 other corporations as members, is the biggest, and most powerful of these corporate think tanks. Since 1994, it has spent more than US $1 million annually to downplay the threat of global warming and climate change. The Information Council for the Environment (ICE), another US-based corporate coalition, was formed in 1991. Comprising the National Coal Associations, the Western Fuels Association and Edison Electrical Institute, ICE launched a US $500,000 advertising campaign roping in Patrick Michaels, a leading scientist from the University of Virginia's Department of Environmental services propagating global warming as a myth not a fact. To create public opinion in their favour, in September 1997, US automobile manufacturers and oil companies launched a US $13 million advertisement blitz convincing the public that a strong climate treaty would result in spiraling price rise and would benefit the poor in the South and the U.S. consumers were to foot the bill. [44] In short, politics intervenes in interpretations of science and policy to address climate change.

Putting a price tag on greenhouse gas (GHG) emissions and putting them on the market will not work. Nor will allowing countries to reach their emission targets by planting trees or using other biological carbon traps like wetlands, farmlands and pasturelands. The reason ignored by the architects of the Kyoto Protocol, is simply the overwhelming uncertainly involved in these methods. With poor data and a poor understanding of how GHGs move between the air, soil, plants, animals and water, it will be impossible to police whether countries have actually reduced their emissions. A study released in August 2000 by the International Institute for Applied Systems Analysis (IIASA), Austria, titled *Full Carbon Account for Russia*, reveals how the protocol is an open invitation to cheat by reporting unreal success in reducing GHGs.

Article 3.3 of the protocol allows industrialized countries to use sinks to meet their emission reduction commitments through afforestation, reforestation and deforestation (ARD) activities. Article 3.4 provides for the possibility of meeting reduction commitments through activities 'additional' to ARD, such as sustainable forest management or adopting farming methods that increase uptake of carbon dioxide by agricultural soils. But these two articles make the Kyoto Protocol impossible to verify, says IIASA. Scientists understanding of carbon movements even on a gross level is fraught with large uncertainly which makes fine calculation such as those needed to verify the protocol virtually impossible. For instance, on the global level, as much as 25 percent of atmospheric Carbon Dioxide remains unaccounted for in the known terrestrial and oceanic sinks.[45]

Yet, uncertainly in reporting carbon movements is an issue that has been largely ignored by the Intergovernmental Panel on Climate Change (IPCC), which actually advocates 'partial accounting'. IPCC argues that in order to implement the protocol, countries need not account for all source and traps of carbon, but can restrict themselves to carbon stock changes since 1990 in lands designated as sinks under the protocol. Partial carbon accounting is restricted to emission from fossil fuel combustion and cement production, as opposed to a more comprehensive exercise of full carbon accounting.

A May 2000 report of IPCC, on 'land use, change and forestry' (LULUCF) mentions various sources of uncertainly but does not define uncertainty and does not provide a way to verify results in the face of this uncertainly. It suggests that countries should learn to eliminate uncertainty over time through a process of trial and error in practice; countries would construct a tool to tell them which direction their emission changes goes but not whether the goal is verifiable.

Uncertainty in Carbon Accounting

IIASA carried out a full carbon accounting for Russia to see whether the accounts add up by the end of the day. A full carbon accounting was done for 1990, the base year of the protocol and for 2010, based on three alternative economic growth paths, generating different carbon emissions. IIASA monitored even those changes in the biosphere, which are not taken into consideration under the protocol. Their study includes all stages of carbon cycle including carbon trapped or released by soils, flora, decomposing organic matter even considering carbon carried by river waters, which becomes, sediment in the sea.

The study goes into great detail to identify interactions between carbon and land, water, air, animals and plants. For instance, IIASA identified 15 different types of soil with different carbon respiration profiles, and calculated mean temperatures that precipitate or decrease respiration. The study found that the emission intensity varies to a great extent depending on soil type and area temperatures with emissions increasing as temperature and humidity increase.

For instance, the steppe zone emits the most carbon in Russia- it occupies 9 percent of the total soil area in the country, but accounts for almost 17 percent of carbon emissions from soil. The tundra zone, on the other hand, has a lower number of biologically active days due to colder weather. Though it occupies 16 percent of Russia's soil surface, it generates only 11 percent of carbon through soil respiration.[46] There is also a large variation in the rate at which carbon accumulates in the soil, depending on the productivity of vegetation, physical and biological conditions in the soil and past history of disturbances. Some scientists go far as to say that no country can present a convincing estimate of carbon content in soils, whereas milder views are that the uncertainty range for carbon content in U.S. agricultural soils, for instance, is plus or minus 40 percent. [47]

Accounting Carbon Contents of Forests

Calculating the exact carbon content of forests presents its own hurdles. An area for potential mistakes is in converting volume of forest into mass of wood and then converting mass of wood into carbon content. Or simply, defining a forest and its boundaries, or insufficient remote sensing data to decide forest densities, or telling 'like' plots from 'unlike' plots. A forest's carbon balance is a delicate equilibrium between the activities of respiration and photosynthesis, and small changes can turn a forest from carbon sink to a source. For instance, a study of 15 European mountain ecosystems found vast differences between their forest carbon balance.[48] High latitude forests show more volatile carbon balances than low latitude forests. Old high latitude forests tend to change from absorbing carbon to releasing carbon during mild winters. In total, forests varied from being net sources to being net sinks. For its study, IIASA classified forests by climatic zones, tree species and age of trees. Forest growth was classified into crown wood, foliage, roots and shrubs. Disturbances such as fires or pests were also taken into account.

Assessing fossil fuel emissions is also fraught with crippling amounts of uncertainty. One of the major sources of uncertainty is related to unmonitored losses during extraction, transportation and storage. For instance, long and aging pipelines may have caused one-half to two-third of annual methane emissions from the gas industry in early 1990s. The total figure of uncertainty in Russian fugitive methane emissions from oil and gas activity is as high as plus or minus 30-40 percent.[49]

IIASA found that in Russia, soil respiration is the largest source of carbon, followed by emissions from the energy sector, animal respiration, and disturbances such as fires, harvests and pests. Meanwhile, primarily forests, followed by grasslands and shrubs, agriculture and wetlands absorb carbon. This full carbon account is complemented by expert assessments of uncertainty for all categories of sinks and sources identified by the study. It was found that Russia emitted 527 million tonnes of Carbon (mtC) into the atmosphere in 1990. But once uncertainty added to this number, emissions for 1990 are anywhere within the range of 155 and 1209 mtC. [50]

With such a large range of uncertainty in emissions, a small decrease such as the 5 percent called for by the protocol is practically invisible. It is impossible to know whether Russia carries out a decrease of 100 million tonnes when the calculation has an error margin of 682 mtC. The stifling uncertainty seems to occur for all nations- for example, another project that developed full carbon accounting for Austria showed the same problems of verification of carbon movements. The findings are not better for Norway, where uncertainty of GHG emissions is as high as plus or minus 20 percent.

Cheating in Carbon Emissions

The uncertainty of whether a tonne of reduced emission claimed by a country trying to meet its Kyoto target is really a tonne or just 700 kg can bring the Kyoto Protocol to its knees. Cheating can range from doing nothing to prevent losses in mining, transportation and storage of fossil fuel to falsifying reports of forestry projects claiming to absorb carbon dioxide, relying on poor measurements, ignoring leakage from biological sinks and many other cases, which will be impossible to monitor. If the architects of Kyoto ignore the risks of uncertainty and allow land management, forestry and other biological sink projects to claim credits; cheating or suspicions of cheating will gain ground and will kill the momentum for an effective global policy to arrest climate change.

Any system that removes carbon dioxide from the atmosphere is a 'carbon sink'. The oceans and terrestrial ecosystems like vegetation and soils are the two known 'natural' sinks. The processes of photosynthesis, respiration and decomposition control their role in the carbon cycle. Over the past 150 years, oceans and terrestrial ecosystems have absorbed about 60 percent of Carbon Dioxide emissions caused by human activities.[51]

Plants remove carbon dioxide from the atmosphere via photosynthesis, a process where sunlight facilitates conversion of Carbon Dioxide and water into glucose and oxygen. Trees rapidly absorb carbon dioxide during growth and as they reach maturity, the rate of absorption stabilizes. A mature oak can contain about 3 tonnes of carbon and a hectare of plantation forest can hold around 200 tonnes of carbon. [52] The complementary process of respiration, which helps plants to derive energy by breaking down organic compounds, releases carbon dioxide back into atmosphere. Carbon dioxide is also returned to the atmosphere when plants decay, burn or are cut. Soils get their carbon content from plant decay, burn or are cut. Soils get their carbon content from plants and store vast amounts of it as compared to plants and forests.

In the ocean, phytoplanktons, which are microscopic plants, convert Carbon Dioxide into organic carbon through photosynthesis. This carbon is stored in the deep ocean when microorganism and other higher life forms that consume them die and settle down at the bottom. However, the uptake by oceanic sinks is limited by the quantity of Carbon Dioxide present in seawater and the slow rate of mixing between water from the surface and deep water. The transfer of carbon deep down into the oceans is important as it is stored for relatively longer periods.

What is LULUCF?

Human activities of 'land use, land use change and forestry' (LULUCF) increase or decrease the amount of Carbon Dioxide absorbed by terrestrial sinks. 'Land use' refers to the sum total of activities undertaken on a certain land area- including grazing and timber extraction, which release carbon trapped in terrestrial sinks, and conservation efforts, which lead to increased Carbon Dioxide sequestration.

Clearing forests for agricultural use, conversion of grassland to cropland and abandoning cropland or pastureland qualify as 'land use' change activities. From 1850 to 1998, land use change led to an emission of about 134 billion tonnes of Carbon (gtC) into the atmosphere. This represents a share of 33 percent of the total emissions in this period due to fossil fuel burning and cement production, and land use change.[53] 'Forestry', meanwhile, includes wide range of activities like planting, and tending of growing trees, pest control, fire management, wildlife protection and production of non-time-products.

How does the Kyoto Protocol deal with LULUCF?

Kyoto Protocol has two articles relating to land use, land use change and forestry activities. Article 3.3 of the protocol allows countries to get credits for reducing Carbon Dioxide concentrations through land use change and forestry activities that are a result of direct actions. Only afforestation, reforestation and deforestation (ARD) activities undertaken since 1990 are eligible under this article. Consequent changes produced in the quantity of carbon present in a system should be measured in each commitment period and should be verifiable.

Article 3.4 discusses changes in content of carbon in terrestrial sinks caused by human induced land-use change and forestry activities, and activities in agricultural soil. Possible examples in this category are forests management, grazing land and crop management. The activities considered here should be additional to those mentioned in the article 3.3. This article does not have a list of eligible activities and advises countries to take a decision on this. A consensus on which activities are to be considered and how they should be included is yet to emerge. This decision is in the second and subsequent commitment periods. A country can claim credit for such an activity in the first commitment period (2008-2012) provided the activity has taken place since 1990.

In addition, a decision on the eligibility of LULUCF projects under article12, on the Clean Development Mechanism (CDM), and article 6, Investment (JI) is yet to be taken. The issue of allowing industrialized countries to buy credits for LULUCF activities under CDM is likely to be particularly contentious.

What are the Problems with LULUCF?

A report released by Intergovernmental Panel on Climate Change (IPCC) at the twelfth meeting of subsidiary bodies highlighted several scientific uncertainties surrounding the definition of terms related to the LULUCF activities.

What is a Forest?

Article 3.3 of the Kyoto Protocol can be implemented only after consensus is reached among countries on the exact of a forest. Most forest definitions are based on a minimum 'canopy cover', but the IPCC report on LULUCF says a common figure for canopy cover for forest in various regions is insufficient. If a forest was defined as a mass of trees with a canopy cover of say 70 percent then areas with sparse vegetation would not be considered forests. They could be cleared without any accounting for the resulting Carbon Dioxide emissions. Similarly, a very low threshold of, say, 10 percent allows dense forests to be heavily degraded without the particular activity qualifying as deforestation. Alternatively, the forests may be enhanced without the actions being considered as reforestation. The IPCC report suggests that bio-specific definitions be adopted, like a low canopy covers for savannas and high canopy cover for moist forests.

Reforestation, meanwhile, is commonly defined as planting of trees on land that has just been harvested. Here too, controversy arises if the definition for deforestation does not include harvesting. Then countries will be able to use the amount of Carbon Dioxide sequestered due to regeneration towards fulfilling Kyoto commitments. However, in such conditions corresponding emissions due to harvesting will go unaccounted for.

The implementation of article 3.4 requires accurate definitions for 'additional' (to ARD activities) land use change and forestry (LUCF) activities and activities that improve sequestration by agricultural soils. When an additional LUCF activity is interpreted broadly, the net effect of all practices such as reduced tillage and irrigation in cropland management, in a specific area is considered to measure carbon content. A narrow definition, on the other hand, means various practices undertaken on an area of land are taken individually to calculate the net change in the quantity of stored carbon. The way an activity is defined has implications in terms of separating naturally occurring changes from those due to human actions. A narrow definition can help in identifying the causes of decrease or increase in carbon content.

Direct or Indirect

A difficult condition attached to ARD activities is that these should be 'direct' in nature. IPCC explains this by saying that the closer in time and space the activity is to impact, the more direct it is. The reasons for engaging in a particular activity would also help in determining how direct it is. 'Indirect' effects would include climate change phenomenon like EI Nino cycles, and Carbon Dioxide 'fertilization' (where higher concentration of carbon dioxide in the atmosphere leads to plants absorbing more of it through photosynthesis). Such effects would significantly affect Carbon Dioxide sequestration during the commitment period of five years as prescribed by the protocol. Terrestrial ecosystems sequester an average of 2.2 gtC per year through natural regeneration and such indirect effects. IPCC warns that if countries are allowed to receive credits for even 50 percent of sinks from these factors, they will be able to meet their Kyoto commitments without lifting a finger.[54]

However, given the present availability of scientific tools, separating direct effects from indirect ones will be very difficult, if not impossible. Existing methods cannot precisely determine either the total or incremental amounts of Carbon Dioxide absorbed due to indirect effects like carbon dioxide fertilization. At a project level, this may only be possible when sequestration in a land area under the LULUCF project is compared with an area where no project is carried out.

Human Induced

LULUCF activities must also qualify as 'human induced', calling for yet another precise definition that distinguishes 'human induced' effects from natural effects. Factors such as natural cycles of disturbance and recovery from fires, pests and diseases could lead to significant changes over the five-year commitment period of the Kyoto Protocol. Sometimes these natural incidents may drive human decisions to undertake a LULUCF activity. When a forest devastated by floods, with no sCoPe for regeneration, is converted into a cropland, the activity cannot necessarily be called human induced – more so when emissions from these natural disturbances are not counted but the subsequent sequestration is considered. Equally confounding is the fact that human actions may contribute towards natural occurrences, like fires and pest infestations. Management practices may specify that certain fires be allowed to burn for ecological reasons.

Techniques are available to measure the changes in carbon content, but attributing a given change to a particular cause is difficult. Even the most direct measurements on small areas cannot distinguish between intentional and natural causes for this change. Narrow definitions facilitate this separation of human induced activities from natural activities. Comparison between managed and unmanaged lands may help in quantifying changes occurring due to factors that are not natural, but even this technique may be expensive when applied over large areas.

No Permanent Fix

Another problem with including LULUCF activities is that they tend not to be permanent. While reducing fossil fuel consumption provides a long-term solution to the problem of global warming, sequestered Carbon Dioxide can easily be released back to the atmosphere by fires, pests, encroachments, or even climatic variations like drought or storms.

The IPCC report suggests that establishing projects in different areas may reduce damages, as geographical separation will prevent fires, pests, and diseases from spreading from one project area to another. Ensuring accounting of reductions even if it happened due to natural reasons, will help in fixing liability on a country in case the project is disrupted. Projects may be assigned a minimum lifetime or limited credits may be issued in view of the risks, However, such measures help only to a limited extent as the stored carbon may eventually be emitted[55].

Leak Proof

A LULUCF project may indirectly lead to Carbon Dioxide emissions outside the project's geographical limits. Since these emissions may not be taken into account, such spillover effects are called leaks. For instance, a forest management activity that restricts the amount of land available for agriculture purposes or logging may compel local communities to clear forest elsewhere leading to Carbon dioxide emissions. It is necessary to include such emissions, which do not fall within the confines of project area, in calculations of changes in carbon dioxide levels. However, it is a daunting and often impossible, task to anticipate these impacts and attribute them to a particular project.

Cost Versus Uncertainty

Measuring changes in the quantity of carbon in plants and soils involves a compromise between precision and investment. Sample land areas are considered to assess variations in stored carbon. The greater is the number of samples, the more precise is the estimate. However, the more the number of samples, the greater is the cost incurred by countries undertaking the project.

Countries need to make substantial investment in human resources, technology and infrastructure to implement measurement methods. Additionally, carrying out such measurements on a regular basis, as required by the protocol, will entail high operational expenses. Most industrialized countries have, at least, a part of the infrastructure, like well-equipped laboratories, accurate maps for the types and vegetation, and trained personnel, in place. Even then the incremental cost to perform these measurements regularly on a national scale may be substantial and particularly taxing for developing countries. For instance, Australia is investing US $5 million annually to upgrade its existing system. Developing countries, with less resources, will be expected to establish similar systems when it is their turn to undertake emission reductions[56].

Moreover, the report points out that the effect of climate change on the sequestration potential of sinks is also uncertain. Forests could behave very differently with increasing concentrations of Carbon Dioxide in the atmosphere. Scientists feel that with rising temperature sinks may absorb lesser amounts of Carbon Dioxide.

The rising concentrations of Carbon Dioxide in the atmosphere and the rise in temperature may eventually turn sinks into sources in a fourth decade. As concentration increases, plants soak more Carbon Dioxide through photosynthesis; this process is called Carbon Dioxide fertilization. Respiration process, on the other hand, releases carbon dioxide. Scientists project that fertilization may start to diminish at higher concentrations while respiration increases with rising temperature. Therefore, the overall capacity to fix carbon sink becomes a source. The IPCC report mentions that the global sink is likely to decline from its current level of approximately 2gtC per year and becomes a source within a few decades.[57]

A parallel hypothesis suggests that the present sink itself may be a temporary consequence of Carbon Dioxide fertilization. Respiratory losses may eventually overtake removal by fertilization and convert sinks into sources.[58]

Should Developing Countries Support LULUCF Activities under CDM?

According to the IPCC, there is a large potential for LULUCF activities in developing countries, particularly for additional activities (like forest and cropland management). In fact, the entire industrialized country reduction commitment of around 700 million tonnes of carbon by 2010 can be met from a additional activities in developing countries alone. LULUCF activities under sinks would provide some of the cost-effective mitigation opportunities.

On the one hand, the annual deforestation rate in developing countries of around 15million hectares (mha) since 1980 is likely to increase, at least for the next 10-30 years. To stop this trend by slowing deforestation as well as enhancing afforestation in the already degraded lands, developing countries need technological developments and transfer, appropriate policies, programmes and funding. Therefore, some scientists are of the view that the developing world should use every opportunity for forest conservation, sustainable forestry and reforestation, including CDM.[59]

Including LULUCF projects under CDM is also one way of ensuring that CDM funds reach the indigenous communities and do not just go into the pockets of the industry. Agro forestry based agricultural development is a traditional practice in many developing countries, offering opportunities to provide benefits to rural societies. In India, for instance, more than 70 percent people live in rural areas and rely mostly on forest for their basic biomass needs, such as cattle feed, fuelwood food and shelter. Establishment and management of village woodlots for fuel wood and fibre, intercropping systems (mixture of tree, agronomic and horticulture crops), and shelter belts or windbreaks are ways to combine improved food production, harvestable wood by the local poor, and carbon sequestration through the forestry component, all within the same system. There are suggestions that establishment of one hectare of agro forestry in the tropics could offset deforestation of 5-10 hectares (ha), for meeting local needs. Such systems may store up to 50 tonnes of carbon per hectare (tC/ha).[60]

In addition, sustainable bioenergy plantations could offer an alternative to fossil fuels. Plantations on 40 mega hectares (Mha) of degraded land in India could produce 160 million tonnes (mt) of biomass per year after 8 successive years of plantation as replacement for fossil fuels. They thus have the potential to reduce total carbon emission of about 1.75 billion tonnes (gt), 3.86 gt and 8.07 gt in the next 25 years, 50 years and 100 years respectively.[61]

But, on the other hand, there is the fear that the race for credits will overpower the immediate concerns of developing countries of improving the quality of life of the rural poor. Many indigenous groups in the developing world have opposed the inclusion of sinks in CDM out of fear that industries will start viewing forests as gigantic carbon sponges, rather than the source of livelihood for the poor. Fast-growing monoculture plantation could replace bio-diverse forests, which provide a wide range of services to poor communities. Old-growth forests could be cut to make way for these plantations.

This is indeed a genuine fear, which is already coming true as industry starts grabbing land for carbon sequestration. India has already seen several attempts on part of the paper and pulp industry to grab so called 'degraded' land, which nevertheless provides a range of services to the poor. The industry has tried to buy this land from the government for commercial plantations that the communities will not be allowed to access.

The Kyoto Protocol had a short-term focus. But any reasonable trajectory of emissions in the future ought to show a rise for same decades and a rapid decline late in the century. There are several reasons as outlined by Thomas C. Schelling[62] First, the technologies needed to drastically reduce fossil fuel consumption through alternative energy sources, greater energy efficiency, and sequestration of Carbon Dioxide or its removal from fuel are not developed.

Second, it is economical to use durable equipment until it is due for replacement; early scrapping is wasteful. Thirdly, the richer countries will almost certainly have higher incomes in the future and be better able to afford drastic changes in energy use. Finally, the economic trajectory for emission over the coming century will differ substantially among the developed countries. Any reasonable rationing scheme should contemplate a time line of at least a century not a few decades. But no possible consensus exists on how much total emission should be allowed for the coming century. In short, the Kyoto Protocol's exclusive focus on the short term neglected the crucial importance of expanding worldwide research and development of technologies to make severe reduction feasible later in the century.

The provision of emission trading is perfectionist and impractical. The problem with trading regimes is that initial quotas are negotiated to reflect what each nation can reasonably be expected to reduce. Any country that is tempted to sell part of an emission quota will realize that the regime is continually subject to renegotiation, so selling any excess is tantamount to admitting it got a generous allotment the last time around. It then sets itself up for stiffer negotiation most time. The proper approach is not a trading system but a financial contribution from the rich countries to an institution that would help finance energy efficient and decarbonized technologies in the developing world.[63]

In contrast with other regimes, what is found in the case of Kyoto Protocol is that commitments were made not to action but to result that were to be measured after a decade or more. This approach has disadvantages. An obvious one is that no one can tell, until close to the target date, which nations are on course to meet their goals.

Uncertainty remains embedded to the Kyoto protocol about how much Carbon Dioxide can be absorbed into various natural sinks- oceans and forests – or sequestered underground or deep in the ocean. IPCC has never proposed what concentration of greenhouse gases would constitute unacceptable damage.[64]

Future of the Treaty Shrouded in Uncertainty

The Kyoto climate treaty seems to be shrouded in uncertainty, as the US could not ratify the treaty on the pretext that India, China and other developing nations did not participate meaningfully in the quantitative emission-reduction commitment programmes, which are so far exempt from such commitments under the treaty. To keep up anti-treaty rumbling alive in the US, Denver-based Western Fuels Association has been financing papers by some scientists who propose that" having more Carbon Dioxide in the atmosphere will be good not bad". This attitude has been reflected in the American Congress.[65]

The U.S. Senators signed the Byrd-Hagel Resolution, which stated that the Senate would not ratify any treaty to reduce emissions until there was meaningful participation from key developing countries. This is a major stumbling block to the ongoing negotiation on climate change. The International Conference on climate change in Buenos Aires saw the developing countries ranged against the U.S. which was trying to impose greenhouse gas reduction targets on them. The U.S. also managed to win over developing countries such as Argentina to its clean development mechanism programmes. The developing countries accused the developed countries of non-performance and the developed countries accused the developing countries of non-participation. A shift was perceptible in the position of the EU away from the U.S. An emerging alliance between EU and G-77 was marked when Dominique Voynet, French Minister for environmental affairs took up cudgels for the G-77 position against voluntary commitment and for a principle of convergence. Given that, under US law an ungratified treaty can remain pending indefinitely, the fate of the treaty hangs in uncertainty. Only strong world public opinion and pressures both from the South, the EU and other countries may bind the US to its commitments agreed to in Kyoto.

The North's advocating of an equity principle on the issue of management of the atmosphere is very much opposed by the South. This will be major stumbling block to future negotiation, unless and until the North provides leadership to the whole world by unilaterally reducing emission of Carbon Dioxide, which encourage other nations to follow suit. According to a U.S. study, if equity was adopted as the guiding principle for managing the atmosphere, the industrialized countries had exhausted their quota of Carbon Dioxide by 1986. Morally, they ought to stop all carbon dioxide emissions right away.[66]

To achieve the goal of equity in controlling Carbon Dioxide emissions will require the apportionment to each of the 169 nations of a permissible maximum release. Such apportionment will have to be based on national area not on population, wealth or past national arrogation. Total land area on earth within national boundaries excluding Antarctica is 133 million square kilometers. One carbon dioxide release chit for each of these square kilometers will have to be created, each one permitting the discharge of 133 millionth of the total permissible amount. Each nation will then be awarded the number of such one-square-kilometer chits corresponding to the size of its national territory. Since many developing nations would not yet be making use of their chits, they may lease temporarily their unused chits to the developed nations who have already gone beyond their permissible chits while building up their industrial and transportation bases.[67] The money earned this way can be harnessed for exploring alternative models of development by the South countries.

Kyoto Alternative Strategy of the United States

US new climate policy in total rejection of Kyoto protocol and the need for capping total GHG emissions, calls for a cut in GHG intensity by 17.5 percent over the next 10 years. The policy announced by President George W. Bush at National Oceanic and Atmospheric Administration on 14 February 2002 will actually cause emissions to increase by about

30 percent over 1990 levels in 2010 contrary to the Kyoto commitments that it had to bring down its emissions to seven percent below 1990 emission levels. Between 1990 and 2000 though GHG intensity fell by about 17 percent, the emissions increased by 14.7 percent. With GDP increase projected to be almost the same as in the 1990s, the emissions will increase by about 14 percent even as GHG intensity declines by 17.5 percent. Among other measures power plant emissions of sulphur dioxide, nitrogen oxides and mercury will be cut by about 70 percent. However, no such reductions are proposed for Carbon Dioxide. The U.S. policy and actions are being guided more by the politics of fuel economy than the wider issue of CO_2 regulation. The U.S. Kyoto alternative strategy has become worthless as far as its effectiveness in reducing total GHG emissions or even lowering their growth are concerned.[68]

After six years of obfuscation and denial, the United States now insists that we find ways to block some of the sunlight reaching the earth. This means launching either mirrors or clouds of small particles into the atmosphere. In a recent U.S. memo to the Intergovernmental Panel on Climate Change, it describes modifying solar radiance as important insurance against the threat of climate change. A more accurate description might be important insurance against the need to cut emissions. A group of nuclear weapons scientists at the Lawrence Livermore laboratory in Calfornia, apparently bored of experimenting with only one kind of mass death, have proposed launching into the atmosphere a million tonnes of tiny aluminium balloons filled with hydrogen every year. One unfortunate deleterious side effect would be to eliminate the ozone layer.

Another proposal from a scientist at the National Centre for Atmospheric Research in Boulder, Colorado, suggests spraying billions of tonnes of sea-water into the air. Regrettably, the production of small salt particles, while generating obscuring mists, could cause droughts in the countries downwind.

Another scheme would inject sulphate particles into the stratosphere. It is perhaps less dangerous than the others but still carries a risk of causing changes in rainfall patterns. As for flipping a giant mirror into the orbit, the necessary technologies are probably century away. All these fixes appear more expensive than cutting the amount of energy we consume. None reduces the concentration of Carbon Dioxide in the atmosphere, which threatens to acidify the oceans, with grave consequences for the food chain. The demand that money and research diverted into these quixotic solutions is another indication that President Bush's avowed conversion to the cause of cutting emissions is illusory[69].

In his State of the Union address in the third week of January 2007, he spoke of the serious challenge of global climate change and announced that he was raising the Government's mandatory target for alternative transport fuels fivefold. This is wonderful news for the grain barrons of the Red states, who will grow the maize and rapeseed that will be turned into biofuel. It is a catastrophe for everyone else. An analysis by the Sarasin Bank published in 2006 found that until a new generation of vegetable fuels made from straw or wood, is developed, " the present limit for the environmentally and socially responsible use of biofuels is roughly 5 percent of current petrol and diesel consumption in the EU and U.S." Now President Bush proposes to raise the proportion to 24 per cent by 2017. Already, though the rich world has replaced just a fraction of 1 per cent of its transport fuels, the U.N. Food and Agriculture Organization reports that using crops to feed cars has raised world food prices, with serious consequences for the poor. Biofuels fall into the same category as atmospheric smoke and mirrors- a means of avoiding difficult decisions[70].

Equal Per Capita Entitlements

In order to maintain equity, the Centre for Science and Environment (CSE) has devised 'equal per capita entitlements' which could be built on the following premises: The emissions absorbed annually by the global atmospheric sinks could be distributed equally amongst all the people of the world thus providing each person with an equal entitlement.[71] A long long-term per emission convergence target could be identified and each person could be given that as an entitlement. On the basis of the latest scientific data about the imminence of threats of global warming, this target could go up and down.

Future atmospheric concentration targets for different greenhouse gases could be agreed upon keeping in mind that the targeted concentration does not threaten to seriously destabilize the global climate, and then the global emissions budget that would allow humanity to reach that concentration target, could be equally distributed among all nations on the basis of equal per capita entitlements. Once, such a concentration and convergence strategy is accepted the national entitlements can be phased in towards a convergence point of equal per capita entitlements over successive commitment periods. At the same time, the targeted atmospheric concentration could be kept subject to review based on latest scientific information available.

According to them, the convergence principle towards a just, equitable and sustainable norm can be the only rational principle those who have higher emission can come down to the norm and those who have lower emission can climb up to the norm. On the grounds of economic efficiency that the developing countries provide the opportunity to reduce emissions more cheaply than the industrialized countries, international cooperation sought from developing countries to combat climate change cannot be said as based on just and equitable principles.

US withdrawal from Kyoto Protocol

Soon after assumption office, US President George W. Bush reneged on a campaign pledge to curb emissions from coal-powered generating plants. He then unveiled his administration's energy plan which is basically a short cut to climate hell. As seen recently in the Hague and Bonn Conference of Parties to the climate change convention, the US withdrew from the rest of the world community working desperately to begin to address the climate crisis. Stabilizing the climate requires global emission reduction of 60 to 80 percent. This will require a far more radical approach than is embodied in the current draft protocol. Against this backdrop, the Kyoto Protocol falls far short of its goal of climate stabilization.[72] According to Prof. Adil Nazam, the net result arrived at the Hague and Bonn conferences with the US shadow falling indelibly large on Japan and EU who acted as its proxies, is that the Kyoto Protocol is now even more (or rather less) of a paper victory than earlier. But more than that, it represents a wasted opportunity. Given that the largest polluter is no longer part of the signatories and the provision of more loopholes for use of sinks and hot air trades, the protocol will now do even less than it was originally going to do in terms of reducing actual emissions or concentrations.[73]

Per Capita the Only Way

Support from unexpected quarters came as a welcome surprise for developing countries such as India, which have demanded that international climate change negotiations be based on the principle of equity. A report released by the UK's Royal Commissions on Environmental Pollution (RCEP) in June 2000 said that an effective, enduring and equitable climate agreement will require greenhouse gas (GHG) emission quotas to be allocated to nations on a simple equal per capita basis.

The UK government is expected to respond in writing in the form of a commentary on the report, an explanation of how existing policies and programmes can be reconciled with it and what new policies- if any- the government is considering in light of the report. So far, the UK has held a position of indifference towards the South's demand to calculate

GHG emissions on a per capita basis as each human being has an equal entitlement to the atmosphere.

As a system of per capita entitlements cannot enter into force immediately, the report proposes 'contraction and convergence'. "Initially shares are 'as is', that is, approximately proportional to each country's income", explains Aubrey Meyer from the London-based Global Commons Institute, a leading advocate of this approach." Over an agreed future period of years however, all countries will converge on the same allocation per head of their population in a base year to be agreed.[74]

This means the quotas of industrialized countries fall year by year, while those of developing countries rise until all nations emit equal amounts of GHG per head (convergence). The RCEP report proposes 2050 as the year for convergence. It will also be cut-off date for national populations, that is, further changes in a country's population will not affect its emission quota.

From then on, after convergence has been achieved, the quotas of all nations would decline together at the same rate (contraction). According to the report, commentators on climate diplomacy have identified contraction and convergence as the leading contender among the various proposals for allocating emission quotas to nations in the long run. To make an agreement based on per capita allocation quotas more feasible, the report supports emission trading between nations. Countries that wish to emit GHG in excess of their respective quotas would be able to purchase unused quotas at prices that incline other countries to emit less than their quotas.

There are other similarities between the conclusions of the RECP report and the Indian position. The commission also recommends that the international community adopt an upper limit for Carbon Dioxide concentration in the atmosphere of 550 parts per million (ppm). Current global concentration levels stand at 368 ppm. A target of 550 ppm is not entirely safe because, according to international scientific community, even stabilization at 450 ppm would result in a temperature rise of 0.7°C and a corresponding 10-65 centimeter rise in sea level.

If the contraction and convergence approach and the target of 550 ppm are adopted, the UK's Carbon Dioxide emissions will have to be reduced by almost 60 percent from their current level by mid-century, and by almost 80 percent by 2100. Though Carbon Dioxide emissions are falling at the moment in the UK, they are expected to rise again as all but one of its existing nuclear power stations will close by 2025. Nuclear power is the main source of carbon-free energy in the country at present.

To achieve the 60 percent reduction target, RECP recommends reductions in energy demand and a large deployment of renewable energy sources, both of which can be achieved partly through the introduction of a carbon tax. Revenues from this tax could be used to fund other measures of cutting down emissions, such as subsidies and tax relief for energy efficiency improvements and research and development of renewable technologies. Future sources of renewable energy for the UK, says the report, could include energy harnessed from waves, undersea turbines powered by the tidal waves, wind energy and even solar energy.[75]

The Third Proposal

In June 2001, Jan Pronk, president of the failed sixth Conference of Parties (COP-6) to the United Nations Framework Convention on Climate Change (UNFCCC), came out with a third proposal in an attempt to resolve 'crunch' issues plaguing the negotiations. He had first come out with a compromise proposal on November 23,2000 at CoP-6, and had revised it again in April 2001. The third proposal, described below, formed the basis of negotiation at the resumed session of CoP-6 in July 2001[76].

Funding and Technology Transfer

Pronk suggested setting up an adaptation fund, financed by taking two percent off the credits generated from projects under the Clean Development Mechanism (CDM). Proceeds from other flexibility mechanism, which involve only industrialized countries, are exempt from such a contribution. He also suggested a special climate change fund to finance technology transfer, capacity building and economic diversification.

Pronk proposed that total annual contributions towards climate change activities should rise to U.S. $1 billion by 2005. Over a certain number of years, the amount to be used towards adaptation programmes should increase to about half of this billion. The commitment is not binding, and unlike the earlier proposal of November 23,2000, failure to contribute does not result in a levy being imposed on Joint Implementation (JI) projects and emission trading.[77]

Trading Cheap

The third proposal said climate change policies and measure should seek to reduce inequalities in per capita emissions of developing and industrialized countries. Therefore, industrialized countries must meet their emission reduction targets chiefly through domestic action undertaken since 1990. No quantitative limit was suggested.

The proposal reiterated the Kyoto Protocol provision allows industrialized countries to bank surplus credits from the first commitment period to meet reduction commitments in the second commitment period. Industrialized countries can therefore buy emission reduction credits at throwaway prices from developing countries and bank them for future use. Developing countries, having sold the cheap options, will be forced to adopt expensive methods when it is their turn to take on emission reductions in the future.

The proposal did not put forward a 'positive list' of projects allowed under CDM. Host developing countries were left to decide what projects were in line with their sustainable development objectives and national priorities. However, the proposal called on countries to refrain from using nuclear projects under JI and CDM. Simplified procedures would apply to specific small-scale projects to facilitate equitable regional distribution of CDM projects. The proposal emphasized that use of public funding in CDM projects should not result in diversion of official development assistance (ODA).

Pronk's proposal directed each industrialized country to keep at least 90 percent of its assigned amount, or five times its greenhouse gas (GHG) emissions in the most recently reviewed inventory, whichever is lower, as reserve. The earlier proposal did not give a choice and asked countries to keep a fixed amount of 70 per cent of their assigned amount as reserve.

The North's Trash Cans

The compromise proposal gave a complex formula to calculate credits from land use, land use change and forestry activities under article 3.3 and 3.4. The Kyoto Protocol had included under article 3.3 the use of afforestation, reforestation and deforestation activities to absorb Carbon Dioxide and gain credits, whereas activities under article 3.4 were still open for future agreements. The proposal considered forest, cropland and grazing land management and vegetation as eligible activities under article 3.4. It offers a three tier method to calculate credits arising from these activities in the commitment period (2008-2012).

In the first tier, countries could fully count Carbon Dioxide removed from the atmosphere through forest management, up to the level of net Carbon Dioxide emissions (if more Carbon Dioxide is released due to deforestation, than is absorbed by afforestation and reforestation) reported under article 3.3. But annual credits in this tier were capped at 8.2 million tonnes of carbon (mtC). The limit could be extended to 13 mtC, if the country meets certain criteria for energy efficiency, forest cover and population density.

Beyond the credits obtained under the first tier, countries could get only 15 percent credits for forest management. A discount factor of 85 per cent was applied to exclude Carbon Dioxide absorbed due to natural reasons, or due to effects of practices employed before 1990. This was done as article 3.4 calls for separating Carbon Dioxide absorbed due to human induced activities from absorption occurring naturally. For example, only forest regeneration done intentionally could be considered, and not regeneration without human assistance. Similarly, Carbon Dioxide absorption attributed to activities undertaken before 1990 was not considered for credits in the first commitment period. It is extremely difficult to attribute causes to the change observed in carbon content and separate human induced effects from natural; and pre-1990 from post 1990 emissions. In order to overcome this problem, the proposal took refuge in an arbitrary discount factor. Strangely, no discounting was applied to the first tier; even though those credits were no less riddled with such problems. In the third tier, full credits were given for agricultural management (cropland, grazing land management and revegetation). The proposal further imposed an overall limit on the sum total of LULUCF credits gained from the second and third tier, CDM projects, and JI projects. For a country required to reduce its GHG emission below base year levels, the total should not be more than 50 percent of the country's Kyoto target. For a country allowed to maintain its base year emission level, or increase its emissions over the base year level, the total should not be more than 2.5 per cent of the country's emissions in the base year. These limits did not apply to credits and debits under article 3.3. The proposal allowed afforestation and reforestation projects under CDM, while forest, grazing and cropland management were excluded.

Ensuing Compliance

The proposal put forward a compliance committee with enforcement and facilitative branches. The facilitative branch would provide advice to countries and assist them in implementing the protocol.

The enforcement branch, which could prescribe legally binding consequences was to assess industrialized countries' compliance with their reduction commitments and their obligation to put in place a national accounting system to estimate GHG emissions and their absorption by sinks at least by 2007. It would decide a country's eligibility to participate in the flexibility mechanisms. If an industrialized country failed to meet these commitments, the enforcement branch could deduct a certain number of tonnes from the defaulting country's assigned amount in the next commitment period. The number of tonnes deducted would depend on the value by which the country exceeds its assigned amount. As the value increases, the deduction becomes higher.

It asks the defaulting country to submit an action plan detailing measures it proposes to take to meet its commitments. The enforcement branch would review and assess the feasibility of this plan, and suspend the defaulting country's ability to sell assigned amount units under the emission trading mechanism.

Pronk proposed that emission reduction targets of industrialized countries in the second commitment period must be decided before 2008 and discussion on the issue should start by 2006.

Constraints

Quite not awake to the danger emanating from global warming, the industrialized rich countries have not attested the goal of global equity in controlling Carbon Dioxide emission as suggested above. Nor have they of their own accord reduced Carbon Dioxide by 50% to the 1965 level. The pressures from NGOs, South countries and above all, the public opinion of the world, may be said as being not enough to bind the North to the South for a target as envisaged above. In spite of the treaty and conventions signed among countries, the fundamental problems remain unsolved. Firstly, the inordinate life style and unrestricted consumption pattern of the North is symbiotically related to Carbon Dioxide emission and pattern of development. Are the western people ready to have a cut in their standard of living by asking their governments to reduce CO_2 emission to the atmosphere?

Secondly, the very cause of this nuisance to the environment is the ethnocentrism of western paradigm of development based on extraction of fossil fuels and industrialization. The problem of climate change puts a challenge to the prevailing pattern of development. To what extent alternative paradigms conducive to the environment, the life pattern and style and future generation's right to exist, are explored, will determine the nature of the future course of action on the part of the nations of the world to combat the crisis

Modern civilization based on oil prepared to go to war to secure oil supplies, but is it prepared to face the situation, if the world's oil wells suddenly dry up? Are multinational corporations and energy sectors dominating the modern state in opposition to change their structure, power and style of functioning?

According to Pad Green, the solution to climate change requires a revolution to the way society produces and uses energy and in the way that people's needs for mobility are met. However, fighting climate change is not just a question of replacing fossil fuels with wind power, biomass, solar or other technologies. As he said, energy renewable technology had environmental impacts, particularly land use (wind power and biomass) and mineral extraction and toxic chemicals.[78]

Thirdly, the question who pollutes the atmosphere needs to be axed, remains central to the solution of the crisis. Whether the rich North shoulders the responsibility to unilaterally reduce CO_2 to an exemplary extent and accept equity in the share of the access to the atmosphere, always remains center stage. The treaties fail to answer the key question about equity, rights of access to resources and the role of multinational corporations in energy sector with the government lacking the political will to tame them. The developing countries always tried to put equity on the global climate change agenda but failed to find to it US and its allies' acceptability. Recently, the U.S. came out with its own version of equity fashioned by none other than the Pew Centre on Global Climate Change, established in 1998 by the Pew Foundation, which in turn was set up by an oil company called Sun. The Pew Report is called Equity and Global Climate Change: The Complex Elements of Global Fairness.[79] This report has little in the common with what the South demands. According to the report, in line with the 'polluter pays principle' responsibility would include not only who emitted in the past, but also who will emit in the future. That means, meaningful participation from South is stressed on. Secondly, if one country can more cheaply reduce emissions than another, and then perhaps it should be asked to do so. Thirdly, all nations should work to the best of their abilities- or with the help of other countries to reduce emissions. So, the report pushes the US argument that developed countries should be allowed to meet their entire commitments under the Kyoto protocol through emission trading without any action at home. This report rejects per capita argument claiming that it creates perverse incentives for population growth.

Fourthly, the countries of the South always trying to oppose any move by the North to bring them within the ambit of climate change treaty, also contribute to the emission of CO_2 to the atmosphere through much less than the North countries do. In their aspiration to attain the level of development the Western countries have reached, the South may add significantly to the emission. Their argument that since they are far behind the western level of industrial development, they should be exonerated from the responsibility to reduce CO_2 emission at their home front sounds logical. Rather than imitating the western pattern of development, the South countries should develop and define development in their own civilization context. The South countries cannot keep pace with the level of development the North has reached unless and until the people in the North change their luxurious and inordinate life style. So the success of the climate change treaty is very much contingent on the kind of revolution needed in ethnocentrism of western consumption pattern, life style and economic thinking.

Fifthly, another stumbling block to rich industrialized countries like the U.S. not agreeing to a major or required reduction of Carbon Dioxide emission to the atmosphere is the great uncertainty associated with climate science. Being a horizon science not a core science[80] global climate change is certainly inter- disciplinary. Since the World's climate involves a continually changing and highly complex set of relations, climate research faces severe obstacles in linking theory and empirical evidence. Climate science relies heavily on elaborate computer models. The most sophisticated of these models are General Circulation Models (GCMs) whose accuracy is tested by comparing their predictions of past global climate with historical data. Modelled predictions of future climate change are based upon incorporating current and projected greenhouse gas emissions into GCMs. "Because of gaps in the data (e.g. cloud behaviour, methane and emissions are to agricultural practices and ability of oceans to absorb CO_2) GCMs should be viewed as heuristic devices rather than reality maps."[81] Since uncertainty is greatest for horizon science like climate change, its perceived legitimacy in policy making should be especially low.[82] That's why this uncertainty is taken advantage of by the rich industrialized North being influenced by their respective industrial lobby to back out from their required commitments to reduction of CO_2. Commitments to reduce green house gas emissions to atmosphere to the level as required for the rich industrialized North, can be binding on these countries only when climate science becomes more certain and accurate.

Lastly, in terms of local pollution and climate effects, the exponential increase in the consumption of fossil fuels contributed to a worldwide quadrupling of greenhouse gas emissions between 1950 and 1995. This corresponds to a quadrupling of Gross World Products during the side period.[83] So this link between economic growth and prosperity, and emissions would be harder to break. If the industrial countries subscribe to the belief that prosperity can be decoupled from greenhouse gas emissions, then governments' willingness to reduce their emissions represents a kind of leap of faith.[84] The only apparent reason for taking that leap is a strong scientific consensus, accuracy and certainty that burning fossil fuels will cause global climate change. Then prosperity will be defined not in terms of fossil fuel-based economic growth, but in terms of what constitutes good for society and recognizes the rights of the future generation's right to atmosphere.

The measures and principles adopted for the implementation of Kyoto protocol, raise different dilemmas as how to distribute the burden reducing emissions among different countries. There is expression of disappointment with the lack of convincing progress in the Kyoto protocol in the five year since Rio World Summit. Instead of consensus of opinion, divergent views and division acted as deterrent to achieve convincing result. All the countries to live in harmony with nature should come forward with a determination to prevent man made changes in climate by rendering their free and unbiased support for the meaningful operation of the Kyoto protocol.

References

1. Mark Storey, "Kyoto Beyond Issues and options in the Global Response to Climate Change", Stockholm Swedishs EPA, Naturvidsverket, 15 November 2002.
2. Antonio G.M.Lavina, "Working paper Globalization, Environment and Communities", from Kyoto to Marrakesh, "Global Climate Politics and Local Communities", World Resource Institute, Washington DC., 31st August 2002.
3. CRS-National Council for Science and the Environment, Washington DC, 1725 K Street, Suete 212, 2006.
4. Sue Fletcher; "Summary of the Kyoto Protocol", CRS report - The Library of Congress Global Climate Change: Washington, 1998, p. 2.
5. Climate Change Convention, The Framework for Action; - Bonn, Germany Climate Change Secretariat (UNFCCC), 26 June 2003.
6. "The Kyoto Protocol in the Convention;" Climate Change Secretariat: Bonn Germany, 1999.
7. The Kyoto Protocol to the Framework Convention on Climate Change (UNFCCC) Bonn, Climate Change Secretariat: Germany, 20 June 2003.
8. *Ibid*, pp. 16-17.
9. *Ibid*, pp. 16-17.
10. Yamin E; "Operational and Institutional Changes in the Issues and Options", The Clean Development Mechanism, United Nations Development Programme, New York–1998.
11. Zhang. Z.X. "Estimating the size of the Potential Markets for all three Flexibility Mechanisms under the Kyoto Protocol", find report prepared by the Asian Development Bank 1999.
12. Vrolijk. C, "The Potential size of Clean Development Mechanism", Presented at the second International Conference Remerging Market for Emissions Trading: London, 26-27 April 1999.
13. Treyur M.C. Kosloff L.H., "The 1997 Kyoto Protocol, what does it mean for project based Climate Mitigation and Adaptation Strategies", 3(1), 1 (1998)

14. James M. Lindsay - "Global Warming Heats up", CFR Publication Brooking Review fall, 2001.

15. Mark Storey, *op.cit*, S-106-48.

16. Grab. Et.al., 2001.

17. Climate Change Convention, FCCC : UN, *op.cit,* 2003.

18. What is Happening to our Climate, Why the USA rejected Kyoto, Climate Change Information Sheets: Chatalaina, UN, Environment programme, 1999. p. 5.

19. In March 2002 the Australian Environment Minister Dr. David Kemp: stated that US policy programme appeals to Australia because it "clearly recognize the importance of taking action in a way that does not undermine the economies of countries like the US or Australia". Environmental New Service March 2002.The Australian Government has since announced that it will not ratify Kyoto.

20. Mark Storey, *op.cit*, S-106-98.

21. Heroshi Ohki, Combating Global Warming: A Common task for man kind, Chairman Special Committee Global Environmental Issues (L.D.P) and Chairman Special Committee for Okinawa and Northern Territories, (H.R) 2001, p. 13.

22. Mark Storey, *op.cit.*

23. *Ibid.*

24. Energy information Administration "Impact of Kyoto Protocol as US Energy Market and Economy Activity: Washington-October 1988.

25. European Environment Agency greenhouse Gas Emission Trends and Projection in Europe - 2004, p. 3.

26. Tito Brago, "Spain Lags in Kyoto Protocol Compliance", Terramerica, Feb-25, 2005.

27. Bartsch Ulrich and Benito Miller, "Fossil Fuels in a Changing Climate Impacts of Kyoto Protocol and Developing Country Participation: Oxford, Oxford University Press, 2000.

28. Joseph Kay, World Specialist website; www.wsws.Org. News and Analysis, North America, 23 February - 2002. Visited on line.

29. Grubb. Michael and Joanna Depledge, "The Seven Myths of Kyoto" A View Point, Climate Policy, Vol-1, no-2, 2001.

30. http:/www.GlobRfox.com/cacc/politics. html.

31. Houghton. J.T.C.T. Jenkinns eds. "Climate Change", The IPCC Scientific Assessment : World Meteorological Organization/United Nations Environment Programme; Inter governmental panel as climate change.

32. Joseph. H. Bial. "Public Choice Issue in International Collective Action," Global Warming Regulation : University of Chicago Law School, Chicago, 2nd November 2000.

33. Carlisie, "On site report from Buenos Aires Global Warming Talks," issues-2 www. National Center org. National Center for Public Policy Research, Washington D.C. November 10, 1988.

34. Campaign Against Climate Change, *op.cit,* p. 3.

35. Jinyue Yan; "Global Warming and Climate Change Mitigation Technologies", Sweden, Royal Institute of Technology.

36. Tarnoff. C. "Global Climate Change" The role of US Foreign Assistance, Report for the Congress Congressional Research Service, The Library of Congress, Washington, 21 November 1997.

37. Anil Agarwal, Down to Earth Vol.6, no.15, 31 December 1997.

38. Pad Green, "Where Climate Change Meets Sustainable Societies", Third World Resurgence, No. 87/88, November/ December 1997, p. 6.

39. Arthur H. Westing, "The atmosphere as a common heritage of humankind: its role in environmental security", scientific World (London), 34(4): 5-6, 1990, p. 207.

40. Robert Repetto and D. Austin, The Costs of Climate Protection: A Guide for the Perplexed, WRI, June 1997.

41. Devra Davis, "Worldwide Deaths Ralated to Fossil Fuel Consumption", The Lancet, 8November 1997; James Mackenzie, Climate protection and the National Interest: The Links Among Climate Change, Air Pollution and Energy Security, WRI, October, 1997.

42. A.B. Lovins and L.H. Lovins, F.Krause and W.Bach, Least-cost energy: Solving the CO2 Problem (Andover, Mass: Brick House, 1981), pp. 184.

43. Peter Nulty, "Global Warming that We Know", Fortune, April 1990. Anil Agarwal and Sunita Narain, Towards a Green World (New Delhi, Centre for Science and Environment, 1992), p. 39.

44. Anil Agarwal, et al in Down to Earth, *op.cit.*, pp. 31-32. see also David L. Levy and Daniel Egan,"Capital Contests:National and Transnational Channels of Corporate Influence on the Climate Change Negotiations", politics and society Vol. 26, no. 3, September 1998, pp. 337-361.

45. Sten Nilson et al, Full Carbon Account Russia, Interim Report,"International Institute Applied Systems Analysis, Luxemburg, http://www.iiasa.ac.at/Admin/Pub/Document/ir-oo-021.pdf, as viewed on August 18, 2001.

46. *Ibid.*

47. *Ibid.*

48. *Ibid.*

49. *Ibid.*

50. *Ibid.*

51. Intergovernmental Panel on Climate Change, Land use, Land Use Change and Forestry, Summary for Policy Makers, 2000, Bonn, p. 25.

52. Janet N Abramouitz, Taking A Stand: Cultivating A New Relationship With The World's Forests, World watch paper 140, World watch Institute, Washington DC, April 1998, p. 14.
53. Intergovernmental Panel on Climate Change, Land Use Change and Forestry, 2000, *op.cit.,* p. 25.
54. *Ibid.*
55. *Ibid.*
56. *Ibid.*
57. *Ibid.*
58. N.H. Ravindranath, Sinking Feeling, India Institute of Science, Bangalore, 2000, mimeo.
59. P.S. Ramakrishnan, Reaction to Intergovernmental Panel on Climate Change's Land Use, Land Use Change and Forestry, JNU, New Delhi, mimeo.
60. Murari Lal, Forests As Carbon Sinks in India, Indian Institute of Technology, Delhi,mimeo.
61. Thomas C. Schelling, What Makes greenhouse Sense? Foreign Affairs Vol.8, No.3, May/June 2002, p. 4.
62. *Ibid,* p. 8.
63. *Ibid,* p. 4.
64. Nikhat Jamel Qaiyum, Climate Change, Meddling Albright, Global environmental Governance, Supplement to Down to Earth, May 31, 1998, pp. 63-64.
65. Kirk Smith, *op.cit.*
66. Arthur H. Westing, *op.cit.*
67. Benito Muller, Creative Accounting, Down to Earth Vol. 10, No. 31, 31 March 2002, pp. 52-53.
68. Anil Agarwal and Sunita Narain, Sharing the Air, Centre for Science and Environment, Down to Earth Vol. 17, no.8, August 15, 1998, pp. 37-42.
69. George Manbiot, " Bush's change on climate is illusory", The Guardian, quoted in Hindu, 31 January, 2007.
70. *Ibid.*
71. Anil Agarwal and Sunita Narain, " Sharing the Air", Centre for Science and Environment, Down to Earth, n. 68.
72. Aubrey Meyer, Director, Global Commons Institute, London, July 20, quoted in Anil Agarwal et al, Global Environmental Negotiations 2, *op.cit.,* p. 237.
73. Energy The Changing Climate, Royal Commission on Environmental pollution, Stationery Office Limited, London, pp. 1-9.
74. Quoted in Anil Agarwal et al., Global Environmental Negotiation 2, *op.cit.,* p. 260.

75. Down to Earth Vol. 10, no. 11, October 31, 2001, p. 52.
76. Quoted inibid., p. 51.
77. Down to Earth Vol.9, no. 15, 31 December 2000, pp. 27-29.
78. Pad Green, *op.cit*.
79. Anju Sharma, 'Shades of Equity' Down to Earth Vol. 7, no. 19, February 28, 1997, pp. 56-57.
80. Eugune A Rose and Thomas Dietz, "climate Change and Society: Speculation, Construction and Scientific Investigation", International Studies Review Vol. 2, no. 2, summer 2000, p. 131.
81. Aant Elzinga, "From Arrhenius to Megascience", Ambio Vol. 26, 1997, p. 99.
82. Karen T. Liftin, "Environment, Wealth and Authority: Global Climate Change and Emerging Modes of Legitimation", International Studies Review Vol. 2, no. 2, summer 2000, p. 131.
83. Lester Brown, Nicholas Lessen and Hal Kane, Vital Signs 1995 (New York: Norton 1995).
84. Karen Litfin, *op.cit*., p. 142.

6

International Cooperation and Constraints

After industrial revolution, a large number of scientists believe that human activities are affecting the heat/energy exchange balance between the Earth, the atmosphere and space, which has increased atmospheric concentrations of Carbon Dioxide (CO_2) inducing global climate change often termed "global warming. Human activities such as burning of fossil fuels, industrial production, deforestation and certain land use practices are increasing atmospheric concentrations of Carbon Dioxide (CO_2) along with other trace gases such as Chlorofluorocarbons (CFCs) Methane (CH_4), Nitrous oxide (N_2O) HydroFlurocarbons (HFCS) Perflurocarbons (PFCS) and Sulferhexafloride (SF_6) may be leading to changes in the chemical composites and physical dynamics of Earth's atmosphere, over the past 100 years. If these gases continue to accumulate in the atmosphere at current rates, most scientists and environmentalists expect global warming would occur through manifestation of Earth's natural heat trapping "greenhouse effect". The effects of extreme weather experienced over the past two decades are attributable to global warming. However, the warming trend at the surface appears to be continuing. A warmer climate would probably have far reaching adverse consequences on human health, agriculture and food production, ecosystems, forests, water resources, marine and coastal resources, sea level and weather patterns and living styles, depending upon climate responses. The damages and devastations caused by global warming year to year in different parts of the world, have already drawn the attention to the possible catastrophic impacts in future. Although causal relationship between projected global climate trends and records showing warm and severe weather events have not been firmly established, attention has been focussed on possible extremes of climate change and need for better understanding of climate processes to improve international response to combat global warming.

Co-operation among countries to reduce greenhouse gas emissions (GHG) is crucial to tackle global warming problem. Climate change is a global problem requiring action from the entire world community.

community. Countries from around the world are working together to share technologies, experience, resources and talent to lower net greenhouse gas emissions and reduce the threat of global climate change. As countries continue to grow and develop, international co-operation becomes increasingly important as the global community searches for ways to meet the climate challenge efficiently and effectively. The key to successful co-operation is finding activities that will help all countries achieve their economic, environmental and developmental goals in a climate friendly manner.[1]

Challenges and emergence of global environmental problems impose an unprecedented requirement for international co-operation. Obviously, a global dimension of climate change problem requires equally global solutions. The chosen way the international community has pursued hovers on how and possibly jointly to respond to the expected future common threats through negotiation and action plans to combat global warming.

The history of mankind's dealing with the global environment problems in the present century has been marked by both co-operation and confrontation at different times and in different contexts between scientific finding and related political economic interests. To be effective and successful, this process requires a large-scale net working among the countries, both developed and developing and international organizations to combat climate change. UN sponsored group of experts has concluded that world wide temperatures will rise 2 degrees within 35 years and more by 6 degrees by the end of the next century if nothing is done to combat global warming.[2]

As scientific data on global warming have gradually accumulated, research institutions and political leaders around the world have recognized that effective measures to tackle global climate change to prevent such warming trends must be developed through international co-operation. Measures to combat global warming must be based upon scientific analysis and knowledge of GHG emissions and reduction potentials to deepen mutual understanding. It is necessary for all countries to further dialogue and interaction to strengthen their combined efforts against climate change.

The dangerous consequences associated with global warming phenomenon are well imagined but it is a matter of deep concern that no appropriate step to curb these effects has been taken so far, large scale deforestation, waste deposits to rivers and seas, burning chemicals and fossil fuels etc have created and still accelerating innumerable problems to nature and environment only careless activities of human beings can be held responsible for the dangerous marks of the global warming. In order to make discussions and negotiations processes of future challenges to successfully mitigate the adverse impacts of global warming it is necessary to broaden the efforts of entire international community.

Climate change has already resulted in global warming the most serious environmental problem that the world faces. The threats in terms of the expected impacts on ecosystems, livelihoods, human health and food security are enormous. While the biggest contributors to global warming are the industrialized countries due to the increasing greenhouse gas emissions, the greatest impacts of climate change will be felt first and seriously by the poorest of under developing countries of the world. These poor and impoverished communities depend greatly on climate conditions and natural resources for their daily survival and sustenance as they do not have resources to adapt to change global warming will bring. The challenge of climate change resulting in global warming and aggravating the problems with all its consequences requires prompt and early international response to address climate change. International response to climate change started from late 1950s by a number of American Scientists in the Mauna Loa Mountains of Hawaii who studied on the density of CO_2 in the atmosphere. However, since the beginning of 1970s, the concern received increasing attention throughout the world. The modern era of international environmental law with its associated political awareness toward transboundary environmental deterioration began with the Stockholm Conference of 1972. The international community and various specialized organizations of the United Nations also showed concern with the issue of global environment. In 1972, a full-fledged environmental conference was held in Stockholm, called the conference on the human environment. The Stockholm conference was determined to raise awareness about the potential of humans to cause environmental damage. The tone of the conference was divisive and differences surfaced among developed and developing nations. One area of agreement was the founding of the United Nations Environmental Program (UNEP). UNEP began to provide leadership and encourage partnerships in caring for the environment by inspiring, informing and enabling nations and people to improve their quality of life without compromising that of future generations."

In 1973, the governing council of UNEP called for a Global Environmental Monitoring Systems (GEMS) to begin collecting the data for Earth science and technology. It was proposed that the new efforts aid other international monitoring programs. In 1974 a second environmental conference was held in Nairobi, Kenya called the intergovernmental meeting on monitoring. It asked GEMS to trade environmental changes affecting the oceans and the world's agricultural supply. Nairobi also become the Head-quarters of the UN Environment programm.[3] Around 1977, the prospect of global climate change evoke international response relating to policy discussion about what is to be done against potential climate change.

The world climate conference sponsored by the WMO (World Meteorological Organization) in 1979 looked at the question from a different angle and issued a statement in the same year that vividly pointed out the possible dangers posed to the welfare of mankind by global warming. The next major step jointly taken by World Meteorological Organization (WMO), United Nations Environment Programme (UNEP) and the International Council of Scientific Unions (ICSU) was the first world climate conference of 1979, attended by scientists from a wide range of disciplines. The conference emphasized upon the need for more scientific research into causes and effects of climate change. The world climate programme was established to further scientific knowledge on climate change. Global climate change received greater support in form of a member of inter governmental conferences which were held in the late 1980's and early 1990's. Realizing the potential threat of the global warming, scientists and environmentalists all over the world expressed their grave concern and called for immediate global action.

The climate change conferences identified the accumulated increase of human generated greenhouse gases in the atmosphere and encouraged the countries to cooperate internationally so as to prevent their deleterious effects on the global climate. A series of international conferences were held until mid 1980s, but failed to achieve substantial progress on the issue of anthropogenic climate change. The issue of climate change steadily acquired response from the different conferences to adopt strategies to counter fossil impacts of global warming. A meeting in Toronto in 1988 hosted by the Canadian government was one such major gathering for this purpose and paved the way in the same year for the creation of the IPCC (Inter Governmental Panel on Climate Change). The task of inter governmental panel was to assess the scientific and technical information about climate change in a comprehensive, transparent, and objective manner. The reports of the panel are made possible through the co-operation of the scientific community around the world. Hundreds of scientists and technical experts were involved in preparing assessment reports and internally thousands more were engaged to provide objective peer review. The panel made a concreted effort to include the broadest possible range of valid scientific opinions. Indeed, the credibility of panel in the eyes of both governments and scientific community rests on its commitment to providing the most upto date balanced scientific information that truly reflects the state of human understanding of climate change science. Since its inception, the IPCC has played a leading role in the world in the compilation and analysis of scientific data to support the control of global warming. The year 1988 was also a turning point in world politics. Reflecting the progress of detente between the United States and the former Soviet Union, Soviet leaders became more active in UN related organizations and showed more interest in environmental issues. Both General Secretary, Gorbachev and Foreign Minister Shevardnadze impressed diplomatic circles by delivering speeches at the UN General Assembly in 1988 in which they stressed the importance of the global environment coupled with substantial arm reductions. Western countries viewed these speeches as reflective of a basic change in the position of the former Soviet Government, which uptill had been indifferent to international co-operation on the global environment.[4]

The most important goal of the intergovernmental panel on climate change (IPCC) is to synthesize the state of climate change science in a way that adheres to the highest standard of scientific credibility. The IPCC sought for consensus among its members about its key findings as well as those areas that require further research. The IPCC gathers data on global climate and issues three assessment reports and fourth assessment report is released in 2007.

After the establishment IPCC in 1989, the United Nations General Assembly taking more interest fixed June 1992 as the time for international conference on Environment and Development. This conference would be the UN's third on the environment. Brazil agreed to host the meeting. The main topic was the increasing concentrations of greenhouse gases in the atmosphere and what to do about them. Global environmental change issues raised the question of international co-operation and collaboration to overcome the problem associated with them. By setting a date every five years in the future the UN was gave politicians, business leaders and scientists in developed and developing nations time to prepare for better understanding.

In 1990, the first assessment report on climate systems and climate change was released by the intergovernmental panel on climate change. The report outlined the scientific knowledge of how the planetary climate system works, the basis for international negotiations towards a framework convention on climate change. The consensus of the report was that global temperature had been increasing during the last century.

The Second World Climate Conference (SWCC) was convened in Geneva, Switzerland between October 29, November-7, 1990 under the auspices of WMO, UNEP and ICSU. It brought together officials from 137 nations. Political division still prevailed, but in the end delegates agreed to a set of principles. They resolved that climate change was "a common concern of human kind that individual nation had different levels of responsibilities based on their levels of development, that global climate policies must also support sustainable economic and social development." The conference called for development of an international treaty on climate change. A framework would allow a continuing series of talks to assess the changing needs of such treaty.[5]

The United States and the Soviet Union among others however were firmly opposed to making any commitment at that time, especially one that would require legally binding reductions of Carbon Dioxide or other greenhouse gases. The United States argued that such matter would be more appropriately considered under the authority of the UN General Assembly and not the World Meteorological Organization (WMO), and further suggested that interested nations reconvene in negotiations that would address specific regulatory actions to combat global climate change. The United Nations General Assembly created Inter Governmental Negotiating Committee recognizing climate change as a common concern of mankind, as a subsidiary body for framework convention on climate change. The United States offered to host the first International Negotiating Committee (INC) meeting entitled "protection of global climate for present and future generations of mankind." It gave the INC the job of preparing for a ministerial conference on the treaty. The ministers met in Berlin to draft a convention on climate change in time for 1992 summit in Brazil. From 1991-92 the International Negotiating Committee (INC) for a framework convention on climate change held as many as five sessions. The last fifth session was held in New York, 150 nations participated and finalized the draft of the convention after intensive talks among the parties. It was adopted on May, 9 1992 at UN Head quarters in New York City, stating a flexible voluntary response by nations to reduce net atmospheric concentrations of green house gases that would be back bone of the climate convention and was opened for signature by June 1992 at the United Nations Conference on Economic Development (UNCED) in Rio. The United Nations taking further steps by convening its third world climate conference at Rio on environment and economic development, which is known as Rio Earth summit. It supported the principle of the second conference whose goals were to global warming while promoting economic and social development. Developed nations were asked to voluntary rollback their greenhouse gas emissions to 1990 levels by the year 2000. Global efforts towards achieving climate change protection reached a significant mile stone with the adoption of UN Framework Convention on Climate Change (UNFCCC) in 1992 in which United States along with 152 nations agreed to the ultimate objective of stabilization of greenhouse gas concentrations in the atmosphere at a level that would prevent dangerous anthropogenic interference with the climate system. The United States and other highly industrialized countries were committed to implement voluntary measures to limit their emissions of greenhouse gases to 1990 levels by the year 2000.

From Rio to Berlin

Global efforts for mitigation and adaptation strategies for climate change received greater support from the Bush administration, when it declared that United states might not be far from the goal of reducing its net emissions of CO2 to 1990 levels by the year 2000. The leadership of United States generated hope among world communities to take further steps to enhance participation to combat the global climate change.

On June 12, 1992 in the Earth summit in Rio, the United States along with 142 nations of the world signed UN Framework Convention on Climate Change. To combat climate change The United Nations Framework Convention on Climate Change (UNFCCC) contained an action framework by dealing with its causes and responding to its adverse effects that called for the world industrialized countries to stabilize GHG concentrations in the atmosphere. The convention also contained other binding agreements for all signatory parties including developing countries. To combat the global warming the convention suggested to continue the negotiations by means of Conference of the Parties subject to the judgment of the ratifying parties after FCCC's entry into force to pursue subsequent actions. Further more, there was less agreement among the nations to set out future reduction targets and timetable. Division and differences appeared relating to the basic question. While the European community and small island states strongly favoured the establishment of a target and time table for limiting the emissions of greenhouse gases, the United States and oil producing states were against this procedure. To ensure co-operation among the signatories, the United States and United Kingdom brought in the compromise formulation, which is now in Article 4 of the UNFCCC with nonbinding call for an attempt to return to 1990 emissions of carbon dioxide and other greenhouse gases not controlled by Montreal protocol. The UNFCCC was signed by 175 states and the European community at the Rio conference in June 1992.[6]

The UNFCCC specified that developed countries should bear the primary responsibility for reducing greenhouse gases and set out a system of voluntary reduction commitment for these countries along with common monitoring and reporting requirements for all countries. The objective of UNFCCC was to stabilize the density of anthropogenic interference of greenhouse gases in the atmosphere so as to prevent their adverse effects on the global climate. The UNFCCC without binding the developed countries and those with economies in transition commits to reduce their CO_2 emissions to 1990 levels by the year 2000. Inter-governmental consultations continued within the UNFCCC framework to meet and negotiate in preparation for the next steps to combat the climate change. The convention also contains other binding agreements for all the signatory parties including developing countries to its establishment support and administration. Furthermore to strengthen international co-operation to counter global warming similar to the 1985 Viena convention that preceded the Montreal Protocol on protection of Ozone layer, the UNFCCC continued negotiations to prepare ground for the conference of the parties to pursue subsequent actions. The inter governmental negotiating committee in its meeting expressed the views that the convention opened for signature at UNCED represented a scientifically first step toward a proactive stabilization of industrial greenhouse emissions. The meeting of the INC in 1994 indicated that parties from developed countries did not generally feel that commitment would be inadequate to meet the ultimate goal of the convention. This led to a general discussion of the necessary next steps, ranging from strengthening the commitment made in the FCCC to agreement on protocol with target and time tables for emission reduction.[7]

The actions aimed primarily at industrialized countries with the intention of stabilizing their emission of greenhouse gases at 1990 levels by the year 2000 and other responsibilities would be incumbent upon all UNFCCC parties. The parties agreed in general that they would recognize "common but differentiated responsibilities" with greater responsibility of reducing greenhouse gas emissions in the near term on the part of developed industrialized countries, which were listed and identified in Annex-I of the UNFCCC and there after referred to as "Annex-I" countries. On September 8, 1992, then President Bush transmitted the UNFCCC for consent of the US Senate for ratification. The Senate consented to the instrument of ratification on October 7, 1992 with a two-thirds majority. President Bush signed the instrument of ratification on October 13, 1992 and deposited it with the UN Secretary General. According to the terms of ratification of the UNFCCC, having received over 50 countries instrument of ratification it entered into force March 24, 1994. Its ultimate objective is "to achieve" in accordance with the relevant provisions of the convention, stabilization of greenhouse gas concentrations in the atmosphere at a level that would prevent dangerous anthropogenic interference with the climate system. Such a level should be achieved within a time frame sufficient to allow ecosystems to adapt naturally to climate change, to ensure that food production is not threatened and to enable economic development to proceed in a sustainable manner. Article 2 of the UNFCCC enunciates "that the global nature of climate change calls for the widest possible co-operation by all countries and their participation in all effective and appropriate international response in accordance with their common but differentiated responsibilities and respective capabilities and their social and economic conditions. After signing of Rio Earth Summit several steps were taken to binds the signatories. After Rio conference, the first CoP was held in Germany with the deposit of fifty ratification on December 1993 and the convention came into force on March 1994. The Association of Small Island States (AOSIS) and Germany submitted a draft protocol calling for negotiation of a protocol with a target and time table, but the United States and oil producing states were against the protocol. The inter governmental negotiating committee set up by UNFCCC was requested to act as an interim coordinating body on business matters relating to global climate change for the UN Secretary General until the conference of the parties to the convention would be established. The intergovernmental negotiating committee between Rio and Berlin dealt with the second controversial topic regarding the joint implementation project or policy in UNFCCC. The purpose of joint implementation can allow one country to help another for the reduction of greenhouse gas to a lowest possible scale. But some countries and actors especially environmental NGOS expressed seriousness against the use of joint implementation project. It appears to offer market oriented countries the chance to implement emissions control but on the other hand, for the cheapest developing countries and some NGOS Joint Implementation as an effort by the rich countries to avoid making substantive changes. "As Victor and Salt (1994) paraphrase the view of opponents "J1 is a loophole through which [the rich countries] will double count existing flow of aid and international investments." Some developing countries express their views relating to limited acceptance of the joint implementation after two years debate.

The United Nations Framework Convention on Climate Change represented a delicate balancing of many different political and economic interest and many scientific issues between developed and developing countries. The political and economic interest reflected differences among various parties, the anticipated impacts of climate change and the equitable apportionment of responsibility for the costs and causes of climate change. The scientific issues included the relationship between atmospheric gases and the nature, degree and location of anticipated climate impacts.[8]

In the early days of climate process it was customary to characterize the issues of climate change as a North South question. Over the years, however, it has become clear that this is a simplistic understanding of a complex political process. For varying reasons industrialized countries have responded politically in different ways with responses ranging from ardent calls for the North to take the lead in cutting emissions to equivocation in the face of lingering scientific and economic uncertainties. Development process has also not responded politically in the same way to climate change. While there is unanimity among the countries of South that technology and new additional resources must be transferred to them if they are to respond effectively to climate change, there is a debate among developing countries on the extent to which they also should take action and participate in the global effort to mitigate climate change.[9]

The other main question with regard to UNFCCC concern for financial and technology transfer will go a long way in making the global response to climate change. The FCCC commits OECD countries and EU to provide "new and additional financial resources to meet the agreed full costs incurred by developing country parties for national reports and some other activities but not for emission control by developing countries. Some financial transfers have been made but little has been done to transfer the technology. Progress in negotiation on transfer question was slow and dominated by major North-South differences in position. [10]

Although a general North-South and developed-developing country divergence amongst issues and interests can be identified with the North promoting environmental protection priorities and cost effectiveness of the measures and the South developmental priorities and historical responsibility. Alliances have also been formed between countries which do not follow strict North-South divisions but, rather are based on consideration such as vulnerability to sea level rise[11] reliance on fossil fuel production[12] and the potential for developmental opportunities. [13] All of these alliances co-exist with countries promoting the diversity of their interests through more than one group. The combination and permutation of interests and issues represented by the alliances underlay the negotiating process and are carefully balanced with the UNFCCC.

International decisions on climate change will have far reaching and long-term effects on global economics, politics and international law, where many of the issues raised have never been confronted before. From a global perspective, the climate change issue is already a vital component of long-term policy and planning. The approach taken by individual countries to address the problem and the extent of their "involvement in the over reaching decision making framework will largely decide their place in the development of global future. Even though the majority of developing countries are highly vulnerable to the potential effects of a changing global climate, the climate change question has not been fully appreciated by these countries. To begin with, South-the developing world saw climate change as a strictly environmental problem. The diversity and complexity of local socio economic development and environmental challenges obscured the global environmental concerns such as climate change. But increasingly, the issue of climate change should enter the real of development action if sustainable results are to be achieved. In fact climate change unites the problems of development and the environment in that each contains the seeds of solutions for the other. At least this is how many of the experts in developing countries understand the issue.

The UNFCCC conference of the parties met for the first time in Berlin, January in the spring of 1995 and voiced concerns about the adequacy of countries abilities to meet commitments under the convention. These were expressed in a UN Ministerial declaration known as the "Berlin Mandate" which established a two year Analytical and Assessment Phase (AAP) to negotiate a comprehensive menu of actions for countries to choose future options to address climate change, which for them individually, made the best economic and environmental sense.

The Berlin Mandate exempted Non Annex-1 countries from additional binding obligations in keeping with the principle of "common but differentiated responsibilities" established in the UNFCCC - even though collectively the newly industrialized countries were expected to be world's largest emitters of greenhouse gas emissions 15 years hence.[14]

The CoP-1 meeting held in mid 1995 found that the voluntary emissions reductions in the Rio treaty were not working properly. The ministers of 117 national parties in order to combat the climate change adopted Berlin Mandate, a call for new talks containing stronger commitments. The international co-operation appears to be searching ways to meet the challenges created by global climate change. In 1995 the second assessment report of the IPCC conducted that there is discernible human influence on global climate. It concluded that 60% to

80% reduction in Carbon Dioxide emissions would be necessary to stabilize atmospheric concentrations of greenhouse gases. But it is generally found that actions of different countries are not conducive to fulfill the obligations under the so called Berlin Mandate. The challenges created by the global warming requires joint venture, and willing co-operation among the parties should be strengthened to fulfill their commitments under the convention. The Berlin Mandate laid the foundation of international co-operation to meet the challenges created by the climate change with greater potential and certainty. The process of collaboration continued with a view to create awareness among the countries to take further actions against climate change.

Despite urgent warning by scientists about disturbing trends, there has been a further increase in the use of fossil fuels and hence in the level of CO_2 emissions on a worldwide scale (IEA 1994). The rapid growth of world population and the quantitative expansion of world economy is certainly responsible for this trend. In this back ground, the first conference of the climate convention in 1995 to fulfill the hopes was declared a failure. Firstly, the conference did not adopt a protocol and secondly the wording of the Berlin Mandate gave rise to worries that the substance of the protocol to be adopted in two years might not match up to original expectations. On the other hand, there is no denying fact that the Berlin conference by acknowledging the inadequacy of existing commitments and adopting the mandate to draw up a protocol, has taken the next steps for an effective climate protection policy. What is important now is that commitments and targets be upheld further in a determined manner in order that the climate convention becomes a powerful instrument of global climate policy.[15]

From Geneva to Buenos Aires

The process of negotiations among parties continued on various possibilities to strengthen actions to tackle the climate change within the framework of the convention. The Conference of the Parties at Geneva, Switzerland in its meeting reviewed the progress of the Berlin Mandate and indicated to carry out the commitments for stabilization of atmospheric concentrations of greenhouse gases. Observing the second assessment report of the IPCC, it was generally held that the global climate is undergoing changes as a result of human activities, which requires urgent precautionary measures to combat such happenings. The scientific findings of the IPCC was confirmed, and needed world wide co-operation for the successful protection of global climate. As the national communication of Annex-I parties revealed that some of them expressed their inability to meet the emission reduction targets of the convention to 1990 levels by the year 2000. Further, the exemption of developing countries from legal binding commitments under the Berlin Mandate acted as a stumbling block in way of its implementation and progress. The Conference of the Parties put utmost importance upon the Berlin Mandate as well as the scientific findings of IPCC relating to global climate, which required urgent joint actions of all countries to address environmental crisis. The countries with myriad problems with limited financial and technological resources expressed their incapacities to implement the adaptation measures to combat the threats posed by global warming. In the light of development of scientific knowledge and information seeking solutions to the problems of reducing greenhouse gas emissions and enhancing sinks, close co-operation and shared commitment were indispensable. Keeping in view the implementation of Berlin mandate, full support of the developed and developing countries was essential to draft a protocol during the present session before third session of the conference. The phase "common but differentiated responsibilities" has become a touch stone for the international climate equity debate. In the second session of the Conference of the Parties, the developing countries ultimately rejected binding commitments, asserting that the historical responsibility for climate change was not theirs, they have less financial ability to pay for reductions and that they have more urgent priorities for their limited resources. There was divergent views on the implementation of the second Assessment report of the IPCC. While the North has had the luxury of time and resources to achieve prosperity the South needs the time and space to fullfil its developmental needs. Hence, the coordinated efforts to combat the climate change at Geneva fully encompass the ambit of Berlin Mandate in particular. Under the circumstances, to calculate the net gains of taking and complying with international agreement to address global warming seems to be difficult to mobilize and sustain.

The co-operation among the countries to reduce greenhouse emissions is crucial to tackle global warming problem. The impacts of climate change are likely to vary considerably by geographic region and occur over a time scale of decades to centuries. The wide differences among the countries relating to economic development stands as a stumbling block to implement the costs of reducing greenhouse gas emission thereby making it difficult for cooperative efforts to meet the catastrophe of global warming. Keeping in view the recommendation of second Assessment Report of the IPCC the United States accepted the legal binding targets to reduce the GHG concentration and exerted influence over other industrialized countries to do the same, which prompted more than 100 countries to express their willingness to follow their path to combat the global warming Thus, the cooperative attitude of the countries showed the sign of appropriate and timely response to progress to combat the global climate change. If the present trend would continue among the world community any effective and meaningful measure would be taken to reduce atmospheric concentrations of CO_2. Thus, the 2nd conference of the parties at Geneva laid the foundation of collaborative efforts searching for more effective ways to bind to the countries to respond the future challenges in a friendly manner.

The threat of global climate change experienced till date has been aggravating the situation that the warming trend will pose major challenges for the survival of mankind on Earth. Intense negotiation and collaboration continued to find out permanent solutions to the problems associated with global warming. Further, it appears that unless and until the nations of the world come forward to fight with the Mother Nature to lower down the temperature of Earth, which is constantly rising and likely to increasing in future.

How to combat the global warming becomes a common task for mankind. After Geneva conference, the process of negotiation continued with a view to bind the world community through a legal document directed towards achieving agreement to stabilize the worldwide CO_2 emissions.

The accumulation of greenhouse gases in the Earth's atmosphere as a result of human activities causing innumerable hazards, required international co-operation to address the climate change. The process of negotiation continued and took a new dimension with the conclusion of historical Kyoto protocol at the third Conference of the Parties in December 1997. The positive participation of the United States in signing the Kyoto Treaty described as an international legal binding document to meet the biggest environmental challenges created by global warming. The progress made towards reducing greenhouse gas emissions has been significantly reflected in the text of the Kyoto protocol. Application of precautionary principles to reduce uncertainty about the threats from global warming united policy makers regardless of difficulties. The progress achieved towards an effective and meaningful international policy can hardly leave the Kyoto participating nations of their obligations to implement the global climate change policies. For the Kyoto protocol to enter into force, 55 parties including Annex-I parties accounting for at least 55 percent of their total CO_2 emissions in 1990 need to ratify it.[16] By October 1999, only 16 countries had ratified it of which Norway was the only Annex-I country to do so.[17] 126 countries then ratified the treaty on 5 October 2004 culminating with Russia in November 2004. With the ratification by Russia, the essential quorum of ratifying countries has now been reached and the Kyoto protocol came into force on 16 February 2005. Thus, campaign against global climate change gained more and more support from the entire world excepting US to be able to tackle the climate challenge effectively. In the recent years, the focus of many of the world's climate change policy makers and negotiators has been on how far Kyoto protocol as an international agreement meets the ultimate objective of international efforts to reduce the concentration of greenhouse gas emissions. The question of how to design a fair and feasible outcome to ensure that the international effort to reduce green house gas emissions is shared equitably remains perhaps the greatest challenge facing the climate change negotiators. There is a growing sense of urgency that international community must take immediate action to counter global warming. Clinton's attempt to sign the Kyoto protocol was resisted by the Senate on the ground that meaningful commitments from the developing countries must be equally sought. Soon after taking office, the Bush administration rejected the Kyoto protocol citing lack of developing countries' participation and possible harm to the US economy.

Many countries of the world ratified the treaty but the US most powerful nation in the world acted against globally coordinated action. The other major developed countries of the world including Australia following the precedent of the US refused to ratify the treaty. The major developed countries of the world instead of cooperating with the protocol have blocked the effective progress to limit the greenhouse gas emissions. Though US government has not initiated any strong measure to reduce their greenhouse gases, still remains as the world's largest polluter. The coordinated actions to fight against climate change were adversely obstructed by the United States. The policies and actions of the United States act as a deterrent to implement the Kyoto protocol making fissures among the world community to meet the challenge of the climate change.

The framework on climate change and the Kyoto protocol sought for global action to mitigate the threat of climate change. The Buenos Aires conference to ensure combined effort of the world community is needed to bring the US and developing countries into a global agreement. The process of negotiation continued in CoP-4 with a view to making rules for implementation of Kyoto protocol. The process of international talks on the protocol began in the summer 1998 in Bonn to set the agenda for the Buenos Aires conference. Representative from the 150 countries participated to formulate the plans to be followed in CoP-4 to combat the global climate change. Irrespective of sincere efforts, the three major plans on mandatory emission cutbacks failed to achieve the consensus.

In the Buenos Aires conference, the plan of action on Kyoto protocol was approved by the parties who agreed to adopt specific policies for achieving emission reduction goals by the year 2000. Uncertainty about the causes and consequences of global warming greatly shaped the negotiation at the Buenos Aires conference. It was hard to motivate countries to act when no one knows whether the problem is big or small, imminent or distant. The developed countries tried to impose the voluntary reductions of greenhouse gases over the developing countries which was certainly hard to ensure co-operation to address the problems of climate change. The rules of the Kyoto mechanisms like emissions trading compliance, carbon sinks and clear development mechanisms failed to achieve consensus both from the industrialized world and developing countries. US demand for meaningful participation in GHG reduction by the developing countries strongly resisted by the China and India. The attitude of developed countries towards developing world was not cordial and favourable to cooperate for global action. The developing countries were not ready to accept the mandatory emissions reduction targets by postponing their development which would adversely affect their economy. Due to the presence of hostile and conflicting interests among the participant countries, the CoP-4 failed to materialize the agreement on Kyoto mechanisms.

The CoP-4 at Buenos Aires generated signs of hope for combating the threat of global climate change through the coordinated action, but experienced the differences of opinion to achieve consensus in desired direction. The atmosphere was not favourable to resolve dead lock and to ensure co-operation to advance climate change negotiation. The Conference of the Parties in Buenos Aires expected to finalize the remaining unresolved issues in Kyoto protocol to mitigate the potential threat of global warming. However, the complexity and difficulty of finding agreements on these issues proved insurmountable and instead, the parties adopted a two year "Plan of Action" to advance efforts and to devise mechanisms for implementing the Kyoto protocol by 2000.[18]

From Bonn to MarraKesh

The combined efforts among the parties continued with a purpose to reflect on principles to enhance the participation of parties to combat the climate change crisis. The Buenos Aires conference failed to achieve substantial progress to implement the Kyoto protocol, which constituted a basis for effective action to address one of the daunting challenges of the present century. The participant countries at the 5th Conference of the Parties expected to resolve the issues in order to meet the rapid changes in climate endangering life on Earth. The process of negotiation began putting emphasis on reconciliation of the hostile attitude between the United State, European union and the developing countries.

To overcome the deadlock and differences among the parties, there needs to a much greater degree of co-ordination as to avoid the current situation. Coordinated action would help to mange successfully climate change policies to adhere to any agreement on a voluntary basis, which ultimately the CoP-5 failed to stimulate international co-operation and collaboration to overcome the problem associated with the "common but differentiated responsibilities". Thus, the Conference of the Parties at Bonn failed largely to achieve international policy consensus to combat global warming.

The problem of achieving effective and lasting international agreements become hardest after Kyoto protocol brought the negotiation process to a stalemate. The Hague (Netherlands) discussion evolved rapidly into a high level negotiation over the major political issues. The politics of combating global climate change resulted in a major controversy over the Unites States' "proposal to allow credit for carbon "sinks" in forests and agricultural lands, which would satisfy a major portion of the US emission reductions in this way. Disagreement over consequences of non compliance by parties that did not meet their emission reduction targets, continued along with difficulty in resolving how developing countries could obtain financial assistance to deal with adverse effects of climate change and meet their obligations to plan for measuring and possibly reducing greenhouse gas emissions. The CoP-6 brought the diplomatic crisis to light over the difference between the United States and some EU countries notably the Unites Kingdom, the EU countries as a whole led by Denmark and Germany who rejected the compromise proposals. Finally, talks and negotiations collapsed in the

Hague conference. Jan Pronk, President of the CoP-6 suspended the CoP-6 without agreement with expectation that the issue would be taken up again at the second round meeting (termed CoP-6 "bis") to be held in the second half of the July in Bonn, Germany. The CoP-6 could have a turning point for all outstanding decisions concerning the negotiations moving out from the diplomatic deadlock between North and South, developed versus developing countries relating to the flexible mechanisms. The Hague conference instead of securing co-operation and collaboration brought the negotiations to a stalemate and exhibited the attitude of conformation between the parties.

CoP-6 in Bonn

When the CoP-6 negotiation resumed on July 16-27, 2001 in Bonn, Germany little progress had been made on resolving the differences that had produced an impasse in the Hague. However, this meeting took place after president George W. Bush had become the US President, and had rejected the Kyoto Protocol in March, as a result the United States' delegation to this meeting declined to participate in negotiation relating to the protocol and chose to act as observer to that meeting. As the other parties negotiated the key issues, agreement was reached as most of the major political issues to the surprise of most observers were given the low level expectations that preceded the meeting.[19]

The real issue is to develop long-term climate change strategy to ensure international co-operation as soon as possible. For successful climate change negotiations, the North-South co-operation is the essential ingredient for greater international co-operation to combat the problems posed by the changing climate and mitigation of its impacts. The role of the European Union was very essential to promote such co-operation by breaking the diplomatic deadlock and stimulate a new impetus to combat the politics of climate challenge. One of the major achievements of the CoP-6 was the isolation of United States from EU, Canada, Japan, Russia and developing countries who under the leadership of the EU, took a major diplomatic initiative to go ahead without US to make the Kyoto Protocol work and combat global warming, which was a common task for mankind and a formidable challenge of the present century requiring co-operation and effective collective action of all nations. After many days of intensive negotiation in Bonn, ministers of environment succeeded in finding a solution to the political issue on the table and adopted a decision that incorporated this political agreement.[20]

At the Cop-7 meeting in Marrakech, Morocco on October 29-November 10, 2001 negotiators in effect completed the work of the

Buenos Aires Plan of Action, finalizing most of the operational details, and set the stage for nations to ratify the protocol.

The Third Assessment Report of the IPCC highlighted that only a small step has been taken and much remained to be done to combat the threat of the climate change. Effective co-ordination and collective action is essential to meet the adequacy of the commitments under Kyoto and common but differentiated responsibilities of Montreal protocol. The United States delegation continued to act as observers, declined to participate in active negotiations. The other parties continued to express their hope that United State would be reengaged in the process at some point to bring the protocol into force. A target date to bring the protocol into force was put forward - from August to September 2002, on which World Summit on Sustainable Development (WSSD) was to be held in Johannesburg, South Africa but this target was not met.

The political momentum generated at 2nd Bonn conference continued to transform substantial decisions as to the progress in the conference and implementation of the Kyoto protocol. Though United States remained aloof from the negotiations it did not affect the implementation of Kyoto Treaty. The 7th Conference of Parties was remarkable from standpoint of winning the co-operation and collaboration to deal effectively in combating global climate change. The main decisions of the CoP-7 included operational rules for international emission trading among parties to the protocol and for the COM and joint implementation, a compliance regime that outlined consequences for failure to meet emission targets but deferred to the parties to the protocol after it was in force to decide whether these consequences were not legally binding according to procedures for the flexibility mechanisms, and to consider at CoP-8 how to achieve a review of the adequacy of commitments that might move forward in discussion of the developing countries' commitments.[21]

The Europeans then announced their intentions to proceed with ratification of Kyoto protocol, while President Bush indicated his willingness to participate in negotiations of the UNFCCC. Parties at CoP-6, which "resumed" in mid July in Bonn.

The CoP-7 certainly made all round success in adopting important decisions about resolving conflicts created in climate change issues. The willing co-operation of all parties was directed towards coordinated action to combat any eventualities standing in the way of negotiations. The progress that has been made on fashioning a global response to climate change is actually remarkable so far as combined efforts of the world community is concerned.

From New Delhi to Buenos Aires

The theory and research regarding collective action to address problems associated with global climate change indicates that achieved success in controlling externalities comes only when there is a consensus on the aggregate benefits to be gained. Agreements reached under these conditions tend to be self enforcing because it is in the interest of all parties to ensure success. [22]

2002 is a pivotal year for climate change. There is optimism that the Kyoto protocol will come into force thus, bringing the climate process to a new stage. Because in the next meeting of the CoP-8 in October 2002 in New Delhi, issues of major concern to South and to North would command greater attention. This is an opportunity that should not be missed in India; it is likely that the role of the developing countries in responding to climate change would occupy center stage.[23]

The process of negotiations at CoP-8 was effective. Collective action relating to sustainable development and implementation of Kyoto protocol expressed in Delhi Declaration, to which the United States and umbrella groups rendered their support, was one of the major achievements of the conference.

The Delhi declaration was strongly resisted by the EU and some other developing countries. The attitude of the United States seemed to be very constructive in the sense that by supporting Delhi Declaration it agreed to relax commitment of emission reductions for the developing nations. The world climate change politics was largely influenced by the industrialized countries of the North particularly by the United States and EU. The presence of differences of opinion between the United States and the European unions supported by other developing countries made the progress of negotiations from bad to worse in combating global climate change. In Delhi Conference of the Parties, several issues were discussed but failed to achieve consensus to adopt draft decisions. The actions of the United States created reaction and confrontation among the developing nations and European Union to make any development in climate change politics. Thus, climate change politics is profoundly influenced by the developed countries. International collective action continued to regulate the problem of global warming meet in Milan, Italy from 1st December to 12 December 2003. From the very beginning parties expressed their willingness and support to adopt decisions on important environmental issues the world is facing today. The EU highlighted that human activities are the principal cause of global climate change as reflected in the Third assessment report of the IPCC. How to combat the new challenges was one of the major issues before Conference of the Parties at CoP-9. Although the Kyoto protocol has not been entered into force, the ratification of numerous countries shows the sign of effecting progress in dealing with the climate threat by world community. The ongoing process of negotiations aimed at bringing the Kyoto protocol into force remained deadlocked and lack of political will stood in the way of achieving consensus to move ahead in combating climate change.

The CoP-9 demonstrated the two faces in negotiation among the parties to adopt decisions on several issues. At the meeting of the conference of parties to the UNFCCC, attempt was made to consider next steps after the 2008-2012 commitment period but these attempts were encountered from developing countries and some other parties. The CoP-9 reflected the representation of various observer constituencies, environmental NGOS, business and industry groups, local governments, indigenous people's organizations and research and Independent NGOs. Substantial progress in negotiation due to lack of collaborative efforts of the parties necessary to meet the UNFCCC's ultimate objective, could not be achieved.

The announced reluctance of Russia at Milan CoP-9 to undertake ratification of the Kyoto protocol called into question whether or when the protocol might enter into force. Without US participation, the required 55% of baseline emissions of parties would be achieved if Russia does not ratify. The meeting centered on largely technical issues and avoided major substantial declarations. The coordinated effort of the parties highlighted the division between developed and developing countries and the apparent reluctance continued to prove leadership and initiative gap between the negotiators and constituency groups. The politics of global climate change demonstrated the lack of co-operation among the parties on many political and technical issues. Increased uncertainty within countries over the aggregate gains from collective action reduces the livelihood of international co-operation.[24]

The tenth conference of the parties to the framework convention on climate change was held in Buenos Aires in December 2004. The CoP-10 was a significant one for the UNFCCC, in that after completion of a decade, it highlighted its role in responding to climate change and progress achieved thereof. The international cooperative efforts succeeded in implementing the Kyoto protocol with ratification of Russian federation in November 2004. The parties at the Buenos Aires conference agreed to go ahead and determined to complete the unfinished issues relating to future climate change policy. Keeping in view the growing accumulation of greenhouse gases in the atmosphere and the recent report of the UN panel on threats, challenges and changes underlines, the only attempt so far made has been to achieve the globally coordinated action in the form of policies and measures urgently needed to combat the threat of climate change. The Conference of Parties at Buenos Aires excepting the co-operation of the United States reached consensus on adaptation policy on climate change, a timely and appropriate step. Attempts to limit global climate change by mitigating GHG emissions would be futile without relatively broad international participation. Global participation is also supported by a powerful economic argument for cost effectiveness. Poorer countries tend to have less efficient technology and more rapid growth rates for population and for capital income than richer countries do. Consequently, poorer countries are likely to have a comparative advantage in developing and supplying the necessary technical opportunities at least to short to medium term. But to achieve a successful international agreement for GHG emissions abatement, cost effectiveness argument must be supplemented with policies for acceptably distributing mitigation costs across countries as well as over time.[25]

A positive development resulting from the withdrawal of the United States from the Kyoto process is that the big developing countries no longer feel compelled to take a defensive stance in the negotiations. For years the negotiating positions of these countries were greatly influenced by a need to parry efforts by the United States to have them take similar commitments (targets and timetables for emission reductions or limitations) as industrialized countries have. Without the United States the developing courtiers have become more receptive to the idea that their participation in the global efforts would result in favourable outcomes for them, given the complexity of these politics it is remarkable that the process has move forward to the stage where it and without vote taken far in any major political decisions. The big question however, is what to do with the United States, the biggest emitter historically at present of greenhouse gases. By abandoning the negotiating process but without offering an alternative to the Kyoto protocol, the United States has endangered the progress that has been achieved.[26]

From Delhi Conference of the Parties to Buenos Aires the negotiation process succeeded in finding a solution to the many technical and political issues that remained on the table and adopted decisions that incorporated in implementing the Kyoto protocol. The international collective action after intensive negotiation completed many unfinished work on the outstanding technical issues and full agreement on the details of Kyoto protocol was achieved in Buenos Aires. By paving the way for the Kyoto protocol to take effect, the Buenos Aires meeting can be judged to be a success. Providing the necessary resources so that developing countries can actively participate in global efforts to reduce or limit greenhouse gas emissions and begin adaptating to the adverse effects of climate change has been the most important issue for developing countries in the climate negotiations. Successful collective action is most likely when each country perceives a large, positive, expected net benefit for their daily survival and sustenance. The ultimate objective of UNFCCC was how to combat the global climate change which required a unified policy response taking the economic, political social and scientific spokes must be connected to round out the wheel and allow international policy to move forward. If one powerful nation refuses to cooperate, industry lobbies weaken regulations, or an electorate will not approve a treaty, no effective policy can be established.[27]

This is the case to date, the world policy makers are not effectively addressing the problem of global warming. Although there is a growing accumulation of greenhouse gases in the atmosphere and possible effects on global temperatures, the international co-operation and action processes against climate change taken so far have been neglected a lot. The kind of response and co-operation needed to combat the global climate change failed to bind the nations to treaties and conventions agreed to. International co-operation on combating climate change probably led to the root of misunderstanding and conflict between the developed and developing countries to achieve a successful international agreement.

Montreal Meet

The eleventh Conference of the Parties to the Framework Convention on Climate Change COP-II and the conference of the parties serving as the first meeting of the parties to the Kyoto protocol was described as a multi lateral efforts to address climate change.

A successful outcome of international co-operation in Montreal would not only serve to operationalize the Kyoto protocol, it could also send a positive signal around the world about the future of the climate regime beyond the end of the first commitment period in 2012. Stephane Dion, COP/MOP president outlined his key goals which he called the three I's became the standard by which success or failures of the meeting would be judged. According to Dion, delegates needed to "implement" the protocol especially the Marrakesh Accords, and other decisions to make the protocol function effectively, "improve" the operation of the protocol and the convention, and "Innovate" by exploring "operations for future co-operation in a manner that reflects the full range of interests of the convention".

By advocating for a process to consider the future under both the Kyoto protocol and UNFCCC, President Dion sought an outcome that maintained the momentum and integrity of the protocol while also engaging the US and other countries that have not ratified the protocol. Highlighting the progress of the COP-II/MOP-I President Dion declared that we have achieved what many claimed unattainable - a process on enhancing implementation under the UNFCCC.

The "Montreal Action Plan" was described as a clear road map for future work under the convention through coordinated action. The international political response to climate change in Montreal conference reached its apex to strengthen co-operation among the parties to fight against global climate change.

Even though the outcomes of COP-II and COP/MOP exceeded expectations, the future of the climate regime is still highly uncertain. The Russian Federation's last gasp's push to have a reference to the voluntary commitments in the decision on Article 3-9 suggests that they have joined the group of countries that may not be willing to take on commitments unless large developing countries are part of a future deal. Other major parties, including the United States, Australia, India and China have begun to focus on technology development and diffusion via the Asia Pacific partnership and this focus on technology also reflected in the decision to discuss future commitments under the convention. How this and other multilateral initiatives ultimately fit with the UNFCCC process is an issue that will need to be assessed in the future. The future may not be clear but at this critical juncture the Kyoto protocol is operational and multiple paths to move forward within the UN framework have been established. Given the real risk of failure in Montreal, it is hard to dispute that COP-II/MOP-I was anything, but a success.[28]

The Montreal meet had overcome so many constraints on the roadmap to achieve consensus in several issues paved the way for concrete steps to identify impacts and measures to adapt to climate change. Excepting the co-operation of United States and Australia, the world community sincerely in search of strategies advanced technologies and action plans to fight jointly to tackle climate change. The atmosphere created in Montreal will certainly develop mutual understanding among the countries to evoke international response to counter the future challenges of climate change through collaboration. 189 nations met in Montreal seeking solutions to the increased global pollutions in the face of atmospheric CO_2 levels now at the highest. Limited regulatory efforts are most likely to generate internal political support within the negotiating countries for international collective action. The Montreal Action Plan is the result of concerted efforts directed towards successful protection of global climate system. The year 2005 was turning point in world climate change politics in implementing the Kyoto protocol, improving the convention and innovating measures for tomorrow giving climate change convention a new dimension. Thus, Montreal conference set effective policies that would determine future course of international action to address the climate change challenges.

Constraints

Article 3 of the 1992 UN Framework Convention on Climate Change (UNFCCC) contains the following language. "The parties should protect the climate system for the benefit of the present and future generations of mankind on the basis of equity and in accordance with their common but differentiated responsibilities and respective capabilities. Accordingly, the developed country parties should take the lead in combating climate change and adverse effect thereof.

The phrase "common but differentiated responsibilities" has become a touchstone for the international climate equity debate. During the first conference of the parties to the UNFCCC (CoP-1; held in 1995 in Berlin, Germany) negotiators debated whether developing countries, in addition to developed countries, would commit to binding reductions for GHG emissions. The developing countries ultimately rejected binding commitments asserting that historical responsibility for climate change was not theirs, that they had less financial ability to pay for reductions and that they had more urgent priorities for their limited resources. However, developing countries at Kyoto did not accept language that would have required them to pursue "best efforts" to reduce GHG emissions through such measures as energy market reforms and also rejected language that would have set future limits on their emissions as a negotiating target.

The differentiated targets among Annex-I countries were not based on a standardized formula but rather on complex negotiations on multiple issues. Article 4 of the protocol allows group of countries to negotiate a redistribution of their collective GHG emission limits. This flexibility has been used by the European Union to set widely varying emission targets for GHG emissions among member countries. These complex procedure may foreshadow ever more complex future negotiations among developed and developing countries over obligations for GHG emissions control.

Debate over a long term equitable sharing of the burden has continued since the negotiation of the Kyoto protocol. While the implementation of Kyoto protocol is still in uncertainty, several developing country representatives continue to press the claim that the Annex-I countries should do even more to reduce GHG emissions given their historical responsibility for GHG emissions. Developed countries accept the concept of differentiated responsibilities but want greater assurance on when and how developing countries would start assuming greater responsibilities, because developing countries are likely to be the primary industrial emitters in the future. This concern was underscored in the Byrd-Hagel resolution passed 95-0 by the US Senate prior to the CoP-3. That resolution opposed ratification of Kyoto treaty until developing countries committed to binding emission limits in the some time frame as the United States. Developing countries counter that developed countries have done little to implement their previous voluntary reduction commitments, even while some developing countries have slowed their emissions growth through reforms in the economic and energy sector. This on going debate about the adequacy of commitments illustrates how differently countries interpret what constitute fairness or equity in mitigating the risk of global climate change.[29]

This debate crisis not only impoverished the developing countries but deteriorated the negotiation processes but also made the rich industrialized developed countries as its sole benefactor. Developed countries are responsible for the largest share of cumulative past GHG emissions so far. Moreover, current emission intensities vary dramatically between rich and poor countries. In addition, developing countries need to increase their emissions over some period in the future as a necessary consequence of critically needed economic growth and improved living standards. Therefore responsibility for resolving the problem also must ultimately be shared. If the current developed world drives its net GHG emissions to zero by the end of this century, the effects on the atmosphere would be small given the expected future growth of emissions in developing countries.

Quite not risen up to the waking up danger emanating from global warming the industrialized rich countries have not attested the goal of the global equity in controlling Carbon Dioxide emissions as suggested above. Nor they have of their own accord reduced Carbon Dioxide by 50% to the 1995 level. The pressure from NGOs, South countries and above all, the public opinion of the world may be said as being not enough to bind the North to a target as envisaged above. In spite of treaty and convention agreed to among countries, the fundamental problems remain unsolved. Firstly, the inordinate life style and unrestricted consumption pattern of the North which is symbiotically related to Carbon Dioxide emission and pattern of development, whether the western people are ready to have a cut in their standard of living by asking their governments to reduce CO_2 emission to the atmosphere.

The environmental debate has been so conducted as evidenced at the Rio Earth summit as if not to punish the culprit but to share his misdeeds. Instead of dealing with systemic causes of environmental degradation such as the unsustainable life style of their own population at the cost of the third world, the rich North is on relating rights of the South to exploit their own resources to the fixing of limits of emission of CO_2 and other gases, which adversely affect the atmosphere and of land and forest use with the ostensible purpose of gaining access to the abundant genetic material available in the South for reinforcing their patents on intellectual rights and dominance. It speaks of the sinister double standards of the North and it proposes a sectoral approach to the environment without being concerned about the demands of the South for inclusion of poverty, development and trade in the debate besides western selective concerns viz, atmosphere, forest, and biodiversity. Nor it is concerned with South's assertion of sovereign rights over the atmosphere and other resources on the basis of equity and the local people's right to be compensated equitably for parting with their unique knowledge of genetic materials to the North.

At the Rio UNCEP conference, the rich nations have taken a position that essentially gets them off the hook for their past deeds and now seek to ram an inequitable system for future global management down the throats of the poor Third World countries.

The climate change convention signed by a record number of 160 nations, prescribed the limits for carbon emissions so as to offset the effects of climate change on the atmosphere caused by greenhouse gases and global warming. It contains much of North's contentions about sharing the management of burden on an equitable basis, while sharing management of the resources of the atmosphere has been denied to the developing countries. The differential responsibility in causing damage to the environment was lost sight of at Rio.[30]

The industrialized North has always been insisting on asserting its right to find an escape route for their emission of CO_2 through forests, needed as carbon sinks to absorb pollution. As one western environmentalist pointed out creating carbon sinks in developing countries through forestry programmes without reducing Carbon Dioxide emissions in their own countries at the same time, is the wrong signal. This means the G-77 are not willing to make their own economics environmentally sustainable. In the face of assertion and determined efforts of India and Malaysia, the developed countries led by United States failed to bring all developing countries into an agreement to a convention on forestry, which prohibited them from cutting down trees on the pretext that they are rain forests and needed as carbon sinks to absorb pollution. The Montreal protocol on protective ozone layer contains anti third world provisions and safeguard the interest of the North. As studies show, while the developing countries share in the depletion of ozone layer remains at 12.4 percent, the developed countries share is 87.6 percent. Adding to this inequity and discrimination, it can be said that fixing quotas for further consumption is unfair and highly erroneous.

A major constraint that affects the Third world is the financial and technological crunch for seeking alternatives to CFCs which remains in the hands of the North. As Z.R. Anasari, former Indian Minister for environment, apprehended at the 1989 London conference, "the technology of substitutes for conservation, recycling and equipment modification will be the monopoly of a few countries in the developed world ... the question that haunts US is the extent of resources required to get the technology as well as products from the companies in the developed world."[31]

Alternatives to CFCS, though claimed to be friendly to the environment, are emerging like new villains. Even when alternatives friendly to the ozone layer are found, they will under the control and monopoly of the developed world, perpetuating their role in their trade to protect their economy. In the scintillating words of an environmentalist.

"Instead of the treaty setting out a system in which a global common resource is shared and managed equitably with equal rights for any citizen, the treaty operates within the context of existing inequalities, creating a legal framework to institutionalize and perpetuate the gap between the poor and rich it does not assign any entitlements to people nor any penalties for the over use or abuse of the common resources of the Earth. Any discussion for corrective action, thus, remains a mere charity from the penalized."[32]

The very cause of nuisance to the environment is that the ethnocentrism of the dominant western economic thinking and pattern of development does not take into consideration the natural threshold, the carrying capacity of the planet Earth and the ecological costs of production based an extraction of fossil fuels and industrialization. The problem of climate change puts a challenge to the prevailing pattern of development. It has also resulted in a western masculine metaphysical understanding of power in terms of dominance over nature; control over economic activities and territorial states. Can such an economic development be called successful if has effected a terrible despoliation of nature and environment and destitution of the people in the Third world. This is what led many to denounce it as antithesis of authentic development or anti development[33] unless and until the prevalent trends and tendencies of the present economic development are reversed, a new global environmental order can not be ushered in.

"Springing from the unending acquisitiveness if our technological way of life and a concomitant decline in our sensitivity to other humans, we have been on a rampage that threatens our common organic bond with the whole of creation- and thus both our own survival and that of other species."[34] The core of the problem is how to impose a moderation on the acquisitive and consumerist man in general and particularly on the exorbitant life styles of the people of the North, which has denied an equitable environmental space to the South, as Centre for Science and Environment argues, riding rough shod over all norms of equity and human rights.

The highest per capita emissions are found in the U.S. followed by Canada, Australia and South Arabia. Alternatively, more countries in Africa, Asia and South America depict low per capita carbon emissions, countries with high standard of living are mostly responsible for the rise of greenhouse gases. These early industrialized countries - Europe, North America, Japan and few others create their wealth in part by pumping into the atmosphere vast amount of greenhouse gases long before the likely consequences were understood. Now the developing countries fear being told that they should curtail their fledging industrial activities - that the atmosphere's safety margin is all used up. Because energy related emissions are the leading cause of climate change, there will be growing pressure on all countries to reduce the amount of coal and oil they use. There also will be pressure (and incentives) to adopt advance technologies so that less damage is inflicted in the future. Buying such technologies can be costly. Countries in early stage of industrialization struggling hard to give their citizens better lives-do not want these additional burdens on economic development. If they agreed to cut back on burning the fossil fuels that are the cheapest, most convenient and most useful for industry, how could they make any progress? The large share of historical and current emissions originates in developed countries. Thus these countries should take the lead in combating climate change and its adverse effect. Although the Kyoto protocol recognizes the right of the developing countries for economic development and acknowledges the vulnerability of poorer countries to the effects of the climate, the developed countries led by North demanding equal share of all developing countries in mitigating the emission of greenhouse gases, constitute major constraints in the way of successful globally coordinated action.

As studies show, there has been an unprecedented growth in the global economy during the eighties. It is much more than that during the several thousand years from the beginning of civilization until 1950.[35] According to a British environmentalist, with world's population increasing more than three times since 1900, the gross world products has increased it times, the consumption of fossil fuels 30 times, industrial production 50 times and the average income of the richest one billion people is 20 times larger than that of the poorest one billion.[36] It seems that the enormous increase in the wealth of the world has not resulted in the equitable distribution of benefits rather it has widened the gap between the North and the South. The major stumbling block is the growing perception of the environmental crisis as mainly a failure of technology and management. What is more horrendous is that UNCED paved the way for the transfer of control of the world's resources to a global technocratic elite by transforming an issue of changing life styles and consumption levels of the lavish rich into one of the population growth and inadequate managerial capacity of the poor? The South environmental degradation is inextricably related to the global process of trade and pattern of economic relations. But the irony is that the most profligate in environmental pollution are demanding that the most frugal and sparing abide by the most stringent rules of environmental protection. According to an analysis if economic progress in North can be said to be sustainable, it is by "importing" it through non-sustainability in other nations. [37]

If sustainable development is understood and couched in the verbiage of western terminology as perpetuating the current system of economic activity, entrenched industrial structures, institutionalizing the economic interests of the weather nations of the world; it will not only be the apotheosis of 'ecological imperialism' but will foreshadow an environmental catastrophe.[38] Uncertainty arises to combat the global climate change because of the lack of conclusive information about the following:

(*a*) The human sources and pace of temperature change; (*b*) The costs and benefits of global warming and their distribution across countries; (*c*) Cost, benefits and effectiveness of different forms of regulation and; (*d*) the extent of treaty compliance by sovereign countries. We argue that uncertainty seriously affects the ability of political constituencies within countries and hence politicians as their agents to calculate net gains of taking and complying with international agreements to address global warming. Under these circumstances, international collective action will be more difficult to mobilize and sustain.[39]

Effective collective action to address potential climate change will be a formidable challenge. The very nature of global externalities presents incentive problems. Abatement by any country benefits others as a public good but if abatement is costly to a country's citizens, its politicians have incentive to invest less in reduction efforts than would be global optimal and free ride on cutbacks taken else where. Research and collective action to address more tractable, local common property resources indicates that these incentive problem can occur even when there is agreement about magnitude of problem and aggregate benefits of resolving it.[40]

As are described, these bargaining issues are more complex in international environmental agreements where the benefits and costs are very uncertain and differentially spread across and within countries and where compliance among sovereign is voluntary. The problem of climate change puts challenge to the prevailing pattern of development. To what extent alternative paradigms conducive to the environment, the life pattern and style and future generations right to exist are explored, will determine the future course of action on the part of the nations of the world to combat the crisis. The modern civilization based on oil is prepared to go to war to secure oil supplies, but weather it is prepared to face the situation its the world's oil wells suddenly dry up. The multi national corporations and energy sectors dominating the modern state are, whether in oppositions to change their structure, power and style of functioning. According to Pad Green the solution to climate change required a revolution in the way society produces and uses energy and in the way that people's needs for mobility are met. However, fighting climate change is not just a question of replacing fossil fuels with wind power, biomass, solar or other technologies. As he said, energy renewable technology had environmental impacts particularly land use (wind power and biomass) and mineral extraction and toxic chemicals.

The question who pollutes the atmosphere needs to be axed remains central to the solution of the crisis. Whether the rich North shoulders the responsibility and unilaterally reduces CO_2 to an exemplary extent and accepts equity in the share of the access to the atmosphere, always remain center stage. The international treaties concluded so far, failed to answer the key question about equity, right of access to the resources and the role of multinational corporations in energy sector with government lacking the political will to tame them. The developing countries always tried to put equity on the global climate change agenda but failed to find to it US and its allies acceptability. Recently, the US came out with its own version of equity fashioned by none other than the Pew Center on Global Climate Change, established in 1998 by the Pew Foundation, which in turn was set up by an oil company called sun. The Pew report is called Equity and Global Climate Change: The Complex Elements of Global Fairness"[23] This report has little in common with what the south demands. According to the report, in line with what the polluter pays principle's responsibility would include not only who emitted in the past but also who will emit in the future. That means meaningful participation from South is stressed on. Secondly, if one country can more cheaply reduce emissions than another and then perhaps it should be asked to do so. Thirdly, all nations should work to the best of their abilities or with help of other countries to reduce emissions. So, the report pushed the US argument that developed countries should be allowed to meet their entire commitments under the Kyoto protocol through emission trading without any action at home. This report rejects per capita argument claiming that if it creates perverse incentives for population growth.

Moreover, the South countries always trying to oppose any move by the North to bring them into ambit of climate change treaty, also contribute to the emissions of CO_2 to the atmosphere though much less than the North countries do. In their aspiration to attain the level of development the Western countries have reached, the South may add significantly to the emission. Their argument is that they are far behind the Western level of industrial development, they should be exonerated from the responsibility to reduce CO_2 emission at their home front sounds logical. Rather than imitating the Western pattern of development, the South countries should develop and define development in their own civilization context. The South countries cannot keep pace with the level of development the North has reached unless and until the people in North change their luxurious and inordinate life style. So the success of the climate change treaty is very much contingent on the kind of revolution needed in ethnocentrism of Western consumption pattern, life style and economic thinking.

The framework convention disappointed many environmentalists and states because it did not provide for mandatory reductions in greenhouse gas emissions. Viewed however, from the perspective of an ongoing process of implementing a common global strategy for addressing climate change, unfortunately industrialized countries have responded politically in different ways with responses ranging from ardent calls for the North to take the lead in cutting emissions to equivocation in the face of lingering scientific and economic uncertainties. Developing countries have also not responded politically in the some way to climate change.

The UNFCCC creating a solid and comprehensive foundation for further national measures and policies, failed to attract the widest possible participation of industrialized and developing states taking into account their respective responsibilities and capabilities. Combating climate change needs a more scientific certainty to bind the nations to the treaties and convention agreed to. But the ongoing negotiation process is caught in the group politics among industrialized and developing countries, which is influenced by their geographic strategic and national interest. Among industrialized countries, the European Union (EU) and the economies in transition of Eastern Europe and the former soviet union (without Russia and the former soviet Republic of Central Asia) collectively called themselves CG-II or the consultative group of 11 countries. Allied with the European countries is a small group of countries (Switzerland, Mexico and South Korea) who are informally called the environmental integrity group. The other industrialized countries have grouped together under an informal coalition known as the umbrella group. This group includes the United States, Japan, Canada, New Zealand, Australia and Norway. Countries of global South negotiate as a collective bloc through the group of 77 and China (G-77). Low lying and small Island states grouped together under (AOSIS) or the Alliance of Small Island States. Developing countries from South East Asia (particularly Philippines, Malaysia, Thailand and Indonesia) fall in between big developing countries and the latter countries. However, International co-operation in combating climate change is bound to be influenced by varying political interests in different ways to extract as many concession as possible. Their participation in the global effort would result in favourable out comes for them. Since UN Conference on Environment and Development the (Earth summit) held in Rio and the recent international conference on global climate change held in Buenos Aires, the 10th conference of the parties, no unified effective policies called for the widest possible co-operation by all countries and their participation in an effective and appropriate international response in accordance with their common but differentiated responsibilities and respective capabilities to address the problem of global warming.

With the support from the G-77 and Association of small Island Nations, the European Union was determined not to negotiate on the basis of US offer on stabilization at 1990 levels. The EU formally proposed in March 1997 that legally binding reduction in emission of CO_2, Methane and Nitrous Oxide by 7.5% by 2010. At the Kyoto conference in December 1997, the EU reneged on its original commitment. Heated exchange and much wrangling marked the conference which ended abruptly to hastily patch up a lukewarm agreement. The US government's view that emission from the South would equal those of the North by 2035 is highly misleading. The biggest polluter tried to shift the yoke of responsibility to the less polluting countries. Thus, policy to combat a global problem is futile without international co-operation. The convention also foresees the contribution of the developed world to a financial mechanism that would help the developing countries to act against climate change through the development of their institutional infrastructure and the use of technologies for reducing greenhouse gas emissions.[41] The recognition that "the large share of global emissions of greenhouse gases has originated in developed countries and that per capita emissions in developing countries are still relatively low and that the share of global emissions originating in developing will grow to meet their social and development needs" appears to be another millstone in the ongoing negotiation to combat climate change. The need for developed countries to take immediate action in a flexible manner on the basis of the clear priorities as a first step towards comprehensive response strategies at the global, national and regional levels that take into account all greenhouse gases with the due consideration of their relative contribution to the enhancement of greenhouse effect. Differences surfaced among developed and developing nations constitute major constraints on climate change and negotiation for a more accurate scientific certitude to combat global warming. Since international environmental treaties are voluntary in nature forcing compliance upon the constituencies in sovereign countries may not be possible at any reasonable cost.

The enhanced greenhouse effect, which causes global warming requires an international treaty to address the global nature of problem, unilateral action, or action by a group of countries would be insufficient to solve the problem. The United States as the world super power and the world's primary greenhouse gas producer is in an unique position to tend negotiations towards treaty but must gain widespread participation in order to succeed. The developed countries, the former Soviet bloc, the debtor nation, and the less developed countries all are bringing conflicting demands to the negotiations.

The GHG treaty comes at time when the United States is the undisputed world superpower, the USSR is gone, the EC is still in the midst of being natured and Japan has not yet assumed a global role. Appropriately, with the responsibility for leadership in solving global warming problem, comes the responsibility for having created the problem. The US is by far the world's worst "greenhouse polluter" in terms of per capita contribution and with the breakup of the USSR, the US will be by far the largest contributor as well. The US House of Representatives, in proposing a CO_2 offset market admits that: 1) The United States has 5 percent of the world's population and yet consumes more than 20 percent of the world's fossil fuels and emits more than 20 percent of the world's CO_2 derived from the combustion of fossil fuels. 2) The United States consumes fossil fuels on a per capita basis at four times the worldwide average of many other highly industrialized countries.[42]

International co-operation in combating climate change is being influenced by the natural interests of the nations, more particularly the United States. There is a clear consensus that the Kyoto protocol is an unfair and ineffective means of addressing global climate change concerns. The US is now the greatest obstruction to the world battle against climate change. The action of US strengthened the hand of those who wanted to weaken the treaty and there by caused it to be (even) weaker than it would otherwise have been.

Nations have a common interest in responding to the risk of climate change, yet many are reluctant to reduce GHG emissions voluntarily or unilaterally. They hesitate because climate change is a global public good-all nations can enjoy protection against the risk of climate change, regardless of whether they participate in a treaty intended to mitigate those risks. Each nation's incentive to reduce emissions is thus limited but it cannot be prevented from enjoying the fruits of other nation's efforts. This incentive to free ride reflects the divergence between national actions and global interests.[43] No nation acting alone can substantially reduce the rate of emission of greenhouse gases. Yet if each nation waits for another to act, all will continue to wait and the rate of building up will be uncomfortably rapid. Such a "tragedy of commons" can only be avoided by international agreement in which some nations take the lead to set the moral (and economic) tone for the rest of the world with the full expectation that others will- by agreement, it is hoped, follow suit. [44] It is not the authority of climate science that is conducting the international negotiation on climate change. It is the sovereign system that is greatly involved in getting the negotiation on, so the regional disparities, super power game and political interests are bound to influence the ongoing negotiations.

The major constraint that hinders the negotiation process to combat the global climate change is prevailing differences and conflicting attitudes between the rich industrialized North and the poor South developing countries. Further, the divergent views between three distinct groups, the United States, the European Union and the developing countries complicated the matter relating to the implementation of Kyoto protocol, which is considered as the first legal binding international agreement to combat the global warming. There needs and among of a much greater degree of co-ordination between different countries so as to avoid current situation where the actions one render meaningless the efforts of another. The ongoing international negotiation on climate change faces the challenges like geographical strategy, national interests of the nations, regional disparities, equity as the basis of meaningful participation. Super Power game and political interests coupled with luxurious and inordinate life style and economic thinking of the North industrialized developed countries has proved to be the greatest obstruction acting against globally coordinated action urgently needed to combat the climate change. There is much that can and should be done to overcome the constraints, the real challenge is to find out the political will that prevents US from reaching the goals.

Thus, lack of co-ordination between the sovereign state systems and the ecological regions in the face of environmental degradation has often resulted in transitional and global environmental problems. Efforts to CoPe with these problems pose a challenge to the sovereign state system. Sovereign territorial exclusiveness pre-supposes that political authority can address problem arising within its jurisdiction. This becomes problematic in the context of global ecological interdependence. Thus, territorial exclusivity stands in sharp contrast to the outlook of global ecology based on holism and the mutual dependence of Earth ecosystems. [45]

The political authority does not take into consideration the interests and rights of the future generations. The intergenerational responsibility, which includes the future generations' right to environment access to fresh and unpolluted water, air and other resources and the present generations' right and obligations provides sufficient ground for reviewing the Sovereign State system. Since environmental problems have become global concerns, transitional environmentalism "aims to transform the modern conception of authority to include not only popular legitimately, which has emerged in tandem with the spread of democracy, but also intergenerational and even interspecies criteria of accountability based on intergenerational equity."[46]

Tackling environmental problems such as acid rain, pollution of air and oceans, ozone layer depletion, global warming and climate change involve non-traditional forms of external interventions, which challenge the sovereign state's omnipotent authority to control events within its territorial jurisdiction. The link between environmental degradation and national Security has recently become the major concern of the Sovereign State system. Tackling the problem of environmental degradation may require new strategies, which may be beyond the capacity of many third world and developing countries. The imperative of environmental degradation may require all nations to compromise their unrestricted freedom in relation to their natural resources, industrial practices and the environment. [47]

Contrary to claims made by some, this requires the concept of merged sovereignty, which comes into existence when nations seek to realize their own national objective along with environmental security through co-operation, voluntary remedial measures and owning responsibility in association with other nations of the world keeping in view intergenerational equity and accountability. Thus, traditional view of sovereignty seems to be inconsistent with the requirements of environmental protection. [48]

Another constraint bound to influence the ongoing negotiations is the interplay between the political authority and authority of science. One of the essential characteristics of modernity is its faith in the role of science to improve consumerist pattern of life linked to the material achievement, economic performance, industrial development with exponential growth in fossil fuel production. The western pattern of development based on industrialization and fossil fuel production has become a standard model for both developed and developing states. It has been associated with modern luxurious life style to improve human life. As a result large quantities of Carbon Dioxide are emitted to the atmosphere causing pollution and an alarming climate change. A majority of scientists believe that this is the primary Greenhouse Gas (GHG) responsible for global climate change, which seriously limit the state authority's capacity to protect its citizens. In spite of efforts to find out alternative energy resources, the authority of science poses a challenge to the authority of state as the sole determinant of wealth production. The signing of 1997 Kyoto protocol to reduce GHG emissions by the industrialized countries 7 to 8 percent by 2012 is a clear recognition of the authority of climate science. More than any other international environmental issue, global climate change envisages the advent of new pattern of authority based on science impacting on the authority of the sovereign nation state.[49]

This dilemma come to the fore when policy makers depend upon it for identifying and addressing environmental problems. Whether the modern nation state is ready to surrender their sovereignty, national interest and protection of citizen's right to the authority of science to combat the global warming.

It has been seen that between 1950 and 1995 a rapid increase in consumption of fossil fuels quadrupled the growth in gross world product to a similar growth in the GHG emissions at the international level. Given the fact that GHG emissions produced in pursuit of prosperity, proposals to reduce these gases have faced strong resistance. A study conducted in 1988, concluded that stabilizing atmospheric concentrations of Carbon Dioxide and bringing it back to 1950 levels, would mean reducing fossil fuel use by 50 to 80 percent.[50]

The Organization of Petroleum Exporting Countries (OPEC) and other states which are dependent on fossil fuels, oppose reduction in Carbon Dioxide emissions. Given the correlation between wealth production and fossil fuel consumption the industrialized nations of the North will be willing to reduce greenhouse emissions only on the basis of scientific certainty and accuracy about the climate change. The targets set by the Kyoto Protocol for the reduction of GHGs in the atmosphere is minimal in view of the dangers the emissions of CO_2 by the industrialized North pose to humanity. Even this minimal reduction target if implemented, the treaty would force the most productive societies on Earth- the ones that had led the way in making human life comfortable, safe and prosperous to slow their economic growth and degrade their standard of living.[51] As the life patterns and economic development are interwoven with the reduction of GHGs emission, thus success of climate change treaty remains uncertain.

The kind of intergenerational accountability involved in the climate change talks and treaties is suggestive of the fact that criteria for consent of future generations to the government is not the fossil fuel based economy but prevalence of a healthy carbon free climate. Thus implies that people may not be willing to choose any other basis of their consent than the production of wealth based on fossil fuel technology. In that case, people are not prepared to sacrifice their present economic gains for the future generations. If so the tension between the authority of science and political authority continues to persist. The uncertainties surrounding scientific predictions may strengthen people's unwillingness to sacrifice their present economic gains and understand the basis of climate hazards.[52]

So long as science does not provide alternative source of energy that would not affect the existing level of economic prosperity, and redefine the present development paradigm linking fossil fuel with wealth production, any attempt to bind the countries with climate treaty may not really be effective.[53]

Increased uncertainty within countries over the aggregate gains from collective action however, reduces the livelihood of international co-operation. That uncertainty arises in global warming regulation and other international accords due to the size, nature and ambiguity of the problem. In particular, a treaty's outcomes might be difficult to predict. The effects of immediate controls on behaviour may not appear until far into the future, and predicting such delayed returns accurately is likely difficult. Additionally, the presence of global externalities means that an accord's benefit depends upon co-operation by all involved parties and the extent of co-operation can itself be difficult to predict. However, the success of combating global climate change is highly circumscribed by a large number of problems and factors, which ultimately are responsible to reach consensus on the road map to be followed to develop interest and incentives.

The governments of rich countries have set the wrong targets to tackle climate change using outdated science. A paper published in 2006 by climatologist Malte Meinshausen suggests that if greenhouse gases reach a concentration of 550 parts per million (ppm) carbon dioxide equivalent, there is a 63-99 per cent chance that global warming will exceed two degrees. At 475 parts per million the average likelihood is 64 per cent. Only if concentrations are stabilized at 400 parts per million or below is there a low chance that temperatures will rise by more than two degrees. The IPCC draft report contains similar figures. A concentration of 510 ppm gives a 33 per cent chance of preventing more than two degrees of warming. A concentration of 590 ppm gives a ten per cent chance. The current level of greenhouse gases in the atmosphere is 459 ppm. To give a high chance to humanity of preventing dangerous climate change, what is needed a programme so drastic that greenhouse gases in the atmosphere end up below the current concentrations. But no government has set itself this task. The EU and Swedish government have established the world's most stringent target, which is 550ppm. It is of carbon dioxide alone. But this target gives the human beings a near certainty of an extra 2 degrees C. When other greenhouse gases are included, this translates into 666ppm, carbon dioxide equivalent. According to last autumn's Stern report on the economics of climate change, at 650 ppm, there is a 60-95 per cent chance of 3 degrees C of warming.

In his book Heat, George Monbiot[54] estimated that to avoid two degrees of warming a global emission cut of 60 per cent per capita between now and 2030 is highly required. This translates into an 87 per cent cut in the U.K. A recent paper in the journal of Climate Change emphasizes that the sensitivity of global temperatures to greenhouse gas concentrations remains uncertain. But using the average figure, to obtain a 50 per cent chance of preventing more than 2 degrees C of warming requires a global cut of 80 per cent by 2050. This is a cut in total emission, not in emissions per head. If the population were to rise from 6 billion to 9 billion between now and then, an 87 per cent cut in global emissions per person. If carbon emissions are to be distributed equally, the greater cut must be made by the biggest polluters: rich nations like US and other western countries. The U.K.'s emissions per capita would need to fall by 91 per cent. But the rich countries appear to quietly have abandoned their aim of preventing dangerous climate change, condemning millions to death. What the IPCC report shows is that the time is to stop treating climate change as an urgent issue. The nations of the world have to start treating it as an international emergency. Since the United States contributes about 25% of the world's CO_2 emissions, its own policy could make a large difference.

Global climate change is different from other environmental problems. First, emissions of CO_2 and other trace gases are almost irreversible; more precisely, their residence time in the atmosphere is measured in centuries. Most environmental problems are mitigated promptly or unfairly short order when the source is cleaned up, as with water pollution, acid rain or sulfur dioxide emissions. Here, reducing emissions today is very valuable to humanity in the distant future. Second, the scale of the externality is truly global; greenhouse gases travel around the world in a few days. This means that the nation-state and its subsidiaries, the typical loci for internalization of externalities, are limited in their remedial ability.[55] The poor countries appear to be most vulnerable to the dangerous climate change, mostly a doing of the rich.

References

1. "Global Warming", US Environmental Protection Agency, July 28, 2004.
2. "World to be Hotter by Two Degrees" Indian Express Daily / 28. 5. 1990, p. 7.
3. Kathy Finberg, "Expanded History of UN Ecological Summits", Facsnet Section Editors, From Stockholm to Buenos Aires, Jan 28, 2000, p. 1. www.facsnet.org/issues/specials/gcc/politics/expand.php$_3$
4. Hiroshi Ohki, "International Co-operation in Combating Global Warming" Chairman of the special committee on global Environmental issues - 2001.
5. Kathy Finberg, op.cit, preparing for Rio.
6. Jill Jagar Tim 'O' Riordan, "History of Climate Change Science and Politics": Routledge, London, New York, 1996, p. -19.

7. *Ibid,* p. 2.
8. United Nations Frame Worked Convention on Climate Change (UNFCCC). A/AC/237 (part-II) Art-1 (1992) 31.1LM-851.
9. Antonio G.M. Lavina, "From Kyoto to Marrakesh Global Climate Politics and Local Communities", World Resource Institute, Washington DC., 31st August, 2002.
10. Jill Jagar Tim 'O' Riordan, *op.cit,* p. 24.
11. For example the Alliance Of Small Island States (AOSIS). The Netherlands although not an Island is one of the most vulnerable developed countries to sea level rise. It was thus able to benefit from the strong position taken on the issue of climate change.
12. For example, OPEC, Norway as a major oil land and gas producer and with an economy heavily dependent on this industry was able to benefit from the position taken by the OPEC Countries which still maintaining its international "green" image in the international political arena.
13. The Potential for Development opportunities is thought to be a significant factor in the breakdown of the g-77 plus china on the issue joint implementation.
14. John. R. Justus and Susan R. Fletcher; "Resources Science and Industry Division." Congressional Research Service- The library of Congress: Washington, 29 October-2004 ORS-9.
15. http/www.globefox/com/cacc/politics.html, visited on the line. WBGU Report summary-1995 p. 1.
16. "Kyoto Protocol to the Convention on Climate Change," Germany Climate Change Secretariat : Bonn, 1999.
17. FCCC/CP/1999/NF "Status of Ratification by the United Nations Frame Work Convention on Climate Change and Kyoto Protocol," visited on line www.unfccc.de.
18. John R. Justus. R. flectcher; *op.cit,* CRS-10.
19. *Ibid,* CRS-11.
20. For an account of Bonn Negotiations see the website of the Negotiation Bulletin (30 July 2001) visited on line www.iisd.linkages, down load./asc/enb/2176c.txt.
21. John R. Justus and others, *op.cit,* CRS-12
22. Ostrom. elinor. "Managing the Commons." New York : Cambridge University Press, 1990.
23. Antonio. G.M. Lavina, *op.cit.*
24. Babcock; Linda George Lowenstein and Yianghongwang, "The Relation Between Uncertainty and Central Zone and Experience in Bargaining Experiment. "Journal of Economic Behaviour and Organization, 1995. 27.475:85.
25. Marina Cazorla and Michel Toman, "Resources for the Future." Washington DC, Climate Issue breef No.-27. December 2000, p. 14. visited on the line internet. http/www.rff.org.

26. A.G.M. Lavina, *op.cit.*

27. Kristin Stewart, "The Problem of Global Warming", Georgetown University School of Foreign Service. Science Technology and International Affairs, 1998. Visited in the line. http/www.Georgetown. edu./sfs/programmes/sita/students/vol-01/Stewartk.htm.

28. A Brief Analysis of CoP-11/Mop –1 Report, New York, International Institute for Sustainable Development(IISD), Vol.12, No. 291, 12 December 2005.

29. Marina Cazirola and Michel Toman, *op.cit,* p.1-3.

30. N. Gann, "Environment and Development : A Search for Economic Rethinking, New Delhi, India Institute of Public Administration, Vol-XXXIX July September No. 3, p. 301.

31. Khorkok Peng, "G-7 Leaders Fails A combat Global Warming in Third World Economics, Trend and Analysis". Third World Network, Penag, Sept. 15 1990.

32. Anon, "China Attacks Unfair Ozone Protocol", New Scientists London, March 11, 1989, "Indian Teams for Signing Montreal Protocol". The Times of India; March 17 1989.

33. Anit Agarawala and Sunita Naraini, "Towards a Green World", New Delhi centre for science and Environment, 1992, pp. 11-13.

34. Denis Goulet, "The Cruel Choice" A New Concept in Theory of Development (New York), Atheneum, 1971, pp. 215-35.

35. Rajani Kothari, Environment Technology and Ethics,in J Ronald Engel and Joan Gibb Engel. ed. ethics of Environment and Development" London Belhaven Press: A Division of Printer Publishers 1990, p. 30.

36. See the state of world 1991, A World Watch Institute, report on progress towards a Sustainable Society, New Delhi, 1991; p. 6.

37. Norman Myers ; "The GAIA Atlas of Future Worlds", New York, Anchor Books (Double Day 1990).

38. David Pearce, Anil Markendya, and Edward B.Barbier; "Blue Print for a Green Economy", Earth Scan Publications, London. 1989.

39. A.W. Crosby, Ecological Imperialism. The Biological Expansion of Eurode, 900-1900. Cambridge University Press, 1986, M.Rediclift. The Multiple Dimension of Sustainable Development. Geography vol. 76 No. 2, 1990, pp. 36-42. D. Pearce, Economics and Global Environmental Challenge, Millennium vol-19, No. 3, 1990, pp.365-87. Robert Pachlke and Douglas Torgerson, Managing Leviathans Environmental Politics and the Administrative state peterboroughont, Broad view, 1990 and Michael Jacobs, The Green Economy Environment, Sustainable Development and Politics of the Future, London, Pluto, 1991.

40. Joseph J.Bial, University of Chicago Law School, Daniel Houser, Department of Economics University of Arizona and Gray D. Libecap. Economics Department and Karl Eller Center University of Arizona and

National Bureau of Economic Research. "Public Choice Issues in International Collective Action - Global Warming Regulation, "November 2, 2000, p. 2.

41. Bac. Mehnet, 1996, "Incomplete information and incentives to free ride on International Environmental Resources", Journal of Environmental Economics and Management 30(3)301-15. Barrant Scott, "Self Enforcing Environmental Agreements", Oxford Economics paper, 46 supplementary, October 1994, pp.878-94. Young, Oram R.ed 1999, "The Effectiveness of International Regimes", Cambridge MIT Press and Libecap, Gary D., "Contracting for Property Rights", Cambridge University Press : New York, 1989.
42. George Strongylis, "International and European action against Cliamte Change", Commission of the European Union, Belgium, p. 1, http:/ www.biopolitics.gr/HTML/PUBS VOL.15/html/Str.bel.html.
43. (HR 2663, 1991) "US greenhouse gas reduction plan, via marketable permits, US governments 1991", CO_2 offsets policy efficiently act 1991, proposed bill before the House of Representatives, June 18, 1991, Washington DC., US Government Printing Press.
44. Marine Cazola and Michael Toman, "International Equity and Climate Change Policy", Resources for the future: Washington DC., Climate Issue brief no. 27, December 2000, p. 4.
45. Schneider 1989, "The Basic fact book for Global Warming", Schenider Stephen H. "Are We entering the Greenhouse Century", San Francisco, CA. Sierra Club books, 1989.
46. John G. Ruggie, "Territoriality and Beyond of Problematizing Modernity in International Relation", International Organization, Vol. 47, 1993, pp. 144-73.
47. Karen T. Litfin, "Environment Wealth and Authority : Global Climate Change and Emerging modes of legitimation" International Studies Review (Special Issue), Vol. 2, no. 2 (summer), 2000, p. 127.
48. Lynton Keith Caldwell, " International Environment Policy: Emergence and Dimensions", New Delhi, Affiliated East West Press, 1991, p. 311.
49. Maurice F. Strong, "One year after Stockholm : A Ecological Approach to Management", Foreign Affairs, vol.51, July 1973, p. 703.
50. Narottam Gaan, "Global Climate Change, Sovereign State System and the Authority of Science", International Studies: New Delhi, London. Sage Publication; Thousands Oaks, 39, 4(2002), p. 411.
51. Christopher Flavin, "Slowing Global Warming", in Lester Brown ed., State of World 1990(New York, Norton 1990), pp. 17-38.
52. Jeff Jacoby, "Scientists do not agree on Global Warming", Boston Glabe 5 November 1998, p. 27.
53. N. Gaan, *op.cit.,* p. 416.
54. George Monbiot, "Policies that could cost millions of lives", The Hindu, 2 May, 2007, p. 13.
55. Kenneth J. Arrow, "Global Climate Change: A Challenge to Policy," Economists' Voice, www.bepress.com/ev June 2007.

7

Climate Change and Threats to Human Security

The debate over the direct connection between climate change and security harks back to the day security threats were outsourced to non-military and non-traditional elements. There are septics who maintain that climate factors will only marginally influence tomorrow's security environment, if at all. They point to significant natural fluctuations in climate patterns and short term cyclical phenomena like El Nino and the recently identified Pacific Decadal Oscillation, the causes of which are not fully understood and deciphered. In their opinion, even if global warming does take place, many of its effects may be localized, benign or favourable. While reductions in rainfall may lead to desertification or water shortages in some regions, others will derive dividends from increased rainfall and higher crop yields. Even where the fabric of the state is torn by environmentally induced conflicts, in all likelihood they will be localized and have negligible effects on existing world order. Sepulchral visions of starving millions from the South on their heels to edge their ways into the North in search of food are far fetched.

On the other hand, mainstream climate scientists and some international security specialists contend that the magnitude of expected climate change will be substantial and certainly beyond the societal and eco-system experience, exposing genuine and multiple risks to global security. The traditional concept of security presupposes that threats arising from outside the state are more dangerous to the state than threats that arise within it. Non- military threats within states- such as poverty, social vulnerability, ecological devastations- are generally not perceived as concrete and tangible. Yet one could argue with equal plausibility that the wrong end of a smokestack can be as much of a security threat to humans as the barrel of a gun.

The late 1970s witnessed a spurt of intellectual fermentation resulting in a myriad of calls to redefine security in non- military terms that include rising poverty, rapid population growth, spread of infectious diseases, and environmental degradation. The realist understanding and definition of security was state centric connected with state secrecy, nuclear and military power. The realist framework of national security as a function of the successful pursuit of interstate power competition through military means continued right through the cold war. According to Dalby, "cold war versions of security have usually been understood in spatial terms as moves of exclusion and protection is a spatial exercise in distancing and boundary making".[1] This means in geopolitical parlance, the spatial limitation of Soviet political control. During the last half century, security has been primarily a matter of concern for states and their military alliances. The legitimacy of the governments is generally understood in terms of provision of internal security for the inhabitants residing within its territorial jurisdiction. Where stability of the regime has been held synonymous with national security serious inroads into the realm of human rights, and internal repressions have been rationalized in the name of national security. Where political instability has been identified as threat, national security is understood as containing and limiting political change and legitimizing the status quo. The intensification of cold war climaxed in the proliferation of nuclear weapons and in the Reagan administration's Strategic Defense Initiative and Star wars merely exposed the paradox of security where the enhancement of nuclear power does not mean the enhancement of security to the people. The problems plaguing the entire humanity in terms of grinding poverty, burgeoning population growth, spread of diseases, scarcity of resources and environmental degradation could not be comprehended within the realist framework based on state centric military capability. Thus, the dominant realist paradigm to understand the current realities seems to be inadequate. It has "become an anachronism that has lost much of its explanatory and prescriptive power."[2]

Environmental Security: The first Dimension

The state-centric and military perspective of security has lost both practical relevance and intellectual credibility in the context of a number of historic forces and events in the contemporary age. These include the end of cold war, global integration of national economies, erosion of national identifies and cultures, the shift in priority from military rivalry to economic competition, and the diminishing role of state as the dominant actor in international politics. On the other hand, there have emerged diverse new issues- ranging from poverty to refugees crises, information privacy to cyber- terrorism, environmental problems to natural disasters

– which requires non-state and non-military policies and strategies. These newly emerging security concerns have been characterized as non-traditional, and are now considered a major component of what is christened as comprehensive security. Among these emergent problems replacing the threat of East-West ideological divide, military aggression and struggle for global preponderance is the global environmental crisis. It looms large in terms of global warming, sea level rise, acid rain, greenhouse effect, diminishing capacity of the agricultural system, depletion of earth's finite resources, punching holes in the ozone layer, and biodiversity loss. Simply put, the global agenda has expanded since the demise of cold war, as has the need for urgent attention to these problems for solution. It is thus seen that "welfare not warfare, will shape the rules and global threats like ozone holes and pollution will dictate the agenda."[3] It is within this context that the environmental question has gained worldwide significance as a security issue. In fact, environmental security stands out as perhaps the most widely debated issue, especially due to its all-pervasive nature, cross national scope and inter- generational implications.[4]

While many of the past, present and future causes of conflict and war may seem to have little or no direct connection with the environment or with resources, a strong argument can be made for linking certain resource and environmental problems with the prospects for political frictions and tensions, or even war and peace. At the centre of ongoing debate is the assertion that resource scarcity and certain forms of environmental degradation are important factors contributing to political instability or violent conflict at local, regional and interstate levels. There is a growing perception that local, regional and global environmental deficiencies or resource scarcities will increasingly produce conditions that may lead to conflict. [5]

This conceptual shift towards environmental security in the context of collapse of Soviet Union and diminution of security threats associated with cold war, pitch forked into the mainstream security debates urging the policymakers to cast about for a new security focus. Despite contentious debates within the field of environmental security, a wide variety of recent comments by senior diplomats and policy makers are symptomatic of the recognition that issues related to environmental security have ascended to the highest levels.

In 1987, the General Secretary of the Soviet Union, Mikhail Gorbachev stated:

> [The World] is not secure in the direct meaning of the word when currents of poison flow along river channels, when poison rains pour down form the sky, when an atmosphere polluted with industrial and transport waste chokes cities and whole regions, when the development of atomic engineering is justified by unacceptable risks...The relationship between man and the environment has become menacing. Problems of ecological security affect all the rich and the poor. [6]

In November 1989, Prime Minister Margaret Thatcher gave a speech to the United Nations General Assembly-saying: While the conventional political dangers – the threat of global annihilation, the fact of regional war- appear to be receding, we have all recently become aware of another insidious danger. It is as menacing in its way as these more accustomed perils with which international diplomacy has concerned itself for centuries. It is the prospect of irretrievable damage to the atmosphere, to the oceans, to earth itself.[7] In April 1997, as United States Secretary of state, Ms Albright went on to say:

> Not so long ago, many believed that the pursuit of clean air, clean water, and healthy forests was a worthy goal, but not part of our national security. Today environmental issues are part of the mainstream of American foreign Policy. [8]

It was in this backdrop of future non-military threats that a number of studies and research institutions undertook works to determine if and how environmental factors were related to the intra and inter state conflicts or violence that appeared to be surfacing around the globe.[9] These studies varied in their approach, their terminology, and their specific findings and consistent in their explanations suggested that environmental stress, operating through a set of intervening variables, could contribute to violent conflicts, and thus constituted a threat to national and international security. Furthering this argument that the mounting environmental problems and the associated issues need an attention with which the conventional outlook of national security appears to be incongruent, Jeremy Rifkin points out: "The environmental threats facing the planet are not simply the result of scientific miscalculation. Nor are they merely the consequences of ill-conceived management decisions. Ironically it is the notion of security upon which our entire modern worldview is based that has led us to the verge of ecocide... In less than a century the practice of geopolitics thus pushed the world to the brink of both nuclear Armageddon and environmental catastrophe forcing us to reconsider the basic assumption of security that animates the modern world view". [10]

Similarly, Lodgaard feels that "the concept of environmental security challenges established frames of mind and political conflicts. It conveys a message that environmental problems have a legitimate claim for status as military problems have."[11]

Another proponent of environmental security in the same vein opines:

> …national security is not just about fighting forces and weaponry. It relates to watersheds, croplands, forests, genetic resources, climatic and other factors that rarely figure in the minds of military experts and political leaders, but increasingly deserve in their collectivity to rank along side military approaches as crucial to a nation's security.[12]

The growing significance of environmental security is quite evident in major international forums. Some well known examples include the UN Conference on Human Environment (1972), Ottawa Conference on Conservation and Development (1986), United Nations Conference on Environment and Development (1992), World Summit for social Development (1995) and UN symposium on the Global Environment in the 21st Century (1997). These conferences and symposia eventually resulted in various international conventions and protocols for environmental protection or security, such as the Vienna Convention for the protection of the Ozone Layer, the convention on Biological Diversity, the Framework convention on climate change, the convention to combat desertification, and the Kyoto protocol. [13] Harking back to as far as 1987, for example, The World Commission on Environmental Development (Brundtland Report) entitled 'Our common Future", stresses the factor of environmental degradation causing the violent relationship between states:

"Environmental stress is both a cause and effect of political tension and military conflict…nations have fought to assist or resist control over raw materials, energy supplies, land, river basin, sea passages and other key environmental resources. According to the report, such conflicts are likely to increase as these resources became scarcer and competition for them will increase."[14]

Environmental security as a concept encompassing non-military aspects was officially mentioned for the first time in the International conference on the Relationship between Disarmament and Development convened by the UN General Assembly in New York from 24 August to 11 September 1987. The final document adopted by consensus states:

> Recently non-military threats to security have moved to the forefront of global concern. Underdevelopment and declining prospects for development as well as mismanagement and waste of resources, constitute challenges to security. The degradation of the environment presents a threat to sustainable development.... Mass poverty, illiteracy, diseases, squalor and malnutrition affecting a large proportion of world's population often become the cause of social strain, tension and strife.[15]

Two distinct features of environmental security are: First, the environmental causes of conflict, i.e. environmental factors behind potentially violent conflicts; Second, the impact of environmental degradation on overall political economy, health and life of the people. If environmental degradation or deficiencies create the conditions that render conflicts, act as multipliers that aggravate core causes of conflict [16] or act as a catalyst factor in creating conflicts, then environmental degradation or scarcity of resources becomes a national security issue.[17]

Environmental Conflict: The second Dimension

In spite of these criticisms, the most influential arguments in the field have concluded that environmental stress is linked to conflict indirectly, but significantly. While the precise character of the linkage varies from case to case, it is made possible environmental stress is supposed to overwhelm the adaptive capacity of some societies while simultaneously introducing and reinforcing forms of conflict and instability. While division and debate characterize the field of environmental security, there is a strong degree of theoretical consensus among researchers. The most prominent and dominant thread that runs through the entire environmental security literature is that the environmental stress simultaneously reduces adaptive capacity and engenders conflict.

The dominant paradigm in the environmental security literature harks back to writers like Thomas Malthus, but it has obtained its contemporarily influential formulation in the work of Thomas Homer Dixon and Toronto Group. From a myriad of empirical case studies conducted by them on Haiti, Chiapas, Gaza, Pakistan and Bangladesh – India, they concluded that environmental scarcity of renewable resources viz., water, forest, fisheries and cropland give rise to a number of deleterious social effects including economic decline, social segmentation and human migration – these social effects in interaction with other political, economic and social factors, can generate conflict and instability. Central to their model was the notion of supply of ingenuity gap or a disparity between the solutions required to cope with environmental scarcity and the human, social and institutional capital that could be mustered to provide these solutions. This ingenuity gap essentially undermines human adaptive responses. That means, according to their studies, resource scarcity and limited or inadequate adaptive capacity coalesce together to generate violent conflicts in various regions.[18]

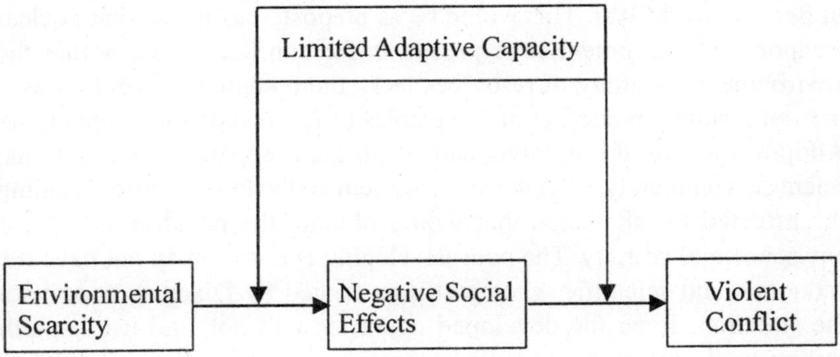

A theoretical representation is made in this figure[19] to understand the linkage between environmental stress and conflict. On theoretical ground it is criticized that even if resource scarcity plays a causal role in conflict, there are other more convincing explanations for conflict. Further, the prospects for adaptation, cooperation or resolution are not as completely bleak as is often presented. At the very prospects of an unlikely nuclear war, the fear of destructibility by the use of nuclear weapons has not any way diminished the universality of nuclear weapon as a main national security issue. It is that fear of destruction, which may have brought many nuclear powers to negotiating table for cooperation or disarmament. The resultant cooperation should not be cited to underrate the holistic perception of nuclear weapons as being a national security concern. Similarly, environmental scarcity of resources with its disastrous social effects may not be everywhere a direct cause of violent conflict, sometimes in combination with other factors, causes conflict. For example, sea level rise a consequence of global warming due to North's mindless pursuit of industrialization based on fossil fuel technology will affect low-lying areas such as Bangladesh below the sea level turning millions of them as refugees fleeing to Indian territories that is likely to exacerbate the already infested ethnic conflict in North-Eastern states. That it would not affect other countries does not any way diminish the environmental causes of conflict not less than the universality of nuclear weapons as a security concern. The consequences of environmental scarcity of resources on political, economic and social life of a state or states may prompt states or nations to cooperate to avoid the negative effects of war on environment. So the environmental co-operation syndrome as argued by some should not be overrated to diminish the role of environmental scarcity of resources causing conflict or violence. No nuclear war has ever been fought in this world after American's dropping of hydrogen bombs on Japan's Herosima and Nagasaki during the course of Second World War. This would be as preposterous to say that nuclear weapon lack the potential or prospects for conflict as to say that the environmental scarcity of resources lacks the potential for conflict as it has not resulted in conflict in some areas or has resulted in cooperation. Adoption means the involvement of all state apparatus, institutions, scientific community, even the social system and value structure including the affected to take steps that would obviate the negative effects of environmental scarcity. The poor developing countries may not have the economic and scientific wherewithal as argued by Dixon to cope with the situation. Even the developed countries will not find it a smooth sailing while responding to the environmental crisis. For example, in regard to stabilization of CO_2 in the atmosphere American steps to renege on its commitment agreed to at Kyoto were a capitulation to the petroleum, coal industrial lobby. What has threatened the world is the Western inordinate life style and pattern of development causing global warming, sea level rise and ozone layer depletion. To ensure environmental security what it requires is to make an overhaul of its pattern of life and development, which is not possible with strong protestations from high-class people. So Bush, American President caving in to the pressure of the industrial class justified his rejection of Kyoto protocol on the ground that countenancing the Kyoto commitment would hamper its economy and life style of its people. [20] Environmental security means overhauling the entire economic development pattern and existing social values related to liberal capitalism that is not possible without politico-socio-economic disruption. So the potential for conflict lies as much in the environmental scarcity of resources as in the very remedies and adaptive measures – a part of fulfillment of environmental security.

In spite of the criticisms above, the main thrust of the studies showing the linkage between environment and conflict, remains paramount: the environmental scarcity operates through a set of intervening variables, contexts or ideational factors that directly cause conflict, and that environmental social effects and stress, as such outstrips attempts to cope with the crisis.

Another study undertaken by Swiss Peace Institute's Environment and Conflicts Project (ENCOP) was in the direction of what the Toronto group suggests. Gunther Bachler belonging to this group in his study used the term transformation by which he meant "the introduction of a heuristic concept in recording those interactions between the three levels – nature, human beings and the economy in a regional context-which have led to conflicts between human communities and will ...increasingly lead to such conflicts."[21]

Degradation is used in this context as an indicator of the degree of environmental transformation. In the words of Kates et al, "the biosphere has accumulated or is on its way to accumulating such a magnitude and variety of changes that it may be said to be transformed."[22] In other words, "transformation conflicts are caused by fundamental anthropogenic changes in the environmental media and by the interactions between the processes of change and their consequences in the eco-regional context."[23]

Another authority Stephan Libiszewski belonging to ENCOP, making a distinction between traditional resource wars and environmental causes of conflict is of the view that an environmental conflict is a conflict caused by the environmental scarcity of a resource that means: caused by a human made disturbance of its normal regeneration rate. Environmental scarcity can result from the overuse of a renewable resource or from the overstrain of the ecosystem's sink capacity, that is pollution. Both can reach the stage of destruction of space of living. Conflicts caused by physical, geopolitical or socio-economic resource scarcity are not environmental conflicts but traditional conflicts of resource distribution.[24]

As found in the Toronto Group's research the ENCOP also walks on the same furrow that scarcity gives rise to conflict. Also it is alleged to be silent about human adaptation to resource scarcity. In these studies, it is mal- development, a condition similar to Homer Dixon's ingenuity gap that undermines human responses and enhances conflicts.[25] Though the ENCOP model is more complex than the Toronto group's general model, but the theoretical argument presented by both is very similar. [26]

In a 1999 NATO pilot study this dominant environmental conflict paradigm was found in the line with the other studies.[27] According to this study, "[it] is not environmental stress in isolation that characterizes the nature of the conflict between groups but other factors".[28] Here too political, economic and social factors intervene between environmental stress and conflict.

The State Failure Task Force (SFTF), another research group marking the same dominant paradigm as with the preceding studies, reiterates the causal weight of environmental stress through intervening variables.[29]. While the researches did find that massive environmental damage in a short time frame could directly cause political collapse, the far more common scenario was that environmental stress operates through the intervening variable of quality of life to generate conflict.

Though highly critical of Toronto group, recent work by Gleditsch and de Soysa appears to have been co-opted by the dominant paradigm. According to their studies, resource scarcity, one component of a multifaceted development problem that they call "poverty" reduces agricultural production that in turn leads to conflict. That is, scarcity leads to a negative social outcome that becomes the proximate cause of conflict.[30] Beyond this however, the Gleditsch and de Soyasa model is similar to the Toronto Group in that there is little room for human adaptation to conditions of scarcity. Indeed, their key independent variable, poverty, is defined by a lack of social and human capital. "Like Homer Dixon's ingenuity gap, Gleditsch and de Soyasa's explanatory variable appears to lock in negative social outcomes, leaving little room for human adaptation."[31]

There is some variation in these models and term presented by these research groups. But in each case the general theory linking resource scarcity and conflict is the same. Homer Dixon focuses on an "ingenuity gap", ENCOP on "mal-development" and Gleditsch and de Soysa on "poverty". Nevertheless, all these phrases describe a similar process- a limited capacity to respond to scarcity.

The model which is critical of all the above models adopted by Richard A Matthew et al finds flaws in current theory in environmental security on two counts. "First, it focuses on too short a time frame. Second, and relatively, it underestimates human adaptive capacity."[32] They were averse to accepting the two extremes, Homer Dixon's lack of adaptive capacity in the poor countries, and Julian Simon and Herman Kahn's faith in the infinite capacity of individuals to adopt. To them, human adaptive capacity lies somewhere between these two extremes. Julian Simon writes, "there is no physical or economic reason why human resourcefulness and enterprise cannot forever continue to respond to impending shortages and existing problems with new expedients that, after an adjustment period, leave us better off than before the problem arose."[33]

Homer Dixon responds to this saying, "while I acknowledge the extraordinary potential of human resourcefulness and enterprise, I nonetheless argue that some societies – especially poor societies – will not be able to supply the unprecedented amounts of ingenuity they will need to solve their emerging scarcity problems."[34] This clearly demonstrates, Homer Dixon never maintains that all societies will not be able to cope with the situation. It is some poor societies because of various factors will be in dearth of required supply of ingenuity to adapt to the situation. This brings Homer Dixon closer to the position taken by Richard A. Matthew and his associates. If adaptation is a dynamic and continuous process, then there may be adoption failure in some and adoption success in others visited with trauma, travails and hardships. When such individual trauma, travails and ordeals while adapting to the environmental stress becomes a collective or group phenomena in a particular political context or in the face of growing incapability of state, the potential for violent conflict exists. Taking a departure from this, Matthew group holds that from a longer time perspective even if the adaptive failures through feedback will result in adaptive success, thus avoiding the prospects for environmental conflicts. Contrary to what Neo-Malthusians such as Paul Ehrlich, Robert Kaplan, and Thomas Homer Dixon contend, "adaptive mechanisms do not simply stall or become overwhelmed while levels of environmental stress continue to escalate."[35] To quote Richard A Mathew further: "This is not to say that all forms of adaptation are socially desirable. Adaptation can mean people of the developing would going further and further into the hinterland to gather fuel, wood and water; parents sending their children to work in factories because of crop failure; and simple belt-tightening people eating less,"[36] or as happened in Kalahandi district of Orissa(India) people eating the dried up Kernel of ripen mangoes died while adapting to food scarcity, or people in these tribal areas of Orissa are forced to sell their children as bonded labourers as a mark of adaptation to the environmental scarcity of crop land and food. These latter examples are certainly unsettling and portent of potential for violent behaviour in an organized form depending on the nature of political system prevailing. If to use the language of Matthew, these starvation, death, or going without food, or half fed situations are the genuine form of adoption, then conflict arising out of these situations created by environmental scarcity in the form of collective or group behaviour or response can be a genuine version of adoption with a view to develop new legitimate and representative political authority and institution and new value structure that would reinvent the political-economic thinking which so far has contributed to environmental scarcity. As Walzer argues, conflict is a normal and important aspect of social development. [37] Then the portrayal of environmental crisis as an environmental conflict paradigm from a broader perspective does not lose its significance or acceptability, as a theoretical framework as argued by Richard Matthew and his group. The conclusion that this group arrived at is not to deny the linkage between environmental scarcity and conflict but stresses on "longer term studies "that might provide deeper understanding of the ways in which concerns about environmental stress and degradation are relevant not only to the those concerned with international security, but also those worried about human rights, social justice and sustainable development. [38]

On the one side the economic deprivation, decreased agricultural production, health hazards, poverty, starvation or half fed or even death situation due to pollution and water scarcity- part of the adoptive success as propounded by Matthew – may cause indirect conflict in association with other factors as nuanced by Volker Boge [39] or Homer Dixon [40]. The other side is the situation of direct conflict or violence arising out of the environmental scarcity of resources - a case of adoptive failure. Hence the conflict emanates directly from the overuse and or pollution / destruction of a renewable natural resource. For example, if a downstream riparian threatens to go to war against an upstream riparian, because the latter pollutes river water so gravely that it cannot be used by the inhabitants of the downstream riparian, who are highly dependent on this water, then the environmental character of conflict is evident. [41] An array of evidences can be cited to show such threats of conflict over environmental scarcity of water all over the globe. [42] That in some cases it has led to cooperation to avoid war does not divest the environmental conflict of its theoretical appeal. Another example of direct violent conflict over environmental scarcity of resources like fish can be cited. The decline in fish catch due to environmental degradation all over the globe and in South Asian regions in particular could result in a series of violent conflict between Tamil Nadu fishermen of India, and Sri Lanka over fishing in waters of Kachchativu Island ceded by India to Sri Lanka as a gesture of friendship and good will in 1974. [43]

The two aspects of environmental scarcity induced situation in terms of adaptive failure and adaptive success can dovetail together into what is called environmental security in a broader sense. What is called as adaptive success at micro level along with adaptive failure in terms of poverty, food scarcity, health hazards or suffering due to environmental degradation at macro level, for example the impact of global warming due to western pattern of development based on fossil fuel industrialization and inordinate life style, poses challenges to redefine development and the vision of and approaches to life.

Human Security: The Third Dimension

The study on environment and security has evolved over the years: from an early primacy on incorporating environmental and its concomitant upshots into the "definition of security" to putting a new premium on how environmental degradation can be a cause or magnifier of violent conflict both intrastate and interstate. An emerging trend within this evolution of non military security threats has been a move toward greater emphasis on the concept of human security. Human security is not in opposition to the earlier trends of redefining security or accounting for the environmental roots of violent conflict. It is an offshoot of these two trends. In a broader sense, human security concerned with security of the people in non-military terms is nothing but an extension of environmental security. The very verbiage used to define the term security in these non traditional and broader senses is today found not dissimilar to that used to understand and define human security.

Those analysts who have focused on explicating the environmental causes of violent conflict have also brought the debate closer to the concept of human security [which] offers a third perspective that allows us to move beyond conventional security thinking, appreciates both the local and global dimensions of the many insecurities experienced by real individuals and groups, and identifies useful ways of linking security and development policies."[44]

While the concept of "human security" has earlier roots, its recent prominence emanates from the 1994 Human Development Report (UNDP, 1994). Its importance was further advanced by the report of the Commission on Global Governance (CGG, 1995). Both reports tried to shift the direction of the security discussion by focusing on issues of human life and human dignity rather than on weapons and territory.

Lorraine Elliott points out two dimensions of the human security paradigm:

> The first is that the concept of "human security" provides an antidote to the more conventional focus on states, borders and territorial integrity. The answer to the question "security for whom" is not the state but the individual and communities, which suggests that even when a state is secure from external threats or internal instabilities, security for its people is not guaranteed. Protecting individuals and communities from the consequences of environmental decline is therefore a security issue. The second dimension is that human

> insecurity (which includes equity, gender, human rights, and identity concerns) is a central factor in social tensions and political instabilities and conflicts that can… become a feature of state insecurity…. If peoples and communities are insecure economically, socially, politically, environmentally, state security can be fragile or uncertain. Environmental security becomes a distributive equity problem rather than one simply of market failure, externalities or zero sum calculations about access to resources and environmental services.[45]

The primacy of state security is strongly embedded in the notion of sovereignty. In its historic meaning, sovereignty implied the security of the sovereign, or "the Prince". The emergence of democratic polity and the transfer of power to the "Citizen" question interestingly the very concept of security rooted in the sovereignty. With sovereignty now ensconcing in the citizenry rather than in the Prince, the notion of security must also be broadened to include the security of the people not the apparatus of the prince. Such a conceptual shift in understanding security does not mince in any way the importance of state security, but it does explicate the need to broaden the term. It is no longer sufficient to hold security of state as synonymous with security of people. Security in conventional parlance understood as synonymous with territorial exclusivity or Prince fails to give security to the individuals and communities. The inadequacy of state security and its brittle impregnability are no where felt so grotesquely than in the case of global climate change. Even the most powerful state well equipped with all modern and sophisticated weapons will come to its knees in the face of climate change affecting millions of people in the both developed and developing world. Environmental security and human security meet the same confluence where the need for sustainable development, and new environmental ethics emerging to redefine western pattern of development and its inordinate life style, meet together.

Climate Change and Human Security

The question how will changing climate patterns affect both inter-state relations and international and national security in a narrow, geo-strategic sense as well as the well-being and survival of human beings and humankind and thus human, water, health and livelihood security, comes to the fore with the findings of scientists about the imminence and impending danger of climate change looming large on the entire humanity.

On 6 April, 2007, the Intergovernmental Panel on Climate Change (IPCC) released the second part of its Fourth Assessment Report demonstrating that the poor of this planet are most likely to suffer the worst effects of climate change. Human security takes on a broader meaning when one considers basic needs for food, water, health – in short, livelihood and a place to live – the issues addressed in the Millennium Development Goals.

> Poor communities can be especially vulnerable, in particular those concentrated in high-risk areas. They tend to have more limited adaptive capacities, and are more dependent on climate-sensitive resources such as local water and food supplies.[46]

Furthermore, within the larger category of 'the poor' lies the frequently invisible (including within that IPCC summary document) group: women. Worldwide, seventy percent of those living below the poverty line are women[47] for whom climate change represents very specific threats to security. When the impacts of climate change are brought home, then women, in their roles as the primary managers of family, food, water and health, must deal very directly with the impacts.

While natural climate variations have existed for millennia, anthropogenic climate change has gradually emerged since the industrial revolution and especially after World War II due to western pattern of development based on the availability of cheap fossil fuels (coal, oil, natural gas) and the dramatic increase in its consumption first primarily in the industrialized countries but now increasingly also in the rapidly growing economies of the BRIC states (Brazil, Russia, India, China), especially of China and India.

Climate Change, Security and Conflicts

Ben Wisner and others have established the linkages between climate change and conflict having implications on national and international security[48]. On 9 January 2004, David King, the UK Government's chief scientific adviser claimed that climate change is a far greater threat to the world than international terrorism. In February 2004, John Reid MP, then British Secretary of State for Defence and now Home Secretary, argued that climate change may spark conflict between nations. He forecast that violence and political conflict would become more likely in the next 20 to 30 years as climate change turned land into desert, melted ice fields and poisoned water supplies. He listed climate change alongside the major threats in future decades, including terrorism, demographic changes, and global energy demand. "As we look beyond the next decade, we see uncertainty growing; uncertainty about the geopolitical and human consequences of climate change. ...Impacts such as flooding, melting permafrost and desertification could lead to loss of agricultural land, poisoning of water supplies and destruction of economic infrastructure. ...More than 300 million people in Africa currently lack access to safe water; climate change will worsen this dire situation."[49] John Ashton, the UK Foreign Secretary's Special Representative for Climate Change, said at a conference on "Climate Change: The Global Security Impact", at the Royal United Services Institute on 24 January 2007: "There is every reason to believe that as the 21st century unfolds, the security story will be bound together with climate change."[50] "Climate change is a security issue because if we don't deal with it, people will die and states will fail," Ashton concluded.

> Ashton pointed out that defense and security planners must face a paradox when assessing their responses to the problem. Most security threats in today's world are amenable to some extent to a "hard power" or conventional reaction, he said, and demand will rise for such responses to climate change-related security problems. "But there is no hard power solution to climate change - you cannot force your neighbour to change its carbon emissions at the barrel of a gun."[51]

Sir Crispin Tickell, the former UK Permanent Representative to the UN, highlighted the environmental factors behind societal collapse. Professor John Mitchell, the chief scientist at the UK Met Office, forecast that the coming decades will see a 30 per cent increase in severe drought. He added that Africa will experience increased desertification, water stress and disease.[52]

Besides the UK, other nations have begun to assess the security implication of climate change. In 2002, the German Ministry for the Environment, Nature Conservation and Nuclear Safety published a commissioned report on climate change and conflicts raised the question whether climate change impacts can increase conflict potentials.[53] n spring 2004 an internal report by Randall and Schwartz for the U.S. Department of Defense on the impact of Abrupt Climate Change on U.S. national security was leaked to the press.[54]

The British initiative during its Security Council presidency to put climate change on its agenda for 17 April 2007 has been the most recent attempt to "securitize" climate change in the context of geopolitics.[55]

Climate Change as a Threat and Challenge to International, National and Human Security

Climate change poses many new threats and challenges to national security and international stability as well as to human security at other scales. The concept of human security was introduced first by UNDP in 1994[56] and then developed further in a report by the Human Security Commission, co-chaired by Sadako Ogata and Amartya Sen, in its report *Human Security Now* (2003).[57] The environmental dimension of human security has been addressed by an international team working on Global Environmental Change and Human Security (GECHS) and in several studies by the United Nations University Institute for Environment and Human Security (UNU-EHS).[58]

In February 1999, during its presidency of the United Nations Security Council, Canada, a founding member of the Human Security Network, put human security on the agenda by addressing the impact of armed conflicts on human beings.[59] In March 2005, then UN Secretary General, Kofi Annan, in his report *In Larger Freedom*[60] wrote of human security in a broad sense, the issue was placed on the agenda of the UN General Assembly in the fall of 2005.

UNDP will take up the relationship between human development and climate change in its *Human Development Report 2007* (HDR), to be launched in November. Over 17 years, UNDP has incrementally developed a sensitive measure of human development (the human development index – HDI). Earlier studies have shown that the HDI correlates well with measures of disaster risk such as UNDP's disaster risk index (DRI), especially for less developed countries.[61] Preliminary analysis for this year's HDR suggests that climate change poses major obstacles to progress in meeting MDGs and maintaining progress raising the HDI: "There is a clear and present danger that climate change will roll back human development for a large section of humanity, undermining international cooperation aimed at achieving the Millennium Development Goals (MDGs) in the process."[62]

Concerning the MDGs individually, UNDP states:[63]

> ...[C]limate change may pose a threat to food security through erratic rainfall patterns and decreasing crop yields, contributing to increased hunger. Furthermore, adverse climate change impacts on natural systems and resources, infrastructure, and labor productivity may lead to reduced economic growth, exacerbating poverty.

> These effects threaten the achievement of MDG 1. Loss of livelihood assets, displacement and migration may lead to reduced access to education opportunities, thus hampering the realization of MDG 2. Depletion of natural resources and decreasing agricultural productivity may place additional burdens on women's' health and reduce time for decision-making processes and income-generating activities, worsening gender equality and women's' empowerment (MDG 3). Increased incidence of vector-borne diseases, increases in heat-related mortality, and declining quantity and quality of drinking water will lead to adverse health effects threatening the achievement of MDGs 4,5,6 and 7. In general terms, the realization of MDG 7 may be jeopardized through climate change negatively impacting quality and productivity of natural resources and ecosystems, possibly irreversibly, threatening environmental sustainability. Climate change, a global phenomenon, calls for a collective response in the form of global partnerships (MDG 8)

Linkages between Climate Change and Security

Some effects of climate change are already evident and will become very clear in the human and climatic short run (2007-2020). They will increase and others will manifest themselves in the medium term (2021-2050); whilst in the long run (2051-2100), they will all be active and interacting strongly with other major trends: the end of the petroleum economy for many producing and consuming nations, possible financial and economic crisis, a larger population of humans, and a much more urbanized humanity – far in excess of the 50% now living in small to very large cities. All these processes will be accompanied by redistribution of population nationally and internationally.[64] Such redistributions typically have significant gender dimensions; for example, extreme event impacts can lead to male out migration in search of work, culminating in an increase in women-headed households – a group often considered particularly vulnerable.[65]

The linkages between climate change and security are complex in many ways. To begin with, climate change involves the interactions of many systems such as the atmosphere, hydrosphere, cryosphere, and biosphere that are immensely complex in their own right. Thus, a recurrent theme in IPCC reports is the significance of thresholds and non-linearities. When human systems are added to the mix, complexity escalates.[66] Livelihood security and other aspects of human security interact with geo-strategic (or "hard") security issues because of the national and regional upheavals that climate stress may put on livelihood systems already vulnerable and incapable of adapting.[67] World wide the rural and urban poor are already under stress, and for some groups such as women headed households in Africa, adaptation to climate-induced stress will be very difficult indeed. As Simon points out, climate change has both intermittent but increasingly frequent, extreme impacts (such as large storms and heat waves) and slow on-set, pervasive, cumulative effects (such as extinction of life forms and sea level rise).[68] Both kinds of effects may have a role in displacing human populations and disrupting their livelihoods. Some major climate changes may actually occur rapidly.

Some efforts by state actors to mitigate and adapt to climate change may also further stress weak and marginal sections of the population such as indigenous groups and ethnic minorities, increasing discontent and alienation. In particular, large scale water management and forestry projects in the past have displaced such groups,[69] and without safeguards are likely to do so as states expand mega-projects as part of their national climate adaptation programs. One example is the new dams being built in Guatemala. Such intra-state tension and possible conflict over the distribution of winners and losers in climate adaptation may spillover into regional conflicts, on the basis of recent experience in Darfur. State actor adaptations may also weaken treaties such as regional water basin management and lead eventually to inter-state conflict. For example, Sudan's decision to build a new dam on the Nile, could have that result.

One must also consider that the world around us in 2007 has in it a large number of weak and crisis-prone nation states.[70] It is not likely that such chronic instability will diminish (although details of the pattern may shift geographically) before severe impacts of climate change are felt. Humanitarian intervention in the crises that are likely will become more difficult and run the danger of exacerbating conflict, especially as civilian humanitarian and military relations become more interwoven.[71]

Figure 1 provides an overview of these complex interactions arranged on a time scale.

Fig. 1. Matrix of Possible Climate Change/Security Interactions over Time

	Direct impact			Indirect Consequences		Slow-onset	
	Water	**Food**	**Health**	**Mega-projects**	**Disasters**	**Bio-fuel**	**Sea level**
Short term (2007-2020)	Local conflict over water	Failure to meet MDGs	Failure to meet MDGs	Long history of develop-ment induced displacement from 1950s	Nation states begin to lose credibility due to inability to prevent large disasters	Isolated food –fuel compe-tition and price spikes	Small number of displace-ments
Medium term (2021-2050)	Increased local & some inter-national conflict over water	Significant displace-ment due to famine	Interacts with food production problems	Displacement of rural poor due to CDM & large scale dams & other state based mitigation & adaptation projects	Significant political unrest due to failure of DRR & inadequate recovery in many countries	Food-fuel competition increases & biodiversity erosion	Increasing displacement & national/ international tension
Long term (2051-2100)	Major inter-national conflict over water	Major displace-ment & political upheaval	Major displace-ment due to epidemics	Major urban upheaval and other political fall out from mega-project displacement	Major upheaval with international implications due to unattended weather catastrophes	Major discontent due to food-fuel competition	Major international tensions due to population displacement
All of these processes strongly interact with each other							

Source: Ben Wisner and others, "Climate Change and Human Security" Simultaneously uploaded to Radix - Radical Interpretations of Disaster: http://www.radixonline.org/cchs.html & http://www.radixonline.org/cchs.doc ;

Disaster Diplomacy: http://www.disasterdiplomacy.org; Peace Research and European Security Studies (AFES-PRESS): http://www.afes-press.de/html/topical.html.

Climate-induced Conflict Constellations

WBGU identifies four conflict constellations[72] in which critical developments can be anticipated as a result of climate change and which may occur with similar characteristics in different regions of the world. "Conflict constellations" are defined as typical causal linkages at the interface of environment and society, whose dynamic can lead to social destabilization and, in the end, to violence.

Conflict Constellation "Climate-induced Degradation of Freshwater Resources":

1.1 billion people are currently without access to safe drinking water. The situation could worsen for hundreds of millions of people as climate change alters the variability of precipitation and the quantity of available water. At the same time, demand for water is increasing due to the world's growing population and its mounting aspirations. This dynamic triggers distributional conflicts and poses major challenges to water management systems in the countries concerned. For example, regions which depend on melt water from mountain glaciers – which are at risk from climate change – will require new water management strategies and infrastructures, as well as political efforts to avert national or even trans-boundary conflicts over the distribution of increasingly scarce water resources. However, the countries which will suffer the greatest water stress are generally those which already lack the political and institutional framework necessary for the adaptation of water and crisis management systems. This could overstretch existing conflict resolution mechanisms, ultimately leading to destabilization and violence.

There is no dearth of evidence in the past to show as a population growth/ demand problem, water scarcity may, indeed, become a source of conflict and instability, but more as a function of supply.[73] International regimes such as the Nile Treaty are old, inadequate, and fragile. Newer, more forward-looking treaty regimes, such as the Nile Basin Initiative, are still in their infancy and subject to similar divisive pressures despite the efforts of multilateral agencies like the World Bank. The other tensions and sources of instability discussed above could also place international water management and sharing agreements under pressure. Management of many of the world's 261 international rivers will face severe tests.[74] Furthermore; many coastal freshwater aquifers will suffer salinization as a result of sea level rise. In Africa alone:

> By 2020, between 75 and 250 million people are projected to be exposed to an increase of water stress due to climate change. If coupled with increased demand, this will adversely affect livelihoods and exacerbate water-related problems.[75]

A team at Keele University and the UK's Centre for Ecology and Hydrology has produced a water poverty index (WPI)[76]. Using the WPI they found that already in 2005 a large number of countries were suffering moderate, high, or severe stress. If this is the baseline situation, what will additional stress due to climate change do in many of these places?

•Conflict Constellation "Climate-induced Decline in Food Production":

More than 850 million people worldwide are currently undernourished. This situation is likely to worsen in future as a result of climate change, as food insecurity in the lower latitudes, i.e. in many developing countries, will increase with a temperature rise of just 2 °C (relative to the 1990 baseline). With global warming of 2–4 °C, a drop in agricultural productivity is anticipated worldwide. This trend will be substantially reinforced by desertification, soil salinization or water scarcity. In South Asia and North Africa, for example, the areas suitable for agriculture are already largely exploited. This may well trigger regional food crises and further undermine the economic performance of weak and unstable states, thereby encouraging or exacerbating destabilization, the collapse of social systems, and violent conflicts.

Food and livelihood pressure due to climate change will lead to populist and/or military coups in a number of countries. After the roll-out of macro-economic "structural adjustment" programs in Africa in the 1980s, one witnessed junior officers in a number of militaries seizing power in the name of workers and peasants who suffered (e.g. in Burkina Faso). This will produce continuing instability in Africa, in particular. Between 1980 and 2001 there were 95 attempted coups in Africa — 33 of them successful. Popular discontent over livelihood security was a contributing cause of many of these.[77] The same pressures as well as the "push" provided by conflict will cause considerable population movements and displacement both within countries and internationally.[78] That, in turn, will increase insecurity – a process that is already occurring. Effects in Africa may include the following:

> Agricultural production, including access to food, in many African countries and regions is projected to be severely compromised by climate variability and change. The area suitable for agriculture, the length of growing seasons and yield potential, particularly along the margins of semi-arid and arid areas, are expected to decrease. This would further adversely affect food security and exacerbate malnutrition in the continent. Local food supplies are projected to be negatively affected by decreasing fisheries resources in large lakes due to rising water temperatures, which may be exacerbated by continued over-fishing.[79]

Women are responsible for around 70 percent of household food production in sub-Saharan Africa, often on the basis of informal resource rights. Climate-induced changes in crop and livestock production could threaten those rights, as well as affect the gendered division of labor with negative effects on women's and men's incomes, livelihoods and household security.[80]

The climate-food connection will not only affect the poor. In some industrial and industrializing nations, as climate change creates new patterns of food production — new exporting and new importing zones – access to supplies and the energy to import them may become strategic concerns and lead to international conflict.

• Conflict Constellation "Climate-induced Increase in Storm and Flood Disasters"

Climate change is likely to result in further sea-level rise and more intensive storms and heavy precipitation. This will greatly increase the risk of natural disasters occurring in many cities and industrial regions in coastal zones. Those risks will be further amplified by deforestation along the upper reaches of rivers, land subsidence in large urban areas and the ever greater spatial concentration of populations and assets. Storm and flood disasters have already contributed to conflict in the past, especially during phases of domestic political tension, e.g. in Central America, India and China. Conflicts are likely to occur more frequently in future, firstly because regions especially at risk from storm and flood disasters, such as Central America and Southern Africa, generally have weak economic and political capacities, making adaptation and crisis management much more difficult. Secondly, frequent storm and flood disasters along the densely populated east coasts of India and China could cause major damage and trigger and/or intensify migration processes that are difficult to control.

• Conflict Constellation "Environmentally-induced Migration"

Experience has shown that migration can greatly increase the likelihood of conflict in transit and target regions. It can be assumed that the number of environmental migrants will substantially rise in future due to the impacts of climate change. In developing countries in particular, the increase in drought, soil degradation and growing water scarcity in combination with high population growth, unstable institutions, poverty or a high level of dependency on agriculture means that there is a particularly significant risk of environmental migration occurring and increasing in scale. Most environmental migration is initially likely to occur within national borders. Trans-boundary environmental migration will mainly take the form of south-south migration, but Europe and North America must also expect substantially increased migratory pressure from regions most at risk from climate change. The question as to which states will have to bear the costs of environmentally-induced migration in future also contains conflict potential..

Health-Climate-Livelihood-Conflict-Security

Health impacts of climate change including epidemics and insect outbreaks will have a similar effect, also compounding food and livelihood crises. This is beginning, but it will accelerate in the medium term. As we have seen with SARS and avian influenza, disease does not respect national boundaries in a globalized world. Changing climate may bring many epidemiological surprises as vector habitats change, sometimes quite rapidly.

Projected climate change-related exposures are likely to affect the health status of millions of people, particularly those with low adaptive capacity, through:

* increases in malnutrition and consequent disorders, with implications for child growth and development;
* increased deaths, disease and injury due to heat waves, floods, storms, fires and droughts;
* the increased burden of diarrhoeal disease; the increased frequency of cardio-respiratory diseases due to higher concentrations of ground level ozone related to climate change; and, the altered spatial distribution of some infectious disease vectors.

Climate change is expected to have some mixed effects, such as the decrease or increase of the range and transmission potential of malaria in Africa[81].

Mitigation-Adaptation-Inequity-Conflict-Security

Adger et al. raise the issue of "fairness" in adaptation to climate change.[82] Mega-projects conceived by nation states as solutions to climate change such as the planting of large scale forestry under the Kyoto Protocol's Clean Development Mechanism (CDM) and the building of more large dams and reservoirs, are beginning to displace other numbers of poor and marginal people, having effects on politics and stability similar to those mentioned above while negatively affecting biodiversity. In the medium term such mega-project investments – already a major feature of rapid urban industrialization in China and India, the world's two most populous countries – will grow rapidly as water shortages intensify. Already "an estimated 40–80 million people have been forcibly evicted from their lands to make way for dams."[83]

The social and economic impacts of climate change focused mitigation projects have not yet been fully assessed. Skutsch, for example, highlights the absence of gender impact analysis of CDM projects.[84] The "clean, green" solution of nuclear energy so heavily promoted in the early years of this century and recently adopted as a climate change-fighting strategy by the EU and others has led to a planet-wide race to capture extractive rights and exploit uranium reserves. At this writing, the historically high value of uranium has led to violent conflict in the Congo and the renewed use of forced labor. The profound, degenerative human health consequences of working and living in a toxic and radioactive environment are only recently being understood. Epidemics of cancer and other radiogenic health problems now prevalent in areas that hosted the Cold War nuclear machine are certain to expand.[85] In addition, a new phase in the growth of nuclear power could exacerbate the problem of "leakage" of weapons grade material into the hands of non-state actors.

Food-Fuel Conflict and Human Security

Large-scale investments in bio-fuels in the medium and long term as a substitute for green house gas-producing petro-based energy sources may have the perverse effect of taking considerable land out of food production and diverting food grains, thus raising food prices and eroding biodiversity. The maize (corn) price in Mexico has already increased because of demand for grain by US ethanol plants, and protests have resulted.[86] If this occurs, then food and livelihood pressures will increase and the desperation of many rural and urban people will increase national and regional insecurity. Rapid expansion of sugar production in Brazil and Africa palm in Colombia, as energy feed stocks, have been a major source of displacement of small farmers from their lands. Also, recent research has shown the energy and carbon efficiency of biofuel production to be variable and often lower than with the burning of fossil fuels.[87]

Disaster-Livelihood-Governance-Conflict-Security

Also in the medium term livelihood security and hence the ability to govern will be undermined by the increasingly frequent occurrence of more and more mega-disasters such as those associated with hurricane Mitch (1998), the Orissa super-cyclone (1999), hurricanes Katrina and Rita, and tropical storm Stan (2005). Even now, the UN reports that over a million people are threatened by erratic weather in five southern African countries.[88] Such catastrophic weather events often produce cascades of secondary physical hazards such as landslides (as Nicaragua during Mitch or in Vargas, Venezuela in 1999) or downstream inundation when dams overflow or dam authorities release large volumes of water to safeguard large dams (as in Mozambique at present and in several recent years). They also trigger changes in social relations, including the exacerbation of unequal gender relations manifested in lack of land and property rights, and rising sexual and gender based violence towards women and girls.[89] In urban industrial landscapes such as greater New Orleans, Manila, or Osaka, storms and flooding often bring further complications by damage done to factories, storage facilities, and pipe lines. The resulting "natural-technological" (natech) hazards are very expensive to clean up and can have long term public health consequences.[90] Institutional systems for anticipating or even timely recognition of the "surprises" that natech hazards may present in the future are not yet been developed world wide.

> Where extreme weather events become more intense and/or more frequent, the economic and social costs of those events will increase, and these increases will be substantial in the areas most directly affected. Climate change impacts spread from directly impacted areas and sectors to other areas and sectors through extensive and complex linkages.[91]

Disasters, development, and conflict have been shown to have complex interactions with one other quite apart from the additional stresses and management challenges likely to accompany increasingly variable weather and more extreme storms.[92]

Sea Level-Displacement-Security

Finally, sea level rise in the long term and its collateral impacts on river flow and ocean discharge regimes will cause displacement of many millions of people currently living in coastal areas. For the small island nations of the world, especially the many cultural groups living on coral atolls, entire nations face complete submersion A recent study calculates that around 634 million people are living less than 10m above sea level. The study notes that "of the more than 180 countries with populations in the low-elevation coastal zone, about 70 percent have urban areas of more than five million people that extend into it." The authors then list Tokyo, Japan; New York, U.S.; Mumbai, India; Shanghai, China; Jakarta, Indonesia; and Dhaka, Bangladesh.[93] One could add other cities as well to the list, for example, Cartagena, Colombia; Lima, Peru; Buenos Aires, Argentina; and Recife and Rio de Janeiro, Brazil. African exposure is high.

Nigerian scholars Ibe and Awosika state: "This coastal zone consists of four major basins which are bordered on the ocean side by low-lying coastlines which are sandy and muddy in some cases. General beach elevations range from 2-3 m above sea level."[94] Most of Africa's major cities are coastal, including Dakar, Senegal; Accra, Ghana; Lagos,

Nigeria; Luanda, Angola; Cape Town and Durban, South Africa; Maputo, Mozambique; Dar es Salaam, Tanzania; and Mombasa, Kenya; and Mogadishu, Somalia. The cost of dislocation – which will include salinisation of coastal aquifers and other low-lying fresh water resources - and loss of infrastructure will be difficult for poor countries to bear, especially in Africa.[95] The Intergovernmental Panel on Climate Change agrees.[96] Considerable political instability may result. Just considering Africa:

> Towards the end of the 21st century, projected sea-level rise will affect low-lying coastal areas with large populations. The cost of adaptation could amount to at least 5-10% of GDP. Mangroves and coral reefs are projected to be further degraded, with additional consequences for fisheries and tourism. [97]

Additional negative feedback can be anticipated as degradation of coastal wetland vegetation and coral reefs reduce or remove their protective influence in the face of storms.

Six Threats to International Stability and Security

In light of current knowledge about the social impacts of climate change, WBGU identifies the following six key threats to international security and stability which will arise if climate change mitigation fails[98]:

1. Possible increase in the number of weak and fragile states as a result of climate change:

Weak and fragile states have inadequate capacities to guarantee the core functions of the state, notably the state's monopoly on the use of force, and therefore already pose a major challenge for the international community. So far, however, the international community has failed to summon the political will or provide the necessary financial resources to support the long-term stabilization of these countries. Moreover, the impacts of unabated climate change would hit these countries especially hard, further limiting and eventually overstretching their problem-solving capacities. Conflict constellations may also be mutually reinforcing, e.g. if they extend beyond the directly affected region through environmental migration and thus destabilize other neighbouring states. This could ultimately lead to the emergence of "failing sub-regions" consisting of several simultaneously overstretched states, creating "black holes" in world politics that are characterized by the collapse of law and public order, i.e. the pillars of security and stability. It is uncertain at present whether, against the backdrop of more intensive climate impacts, the international community would be able to curb this erosion process effectively.

2. Risks for global economic development

Climate change will alter the conditions for regional production processes and supply infrastructures. Regional water scarcity will impede the development of irrigated agriculture and other water-intensive sectors. Drought and soil degradation will result in a drop in agricultural yields. More frequent extreme events such as storms and flooding put industrial sites and the transport, supply and production infrastructures in coastal regions at risk, forcing companies to relocate or close production sites. Depending on the type and intensity of the climate impacts, this could have a significant and adverse effect on the global economy. Unabated climate change is likely to result in substantially reduced rates of growth. This will increasingly limit the economic scope, at national and international level, to address the urgent challenges associated with the Millennium Development Goals.

3. Risks of growing international distributional conflicts between the main drivers of climate change and those most affected

Climate change is mainly caused by the industrialized and newly industrializing countries. The major differences in the per capita emissions of industrialized and developing/newly industrializing countries are increasingly regarded as an "equity gap", especially as the rising costs of climate change are mainly being borne by the developing countries. The greater the damage and the burden of adaptation in the South, the more intensive the distributional conflicts between the main drivers of climate change and those most affected will become. The worst affected countries are likely to invoke the "polluter pays" principle, so international controversy over a global compensation regime for climate change will probably intensify. Beside today's industrialized countries, the major ascendant economies whose emissions are increasing substantially, notably China but also India and Brazil, for example, will also be called to account by the developing countries in future. A key line of conflict in global politics in the 21st century would therefore divide not only the industrialized and the developing countries, but also the rapidly growing newly industrializing countries and the poorer developing countries. The international community is ill-prepared at present for this type of distributional conflict.

4. The risk to human rights and the industrialized countries' legitimacy as global governance actors

Unabated climate change could threaten livelihoods, erode human security and thus contribute to the violation of human rights. Against the backdrop of rising temperatures, growing awareness of social climate impacts and inadequate climate change mitigation efforts, the CO2-emitting industrialized countries and, in future, buoyant economies such as China could increasingly be accused of knowingly causing human rights violations, or at least doing so in de facto terms. The international human rights discourse in the United Nations is therefore also likely to focus in future on the threat that climate impacts pose to human rights. Unabated climate change could thus plunge the industrialized countries in particular into crises of legitimacy and limit their international scope for action.

5. Triggering and intensification of migration

Migration is already a major and largely unresolved international policy challenge. Climate change and its social impacts will affect growing numbers of people, so the number of migration hotspots around the world will increase. The associated conflict potential is considerable, especially as "environmental migrants" are currently not provided for in international law. Disputes over compensation payments and the financing of systems to manage refugee crises will increase. In line with the "polluter pays" principle, the industrialized countries will have to face up to their responsibilities. If global temperatures continue to rise unabated, migration could become one of the major fields of conflict in international politics in future.

6. Overstretching of classic security policy

The future social impacts of unabated climate change are unlikely to trigger "classic" inter-state wars; instead, they will probably lead to an increase in destabilization processes and state failure with diffuse conflict structures and security threats in politically and economically overstretched states and societies. The specific conflict constellations, the failure of disaster management systems after extreme weather events and increasing environmental migration will be almost impossible to manage without support from police and military capacities, and therefore pose a challenge to classic security policy. In this context, a well-functioning cooperation between development and security policy will be crucial, as civilian conflict management and reconstruction assistance are reliant on a minimum level of security. At the same time, the largely unsuccessful operations by highly equipped military contingents which have aimed to stabilize and bring peace to weak and fragile states since the 1990s show that "classic" security policy's capacities to act are limited. A climate-induced increase in the number of weak and fragile states or even the destabilization of entire sub-regions would therefore overstretch conventional security policy.

Overstretching the Capacities of the Global Governance System

The greater the scale of climate change, the greater the probability that in the coming decades, climate-induced conflict constellations will impact not only on individual countries or sub- regions but also on the global governance system as a whole. These new global risk potentials can only be countered by policies that aim to manage global change. Every one of the six threats to international stability and security, outlined above, is itself hard to manage. The inter-action between these threats intensifies the challenges for international politics. It is almost inconceivable that in the coming years, a global governance system could emerge with the capacity to respond effectively to the conflict constellations identified by WBGU. Against the backdrop of globalization, unabated climate change is likely to overstretch the capacities of a still insufficient global governance system.

As the climate-induced security risks of the 21st century have their own specific characteristics, they will be difficult to mitigate through classic military interventions. Instead, an intelligent and well-crafted global governance strategy to mitigate these new security risks would initially consist of an effective climate policy, which would then evolve into a core element of preventive security policy in the coming decades. The more climate change advances, the more important adaptation strategies in the affected countries will become and these must be supported by international development policy. At international level, the focus will be on global diplomacy to contain climate-induced conflicts, as well as on the development of compensation mechanisms for those affected by climate change, global migration policy, and measures to stabilize the world economy. The opportunities to establish a well-functioning global governance architecture will narrow as global temperatures rise, revealing a vicious circle: climate change can only be combated effectively through international cooperation, but with advancing climate change, the basis for constructive multilateralism will diminish. Climate change thus poses a challenge to international security, but classic, military-based security policy will be unable to make any major contributions to resolving the impending climate crises[99].

The Link between Carrying Capacity and Warfare

Today, carrying capacity, which is the ability for the Earth and its natural ecosystems including social, economic, and cultural systems to support the finite number of people on the planet, is being challenged around the world. As predicted, abrupt climate change is likely to stretch carrying capacity well beyond its already precarious limits. As abrupt climate change lowers the world's carrying capacity aggressive wars are likely to be fought over food, water, and energy. Steven LeBlanc, Harvard archaeologist and author of a new book called Carrying Capacity, describes the relationship between carrying capacity and warfare. Drawing on abundant archaeological and ethnological data, he argues that historically humans conducted organized warfare for a variety of reasons, including warfare over resources and environment. Humans fight when they outstrip the carrying capacity of their natural environment[100]. Peace occurs when carrying capacity goes up. But such peaceful periods are short- lived because population quickly rises to once again push against carrying capacity, and warfare resumes. Indeed, over the millennia most societies define themselves according to their ability to conduct war, and warrior culture becomes deeply ingrained. With carrying capacity lowered by abrupt climate change, humanity would revert to its norm of constant battles for diminishing resources, which the battles themselves would further reduce even beyond the climatic effects. Once again warfare would define human life. As famine, disease, and weather-related disasters strike due to the abrupt climate change, many countries' needs will exceed their carrying capacity. This will create a sense of desperation, which is likely to lead to offensive aggression in order to reclaim balance[101].

Conclusion

Premised on Newtonian and Cartesian epistemology, the western political and economic thinking employed science to the ends of human beings- a commodious and luxurious life. Not only that, it borrowed the insights of science to view nature as the lifeless other to be exploited for the attainment of these ends. This resulted in defining development based on fossil fuel technology and industrialization, which destroyed the nature with ramifying consequences upon the entire mankind. The result of following the western pattern of development since the beginning of industrialization has been the accumulation of greenhouse gases in the atmosphere with the devastating consequences as noted above. The more a country is industrialized and considered developed, the more greenhouse gases it has emitted to the atmosphere. On this account, the industrialized North through its centuries of progress on this development trajectory has usurped the resources of the atmosphere at the cost of the developing and underdeveloped countries, and polluted the atmosphere. As the rich industrialized countries have unilaterally and inequitably messed up the atmosphere, they have squarely the historic responsibility of disabusing it of the debris. This is the argument put forth in the climate change debate by developing countries in response to American attempt at bringing the former into the task. Today, the debate remains hanging on a crucial contradiction between the principle of inequity the North have been practicing since industrial revolution as to the uncontested access to the atmosphere denying the same to the South and at the cost of nature and future generations, and the preachment of equity principle and meaningful participation to the South on the question of cleansing the atmosphere.

Coming to the very root of the crisis, Science provided the ontological foundation to Political Science to look at the nature and the poor who do not have the wherewithal to have a commodious living as "the other" to be exploited or harnessed for one's end. The entire Earth was looked down upon as a compendium of lifeless raw materials to cater to the materialistic ends of those humans who are propertied or rational in the words of English philosopher Locke, because they have property. To attainment of these goals- wealth production and commodious living by the wealthy few believing in exorbitant consumption and inordinate life style as quintessential of development, the entire Earth has been subjugated and robbed of its bounties at the cost of nature, other humans, non-human living and future generations. That every body is a self sufficing and aggrandizing part disjointed from the whole has resulted in a mechanical view of the universe. The concept of development based on this paradigm has been the development of one against the other. Woven into this paradigm was the concept of security, which was the security of one or one group, or one state against the other. But today, the devastating consequences of climate change and its pervasiveness impacting the very survival of entire humanity have spurted the traditional security planners into thinking anew what so far they have defined as development and established frame of mind about security in terms of disjointed parts and others as mere objectivities not as inter subjectivities A profound affirmation of this is found in Eastern insight epitomized in the Indian Upanishads: "The entire universe is like a family" [Basudheiba kutumbakam]. No man is like an island. Everybody is the inseparable whole. In more mundane terms, as the rich countries and wealthy people have enjoyed, usurped, and destroyed the atmosphere at the cost of the other (humans, nature, living and non-living, and the future generations), they must not only come forward to cut down its consumption, rethink its life style and pattern of development, and follow exemplarily new environmental ethics but also help, support and promote the rest of the world in adapting to the changing planetary system. Martin parry, a climate scientist with the United Kingdom's Met Office, said destructive changes in temperature, rainfall and agriculture were now forecast to occur several decades earlier than thought. Vulnerable people, such as the old and poor, would be worst affected, and, world leaders had not yet accepted that their countries would have to adapt to the likely consequences. Co- chairman of the IPCC working group, Professor Parry said: "We are all used to talking about these impacts coming in the lifetimes of our children and grand children. Now we know that it is us." He added that politicians had wasted a decade by focusing only on ways to cut emissions, and had only recently woken up to the need to adapt. "Mitigation has got all the attention, but we cannot mitigate out of this problem. We now have a choice between a future with a damaged world or a severely damaged world."[102]

References

1. S.Dalby, "American Security Discourse: The Persistence of Geopolitics," Political Geography Quarterly, 9, 1990, pp. 171-88.
2. O.R.Holsti, "International Systems, Systems Change and Foreign Policy," Diplomatic History, 15, 1991, p. 94.
3. J.Joffe, "Entangled for ever", in C.W.Kegley Jr. and E.R.Wittkoff, eds., The Future of American Foreign Policy (New York: St. Martin's Press, 1992), p. 35.
4. M.Shamsul Haque, "Non-Traditional Security and the Environment in North east Asia", Work in Progress Vol. 16, No. 3, Summer 2002, p. 24.
5. Peter H.Gleick, World's Water: The Biennial Report on Fresh Water Resources (Washington D.C.: California: Island Press, 1998), pp. 105-106.
6. M.Gorbachev, "Reality and guarantees for a secure world", Moscow News, No. 39, 1987, p. 3287.
7. Quoted in Peter H.Gleick, World's Water, op.cit, p. 106.
8. U.S. Department of State, "Environmental Diplomacy: The Environment and U.S. Foreign Policy", U.S. Department of state, Washington, D.C.: 1997.
9. Ted Gurr, Minorities at Risk: A Global view of Ethnopolitical Conflicts (Washington DC: US Institute of Peace Press, 1993)
10. J.Rifkin, Biospheric Politics: A New Consciousness for a New Century (New York: Crown, 1991), p. 2.

11. Sverre Lodgaard, "Environmental Conflict Resolution," paper presented at the UNEP meeting on Environmental Conflict Resolution, Nairobi, 30 March 1990, p. 18
12. Norman Myers, "The Environmental Dimension to Security Issues", The Environmentalist Vol. 6, Winter 1986, p. 251
13. See M.Shamsul Haque, "The Fate of Sustainable Development Under the Neoliberal Regimes in Developing Countries", International Political Science Review 20/2 (1999), pp. 199-222.
14. World Commission on Environment and development, Our Common Future (Brundtland Report (New York / London: Oxford University Press, 1987)) p. 290
15. Quoted in Dietrich Fisher, Nonmilitary Aspects of Security: A system's Approach, United Nations Institute for Disarmament and Research (UNIDIR), (Aldershot: Dartmouth Publishing Company Ltd, 1993), p. 10.
16. Norman Myers "The Environmental Dimension to Security Issues," The Environmentalist Vol. 6, Winter 1986, p. 253.
17. Gareth Porter "Environmental Security as National Security Issue", Current History, May 1995, p. 218.
18. Thomas F. Homer Dixon, Environment, Scarcity, and Violence (Princeton, New Jersy: Princeton University Press, 1999); Thomas F.Homer Dixon and Jessica Blitt, Evidences: Links Among Environment, Population, and Security (New York: Rowman and Littlefield, 1998); Thomas F.Homer Dixon, "Environmental Scarcities and Violent Conflict: Evidence from Cases", International Security Vol. 19, 1994, pp. 5-40.
19. Thomas F. Homer Dixon, Environment, Scarcity, and Violence, p. 7 and Daniel Esty et. al., "The State Failure Task Force Report: Phase II Findings", Environmental Change and Security Project Report 5, 1999, p. 63; S.C. Lonergan, ed., Environmental Change, adaptation and Security, (Boston: Klewer, 1999); David Dessler, "Review of Environmental Scarcity and Violence", Environmental Change and Security Project Report 5 (1999), pp. 100-101.
20. David L. Levy and Daniel Egan, "Capital Contests: National and Transnational Channels of Corporate Influence on the Climate Change Negotiations", Politics and Society Vol. 26, no. 3, September 1998, pp. 337-361. See also N.Gaan,"Politics of Governance of Global Climate change: Not on Equity but on North's Interests", India Quarterly Vol. VIII, no. 4, October-December 2001, pp. 89-112.
21. Gunther Bachler, Conflict and Cooperation in the Light of Global Human- Ecological Transformation, ENCOP, occasional paper 9, October 1993, p.5

22. Robert W. Kates and B.L. Turner II and William Clark, "The Great Transformation", In B.L. Turner II, and William C.Clark, Robert W. Kates, John F. Richards, Jessica T. Matthews, William B. Mayer, eds., The Earth as Transformed by Human Action: Global and Regional Changes in the Biosphere over the Past 300 years (Cambridge: Cambridge University Press with Clark University, 1990), p.1
23. Gunther Bachler, Conflict and Cooperation, Ibid. p. 16
24. Stephan Libiszewski, What is an Environmental Conflict? ENCOP, Occasional paper no. I, July 1992, p.6
25. Richard A. Matthew, Ted Gaulin, and Bryan McDonald, "The Elusive Quest: Linking Environmental Change and Conflict" submitted to Canadian Journal of Political Science, Revised Manuscript submitted; Dec 21, 2001, File Number: 01-12, p. 7.
26. See for details Nancy Peluso and Michael Watts, ed., Violent Environments (Ithaca: Cornell University Press, 2001), pp. 15-24.
27. Committee on the challenges of Modern Society, NATO, "Environment and Security in an International Context", NATO Report 232, 1999.
28. Ibid, p. 22
29. Daniel Esty et.al., "The State Failure Task Force Report: Phase II Findings", Environmental Change and Security Project Report 5, 1999.
30. Ted Gaulin, "To Cultivate a New Model: Where do Soyasa and Gleditsch Fall Short", Environmental Change and Security Project Report 6, 2000, pp. 104-107.
31. Richard A. Matthew, et al., "The Elusive Quest", op. cit, p. 9.
32. Ibid, p. 25.
33. Julian Simon, The Ultimate Resources (Princeton, N.J.: Princeton University Press, 1981), p. 345; and Julian Simon, The Ultimate Resource 2 (Princeton, N.J.: Princeton University Press, 1996)
34. Thomas F. Homer Dixon, Environment, Scarcity and Violence, p. 114.
35. Richard A. Matthew, et.al., The Elusive Quest, p. 21.
36. Ibid, p. 16
37. Michael Walzer, Just and Unjust Wars: A Moral Argument with Historical Illustrations (New York: Basic Books, 1992); Michael Walzer, Spheres of Justice: A Defence of Pluralism and Equality (Oxford: M. Robertson, 1993); Michael Walzer, Thick and Thin: A Moral Argument at Home and Abroad (Notre Dame: University of Notre Dami Press, 1994); and Michael Walzer, "The politics of Rescue", Social Research 62, 1995, pp. 53-67.
38. Richard A. Matthew, et.al, "Elusive Quest, p. 24.
39. Volker Boge, "Proposal for an Analytical framework to grasp environmental conflict", ENCOP, occasional paper no. I, July 1992, Swiss Peace Foundation. p. 5.

40. Homer Dixon, Environment, Scarcity and Violence, op. cit.
41. Volker Boge, op. cit.
42. Peter H.Gleick, World's Water: The Biennial Report on Fresh Water Resources (Washington D.C.: Covels, California, Island Press, 1998); Haleh Hatami and Peter H.Gleick, "Chronology of Conflict over Water in the Legends, Myths and History of the Ancient Middle East", Report of the Pacific Institutes of the Studies in Development, Environment, and Security," Oakland, California, October 1992; Helga Haftendorn, "Water and International Conflict", Third World Quarterly vol.21, no.1, 2000, pp. 51-68; Marq De Villiers,Water Wars, London: Weidenfeld and Nicolson, 1999) ; World in Transition: Ways towards Sustainable Management of Fresh Water Resources, German Advisory Council on Global Change, Annual Report 1997 (Heidelberg: Springer – Verlag Berlin, 1999)
43. N Gaan, Environmental Scarcity of Fish and Conflict: The Case of India and Sri Lanka over Kachchativu Waters", International Studies Notes Vol-22, No. 3, Fall 1997, pp. 17-23.
44. Geoffrey D. Dabelko, Mark Halle, Steve Lonergan and Richard Matthew, State of the art review on environment, security and development co-operation. Prepared for the Working Party on Development, Co-operation and Environment, OECD Development Assistance Committee, Paris. p. 48.
45. Lorraine Elliott, "Regional environmental security: Pursuing a non-traditional approach" In Andrew T.H. Tan and J.D. Kenneth Boutin (Eds), Non-Traditional security issues in Southeast Asia (Singapore: Select Publishing, 2001), p. 449.
46. Quotations from the IPCC rely on "Working Group II Contribution to the Intergovernmental Panel on Climate Change, Fourth Assessment Report Climate Change 2007: Climate Change Impacts, Adaptation and Vulnerability, Summary for Policymakers, 6 April 2007 http://www.ipcc.ch/SPM6avr07.pdf .
47. See: Ulrike Röhr (2006) "Gender and climate change," *Tiempo* 59 (April): 3-7 http://www.tiempocyberclimate.org/portal/archive/pdf/tiempo59high.pdf .
48. **Ben Wisner and others, "Climate Change and Human Security"** Simultaneously uploaded to **Radix - Radical Interpretations of Disaster:** http://www.radixonline.org/cchs.html & http://www.radixonline.org/cchs.doc ;

    Disaster Diplomacy: http://www.disasterdiplomacy.org; **Peace Research and European Security Studies (AFES-PRESS):** http://www.afes-press.de/html/topical.html .
49. Ben Russell and Nigel Morris (2006) "Armed forces are put on standby to tackle threat of wars over water", *Independent*, 28 February http://news.independent.co.uk/environment/article348196.ece .

50. Quoted in Ben Vogel (2007) "Climate change creates security challenge 'more complex than Cold War'," *Janes.com* http://www.janes.com/security/international_security/news/misc/janes070130_1_n.shtml .

51. Quoted by Chris Littlecott (2007) "Climate Change: The Global Security Impact" February http://www.e3g.org/index.php/programmes/climate-articles/climate- change-the-global-security-impact /.

52. Sir Crispin Tickell (2003) "Risks of conflict: Population and Resource Pressure", In: Hans Günter Brauch, P.H Liotta, Antonio Marquina, Rogers, Paul; Selim, Mohammed El-Sayed, eds. *Security and Environment in the Mediterranean. Conceptualising Security and Environmental Conflict*, pp. 13-18. Hexagon Series on Human and Environmental Security and Peace, vol. Springer: Berlin-Heidelberg.

53. See: Hans Günter Brauch (2002) "Climate Change, Environmental Stress and Conflict," In: Federal Ministry for the Environment, Nature Conservation and Nuclear Safety, ed. *Climate Change and Conflict*, pp. 9-112. Federal Ministry for the Environment, Nature Conservation and Nuclear Safety: Berlin http://www.afes-press.de/pdf/Brauch_ClimateChange_BMU.pdf.

54. Hans Günter Brauch (2004) "Abrupt Climate Change and Conflicts: Security Implications from a European Perspective - Hobbesian vs. Grotian Analyses," Friedrich Ebert Foundation and Carnegie Endowment for International Peace, Washington, DC, 29 March http://www.afes-press.de/pdf/Brauch_ClimateChange.pdf

55. See: "Press Conference by Security Council President, 4 April 2007" http://www.un.org/News/briefings/docs//2007/070404_Parry.doc.htm .

56. UNDP (1994) *Human Development Report: New Dimensions of Human Security*. UNDP: New York.

57. On the narrow and broad definitions of 'security', see: Hans Günter Brauch: *Environment and Human Security*," InterSecTions, 2/2005 (Bonn: UNU-EHS); at: http://www.ehs.unu.edu/file.php?id=64; and Hans Günter Brauch: *Threats, Challenges, Vulnerabilites and Risks in Environmental and Human Security*. Source 1/2005 (Bonn: UNU-EHS) http://www.ehs.unu.edu/file.php?id=63 and Commission on Human Security (2003) *Human Security Now*. Commission on Human Security: New York http://www.humansecurity-chs.org/ .

58. For GECHS see http://www.gechs.org/ ; Janos Bogardi and Hans Guenter Brauch (2005) "Global Environmental Change: A Challenge for Human Security – Defining and conceptualising the environmental dimension of human security", In: Andreas Rechkemmer, ed. *UNEO – Towards an International* Environment, pp. 85-109. Nomos: Baden-Baden. GECHS will also be holding a conference on the mainstreaming of human security, "The International Conference on Human Security

in Asia: Theory, Practice and Impacts will be held in Bangkok, October 4-5 2007 http://www.ids.polsci.chula.ac.th/humansecurity.htm .

59. Jürgen Dedring (2007) "Human Security and the UN Security Council", In: Hans Günter Brauch, John Grin, Czeslaw Mesjasz, Pal Dunay, Pal Chadha, Navnita Pal, Béchir Chourou, Ursula Oswald Spring, Ursula, P.H. Liotta, Patricia Kameri-Mbote, eds. (2007) *Globalisation and Environmental Challenges: Reconceptualising Security in the 21st Century.* Chapter 48. Hexagon Series on Human and Environmental Security and Peace, vol. 3. Springer: Berlin (in press).

60. Kofi Annan (2005) *In Larger Freedom: Towards Development, Security and Human Rights for All.* United Nations: New York http://www.un.org/largerfreedom/ .

61. UNDP (2004) *Reducing Disaster Risk: A Challenge for Development.* Geneva: UNDP, Bureau for Crisis Prevention and Recovery http://www.un.org/special-rep/ohrlls/ldc/Global-Reports/UNDP%20Reducing%20Disaster%20Risk.pdf .

62. UNDP (2007) *Human Development Reports* http://hdr.undp.org/ ; see also UNDP, UNEP, World Bank,

    ADB, AfDB, GTZ, DFID, OECD, and EC (2003) *Poverty and Climate Change: Reducing the Vulnerability of the Poor through Adaptation.* World Bank: Washington http://www.undp.org/climatechange/adap01.htm .

63. UNDP (2007) "Poverty Eradication, MDGs and Climate Change"

    http://www.undp.org/climatechange/adap01.htm .

64. David Simon (2007), "Cities and Global Environmental Change: Exploring the Links," *The Geographical Journal* 173, 1 (March): 75-79 & see chapters 3 & 4 of Sir Nicholas Stern et al. (2007) *Stern Review on the Economics of Climate Change*. London: UK, Department of the Treasury

    http://www.hm-treasury.gov.uk/independent_reviews/stern_review_economics_climate_change/stern_review_report.cfm

65. Delaney and Shrader (2000) report the percentage of women-headed households more than doubled in both Honduras and Nicaragua following Hurricane Mitch in 1998. See: Patricia L. Delaney and Elizabeth Shrader (2000) "Gender and Post-Disaster Reconstruction: The Case of Hurricane Mitch in Honduras and Nicaragua", LCSPG/LAC Gender Team, The World Bank, Decision Review Draft, page 24 http://www.gdnonline.org/resources/reviewdraft.doc .

66. Millennium Ecosystem Assessment (2006) *Our Human Planet: Summary for Decision Makers*, p. 6, Box 1.2, "Millennium Ecosystem Assessment Conceptual Framework" http://ma.caudillweb.com//en/Products.Global.Summary.aspx .

67. On the definition of "vulnerability" at the scale of household livelihoods and its linkage with macro-scale processes, see Ben Wisner, Piers Blaikie, Terry Cannon, and Ian Davis (2004) At Risk: Natural Hazards, People's Vulnerability and Disaster. 2nd Edition. Routledge: London.
68. David Simon (2007) Ibid.
69. Art Hansen and Anthony Oliver-Smith (1982) Involuntary Migration and Resettlement: The Problems and Responses of Dislocated Peoples Westview Press: Boulder, Co; World Commission on Dams (2000) "People and Large Dams: Social Performance," In: Dams and Development http://www.dams.org//docs/report/wcdch4.pdf ; Chris de Wet, compiler (2002) Improving Outcomes in Development-Induced Displacement and Resettlement

    (DIDR) Projects. Oxford University, Refugee Studies Centre http://www.rsc.ox.ac.uk/PDFs/rrimprovingoutcomes02.pdf ; W. Courtland Robinson (2004) "Minimizing Development-Induced Displacement," Migration ***Information Source*** **http://www.migrationinformation.org/feature/display.cfm?ID=194** .
70. See: Crisis States Programme, Development Studies Institute, London School of Economics:

    http://www.crisisstates.com/News/seminars1.htm .
71. International Famine Program (2004) *Ambiguity and Change: Humanitarian NGOs Prepare for the Future.* A report prepared for: World Vision, CARE, Save US, Mercy Corps, Oxfam USA, Oxfam GB & Catholic Relief Services http://famine.tufts.edu/pdf/ambiguity_and_change.pdf .
72. German Advisory Council on Global Change – WBGU Secretariat Reichpietschufer 60-62, 8. OGD-10785 Berlin.The summary can be downloaded through the Internet from the websitehttp://www.wbgu.de/wbgu_jg2007_kurz_engl.html.
73. On the neo-Malthusian roots of "environmental conflict" discourse, see Elizabeth Hartmann (2003) *Strategic Scarcity: The Origins and Impact of Environmental Conflict Ideas*, PhD Thesis, Development Studies, London School of Economics & Betsy Hartmann, "Degradation Narratives: Over-Simplifying the Link Between Population, Poverty and the Environment," *IHDP Update, Newsletter of the International Human Dimensions Program on Global Environmental Change*, No. 4, 2002: 6-8 & Elizabeth Hartmann (1998) "Population, environment and security: a new trinity," *Environment and Urbanization* 10,2: 113-127 — summarized in http://popdev.hampshire.edu/projects/dt/dt27.php.
74. Twin Basin, "International River Basins of the World"
75. Quotations from the IPCC rely on "Working Group II Contribution to the Intergovernmental Panel on Climate Change, Fourth Assessment Report Climate Change 2007: Climate Change Impacts, Adaptation and

Vulnerability, Summary for Policymakers, 6 April 2007 http://www.ipcc.ch/SPM6avr07.pdf . P.10.

76. Water Poverty Index http://www.ceh.ac.uk/sections/ph/WaterPovertyIndex.html
77. See: Patrick J. McGowan (2003) "African Military Coups d'Etat, 1956-2001: Frequency, Trends and Distribution.." *Journal of Modern African Studies*, 41, 3: 339–370; at:

    http://journals.cambridge.org/download.php?file=%2FMOA%2FMOA41_03%2FS0022278X0300435Xa.pdf&code=aad776a39cf997c090aecae20ceafeb1.
78. See: Spanish Environment Ministry (2006) *Conference on Desertification and Migration*. 25-27 October 2005, Almeria, Spain http://www.sidym2006.org/eng/eng_ponencias_conclusiones.asp .
79. Quotations from the IPCC rely on "Working Group II Contribution to the Intergovernmental Panel on Climate Change, Fourth Assessment Report Climate Change 2007: Climate Change Impacts, Adaptation and Vulnerability, Summary for Policymakers, 6 April 2007 http://www.ipcc.ch/SPM6avr07.pdf . P.10.
80. CIDA (no date) *Gender Equality and Climate Change. Why consider gender equality when taking action on climate change?* Canadian International Development Agency www.acdi-cida.gc.ca/INET/IMAGES.NSF/vLUImages/Climate%20change3/$file/Gender-2.pdf .
81. Quotations from the IPCC rely on "Working Group II Contribution to the Intergovernmental Panel on Climate Change, Fourth Assessment Report Climate Change 2007: Climate Change Impacts, Adaptation and Vulnerability, Summary for Policymakers, 6 April 2007 http://www.ipcc.ch/SPM6avr07.pdf . P.9.
82. Neil Adger, Jouni Paavola, Saleemul Huq, M.J. Mace, eds. (2006) *Fairness in Adaptation to Climate Change*. Cambridge, MA: MIT Press; See also: Michael H. Glantz (1990) "On the Interactions between Climate and Society," *Population and Development Review* 16: 179-200 & Michael H Glantz and Dale Jamieson, co-convenors (2001) "Climate Ethics and Equity," *NCAR Working Group Web Page* (October) http://www.ccb.ucar.edu/ethics/ .
83. International Rivers Network, "About Rivers and Dams" http://www.irn.org/basics/ard/ .
84. Margaret Skutch (2004), "CDM and LULUCF: what's in it for women? A note for the Gender and Climate Change Network, Technology and Sustainable Development TDG, University of Twente; at: http://www.gencc.interconnection.org/skutsch2004.pdf .
85. Johnston, Barbara Rose (2007) Half-lives & Half-truths: Confronting the Radioactive Legacies of the Cold War. SAR Press: Santa Fe, NM.

86. Brittany Sauser (2007) "Ethanol Demand Threatens Food Prices," *Technology Review* (13 February) http://www.technologyreview.com/Energy/18173/ .

87. Jeffrey A McNeely (2006) "Bio-Fuels: Green Energy or Grim Reaper?" *The Green Room*, 2 September http://news.bbc.co.uk/2/hi/science/nature/5369284.stm .

88. United Nations Office for the Coordination of Humanitarian Affairs - Integrated Regional Information Networks (IRIN) (5 April 2007) "Southern Africa: Extreme weather threatens over a million people" http://www.reliefweb.int/rw/RWB.NSF/db900SID/SHES-6ZYQST?OpenDocument .

89. Maureen Fordham with Madhavi Malalgoda Ariyabandu, Prema Gopalan and Kristina J Peterson (2006) "Please don't raise gender now – we're in an emergency!" *World Disasters Report 2006*, Chapter 6. International Federation of Red Cross and Red Crescent Societies: Geneva http://www.ifrc.org/publicat/wdr2006/summaries.asp .

90. A.M. Cruz, L.J. Steinberg, A.L. Vetere-Arellano, J.P. Nordvik, and F. Pisano, (2004). *State of the Art in Natech (Natural Hazard Triggering Technological Disasters) in Europe.* DG Joint Research Centre, European Commission and United Nations International Strategy for Disaster Reduction, Ispra, Italy.

91. Quotations from the IPCC rely on "Working Group II Contribution to the Intergovernmental Panel on Climate Change, Fourth Assessment Report Climate Change 2007: Climate Change Impacts, Adaptation and Vulnerability, Summary for Policymakers, 6 April 2007 http://www.ipcc.ch/SPM6avr07.pdf . P.16.

92. Ben Wisner (2008) "The Interactions between Conflict and Natural Hazards in an Unstable, Globalizing World: Swords, Plowshares, Earthquakes, Floods, and Storms," In: Hans Guenter Brauch, et al., eds.*Globalisation and Environmental Challenges: Reconceptualising Security in the 21st Century*, Vol. II, Chapter 15. Springer-Verlag: Berlin (in press); See earlier version *Journal of Natural Disaster Science* (Kyoto, Japan)26,2 (2004): 63-72

    http://www.drs.dpri.kyoto-u.ac.jp/jsnds/download.cgi?jsdn_26_2_3.pdf.

93. Thomas Wagner, (28 March 2007) "Major Cities Warned against Sea Level Rise" *Independent (South Africa) On Line* http://www.iol.co.za/index.php?set_id=1&click_id=31&art_id=nw20070328024424684C606123

94. A.C. Ibe and L.F. Awosika (1991) "Sea level rise impact on African coastal zones," In: S.H. Ominde and C. Juma, eds., *A change in the weather: African perspectives on climate change*, 105-12. African Centre for Technology Studies: Nairobi, Kenya [Reprinted with permission by CIESIN http://www.ciesin.columbia.edu/docs/004-153/004-153.html .

95. Simon (2007) *Op. Cit.*

96. IPCC (1997) "African Coastal Zones", in: *IPCC Special Report on The Regional Impacts of Climate Change: An Assessment of Vulnerability* http://www.grida.no/climate/ipcc/regional/030.htm .

97. Quotations from the IPCC rely on "Working Group II Contribution to the Intergovernmental Panel on Climate Change, Fourth Assessment Report Climate Change 2007: Climate Change Impacts, Adaptation and Vulnerability, Summary for Policymakers, 6 April 2007 http://www.ipcc.ch/SPM6avr07.pdf . P.10

98. German Advisory Council on Global Change - WBGU Secretariat Reichpietschufer 60-62, 8. OG D-10785 Berlin.The summary can be downloaded through the Internet from the website http://www.wbgu.de/wbgu_jg2007_kurz_engl.html

99. Ibid.

100. Peter Schwartz and Doug Randall, An Abrupt Climate Change Scenario and Its Implications for the United States National Security, October 2003.

101. Ibid.

102. Quoted by David Adam, " How climate change will affect the world", Guardian Newspapers in The Hindu, 20 September,2007.

8

Conclusion

The recent report by Intergovernmental Panel on Climate Change supported and hammered out by a bevy of scientists across the world is of the view that it is nearly certain to conclude that there is at least a 90 per cent chance that human caused emissions are the main factor in warming since 1950. A large number of scientists believe that human activities, which have increased atmospheric concentrations of Carbon Dioxide (CO_2) by one third over the past 100 years may be leading to an increase in global average temperatures. Scientists have found that the four important variable greenhouse gases whose atmospheric concentrations can be influenced by human activities are Carbon Dioxide (CO_2), Methane (CH_4) Nitrous Oxide (N_2O) and Chlorofluorocarbons (CFCs). Historically CO_2 has been the most important but over the past several decades the other gases have assumed increasing significance and collectively are projected to contribute as much to potential global warming over the next 60 years as CO_2. It is an established fact that anthropogenic interference is responsible to add more and more gases to the atmosphere. The concentration of CO_2 in the atmosphere is steadily increasing due to the combustion of fossil fuels, deforestation, desertification and agricultural activities. Almost all greenhouse gases reached their highest recorded levels in the 1990s and continue to increase. The Earth climate system has drastically changed since the pre industrial era on both global and regional scale. The concentrations of greenhouse gases and their radiative forcing have generally increased due to the result of human activities. There is strong scientific consensus that there has been an increase in the atmosphere in concentrations of greenhouse gases especially of Carbon Dioxide over recent decades and centuries.

The amount of carbon cycling from natural occurring processes each year through the biosphere as CO_2 is enormous some 800 billion tonnes. Ice cores and other proxy climate data, which all indicate CO_2 concentrations in the atmosphere, have shown, in general a relatively stable global climate at least over the past 10,000 years. As such many scientists suggest that the amount of CO_2 generated by natural processes is about equal to the amounts absorbed and sequestered by natural processes. However human activity since the industrial revolution in 1850 and primarily in the form of burning fossil fuels, is now generating some additional 24 billion tonnes of CO_2 per year. Available evidence shows that about half this amount is absorbed by natural processes on land and in the ocean and that atmospheric concentration of CO_2 is now about 35% higher than they were some 150 years ago. Some scientists believe that a large amount of CO_2 may be stored in Northern latitude, soils and temperature and tropical forests, suggesting a greater importance of role of natural resources and land use practices in these regions including burning of biomass and deforestation. Scientists estimate that anthropogenic emissions of CO_2 alone may account for as much as a 60% increase in global mean temperatures of 0.4F since 1850.

The most recent Global Climate Models (GCM) have projected globally averaged warming ranging from 3 to 10.7 degrees F. Over the next 100 years, if greenhouse gases continue to accumulate in the atmosphere at the current rate. Climate scientists believe that such a warming could shift temperate zones, rainfall patterns, and agricultural belts and under certain scenarios cause sea level to rise. They further predict that global warming could have far reaching effects- some positive some negative- depending on how it may be experienced in a given region - on natural resources, ecosystems and food production, energy supply, use and distribution, transportation, land use, water supply and control and human health.

Even if the levels of atmospheric greenhouse gases were stabilized tomorrow, the world would go on warming for centuries. The recent episodic weather events may seem extreme in nature and that this may be indicative of long term climate change. Much of the global Carbon Dioxide emissions today emanates from the industrialized North countries. That is to say from only 27 of all the sovereign states, accounting for 43% of global land and 20% of global population on the contrary comparatively little of the Carbon Dioxide emissions today flow from the remaining nations accounting for 57% of global land area and 80% of the global population. Again, the issue of climate change politics is closely associated with political and economic strategy between North and South countries. The North industrialized countries led by the United States of America reached the apex of development based on combustion of fossil fuel technology. Following the Western pattern of development, the developing world ubiquitously imitated the path, which resulted in the emission of Carbon Dioxide into the atmosphere in an unprecedented way dangerously aggravating the situation.

The inordinate life style and unrestricted consumption pattern of the North is symbiotically related to the Carbon Dioxide emission and pattern of development. The rich industries North being 20% of the world population is responsible for 50% of the world's total emission. As Clinton himself admitted, the US with less than 5% of the world's population contributes over 25% of the world's greenhouse gas emission. The quantities of gases emitted from different sources from different countries of the world into the atmosphere exceed the ability of the atmosphere to absorb them. This relentless and continuing emission of greenhouse gases causes global warming.

It is predicted that the rise of temperature to 2 degrees would be throughout the globe. The range of global warming would be 10 degrees increase in polar region, 2 to 3 degrees increase in the middle latitude and all most imperceptible increase in the tropics. As the gases are expected to continue accumulating in the atmosphere, serious dramatic consequences for climate changes are impending.

Some skeptics of the global warming theory have called into question the reliability of computer climate models and their output used to make projections of future warming that supported Kyoto protocol negotiations. They also challenge some scientists' assertions that recent episodic weather events may seem more extreme in nature that this may be indicative of long term climate change. The levels of greenhouse gases in the atmosphere have been increasing rapidly over the century and reached their highest recorded levels in the 1990s and the trend is continuing till date. The concentration of CO_2 in the atmosphere increases due to rapid industrialization, urbanization coupled with combustion of fossil fuels, deforestation, desertification and agriculture, attributable to human activities. Most recently, in the TAR, the IPCC have further strengthened their statements expressing greater confidence that human activities are altering climate patterns. There is new and stronger evidence that most of the warming observed over the last 50 years is attributable to human activities. "Human influence will continue to change atmospheric composition through out the 21st century".

The global averaged surface temperature is projected to increase by 1.4 to 5.8C over the period 1990 to 2100. The projected rate of warming is much larger than the observed changes in the 20th century and it is very likely to be without precedent in coming decades. If the atmospheric concentration of heat trapping gases increases sufficiently, the Earth temperature will rise. Equally indisputable is the fact that human spewing heat-trapping gases into the atmosphere increases. The main culprit is Carbon Dioxide released by burning of fossil fuels. Methane gas, which has more than double in concentration over the past three centuries as the result of cultivating rice, raising live stock and exploring for oil is a secondary factor as is Nitrous Oxide a product of burning fossil fuels and producing nylon and fertilizer. And human innovation has injected synthetic gases such as fluorocarbon and Sulphur Hexafloride into the atmosphere. Although these gases are found in true amounts they are thousands of times more efficient than Carbon Dioxide in absorbing heat. The average surface temperatures have increased roughly one degree Fahrenheit during the 20th century. This number sounds unimpressive but small variations in global temperature can cause dramatic climate changes. The Carbon Dioxide emanating from burning of fossil fuels has already warmed up the world and that if nothing is done it will have disastrous consequences. The term global warming refers to additional heating caused by greenhouse gases released by human activities, primarily the burning of fossil fuels. Owing to the rise in atmospheric Carbon Dioxide caused by modern industrial societies, widespread combustion of fossil fuels (coal, oil and natural gas) the effects on Earth may be intensified and long-term climate changes may cause drastic consequences. The levels of Carbon Dioxide in the atmosphere is increasing with the likelihood that it will double by middle of the next century. Post Second World War industrialization has caused a dramatic jump in the amount of Carbon Dioxide in the atmosphere. The increased concentration of greenhouse gases in the atmosphere has led to concerns that human activities could warm the Earth and fundamentally change the natural processes controlling climate. In recent years, the statistical and scientific evidence has shown that the climate is being disrupted by building up of greenhouse gases as a result of western pattern of development. According to Intergovernmental Panel on Climate change since 1990, global warming has been speeding up. Global climate change is one of the most pressing challenges for future generations and will make ramifying impacts on many aspects of human life. The impacts of climate change are likely to vary considerably by geographic region and occur over a time scale of decades to centuries. It will affect the way societies are organized, the way cities are built and the way transport and energy systems are designed.

There is a growing concern that if the trend towards a warmer climate continues at its present rate, it will disrupt weather patterns, ecosystems and agriculture around the world with disastrous consequences for the human race. Experts predict that unless the trend towards is reversed, the amount of greenhouse gases emitted into the atmosphere is expected to triple and temperatures to rise by two to six degrees Celsius by the end of this century. The effects of such development will be disastrous. Satellites monitoring the polar atmosphere show that the hole, which opens in the ozone layer over Antarctica each spring was bigger than ever this year. As warmer temperature melts the ice caps in the North and South poles, sea levels will rise and flood the low lying coastal countries wide areas of land. We can also expect strange climatic disturbances such as hurricanes, earthquakes and floods in unexpected places. The scourge of devastating floods and storms that swept many parts of the world, has already caused numerous hazards to life and settlements of mankind. Although health considerations are yet not of priority concern, the continued rise in global temperatures is certain to have extremely adverse effects on the health of future generations as they struggle to CoPe with climates hotter than any experienced in millions of years. Global warming could have catastrophic and undesirable effects including a greater incidence of tropical diseases, more heat related mortality, reduced agricultural outputs in certain areas and rise in sea levels that would threaten low lying areas of the world.

The IPCC report comes out with a plethora of consequences that global warming will be having on the Earth: changes in weather patterns, frequency of more floods and droughts in some areas and far reaching effects on agricultural production, environment, farming systems and forestry. Today, climate change experiences more hot days and heat waves and fewer cold and frost days affecting the weather systems.

Too much of heat and cold resulting in extreme types of summer and winter droughts, extreme rainfalls, torrential rain causing high floods, will lead to unusual weather repeated disasters. Scarcity of drinking water and sanitation will become as menacing as its consequences on political and economic set up. Millions would be affected within the developing countries especially in arid and semiarid regions where available water is already a limiting source. The potential impacts of climate change on agriculture are quite large. The potential disruption of food production in tropics and sub-tropics despite steady global production in developing world, could be far reaching to meet the basic human needs of growing populations. Extreme weather conditions resulting from high temperatures in terms of heavy rainfalls, floods and droughts will adversely affect the food productions.

The consequences of global warming could be serious for many densely populated low lying costal villages and island countries of the world. Many will be affected seriously by flooding and sea level rise depriving them of their housing, shelters, and land resources causing major problems for human settlements, and millions would be driven out of their homes as refugees. Tropical cyclones, hurricanes and floods are expected to increase in the coming century resulting in innumerable hazards affecting shelters and crops of the coastal areas. It adversely affects structures and constructions of building, roads and bridges, causing migration and resettlement due to loss of housing and shelter.

Marine ecosystems and coastal resources are vulnerable to the impacts of climate change due to the increasing intensity of weather events and rising sea levels. It affects fisheries, coral reefs, shore line displacement, coastal erosion, public work infrastructure, hydrological systems, terrestrial and marine ecosystems, human settlements, tourism, lives and property, estuaries, and substantially alters the distribution and abundance of major fish stocks of the coastal areas of the world.

The global warming is predicted to have far reaching impacts on human health. Deaths and diseases, heat stress vector borne diseases would claim more lives as the tropical habitant of insects expands northwards. There are increased risks of heat related morbidity, air polluted diseases, chemical pollution, water borne diseases, vector borne diseases causing innumerable hazards to human health. The diseases like cancer, asthma, chest pains, malaria, dengue fever, respiratory diseases, lung diseases and other serious diseases are increasing in the number leading to large deaths in future.

As the temperature rises, the melting of ice, and thermal expansion will lead to the sea level rise causing major problems to small island states, low-lying deltas, coastal regions throughout the world. Sea level rise could have profound implications on coastal areas making ground water saltier, endangering loss of land due to inundation and erosion and increased flooding could adversely affect agriculture, tourism, freshwater resources, fisheries and aquaculture, human settlements and health.

Millions of climate refugees could be created by sea level rise in countries like Bangladesh, Egypt, China, Vietnam, India, Thailand, Philippines and Indonesia. The world has been experiencing the 12 warmest year in the past two decades in 1990 and 1998 among the warmest. Climate change is likely to disrupt ecosystems, which provides valuable services and benefits to mankind. Irregular and large scale losses of cool temperate forests, loss of biological diversity species adapted to cool climates would cause extinction as habitats disappear and they are unable to migrate and with heavy damages to sensitive ecological systems, these which may not recover for centuries. Too much heat or cold or extreme type of summer, winter, drought or torrential rain, frequency of flood or drought, formation of low pressures of air amidst the seas and oceans, land slides and land erosion, extension of deserts and heavy rainfalls would lead to more and more natural disasters every year.

The impacts of global warming and climate on water resources are likely to be serious due to low availability of drinking water throughout the world. Warmer temperatures, drier conditions and sea level rise would further worsen demand for water resources threatening the survival of human beings on Earth. The continuation of this trend would exacerbate water shortages, directly affect water demands with respect to agriculture and food production, industrial operations, navigation, hydroelectric power generation, which ultimately would affect the economy, trade and commerce, employment and income of the ever growing population of the world. According to the report of the Inter governmental Panel on Climate Change, the developing countries are twice as vulnerable as developed countries and small island nations are three times as vulnerable to the adverse effects of climate change.

Thus, global warming will have profound and far reaching consequences on agriculture, food production and forestry causing major problems for human settlements. Intense and extreme weather patterns affect coastal zones and marine ecosystems, exacerbate availability of fresh water, diminish surface water and ground water supplies, threaten managed and unmanaged ecosystems, including natural habitats, and human health causing death and diseases of millions, and rising sea level would submerge small island states, low lying deltas and coastal regions resulting in drowning of millions of lives and property around the world. Further climate change will aggravate the problems by the threats of desertification in the arid and semiarid zones of Africa. Extreme weather events are expected to result in more catastrophic and damaging natural resource induced disasters.

International response was created since 1950 to combat the catastrophic effects of climate change. The scientists all over the world express their serious concerns relating to concentrations of greenhouse gases in the atmosphere, probably the most serious environmental problem that the world faces. After the global consensus of 1953 and oceans conference of 1970, environmental issue became an integral part of United Nation's agenda. In 1972 a full-fledged UN Environmental Conference was held in Stockholm on international environmental issues to raise awareness about potential for humans to cause environmental damages. In 1974, second environmental conference was held in Nairobi,

Kenya on environmental changes. In 1979, the official first world climate conference was held in Geneva. It considered how climate change would impact human activities and what the nations of the world could do to avoid climate disruptions. The next meeting of experts was held in Villach, Austria in 1980 to assess the concentrations of greenhouse gases and its impacts upon the Earth. The third Villachs conference was held in 1985 about the problem of anthropogenic climate change and how to reduce greenhouse gas emissions. The Villach conference thus was confined to stimulating awareness and efforts in international sphere to combat the impacts of global warming through coordinated action.

The Toronto Conference of 1988 highlighted the threats of global warming and increased the attention relating to stabilization of greenhouse gases concentration in the atmosphere. In 1988, the UN voted to make environmental issues as a part of programme of all its agencies. The Intergovernmental Panel on Climate Change, a committee of thousands of scientists was founded. The IPCC gathers data on global climate and issues assessments. It issued it first report in 1990, second in 1996, third in 2001 and fourth is released in 2006. The IPCC and its three working groups are to assess available scientific and socio economic information on climate change and its impacts and the options for mitigating climate change and adapting to it and to provide on request scientific/ technological/ socio economic advice to the conference of the parties to the United Nation's Framework Convention on Climate Change (UNFCCC). Concerns about the accumulation of greenhouse gases in the atmosphere and possible impacts on global temperatures have led to a series of international initiatives for collective action. The IPCC report formed the intellectual basis on which the United Nations conference on environment and development was held in Rio in June 1992. It supported the principles of second conference. Its goals were to slow or halt environmental degradation while promoting sustainable economic and social development. Developed nations were asked to voluntarily reduce Carbon Dioxide emissions to 1990 levels by 2000. This conference coming 20 years after Stockholm conference of 1972, was attended by the totality of the world's countries, and marked for the first time, the fact that the world was willing to discuss all the challenges posed by the need for world wide co-operation especially between North and South in order to take effective action against climate change. One notable success of the Rio Conference was the signature of the United Nations Convention on Climate Change by 186 countries.

In 1994, the convention entered into force. Developed nations were required to submit greenhouse gas inventories of emissions and carbon sinks. Also in 1994, the intergovernmental negotiating committee met six more times to debate on details of treaty, financing support for developing countries and procedures. In early 1995, the INC dissolved and the Conference of the Parties (CoP) replaced it. The CoP became the primary governing body of the Framework Convention on Climate Change.

The Conference of the Parties in its first meeting intensified their efforts to implement the adequacy of commitment under the Berlin Mandate. In Berlin meeting in 1995, the Conference of the Parties (CoP) created at Rio conference defined the structure for the action. The Conference of the Parties to the climate conference in 1995 to fulfill the hopes has been declared a failure. Firstly, the conference did not adopt a protocol, and secondly, the wording of Berlin Mandate gave rise to worries that the substance of the protocol to be adopted in two years might not match up to original expectations. On the other hand, there is no denying that the Berlin conference by acknowledging the inadequacy of existing commitment and adopting the Mandate to draw up a protocol, has taken the next steps for an effective climate protection policy. In 1995, the Second Assessment Report of the IPCC concluded that "the balance of evidence suggests that there is a discernible human influence on global climate". It concluded that substantial reduction of Carbon Dioxide emissions would be necessary to stabilize atmospheric concentrations of greenhouse gases. The Berlin Mandate exempted Non Annex-1 countries from additional binding obligations in keeping with the principle of "Common but differentiated responsibilities" established in the UNFCCC - even though collectively, the new industrialized countries are expected to be the world's largest emitters of greenhouse gas emissions 15 years hence.

The second conference of the parties to the UNFCCC - (CoP) met in 1996 in Geneva. It accepted the Second Assessment Report of the IPCC representing the most comprehensive and authoritative assessment of scientific and technological information to combat the global climate change. Secondly, it rejected uniform "harmonized policies" in favour of flexibility and called for "legally binding mid term targets" requiring industrial nations to reduce their source of greenhouse gas emissions. The US announced that it would support legally binding targets and timetable in the near future to reduce the accumulation of greenhouse gases, and challenged other industrialized nations to do the same. More than 100 countries announced that they would develop such targets. The EU however reiterated its commitment to work towards the year 2000 goal. For successful protection of global climate, action was to be taken on a worldwide level.

A key achievement of the UNFCCC process was the adoption of the Kyoto protocol on climate change at Kyoto, Japan, on 11th December 1997. The Kyoto protocol broke new ground with its legally binding constraints on greenhouse gas emissions and its innovative "mechanisms" aimed at cutting the cost of curbing emissions. Today, 186 countries (including the European community) are parties to the convention. It contains provisions intended to advance the implementation of UNFCCC obligations shared by all parties including commitments by developing countries. The complexity of the negotiations however, meant that considerable "unfinished business" remained even after protocol itself was adopted. The protocol sketched out the basic features of its "mechanisms" and compliance system for, example, but did not flesh out the all-important rules of how they would operate. Although 84 countries signed the protocol indicating that they intended to ratify, many were reluctant to actually do so and bring the protocol into force. Since its adoption, governments have been negotiating the details of the Kyoto protocol to enable its ratification by key players. The negotiations have been protracted and difficult involving complex technical and political issues. In early 2001, the Bush Administration decided to abandon the negotiating process on the supposed ground that it was too costly for the US economy and unfair because it excluded developing countries. Nevertheless the negotiations continued. There was high expectation that Kyoto protocol would come into force perhaps by September 2001 when world summit on sustainable development convened in Johannesburg. Many nations subsequently ratified the treaty, culminating with Russia in November 2004. The ratification by Russia meant that the essential "quorum" of ratifying countries had now been reached and the Kyoto protocol therefore came into force on 16th February 2005.

The CoP-4 took place in Buenos Aires in November 1998. It had been expected that the remaining issues unresolved in Kyoto would be finalized at this meeting. However, the complexity and difficulty of finding agreement on these issues proved insurmountable and instead the parties adopted a two year "plan of action" to advance efforts and to devise mechanisms for implementing the Kyoto protocol, to be completed by 2000.

The 5th Conference of Parties to the UN Framework Convention on Climate Change met in Bonn(Germany) between October 25 and November 4, 1999. Diplomacy and bargaining dominated the conference, many delicate issues were discussed and did not reach major conclusion. It was primarily a technical meeting raising many different dilemmas and dealing with many scientific uncertainties marking the lack of consensus among the parties to reach any conclusions.

When the CoP-6 convened on November 13, 2000, in the Hague, discussions evolved rapidly into a high level negotiations over the major political issues. At this meeting, despite some compromises agreed between the United States and some EU countries notably the United Kingdom, and the EU countries as a whole led by Denmark and Germany rejected the compromise positions, and the talks in the Hague collapsed. Major substantial differences between parties on compliance with the Kyoto mechanism for sinks and mechanism for financial and technology transfer to developing countries persisted. CoP-6 negotiations resumed on July 16-27, 2001 in Bonn. Little progress had been made on resolving the differences that had little produced an impasse in the Hague. The other parties with United States as observer at the meeting negotiated the matter like flexible mechanisms, carbon sinks, compliance and financing. Agreement was reached on a host of major political issues. CoP-6 therefore, would have been a turning point for all outstanding decisions concerning the negotiations on critical issues related to climate change.

The climate change process continued rapidly at the CoP-7 meeting in Marrakesh in 2001 with the adoption of Buenos Airs plan of action finalizing the most of the operational details and setting the stage for nations to ratify the Kyoto protocol. But the United States continued to act as an observer declining to participate in active negotiations. The attitude of United States raised a storm of international criticism, and united the most of the countries of the world in opposition to the US action. Agreement among other parties was also found on the remaining protocol issues, and they announced that they would seek ratification of the protocol and its entry into force even without the participation of United States. At the CoP-7, decisions on all-important issues showing international co-operation were reached on the basis of Buenos Airs plan of action. However, progress in achieving the objectives of the convention has also been of critical importance to forging an effective response to combat the climate change.

The United Nations Frame work Convention on Climate Change at CoP-8 meeting adopted at the Delhi Ministerial declaration on climate change and sustainable development, rules of procedure of development mechanism, assessment of the reporting of developed countries, compliance under the Kyoto protocol, global environmental facility to assist developing countries and new guidance of national communications for developing countries to meet their commitments under the frame work convention. In the conference of the parties, attempts were made to consider next steps after the 2008-2012 commitment period but all these attempts encountered resistance from the developing countries and some other parties to make the negotiations meaningful and effective in order to promote technological advances through research and development to substantially increase renewable energy sources and to promote the transfer of technologies, making the CDM fully operational. Ninety six parties have ratified including developed countries accounting for 37.4% of CO_2 emissions without US participation, the required 55% of the base line emissions of parties would be achieved. Many parties to the UNFCCC continued to express the hope that the United States will reengage in international efforts to reduce greenhouse gas emissions. The progress that has been made on fashioning a global response to combat climate change is actually remarkable given the complexity of politics of climate change. Ninth Conference of the Parties on climate change was held in Milan, in 2003. The meeting centered on largely technical issues and avoided major substantial declarations.

At the CoP-9, attempts were made to discuss several issues, which encounter resistance and challenges to adopt decisions. Two faces of the CoP-9 highlighted the division and disputes between the developed and the developing countries, which was obstacle to taking concrete steps and measures to combat the threats of the climate change. The U.S. continued refusing to ratify the Kyoto protocol, along with Russian reluctance at Milan CoP-9 to undertake ratification calling into question whether or when the protocol might came into force. The overall performance of CoP-9 demonstrated the lack of political will and understanding to implement the decisions by enhancing participation in the global efforts to address the climate change. The very purpose of the convention with the aim of arriving at political agreement on the issues that prevented countries from ratifying the protocol was defeated. Progress in the struggle against global warming was no longer in sight. The process of negotiation continued in order to facilitate early steps in addressing the dangerous implications of global warming. The importance of further dialogue and interaction between the parties on climate change was held in Buenos Aires in 2004, to resolve the unfinished issues in fulfilling the objectives of the UN Framework Convention on Climate Change. The UNFCCC completed a decade and is going to celebrate the tenth anniversary year of the adoption of the convention. The conference of the parties has assumed increasing significance and greater roles in combating global climate change. Strong determination and collaborative efforts succeeded in getting the Kyoto protocol ratilied by Russian Federation in November 2004, to facilitate early entry into force of Kyoto protocol. Though United States remain adamant not to ratify the Kyoto protocol, the entry into force of Kyoto protocol from 16th February 2005 marked a greatest achievement.

To combat climate change it is necessary for all countries to further strengthen their actions to bind the nations to take treaties and conventions into meaningful operation. The eleventh Conference of the Parties to the UN Framework Convention on Climate Change, and the first meeting of the parties CoP-11/Mop-1 was held in 2005 at Montreal. Key decisions were made in several areas. The Marrakech accords the rulebook for the Kyoto protocol. Numerous decisions were agreed upon - components of the "Montreal Plan of Action." The implementation, improvement and innovation became the standards to judge the outcomes of the conference. The CoP-11/Mop-1 achieved tremendous success in overcoming strong pitfalls and exceeding the expectation to strengthen the global efforts to combat climate change. Thus, it sets a strong structure for future action on global climate change.

The threat of global climate change is the biggest environmental problem of the present century impinging upon all the countries around the world to work together toward lowering net greenhouse gas emissions to address the global warming. The negotiation process conducted to take further actions in the conference of the parties on mitigation and adaptation activities in a more comprehensive way to prevent anthropogenic interference with the climate system.

The UNFCCC specified that the developed countries should bear the primary responsibility for reducing GHG emissions and setout a system of voluntary reduction commitments for the developing countries. Transition economies were allowed to use a different base year and developing countries were not required to take any action. At current rate of economic development and fossil fuel use, China, India and Brazil and other developing countries will surpass the emissions of industrialized countries early in the 21st century. Hence, there is concern that the special exemption afforded to developing countries might preclude any real reduction in GHG accumulation. It follows that targeted level of GHG in the atmosphere might require greater reductions within developed countries at corresponding greater costs. These higher costs will stimulate political opposition and possible shifts in position regarding international co-operation.

Developed countries accepted the concept of differentiated responsibilities but want a greater assurance on when and how developing countries would start assuming greater responsibilities to reduce GHG emissions because developing countries are likely to be the primary industrial emitters in the future. The developing countries' exemption was just one of the problem standing in the way of implementing the Kyoto protocol. The protocol sketched out the basic features of its three mechanisms and compliance system but failed to establish all important rules for its implementation except through Clean Development Mechanism and emission trading introduced into the strategy as outlined in the protocol, it does not insist on the developing countries participation. The Kyoto protocol is all along opposed by the United States on the ground that it fails to establish a long-term goal based on science, and it poses serious and unnecessary risks to the US economy and ineffective policies in addressing climate change because it excludes major parts of the world. The kind of response and address needed to combat the crisis, the Kyoto Protocol failed to win the co-operation from the rich industrialized North who are being the biggest polluters and expected to meet the targets. The cooperative efforts made by the world community over the courses of many years to create an effective system for combating global climate change seem to be shrouded in uncertainty with the pronouncement made by the Bush administration's rejection of the Kyoto protocol.

The treaty requires developed nations to reduce their emissions below 1990 levels by 2008-2012. Most of the 15 western European nations that ratified the treaty are not on track to meet their emissions reduction targets due to the unacceptable high impact of compliance on energy costs. This is particularly true of these European nations with an energy wise and emission history similar to that of US. These initial difficulties provide an indication to the world that compliance with the Kyoto protocol will be very expensive and that America's decision to stay out is based on a solid rationale.

The most difficult challenge was how to bring the United States back to the negotiation table. Again the United States all along opposed to the idea of strong climate treaty and the issue it has raised against the Kyoto protocol are not particularly persuasive.

The six-country Asia Pacific partnership on clean development and climate has put paid to any hopes of getting the US into the Kyoto protocol. The six-country partnership focuses on the importance of the development agenda in considering any climate change approach and thus, signals a deviation from the Kyoto agenda. The partnership has some strange bed follows- China and India two of the world's most populous nations requiring abundant quantities of energy to fuel their development in addition to Australia, Japan and South Korea. This group is led by US itself, a huge energy guzzler and the world's biggest polluter, accounting for 36.1 percent of global Greenhouse Gas (GHG) emissions. The US had elected not to join the Kyoto protocol citing non-inclusion of the three large developing countries- China, India and Brazil in the first commitment round of 2008-12. Australia, which emits 2% percent of global GHG is a signatory to Kyoto protocol but has not ratified the protocol and as such is not subject to commitments of the other four Kyoto signatories in the partnership only Japan with 8.5 percent of global GHG emissions is subject to emission reduction target during the first commitment period. The European Union and other members were hoping to persuade the US to chip in. After all without the US, the Kyoto protocol is not really effective. Roping in the mighty haves meant imposing commitment on China and India as well. But the partnership seems to have put paid to any hope of getting US into the Kyoto. Worse, now there are fears that the US may effectively lure China and India a way with promises of technology transfer for clean development. No wonders there are fears that the partnership has severely weakened Kyoto and its objectives.

Crucial talks aimed at combating the threat of global warming opened with the US government signaling that it would resist attempts at being drawn into a new international process to cut emissions. Delegates at the United Nations Climate Conference, the first since the Kyoto protocol came into force in 16th February 2005, will discuss what action to take to reduce emissions of greenhouse gases when the Kyoto agreement expires in 2012. The US has refused to sign the Kyoto protocol and sent a clear message that it was in no mood to rethink its opposition to binding international agreements. US chief negotiator Harlan Watson said, he would strongly resist conditions and plans to combine the US with other developed nations and other developing countries in a joint commitment to action. He told to the BBC, "we feel very strongly that it is not appropriate that the ground is not there yet, there are many different ideas, people are not yet ready to move ahead under the convention". Despite not joining the Kyoto process, the US participates in the UN Framework Convention on Climate Change, which gave rise to the protocol. Large developing countries such as China and India, which are exempted from Kyoto restrictions are a focus of the Montreal meeting because their emissions are rising sharply and threatening to swamp cuts promised by developed countries. The Kyoto protocol manifested the issue of climate change with disappointments and problems because the "common but differentiated responsibility" could not be implemented within a relatively homogenous manner due to lack of coordinated action. The future of the treaty remains uncertain as the US has not only refused to ratify the treaty but also continues to insist on meaningful participation of the developing countries. The US position is not accepted by China, India and the European Union. Without a major move towards zero carbon energy system by the industrialized countries and without the acceptance of equity, all negotiations toward reducing Carbon Dioxide emissions will remain hostage to the interests of the industrialized North. More than 180 nations on 28th November 2005 began grappling with the gloomy prospects of increased pollution and global warming at the first meeting of the United Nations Kyoto protocol as a political storm unfolded in host nation Canada. Its challenge will be to frame the first step for crafting pledges on greenhouse gas pollution after Kyoto protocol runs out in 2012. Montreal meeting is the first convention since the Kyoto protocol signed by 156 countries took effect in February, 2005.

But the present commitment period does not include the planet's worst polluter, the United States, which whisked away from the binding GHG reduction commitments agreed to in the protocol in 2001, nor does it include fast growing developing countries such as China and India in its pledges on targeted reductions. The present Kyoto period is only a tiny first step toward tackling greenhouse gases that have been increased dramatically in recent decades as fossil fuels are burned to power economic growth. Atmospheric CO_2 levels are now at the highest during the last 650,000 years, scientists say and 2005 is likely to go into history books as the warmest year on record. Keeping in view increased global pollution, the parties in Montreal are concerned with how to take concrete steps and measures to combat the global warming.

The present day world passes through an ordeal of threats and catastrophic consequences of global warming due to the accumulation of greenhouse gases in the atmosphere. Tackling the problem of environmental degradation may require co-operation among the countries to address the challenges of climate change. The dangerous consequences of global warming require early and prompt actions for environmental security through co-operation.

Any international treaty in order to be effective requires co-operation, consent and willingness of the parties to implement so as to fight against the threats of the global warming effects. However conclusion of treaties, protocols and agreements may not be self-enforcing to achieve the objectives. There are many hindrances and obstacles in the way to respond in the desired direction, the decisions taken in various international conferences. The climate protection actions under the UN framework convention facing the constraints in moving the process forward for action are quintessential. Conflicting attitude of both North and South countries relating to the issues and interests represented by the alliances stands in the way of effective coordinated action. Another question relates to financial and technology transfer, and new additional resources to the developing countries must be transferred to take action and participation in the global effort to mitigate climate change, which has not yet been fulfilled.

Benefits and cost issues also endangers the global environmental issues based upon international co-operation and collaboration. As the benefits are unequal so how can the cost mitigation be equal for all countries. It is far from justice and fair play. In combating global warming the benefits and cost should be proportionate to curb discontentment. The inordinate life style and exorbitant consumption of western countries based upon fossil fuel production needs to be reexamined. It is not possible to abandon the present day fuel burning over night in order to give effect to the climate protection treaties. The principle of equity and responsibilities in meeting the commitments of emission reduction targets in a stipulated time table making division among the world community still remains uncertain and hazy to ensure co-operation by all countries and their participation in an effective and appropriate international response in accordance with their common but differentiated responsibilities and respective capabilities and their social and economic conditions to address the problem.

The largest share of historical and current global emissions of greenhouse gases has originated in developed countries that per capita emissions in developing countries are still relatively low, but the developed countries are continuously pressing to impose emission reduction targets over them. How can it be acceptable to them by endangering their social and developmental needs? This acts as a deterrent to implement the protocol agreed to so long as the alternatives to fossil fuel consumption are devised. Without providing better living and economic development to developing countries, any attempt to bind the developing countries to cutback fossil fuels burning is surely to fail in addressing the global problem. The super power game played by the United States in international politics, aggravates the problem of present day global warming. By discarding the ratification of Kyoto protocol, showing scant respect to the collective action, exploiting scientific uncertainties and dishonoring the previous commitments to reduce GHG emissions on targeted timetable, America is blocking the progress of environmental protection. Without the participation of US, the international co-operation and kind of response needed to combat the politics of global climate change is bound to be defeated to achieve the basic objectives of the UNFCCC.

The environmental security is closely associated with the national interests of the parties. No international treaty or agreements can be effective unless and until the national interests remain open to be redefined in terms of the greater interest of the environmental protection. Effective realization of climate protection treaties fails to coincide with the vested national interests of the countries.

Another major stumbling block in the progressive realization of the environmental protection regulations is the lack of sincere co-operation from the entire international community. But existence of differences, divisions, and discord among nations acts against maintaing a balance to secure co-operation among the parties, which has not become conducive to tackle the problem in a friendly manner.

The developed countries have already reached the apex of the development in exploiting nature. Sudden imposition of restrictions on the developing countries to stop their development by lowering emissions creates embarrassing situations to ruin their economies, which is highly unfair for continuing regulations through collective action. The difference between the lùxurious emission of the rich industrialized nations and the survival emissions of the poor developing world is to be taken note of, while arguing for the meaningful participation of the developing countries.

The climate change challenges the very sovereign state system and the legitimacy on which it is premised. The very grounds on which the present citizens of a country tend to give consent to the state have temporal and space limitations. It would mean transgression of the legitimacy to act in a way to satisfy the needs of the people on whose consent the authority is legitimized, that will deprive the future generations' right to live on this earth at a level that will match the life style of the western people. In this sense the legitimacy is temporal as the consent of future generations to the authority should not be taken for granted. The space limitations are very much inherent as the future generations both living human and non human have a right to live on this earth. The ontological foundation provided to the modern liberal market state by the Newtonian and Cartesian metaphor needs to be revised as its very premise that the nature is lifeless other to be exploited for the inordinate life style and commodious living of the people, has been the principal cause of environmental degradation. The faith in science that provided the talisman to the state to develop mankind in a materialistic way needs to be reviewed calling for a leap of faith.

The very cause of this nuisance to the environment is the ethnocentrism of western paradigm of development based on extraction of fossil fuels and industrialization. The problems of climate change put a challenge to the prevailing pattern of development. To what extent alternative paradigms of development conducive to the environment are devised rethinking the existing life pattern and style of people and recognizing the future generations' right to exist, will play a major role in combating the climate change. The modern civilization based on oil is prepared to go to war to secure oil supplies, but whether it is prepared to face the situation if the world's oil wells suddenly dry up. The modern life is so intimately connected with oil consumption that it is difficult to change the style of functioning to implement the climate treaties.

Further, the bargaining attitude of the developed countries to limit the CO_2 emissions causes consternation among the South countries to accept the voluntary reduction targets as set by the climate change treaty. The South countries always persist in opposing any move by the North industrialized countries to pitchfork them into the ambit of climate treaty on the ground that they have not yet reached the level of development with that of the industrialized North. So the success of the climate change treaty very much revolves round the ideological differences and bargaining and conflicting attitude of the North and South countries.

The treaties and agreements concluded for global warming regulation lack scientific certainty to bind the countries to the commitment of reduction targets within stipulated timetable. Addressing climate change is not an easy task. It raises different dilemmas as how to distribute the burden of reducing emissions among different countries and deal with scientific uncertainty. Any international or domestic policy instrument can be effective only if accompanied by adequate system of monitoring and enforcement. There is a linkage between compliance enforcement and the amount of international co-operation that will actually be sustained. Many multilateral environmental agreements impose no compliance obligations to bind the nations under UNFCCC to meet the objectives. Without accurate and scientific certitude about climate change on regional basis, meaningful negotiations are difficult to sustain today.

The common but differentiated responsibilities targets are not based on a standardized formula, and debate over long term equitable sharing of burden continues with different countries interpreting what constitutes fairness or equity in mitigating the risk of global climate change. A major constraint, which affects the developing countries is the financial and technological crunch for seeking substitutes to the existing traditional sources of energy, which happen to be the monopoly of a few countries in the developed world.

The United States is now the greatest obstruction to the world battle against climate change. The action of US not only strengthens the hands of those countries who wanted to weaken the treaty, but also makes it more weaker than it would other wise have been. To address the global warming unilateral action or action by group of countries would be insufficient to solve the problem. So long as the United States remains outside the orbit of the negotiation process, the global effort to mitigate the climate change will remain uncertain. In view of the above stated constraints, the global climate change politics passing through formidable challenges to tackle the environmental crisis through collective action is very much inherent in the nature of world politics. Concerted efforts and coordinated actions should be the fundamental principle to fight against the threat of imminent implications of global climate change.

Unfortunately, conferences and negotiations do not stop a process like global warming. The latest document to add to the mounting evidence that things are going very wrong in the world was the report by a former Chief Economist of the World Bank, Sir Nicholas Stern to the British government. The Stern Review stated that global temperatures have risen by half a degree Celsius as a result of carbon emissions and that if nothing is done, there is a 75 per cent chance that temperatures will rise by two to three degrees Celsius over the next 50 years. This will have a devastating effect on weather patterns resulting in floods, droughts, melting ice caps, and rising sea levels. The countries that will bear the brunt of this are the poorest. The Stern report estimated that there would be a loss of one per cent of the global gross domestic product caused by extreme weather. This report coming out in October 2006 suggested a remedy immediately to be adopted is that the world must cut back on Carbon Dioxide emissions by 50 billion tonnes to 70 billion tonnes a year by 2050 to avoid catastrophic climate change.

So far as clean energy programmes under CDM as outlined in Kyoto protocol, are concerned, what made the rounds in Nairobi about the future of Kyoto protocol is the misgivings and irk many raised about the viability of these projects. These are new ways to exploit the developing world, exacting a terrible price, with communities being robbed of their land and livelihood damaged by projects such as hydro-electric dams and fast growing tree plantations. As critics being buttressed by Stern report opine, these projects are encouraging destructive development and lining the pockets of the rich. For Larry Lohmann, author of Carbon Trading, carbon credits are just a new instrument for northern energy companies to exploit the developing world. Added to classic local conflicts over extraction, pollution, and labour abuse are now, increasingly, local conflicts over carbon offsets- the projects that license and excuse the extraction, the pollution and the abuse.

Patrick McCully of International Rivers Network says additionality is largely a joke: "We thought carbon credits would allow destructive projects to go forward that would not otherwise have been built. But we found the opposite. The carbon credits were going to projects that would have gone ahead anyway- they were the icing on the cake for developers."

What is the Way out: Prescriptions Toward Rethinking Development

Since the present and ubiquitously practiced western pattern of development based on fossil fuel technology and relentless industrialization thinking the nature and the living non human beings as " the lifeless other" to be exploited for a very commodious living for the few, is the root cause of the historical emission of Carbon Dioxide and other greenhouse gases to the atmosphere with all diabolic consequences upon the very survival of the present human civilization, what stands as a great desiderata raising the prospects of hope is to rethink the very pattern of development and the way of our life and the view of the universe formed by following the Newtonian and Cartesian metaphor for centuries together.

If there is any idea or word or concept in the present world that will match God's uncontested power beguiling the entire universe into its fold, it is the current concept "development" that has occupied the entire universal, individual, societal, nature, cultural and time space decimating many cultures and civilizations. The only highest intellectual achievement worth the name is acquisition of knowledge and mastery over the technological and scientific gadgets of development in western epistemology. It is all devastating, engulfing and rapacious enough to destroy nature and subject human beings to constant penury and suffering and divide hierarchically and vertically the entire humanity as developed and developing or underdeveloped on the criterion of their progression on the trajectory to what is understood as development in the western parlance. Its omnipotence is to cram the immeasurable diversities in culture and civilization, which the entire humanity in both North and South represents, into a single western straightjacket. Its acceptability is found in its success to ruin the nature and human beings and their inherent potentiality to live in their own defined ways.

If gone by civilizations are likened to dilapidated buildings, archeologists shovel in hand work through layer upon layer of the ruined buildings to unearth the secrets and underpinnings of a dilapidated monument hidden under piles of earth and rubble. Similarly, divergent and enriched ideas, cultures and civilizations have turned out to be ruins with their foundations covered by years or even centuries of western practice of development. Today, the idea of development, which stood like a monumental structure in the intellectual landscape with its shadows obscuring the vision and foresight of human beings. The grand edifice built over these years by the West yet nourished, maintained and beatified by the exploitation of both nature and the poor, is on the verge of falling apart and in danger of total collapse.

The Newtonian and Cartesian image and view of the world as mere lifeless particles in motion to be harnessed and exploited for human ends became the guiding metaphor in the emerging mechanistic world view and liberal conception of possessive and atomistic individualism. The liberal and market based polity and economy founded on such a view aims at ensuring abundant economic growth, wealth production and luxurious, materialistic and inordinate commodious living. To this end, science provided the ontological foundation sharing with which the political and economic thinking of US and the entire west constitutes the ideological foundation of what is today universally christened as development. The consequences of imposing a unitary western ideological and culture upon the entire universe trampling on many hallowed cultures and civilizations have already played havoc with nature and humanity, propelling us to redefine development because of its anti nature and anti human moorings.

Development is the Unfolding of a Culture: Realizing the Code or Cosmology of that Culture

There is no gainsaying the fact that what is today universally accepted as development is rooted very much in western culture and its Judeo-Christian tradition. Unlike Marxian economic determinism there is a cultural determinism of development. So like the people of western culture, every society, culture and civilization has an inalienable right to define what is development. Non-recognition of this right means reinforcement of a western cultural hegemony upon all other people. There are a myriad of cultures in the world, even civilizations, or macro cultures spanning vast regions in space and time. So a consequence of recognizing this definition would be that there are many developments. The universalization of western pattern of development based on fossil fuel technology, industrialization, exorbitant consumption and production and inordinate life style, liberal market economy and a world view formed by Newtonian and Cartesian understanding of matter made one thing certain, all the people of the earth are to move along the same track and aspire to only one goal- development. In other words, if one civilization imposes its definition of development on another, then it leads to a major case of cultural violence and it grafts another cultural code onto another people's culture, thereby legitimizing what is illegitimate and vice-versa. Straitjacketing all other people into a single cultural code means exposing all them to culturocide, killing of their own culture, leading them to gross alienation[1].

The word 'development' may be likened to a flower metaphor. The unfolding of a flower is already preprogrammed in the seeds as genetic code in the flower as a cultural code or cosmology in the civilization. So development is a programme to be realized or fulfilled according to the cultural code; neither the flower nor the civilization has real freedom of choice. That means, the flower or fruit or civilization is the end product according to genetic code preprogrammed in the seed. No change to the flower or civilization can be brought in unless and until there is a change in the genetic code. Why a change to this flower is warranted upon it is because this has been ruinous to both nature and humans. So non-acceptance of this flower or civilization as a universal model of development implies recognition of other existing divergent cultural codes on which different flowers or developments can be preprogrammed friendly to both nature and humans.

The western imperatives and imposition of what constitutes development means that the societies of the Third World are no longer seen as diverse and incomparable possibilities of human, nature and non human living arrangements but are rather placed on a single progressive track judged more or less advanced according to the criteria of the western industrial nations.

Development Means Progressive Satisfaction of the Needs of Human and Non Human Nature

Development can be defined as the progressive satisfaction of the needs of human and non human nature, starting with those in most need. Human beings have needs. If these are not satisfied or met, they are no longer human beings, meaning for the more material/ somatic needs they are no longer beings with life.[2] Suffering means needs deprivation. The more intensive (total deficit of one need) and extensive (deficit of several needs) of needs is deprivation. Nature and non human beings have also needs. The concept "needs" extends to all forms of sentient life. At all levels of deprivation there is an element of suffering. The extreme form of suffering is death, individual extinction whether from trauma inflicted on the body (direct violence), or lack of inputs (structural violence). But before extinction of the individual enters another key concept in development theory and practice, exploitation. It is defined as the use of life beyond its capacity for reproduction. Like a flower wilts, due to exploitation man or nature moves in a downward succession ending with death sooner or later, if every morning appears to be less than the morning before. When this happens for all individual species, plants, animals or human beings then that species is endangered, threatened with extinction. Renewability in case of non-living nature and reproducibility or sustainability are the better words to understand this.

If development is the progressive satisfaction of needs of humans and non human nature then the problem of environmental degradation is a matter of central concern. The present concept of development is homocentric whereby human needs are given priority to the exclusion of nature's needs. It often takes the enlightened form of environmental protection, lamenting that nature sets limits to growth, trotting about how nature can be sustained. Nature is conceived of as existing for the sake of human beings. This attitude to nature resembles to that of certain elites to people, who think they exist for the sake of elites as a means to their reproduction.

The somatic needs can be put under two heads: survival as opposed to extinction, and a minimum well-being. But human beings have also spiritual needs which can be kept under the headings of identity, something with which to identify in nature, personal, social, world, time and cultural spaces giving meaning to life; and freedom is defined partly as mobility in world space, social space and inner personal space with the possibility of making choices.

The western economic thinking has reduced 'the whole man' to an economic or consumer man[3] who is apt to think of satisfying his economic interests in terms of utility. The neo classical economics- the mainstream of present day economics remains impervious to the difference between human needs and wants. It has reduced all hierarchy of human needs to mere wants, which are measurable or additive quantitatively or to use the technical term commensurable and translated into consumptive goods in terms of utility and entered as inputs into the market mechanism. On the other hand, needs are incommensurable, they simply cannot be added. "Thus the economics of utility comes out of a world view, or an image of society in which all needs have been met. Only in that context, does it make sense and carry any realism. The shocking thing about an economics that relies on this picture is that it begins at a place where the fundamental economic problems already assumed to have been solved."[4] Maslow has listed the growth necessities in their order of priority for the human beings: These are

Deficiency needs, which include material needs and social needs

(*i*) Material needs- physiological needs, air, water, food, shelter, sleep, safety, security (*ii*) Social needs- self esteem, esteem by others, belongingness, love, affection, acceptance

Self – Actualization needs- moral needs- love, truth, service, justice, perfection, aesthetics, meaningfulness.

Not that after the fulfillment of deficiency needs motivations for self-actualization needs start. To quote him:

> "If we define growth as the various processes which bring the person towards ultimate self-actualization, then this conforms better with the observed fact that it is going on all the time in the life history. Growth is seen then not only as progressive satisfaction of basic needs to the point where they disappear, but also in the form of specific growth motivations over and above these basic needs."[5]

'Hierarchy of human needs' has been subject to controversy. It has a tendency to be universalized and freezed into a general law giving significance to the priorities and thus, derecognizing the diversities and ignoring the important classes of basic needs for a large section of society. But the hierarchy thesis invites usefully a pinpointed attention to the material deprivation of a large section of the society, when there is a lot of disagreement about what constitutes the non-material needs. Another important aspect, which this thesis serves, is while building alternatives, to take into account not only the consumer wants but also all hierarchy of needs.

Development has been Synonymous with Economic Growth

To hold development as nothing but economic growth has become platitudinous in the present economic thinking. What has risen to a standard of universal rule is the concept of development defined in terms of abundant economic growth at every body's cost. The costs of such a definition are enormous:

So far as **nature space** is concerned, the current western pattern of development has resulted in depletion of natural resources such as land, water, air, minerals, forests, and bio diversity and production of wastes or pollution of wastes or pollution and extinction of living and non living nature.

In human space as human needs deficits, it has resulted in threatening reproduction. Hence reproduction means to look afresh, fit and born again after sleep/rest, excretion and food every morning to start a new day. 'Not to be reproduced' means the growing human needs deficits, which make humans every morning look less than the morning before. That means, like a wilted flower in a downward succession human beings end with death sooner or later.

A growth oriented economy aiming at mindless and limitless exploitation of natural resources has ignored the human space and made it plagued by human needs deficits. It has resulted in economic exploitation, yawning gap between rich and poor and abysmal grinding poverty. The space naturally belonged to the humans has been usurped by the rich and the elites. In this definition, development means the development of natural resources not people. So development should be redefined in terms of reproducibility, which is sustainability, reproduction by its own forces as opposed to being propped up by external assistance.

The social space has been usurped by the imperatives of economic growth. Social space otherwise known as individual interaction system through culture, tradition, belief and other age old venerated values has been negated by economic growth. All aspects of individual life have been subject to countless intervention, regulation, straightjackets, organization and standardization by unprecedented flowing of agencies and administration in the name of development. Tradition, hierarchies, mental habits- the whole texture of societies have all been dissolved in the whirlpool of economic growth and mechanistic models of economists.[6] From this view point, the economy overshadows every other reality; the laws of economy dominate society and not the rules of society the economy.[7] All diversities have been crammed into an economic straitjacket.

The world space characterized by diversities and symbiosis in terms of culture, civilization, religion and values has been reduced to a mere economic activity. The world resembles a mere market place where everything is counted in terms of money. Under the banner of economic growth as development, the west has succeeded in its grand project of enforced reorganization of many societies into an economy. All nations and states have been reduced to mere factors of production in a world economy controlled by the west. The divergent pattern of subsistence economy prevalent in Asia and Africa was replaced by western national economy as propounded by Adam Smith. The western norms of organizing society into factors of production and distribution or mere economic units have been universalized. The whole world stands divided on the western criteria as developed, developing, civilized and uncivilized. This pattern of economic rules, norms and structures as shaped at Brettenwoods threatened traditional cultures, fostered economic inequality, weakened existing social structures and above all deliberately attempted to expropriate these developing and third world countries of their economic base and sustenance. The degree of civilization in a country could be measured by the level of its production. The third world and developing countries are no longer seen as diverse and incomparable possibilities of human living arrangements but are rather placed on a single track factorized into western production paradigm as mere economic units and judged more or less advanced according to the criteria of the western industrial nations.

Development as defined in the west and ubiquitously imitated in all parts of the globe is one of immediacy in meeting its domestic economic imperatives. Like a business concerned with immediate gain or profit, economic growth aims at exploitation of resources to the full available at present without looking to future implications. Nature, human beings, and non human beings are considered as the other to be exploited for the economic benefits of the exploiter. While defining development no concern is shown to sustainability or reproducibility or renewability. Even the attention to intergenerational equity and interspecies accountability in the conceptualization of what is development is very slim. The very recognition of the right of both animate and inanimate, plants, trees, animals and other human beings to live on this earth with reproducibility, sustainability and renewability should form the epithet of what is understood as development.

In the **cultural space** the west has been able to reinforce its value structure upon the entire world in the name of development. The imposition of western technological and materialistic culture upon the entire globe has sidelined other cultures and civilizations as mere folklores or remnants of barbarism. All other roads or moccasins seen on the paths to development are either rejected or not tried. Deification of western culture, value pattern and development has been universalized as a mark of progression on the trajectory to a civilized life. Naturally, a question crops up in the mind whether the people in the developing world are destined to be led by west as if to justify Huntington's clash of civilization. Have not they the distinguished philosophy of their own or intellectual adequatio to shovel their paths to development? If development is growth centered then it contradicts development which is culture centered and needs centred. What is development to one, may not be development to other.

Development can be Understood in Plural as Developments, not in Singular

There are as many cultures or civilizations, as many developments. Every culture or civilization has its own way of looking at life and defining what is development. If this were not so, then human history would not have been a record of many cultures and civilizations. To understand development as merely a western monolithic orthodoxy means to misrepresent the very diversities into which human beings are organized in their political and economic life. If the development of one culture is imposed upon another culture, it will sooner or later be experienced as a straitjacket. Under the weight of western ethnocentrism of development, all other cultures and civilizations have faded into insignificance. Rise of fundamentalism and terrorist forces can be partly explained as a manifestation of their reactions against the superimposition of western cultural ethnocentrism. This kind of reaction with violence to external imposition refers to people who believe enough in their own culture to stand up for it not caving in to a dominated culture from the outside. To look down upon other cultures or civilizations with disdain has been the foundation of the western pattern of development born in a Judeo-Christian tradition. This was even seen in the British colonial masters when they came as masters to rule over the nations in Asia, Africa and their colonies. British imperial administrator Lord Lugard had formulated the doctrine of the double mandate, economic profit of course, but above all the responsibility to elevate the coloured races to a higher level of civilizations[8]. The foundation of all encompassing globalization of American empire harks back to the 1840s when the Doctrine of Manifest Destiny (DMD) was invoked to justify the conquest of North America[9]. That means it is not man but God who had ordered the destruction of Indians, forests and buffaloes, the draining of swamps and the channeling of rivers and the development of an economy that depends on the continuing of exploitation of labor and natural resources. The context of Manifest Doctrine was also in vogue in the late 1800s and early 1900s to justify the US invasion of countries in Central and South America that declined to kowtow to American policies. Even the First World War, Second World War and the great depression compelled America to determinedly defend itself and spread its sphere of influence. The post second world war American onslaught on communism, military intervention in Vietnam, Iran, Indonesia, Guatemala or Nicaragua and the present military intervention in Afghanistan and Iraq after September 11 terrorist attack are some few examples to buttress the working of the Doctrine of Manifest Doctrine in American Foreign policy to reinforce its empire. US President George Bush claimed that he was on a mission from God when he launched the invasions of Afghanistan and Iraq, according to a senior Palestinian politician in an interview to the BBC.[10]

Western History and Civilization as Universal History of Development and Economic Growth

Every nation or state has its own history and civilization and its own way of defining what constitutes development. Before western concept of development dented into the myriad concepts and patterns of development prevalent in many civilizations and cultures, the people in the world had divergent ways of looking at the universe and relating it to what was development to them on the indices of their own cultures and value structures. The spread of colonialism, imperialism, industrialization, liberal market economy and science and technology by the west in 19th and 20th century and under American supremacy in the post second world period put into backburner many cultures and civilizations, and universalized western view of universe and life as synonymous with development. Today, all the nations of the world seem to have put on a western cultural straightjacket as the only road to development despite their having divergent cultural and civilizational ways of defining development. The supremacy of western culture has culminated in what is called as globalization- the crown of western liberal market economy. The adjustment pangs born of the overweening zest with which they are transforming their socio-economic and cultural societies to match the western pattern of development, could be a predominant factor explaining the ongoing orgy of violence in various parts of globe.

Organization of the society into economic functional units as per the nuances of liberal market economy, increasing division of labour, increasing specialization and increasing production of goods and savings, limitless consumerism and inordinate and luxurious life style and accumulation of wealth have been hallmarks of modernity and progress. The major inconsiderates of western pattern of development and economic thinking are hard work, saving, investment and greed. Since the development is resource based, their scarcity and exploitation requires hard work, savings and investment to obviate future uncertainty, to ensure a life of plenitude in future that means to postpone gratifications to enjoy later. The overriding motive behind all these is greed without paying attention to rests in terms of exploitation of nature, of the internal proletariat and of external proletariat in world space and even of culture and self.

The value pattern and ethics associated and developed with the evolution of a civilization or culture of a society or nation were ignored while defining development in western verbiage. On the other hand, the dominant value structure of the west became the major carriers of inconsiderateness of the western capitalist mode of development and economic growth. Historically, the value pattern derived from Judeo-Christian tradition and Protestant ethics in terms of greed, hard work, saving, investment and postponement of gratification evolved gradually to become the mainstay of what the West defines as development, and was universalized as the ethnocentric values in all societies and nations. An excerption here would sport how the western values derived from their religious tradition have come to be imbibed into mainstream of socio-economic and political life of the South as universal values by eschewing their own timeless values evolved during the ages:

> "One of the basic features of the Lutheran theoscape was the construction of paradise as a scapegoat. Access should not be seen as guaranteed by any formula controlled by human beings themselves. To the contrary, with God being His own cause, humans have little or no leverage. This means, uncertainty, but also standing in line in front of paradise. Given the super-individualization of the protestant soul standing in line would mean competition to get into paradise."[11]

On the other hand, the values of frugality, limited desires, shunning greed, decrying accumulation of wealth as sin, and renunciation in place of inordinate consumption and exorbitant life style, associated with other societies and civilizations were simply jettisoned as uncivilized to give primacy to western values.

Uncontested acceptance of western development and its concomitant value system as universal has resulted in the reculturation of other societies into a western consumerist cultural system that has become a planned and unstated objective of western powers with the sole leit motiv of bringing people from diverse cultures into a single civilizational model.[12]

Economist's Blind Eye

What is at the core of the western concept of development is that the essential reality of a society consists in nothing else than its functional achievements: the rest is just folklore or private affairs. From this view point the economy overshadows every other reality; the laws of economy dominate the society and not the rules of the society the economy. This is why, whenever development strategists set their sights on a country, they do not see a society that has an economy, but a society that is an economy. In the scintillating words of Galtung:

"Mainstream economics, like any science is an effort to make certain aspects of reality transparent and amenable to processing by the human mind in general, and the faculties for abstraction and generalization in particular, but always with the cost of making other aspects of reality opaque."[13] The direct side effects, positive and negative consequences which are made invisible in the mainstream economics are not accounted for in the mainstream economics.

There are six holes or caveats in the mainstream economics never looked for:

Nature Space

Nature is not seen in its own right as having a life of its own coming to creation even prior to human beings come to earth. The religious scriptures aver that the power of God is as much reflected in human beings as reflected in both animate and inanimate. They are not the lifeless other to be exploited using the Newtonian and Cartesian logic or to be considered by developmentalists as a resource cornuCoPia or a dumping thrash can for pollutants. Scoffing at the scant attention the proponents of liberal market economy used to pay to the nature, Peter Kropotkin stated: "Treating nature as whole while observing its rich diversity, it would appreciate the patterns of mutual aid and the complexity of natural phenomena, and question arguments based on ontological stratification or linear thinking."[14] In a similar tone, Eric Laferriere pointed out that "understanding nature historically, as a rich and long process of biological change, should put the presumed superiority of human kind into perspective and illuminate the sheer absurdity of ideologies based on consumption."[15] Indian Philosophy expresses that in the heightened stage of God–realization, the individualized self is transcended into Universal or Larger Self in which he/she perceives both the living and non- living as the power of God. The aura of holism strewn around nature rarely finds a mention in the mainstream economic theory. The assumed uncontested right of human beings to destroy nature has been challenged by Murray Bookchin. While explicating the concept "ecology of freedom", he stated that the respect for life, human and non-human, hinges on a recognition of difference, but not on a spurious notion of justice seeking to attribute rights indiscriminately.[16]

Human Space

Mainstream economists tend to view the human space as mainly production factors at various levels and as consumption potential. Other non-economic and humanistic aspects such as fellow feeling, frugality, honesty, modesty, austerity remain opaque or sidelined in economic thinking. Applying the Newtonian metaphor of atomism, the society is considered an assemblage of atomistic individuals solely concerned with aggrandizement of their own selfish interests. The human beings are not measured in terms of their inherent intrinsic worth but in terms of their being factorized into the mechanism of production of wealth. The western liberal market economy and polity founded on Hobbes and Locke's possessive individualism aims at ensuring abundant economic growth, wealth production and luxurious life style. To this end science provided the ontological foundation. Newtonian image of particles in motion becomes the guiding metaphor in the emerging mechanistic world view and liberal conception of possessive and atomistic individualism.[17] In contrast to the organistic world view linking the individual with God in a great chain of being, Hobbes conceived of both the state and the individual as machines, and may thus be considered founder of modern thinking on the basis of his contribution to mechanistic world view.[18] Similarly, Locke grounds his understanding of individual property rights in Biblical injunctions. Because He commanded man to "subdue the Earth", God gave the world " to the use of the industrious and rational". Land that is left to nature is wasted.[19] Thus, human being as a subjective self in terms of his/her intrinsic worth is ignored and viewed exclusively as an objectified and mechanized factor related to production and consumption in a market society.

A prominent psychologist Edward Diener pointed out that while poverty certainly causes unhappiness, wealth does not necessarily bring happiness. Since 1957, the average America's real income has trebled. But the fraction of Americans who describe themselves as very happy has remained static at one third throughout this period. One reason is, as economist Julliet Schor likes to point out, materialism causes people to spend rather than save, embedding anxiety in daily life. Besides, runaway consumerism puts the individual onto a never ending over-accelerating treadmill aptly summarized by David Myers' wry comment, " The victor belongs to the spoils." Such a wealth driven happiness is ethically vacuous, not impelled by basic values, and not anchored in concepts of rights and responsibilities. Not every nation with a high per capita income is truly developed."[20]

The liberal market economy tended to view man as wholly a consumer or economic one ever inclined to satisfy his/her desires in terms of consumption or utility. It has reduced all hierarchy of human needs to a mere compendium of wants which are measurable or commensurable quantitatively or translated into consumption items in terms of utility, and entered as inputs into the market mechanisms. On the other hand, needs are incommensurable and as such cannot be added. Thus, the economics of utility comes out of a world view or an image of society where all needs are purported to have been met. Only in that context does it make sense and carry any realism. The shocking thing about this market economy, which relies on this unrealistic picture, is that it begins at a place where fundamental economic problems remain grotesque and are assumed to have been solved. An economy, which reduces all human activity and even existence and values to a sheer commercialization and utilizable commodities in a market place , has ruined the moral, social and ecological foundation of the society. An excerpt would buttress this point:

> The human enrichment of economics involves the recognition that we have a dual self. The self that we feel we are is at the same time perceived as divided. Its lower aspect- self interest in its unambiguous interpretation – seeks one's own advantage regardless of the interests or well being of others. This is the self that finds it rational to free ride. In contrast, the higher self is that which identifies with a common humanity and finds its rationality in objectivity, fairness and the truth. The recognition of the existence of the higher self as well as the lower is necessary for an economics that is responsive to human needs and not merely human fancy driven by dollars. This an economics that promotes the well being of all rather than just a commercialization of human activity which by itself eats away the moral, social, and ecological fibre of society.[21]

What needs to define the individual is not certainly consumerism, acquisitive individualism, unbridled avarice for wealth production and a particular economic and technological way of life that has already spelt a doomsday for the present civilization. Amitai Etzion in his "Moral Dimension" is of the view that apart from rationality, which should not be confined to a mere cost- benefit calculus of maximum self interest, altruism and moral duty are equal motivators of human behaviour in the economic realm. But the widely acclaimed liberal market economy is completely oblivious of this moral aspects of human behaviour. The intrinsic human values such as selflessness, sacrifice, and community feeling inherent in many great civilizations and cultures are undermined at the cost of providing a humanistic visage to the current capitalist economy. Adam Smith, the father of classical economics in his "The Theory of Moral Sentiments' assumed that a higher providence ordains that the working of market economy remain within certain moral and ethical bounds not resulting in total selfishness. As one philosopher of science, Stephen Toulmin opines:

> "Instead of viewing the world of nature as onlookers from outside, we now have to understand how our human life and activities operate as elements within the world of nature. So we must develop a more coordinated view of the world, embracing both the world of nature and the world of humanity."[22]

Societal Space

It is seen as a locus for production- distribution- consumption cycles, and as a market place where everybody animate and inanimate is considered as a commodity to be sold or purchased. Society is understood not as a whole, diverse or plural but a disparate, disjointed, divisive and fragmented compendium of atomistic individuals tied with each other in a production- distribution nexus. One views the rest as the other to be exploited to one's advantage or discarded to avoid one's disadvantage. Society is understood as hierachically organized production- distribution set up with individuals embedded in it vying for wealth, inordinate life style and exorbitant consumption. To an economist's eye the entire societal space appears as a mere economic space. All aspects of society are viewed as mere economic units to be monetized.

Mainstream economics has been able to construct a homogenizing view in its economic framework. It reduces motives to a few universals such as needs or wants. In the process, it has also homogenized the plural and divergent society as mere economic unit by emphasizing a statist ontology that not only ascribes a natural aura to such a form of association, but also close its eyes to its internal variance and beauties. By reducing all aspects of a society to a mere narrow groove of economic motives or desires, and holding these as immutable and permanent, mainstream economics imposes a standard straitjacket upon all cultural diversities and anthropological insights forming the society. The economic view point is notoriously colour blind. It easily recognizes the human relations in terms of cost-yield or production dimension with extreme clarity, but is hardly able to perceive other dimensions of reality equally important. It fails to take note of collectivity, community feeling, cooperation, integration and other centripetal forces working in the society. At worst, the western mainstream economists, sociologists and Marxist historians have succeeded in universalizing the unidimensional economic factor to such an extent that other important factors and aspects of the society remain opaque. The hitherto unimportant fissures, divisive or centrifugal forces in the society are tried to be understood or overemphasized as dysfunctionally causative factors of economic production.

Not everything that looks like an economic activity is necessarily a part of economics. Indeed, economics offers only one of many ways of looking at goods oriented activities and putting them in a larger context. In every society things are produced, distributed and consumed; but only in modern westernized societies are prices and products, conditions of ownership and work predominantly shaped by the laws of economic efficiency. This is a paradox to hold that economic efficient production of goods as outlined by the west can be a universal pattern. There are different rules other than what the west suggests.

In societies that are not built on the compulsion to amass material wealth, economic activity is not geared to slick, zippy output. Rather, economic activities like choosing an occupation, cultivating the land, or exchanging goods are understood as ways of enacting that particular social drama in which the members of the community happen to see themselves as the actors. Economic activity is mere a chapter in the social drama not overarching other chapters of human life. That drama's story largely defines what belongs to whom, who produces what and how it is exchanged. This economy is closely bound up with life but it does not stamp its rules and rhythms on the rest of the society. It is now the west which through its universalization of economic imperatives dictate the drama and everyone's role in it.

World Space

Mainstream economics sees the world space as an international social space. What is true of social space within a state has become also true of the social space in international sphere. The entire world space has been reduced to a mere economic activity. Usurpation of the world space by the western liberal economy has been crowning achievement of globalization. In other words, it is an extension of western economic imperatives of abundant economic growth, wealth production and exorbitant life styles. The word "market" originally coined by Zedler's Universal Encyclopedia, meant a specious public place, surrounded by ornate buildings or enclosed by stands where, at certain times, all kinds of victuals and other wares are offered for sale. Adam Smith was the first thinker to extend the term market to society- wide space occupying the entire nation state. Then, it occupied the entire world space in the name of globalization. At present, the economy has finally achieved worldwide dominion, social disruptions and environmental destruction have become rampant. Societies find themselves cornered. They cannot afford to surrender to this monster, but they cannot escape from it either. In fact, the economy during its ascension to the top has blotted out alternatives to itself, which are not hazardous for both humans and nature. Even John Keynes, father of neo-classical economics and the chief architect of the post- world war II institutions shaped at Bretton-Woods, had proposed a toast to economics and economists, saying, you are not the trustees of civilizations but one of the possibilities of civilizations. But mainstream economics has dominated the entire world and all aspects of human life by arrogating to itself the authority of a trustee to define the destiny of mankind.

The mainstream economics has portrayed the world as a giant machine fixated on the goal of wealth production. It has trivialized culture and acculterd individuals, and societies in the process of social creation. Its anthropogenic view of nature and universe and consequent emphasis on economic growth leads to a relative lack of concern for the stability, integrity and beauty of the earth. Obsessed with growth fetish the western liberal market economy pauperized both the nature and human beings. In other words, "if Judeo-Christian monotheism took nature out of religion, Anglo-American economists took nature out of economics."[23]

The worst nightmare for the ecologists is the current spread of western liberal market economy throughout the world culminating in globalization. It involves the most fundamental centralized restructuring of socio-economic and political relations since the industrial revolution. It has created a new corporate colonialism in the form of TNCs to which all individuals, societies and nations must adjust. The new corporate colonialism is likely to dispossess, impoverish, and marginalize more people, destroy more cultures and cause more environmental devastations than either the colonialism of old or development of the last 50 years.[24]

In the current it means the homogenization of prices, products, wages, rates of interest and profits to become the same all over reinforcing the economic interests of the North countries. The process of economic globalization advanced by the Bretton-Woods institutions promoted the interests of the superrich so successfully that it also damaged their concern for and obligations to less fortunate inhabitants and their natural ecosystem in the developing world. It becomes another euphemism for the continuing exploitation of the underdeveloped by the developed, and redistribution of resources and wealth from the less to the more developed.[25]

Time

The mainstream economics looks at things for the shorter time horizons. It is more concerned with immediacy than with sustainability for the future. It depletes the nature, exploits others and exhausts to the full what is at the present with the calculation that it is more conducive and gainful to its interests for the time. It never looks beyond the immediacy and thinks over the ramifying implications of its relentless exploitation. It views both living and non-living as separate, independent, objectified and unconnected raw materials to be harnessed for one's own material aggrandizement. It is never aware of the fact that all these living and non-living are inseparable and inextricable parts in the web of relations that spans beyond the shorter horizon into the infinite timelessness frame of ever dynamic sustaining biotic system. Because of its shorter time horizon outlook, the mainstream economics disavows inter-species accountability, inter-generational equity, and responsibility to future generations.

Culture

Culture has been tailored to serve economics as constructed by economists rather than vice versa, by relativizing all values and making them comparable through monetization so as to permit inter-personal and inter value cost-benefit analysis. Mainstream economic culture of the west has been super-imposed upon all the cultures of the world. Western culture has been universalized and homogenized all over the world. The western culture has been ethno-culture killing varieties of cultures and value structures prevalent in the world. This has led to culturocide. The western culture of consumption, inordinate life style, and approach to life and nature , and primacy to monetization over all other values has replaced the other cultures of the world.

Poverty of Philosophy

Philosophy denotes the capacity to develop awareness of the holes in one's own reasoning i.e to see the other six holes mentioned above. Western philosophy and science has been ethno-philosophy and ethno-science. The South countries have with a religious attitude shown adherence to the western philosophy and approach to development without exploring other possibilities based on their own culture and civilization. In the post second world war period, the unequivocal acceptance of western philosophy and science as the ontological foundation of development by the South countries, shows whether there is poverty of philosophy in these countries.

The superimposition of western philosophy, science and economic thinking in the name of globalization and development has been carried on so successfully and incontestably that the western mind has been impervious to its own holes and the pool of eternal values lying embedded in other cultures and civilizations.

The indoctrination of western philosophy, science, and economic thinking as development has been carried on so successfully and incontestably throughout the world that the mainstream economics' blind eye has been impervious to its own holes and the other possibilities lying embedded in other cultures and civilizations. The western paradigm of development based on a world view, which is formed by the Newtonian or Cartesian classical scientific understanding of the universe in the 16th century requires an ontological revisionism, as science has already strode away from the classical foundation towards the eastern insights. There is no reason why a view of development belonging to a particular age, culture and history should bind all other nations to its lexicon when that view of the universe has already undergone a revolutionary change in the realm of science.

A leap of faith of all scientists, policymakers and human beings in the Cartesian spilt and mechanistic world for human liberation needs to be shifted to faith in cosmic worldview and its idea of unity and oneness between matter and spirit. Though a shift in the twentieth century science is perceived from this fragmented, mechanized and distorted view of matter to the idea of unity advocated in Eastern Philosophy, it has not been universalized and yet to form the premise of modern concept of development. In such a situation the locus of majestas will not emanate not from a view of universe built upon matter but from a transcendental vision looking beyond matter.To persist in such an old Cartesian mechanized, fragmented and distorted view of the universe comes as a testament to our immaturity and failure to identify ourselves with the real self. From this arrogant rational instrumentality of world view based on matter, emerges the creeping ecological crisis challenging us, the individual human beings and collectivities to evolve body, mind and soul consciously towards the realization of the universal self. The experience of the universe in modern physics as a dynamic, inseparable whole makes the traditional concepts of space and time, of isolated objects, and of cause and effect lose their meaning. Such an experience, however is very similar to that of the Eastern mystics, but very seldom has it been realized that this seems to lead in the same direction, towards a view of the world which is very similar to the views held in Eastern mysticism. The developments in modern physics are nothing new but a reflection of the ancient wisdom. This has been buttressed by no less a person than Julius Robert Oppenheimer:

> "The general notions about human understanding…which are illustrated by discoveries in atomic physics are not in the nature of things wholly unfamiliar, wholly unheard of, or new. Even in our own culture they have a history, and in Buddhist and Hindu thought a more considerable and central place. What we shall find is an exemplification, an encouragement, and a refinement of old wisdom".[26]

As Capra points out: When the concept of human spirit is understood as the mode of consciousness in which the individual feels connected to the cosmos as a whole, it becomes clear that the new vision of reality as understood by modern scientific development is in harmony with the visions of spiritual traditions[27]. If the modern science has already changed its perception of matter, the western paradigm of development built upon the foundations of the classical view of matter, needs a rethinking in terms of Eastern values, modern science, and vision of reality. The western liberal political tradition, which shared the same ontological foundation with Newtonian science, needs to part with it and renew its company with the new paradigm thinking in science in the changing scenario from a cosmic whole perspective.

Man's spiritual challenge today is to apply both faith and reason to find ways to live in harmony with nature. If contemporary environmental problems are to be solved, then moral teachings must be part of the effort to end environmentally destructive behaviour. As Weis wrote,

> No longer can we humans see ourselves and our selfish desires as the center of living and the sole criterion for decision making. Our vocation is not to dominate the earth. Our vocation is to discover community with it. Understanding our true position as one living species on this living planet is... a recognition of ourselves as made of the very stuff of the planet.[28]

Environmental degradation is a prideful arrogance toward God's creation and an abdication of our responsibility to find harmony with it. To distance nature from ourselves, by treating it as an object to our subject or by seeing it as inanimate and subservient to our material desires, is to falsify its truth, which is that it is, as we are, a creation of God.[29] In the Encyclical Letter, Centesimus Annus, Pope John Paul II offered a provocative counterpart to too widely accepted view of man's domination of nature, a counterpoint that should be brought to the center of the ethical resurgence in man:

> In his desire to have and to enjoy rather than to be and to grow, man consumes the resources of the earth and his own life in an excessive and disordered way. At the root of the senseless destruction of the natural environment lies an anthropological errot, which unfortunately is widespread in our day. Man, who discovers his capacity to transform and in a certain sense create the world through his own work, forgets that this is always based on God's prior and original gift of the things that are. Man thinks he can make arbitrary use of the earth, subjecting it without restraint to his will, as though it did not have its own requisites and a prior God given purpose, which man can indeed develop but must not betray.[30]

Given our ability to alter the environment in globally catastrophic ways, we must protect nature for a reason greater than that provided by the Newtonian view of the planet and man's material deterministic role in it- namely, that God wants and expects us to do so.

References

1. Johan Galtung, Development and Alternative Economics, Fall 1993.
2. *Ibid.*
3. See Herbert Marcuse, An Essay on Liberation (Boston: Beacon Press, 1969), p.11. William Leiss, The Limits to Satisfaction: An Essay on the Problems of Needs and Commodities (Toronto: University of Toronto Press, 1976), pp. 49-71.
4. Mark. Lutz and Kenneth Lux, Humanistic Economics: The New Challenge (New York: The Bootstrap Press, 1988), p. 29.
5. Abraham H. Maslow, Toward a Psychology of Being (New York: Van Nostrand Reinhold, 1968), p. 26.
6. Wolfgang Sachs, "Development: guide to the ruins", New Internationalist, June 1992, p. 6.
7. *Ibid,* " The economist's blind eye", New Internationalist, June 1992, p. 16.
8. Wolfgang Sachs, Development: a guide to ruins, *op.cit.* p. 5.
9. John Perkins, "American Empire: Slaver or Saviour?", World Affairs, Vol. 9, no. 1, pp. 19-20.
10. The Hindu, October 8 , 2005.
11. Johan Galtung, *op.cit.,* p. 11.
12. J.C.Kapur, "Towards a Philosophy for a New Human Order", World Affairs, Vol. 7, no. 4, October- December 2003, p. 39.
13. Johan Galtung, *op.cit.,* p.12.
14. Peter Kropotkin, Mutual Aid: A Factor of Evolution (Boston, MA: Extending Horizon Books, 1955).
15. Eric Laferriere, " Emancipating International Relations Theory: An Ecological Perspective", Millennium: Journal of International Studies, Vol. 25, No. 1, 1996, p. 57.
16. Murray Bookchin, The Ecology of Freedom: The Emergence and Dissolution of Hierarchy, Revised Edition (Montreal and New York, NY: Black Rose Books, 1991).
17. N.Gaan, " Post-Iraq War World Order: American Script, Pax Romana or Pax Brittanica", BIISS Journal, Vol. 25, No. 3, 2004, p. 208.
18. Carolyn Merchant, The Death of Nature: Women, Ecology and the Scientific Revolution (San Francisco: Harper Collins, 1990).
19. John Locke, Two Treaties of Government (New York: New American Library, 1965), p. 333.
20. Denis Goulet, "The United States: A Case of Anti- Development", Motive, January 1970, pp. 6-13.

21. Mark A Lutz and Kenneth Lux, Humanistic Economics: The New Challenge (New York: The Bootstrap Press, 1988), p. 319.
22. Stephen Toulmin, The Returen to Cosmology: Postmodern Science and the Theology of Nature (Berkeley: University of California Press, 1982), pp. 255-56.
23. J.R. McNeill, "Ideas matter: A Political History of the Twentieth Century Environment", Current History, Vol. 99, No. 640, November 2000, p. 374.
24 . Edward Goldsmith, "Development as Colonialism", World Affairs, Vol. 6, No. 2, April-June 2002, p. 36.
25. Ismail Shariff, and David M. Littig, " Globalization Old Wine into New Bottles", World Affairs, Vol. 6, No. 2, April-June 2002, p. 42.
26. J. R Oppenheimer, Science and the Common Understanding (London: Oxford University Press, 1954), pp. 8-9.
27. Fritjof Capra, The Tao of Physics (London : Flamingo 1991), p. 358.
28. M. Weis, "Living beings call us to reflective living", Merton Seasonal, Autumn 1992, pp. 8-9.
29. Andrew J. Hoffman and L.E. Sandelands, "Getting Right with Nature", Organizations Environment, Vol. 18, No. 2, June 2005, p. 159.
30. Pope John Paul II, Encyclical letter centesinus annus (Boston : Pauline, 1991), p. 56.

Bibliography

REPORTS AND DOCUMENTS

Berlin Mandate, 1995, United Nations Framework Convention on Climate Change: First Conference of the parties Report.

Climate Change 1995, Intergovernmental Panel on Climate Change; Second Assessment Report 1996.

Climate Change Action Report 2002, Earth Summit Report: Riodejanerio, June 1992.

CRS Report, Library of Congress, Washington, January 7, 2000.

First Assessment Report of IPCC, 1990

First World Climate Conference Report; Geneva, Switzerland, 1979

Fourth Meeting of the Conference of the Parties to the UN Framework Convention on Climate Change Report; Buenos-Aires, Argentina, 1998.

Hague Conference; Conference of the Parties, CoP-6, Report 1999.

Ninth Conference of the Parties to the UN Framework Convention on Climate Change; CoP-9, Report Milan, Italy, December 2003.

Second Conference of the Parties Report, CoP-2, Geneva, Switzerland, 1996.

Second World Climate Conference Report, Johannesburg, 2002.

Seventh Conference of the Parties to the UN Framework Convention on Climate Change, CoP-7, "Marrkesh Accord", October 2001.

Summary of Workshop Villach Conference Report, 28 September 1987 and Bellagio Conference Report November 1987.

Tenth Conference of the parties to the UN Frame work Convention on Climate Change Report; CoP-10, Buenos Aires, Argentina, December, 2004.

Toronto Conference Report, 1988

UNFCCC, "Review of the Implementation of Commitments and of their Provisions of the Convention", Conference of the parties, Fourth Session; Buenos Aires, November 1998.

UNFCCC, Eleventh Conference of the Parties, CoP-11/Mop1 Report, Montreal Canada, November-December 2005,

UNFCCC, Fifth Conference of the Parties Report, CoP-5, Bonn, Germany, November 1999.

UNFCCC, Third Conference of the parties, CoP-3, Kyoto Protocol, December 1997.

UNFCCC, Eight Conference of the Parties,CoP-8 Report, New Delhi, October 2002.

United Nations, "Framework Convention on Climate Change", Riodejanerio, Brazil,1992.

United States Environmental Protection Agency, Internet Report Entitled "The Kyoto Protocol and the President Policies to address Climate Change", www.epa.gov.11/23198.

Villach Conference Report, 1985.

WRI (World Resources Institute) World Resources 1998-1999. A Guide to Global Environment, New York, Oxford University Press, 1998.

ARTICLES

Regional Study on greenhouse Effect and its Impact on the Region", Kathamandu, SAARC Secretariat, December 1992.

Anderson Theodore, New Scientist, and Environment Report/Climate Change: Washington, vol. 300, May 1999, p. 1103.

Arthenius Svante; " A Discussion of greenhouse gases: Stockholm", Nebraska Cooperative Extension, NF-91-27, 1996.

Austin D. Goldemberg. J and Parker. J. "Contribution to Climate Change are Conventional metrics misleading the debate", Climate Notes; Climate Protection Institute; World Resource Institute, Washington DC., 1998.

Bach William, "Coal Policy and Climate Protection: Can the Tough CO_2 Reduction Target be met by 2005", Energy Policy, Vol.23, No.1, 1995.

Bhandari P. "Historical Perspective on Negotiations in Climate Change: Post Kyoto Perspectives from the South Tata Energy Research Institute, New Delhi, 1998, pp. 44-60

Birdsall N. "Another look at Population and Global Warming", Policy Research Working papers, The World Bank, Washington DC., 1992.

Boni Biagini and John Virdin, " Proposal on Climate Change Impacts on Coastal and Marine Resources", World Resource Institute, 2001.

Briedenich Claire, Danniel Magraw, Anne Rowley and Jammes W. Rubin, "The Kyoto Protocol to the United Nations Framework Convention on Climate Change", 92 American Journal of International Law, 1998, p. 315.

Burtraw, Dallos and Micheal Tomam, "Equity and International Agreement for CO_2 containment", Journal of Energy, 1992, 118(2), pp. 112-35.

Carlisle Johm and David Ridenour, "On sight Report Buenos Airs Global Warming Talks", www.nationalcentre.org, issue2, November 10, 1998.

Carraro C and B. Buchner, "Economic and Environmental Effectiveness of a technology based protocol", CEPR Discussion paper no. 4412, 2004.

Chanton Jeffrey, Ph.D., "Global Warming and Rising Oceans", American institute of Biological Sciences, 2002.

Choudhuri Pramatipal, "Global Warming is Earth too hot to handle: Statesman, 5-8, 1990.

Christopher Flavin, Odil Runali, "Reporting on Climate Change", June 1996.

Cooper Richard, "Toward a Real Global Warming Treaty", Foreign Affairs, 1998, 77(2), pp. 66-79.

Dasgupta Rupak, "Consciousness of Environment", Indian Express Daily, 21.05.1991, p. 18.

Dorwin Roy, "The Impacts of Global Warming on Agriculture: A Ricardian Analysis", American Economics Review, 1999, 89(4), pp. 49-52.

Douglas B.C., "Global Sea Level Acceration" J. Geography, 97(C8)12699-12, 706, 1992.

Drago Titu, "Spain lags in Kyoto Protocol Compliance", Terramerica, February 25, 2005.

Dunn S., "Hydrogen Futures : Toward a Sustainable Ecosystem" International Journal of Hydrogen, vol.27, 2002, pp.234-264.

Eichammer W. et.al., "Greenhouse Gas Reductions in Germany and UK-Coincidence or Policy induced? An Analysis for International Climate Policy", Elsevier, vol.1, no.3, 2001.

Eucom 230 final, "European Commission preparing for the Implementation of Kyoto Protocol", 19 May 1999.

European Environmental Agency, "Greenhouse gas Emission trends and Projection in Europe", 2004, p.3.

Eyckmans J. and M. Finus, "New Roads to International Environmental Agreements; The Cause of Global Warming", Mimeo, 2004.

Eyre N. "Carbon Reduction in the Real World, How the UK will Surplus its Kyoto Obligations Climate Policy", Elsevier, vol.1, no.3, 2001.

Finberg Kathy, "Expanded History of UN Ecological Summits: From Stockholm to Buenos Aires", Facsnet Section Editors, no.4, January 28, 2000, p. 1.

Fletcher Sue, "Summary of the Kyoto Protocol", CRS Report. Library of congress, Global Climate Change : Washington, 1998, p. 2.

Gerlogh R and B.C.C. Vander Awan; The effect of Ageing and an Environmental Trust Fund in an Overlapping generations model on Carbon Emission Reduction", Ecological Economics, (2001b)36(2), pp. 311-326.

Glebson Ross, "Boiling Point : How Politicians big oil and coal, Journalists and activities have fueled the Climate Crisis – what can we do to avert disaster, New York basic Books, 2004, www. heatsaline.org.

Glebspan Ross, "Global Warming and Political Power: The End of Nature and Beyond", Organization and Environment, London, New Delhi, Sage Publication(s) Thousand Oaks, Vol. 18, no. 2, June 2, 2005.

Glebspan Ross, The Heat is on : The Climate Crisis, the coverup the prescription (paper ed.) Reading M.A., Perseus,1998.

Glebspan Ross, The Heat is on : The High Stakes battle over Earth's threatened Climate, Reading MA, Addison Wesley, 1997.

Global Common Institute, "Contraction and Convergence: A Global Solution to Global Problem", London, UK Global Common Institute, July 1997.

Goodland R and Daly H, " Why Northern income growth is not Solution to Southern Poverty", Ecological Economics, Vol. 8, No. 2, 1993, pp. 85-101.

Goulet Denis, "The Cruel Choice: A New Concept in Theory and Development", New York, Atheneum, 1971, pp. 215-35.

Green Peace internet site on Global Warming: www.greenpeace.org, 20/11/98.

Grubb M. Vrollk C., Brack D., "The Kyoto Protocol a guide and Assessment", London , Royal Institute of International Affairs and Earth Scan Publications Ltd, 1999.

Hazaraff. Cat, " Global Could Threaten Human Ecosystems", Washington, DC., Health Environment New Service.(ENS), December 13, 2000.

Helm Carsten, "International Cooperation Behind the Veil of Uncertainty". Environmental and Resources Economics, 1998, 21, pp.185-201.

Holtz Eakin, Douglas and Thomas M. Selden, "Stocking the Fires", CO_2 Emissions and Economics Growth", Journal of Public Economics, 1995, 57, pp. 85-101.

Howrath R.B. , "Climate Change and Representative Agent", Environmental Resource Economics, 15, 2000, pp. 135-148.

Howrath R.B., "Climate Change and Overlapping Generations", Contemporary Economic Policy, 14,1996, pp. 100-111.

Jacoby Henery and Davod Reiner, "Getting Climate Policy on Tracks after the Hague", International Affairs(Blackwells), Vol. 77, No. 2, April, 2001.

Jacoby Henery D., Ronald, G. Primn and Richard Schmaleensee, "Kyoto Unfinished Business", Foreign Affairs, 77, 4 July –August 1998, pp. 54-56.

Janetus Anthray. C, et.al. 2000, "Impacts of Climate Change on Agriculture", Synergies of Rio Convention, 2000.

Jodha N. S., "Political Strategy for Adopting greenhouse Warming Perspective from the Developing World," Washington, USNAS, 15 June 1998, p. 12.

John A and R.A. Pechenino, "International and Intergenerational Environmental Externalities", Scandinavian Journal of Economics, 1997, 99(3), pp. 371-387.

Kane Sally, John Reilly, James Tobey, "Climate Change Economics Implications for World Agriculture," USDA Economic Research Service, Agriculture Report 647, October 1991.

Kelling C.D, T.P. Whorf, "Reporting on Climate Change", Scripps Institutions of Oceangraphy, Lajolla, California,1998.

Kevin Baumert and Namcy K. Kete, The US Developing Countries and Climate Protection Leadership or Settlement? Issue Brief; World Resource Institute, 2001.

Khorkok Peng, "G-77 leaders fails to Agree Combat Global Warming in Third World Economics", Thrend Analysis, Third World Outlook, Penag; September 15, 1990.

Kolstad Charles D., "Learning and Stock effects in Environmental Regulations", Journals of Environmental Economics and Management, 31,1996, pp. 1-18.

Larry Parker and John Bladget, "Climate Change", Three Policy Perspectives, CRS Report, Washington, ENR-1994.

Lavina M. G. Antonia, "From Kyoto to Marrakesh Global Climate Politics and Local Communities", World Resource Institute, 31st August 2002.

Ledley S. Tamaras, Eric T. Sundait, Stephen E. Schwartz, Borothy K. Hall, Jack D. Fellows and Timothy L. Killen, "Climate Change and greenhouse Gases", Massachusetts Ave, Cambridge, Vol. 80, No. 39, 28 September 1999, p. 453.

Lindsay M. James, Global Warming Heats Up", CFR Publications, Brooking Review, Washington, Fall 2001.

Ling Bing, "Developing Countries and Ozone Layer Protection: Issues, Principles and Implications", 6. Tulane Environmental Law, Journal 91, 1992.

Lutz W., PrinZ C and Langgassner J, "World Population Projection and Possible Ecological Feed Backs", POPNET, IIASA, No. 23, Summer 1993.

Manne Alan and Richard Richels, "The greenhouse Debate; Economic Efficiency, Burdern Sharing and Hedging Strategic", The Energy Journal, 16(4), 1995, pp. 1-37.

Maste Panov A and Pluzhnikov O. Berdin V, "Post Kyoto Energy Strategy of the Russian Federation: Outlooks and Prerequisites of the Kyoto Mechanism Implementation in the Country", Climate Policy Elsevier, Vol. 1, No.1, 2000.

Matsumura H., "Japan and Ratification of Kyoto Protocol Climate", Elsevier, Vol. 1, No. 3, 2000.

McKibben B, "The End of the Nature", New York, Random House, 1989.

McKibben Warwick J and Peter J. Wilcoxen, "Beyond the Kyoto Protocol: Presented at the International Conference on the Sustainable Future of the Global System", United Nations University, Tokya, Japan, May 24-25, 2000.

McKibbin Waraick, "Moving Beyond Kyoto Policy Brief 66", Brooking Institution, Washington DC., 2000.

McKibbin Warwick and Willcoxen P., "A Betteer Way to Slow Climate Change", Brooking Policy Brief 17., Brookings, 1997.

McKibbin Warwick, "Moving Beyond", Kyoto Policy Brief 66, Brooking Institution, Washington DC., 2000.

Meyer Sieve, Ken Hubbard, "Discuss of greenhouse gases", Stockholm, Nebraska Cooperative Extension, NF. 91-27, May 1991, p. 2.

Michel Chris, "greenhouse and Science of Uncertainty", Australian Broadcasting Corporation, 1997.

Milly Christopher, "Atmospheric Scientist of the US Geopolitical Survey" National Geographic Climate Studies more Floods in this Century, 30.1.2002.

Mintzer and Miller, "The Ozone Layer : Its Protection Depends on International Cooperation", 21-Environmental Science Technology, 1987, p. 1167.

Moore Thomas Gale, "Climate of Fear : Why we should not worry about Global Warming", Washington Dc., Cato Institute, 1998.

Morgan Granger, "Climate Change Managing Carbon from the ground UP Science", 289(5488), 2285, 2000 eds.

Muller B., 'The Kyoto Mechanisms Linking Technology to Ratification Climate Policy", Elsevier , Vol. 1, No. 3, 2000.

Nagle Oral E., "Stratospheric Ozone: United States Regulation of Chlorofluorocarbons", 16 Boston College, Environmental Affairs Legal Review, 1989, p. 531.

National Academy of Sciences, "Policy Implications of greenhouse Warming", Washington DC., NAS Press, 1991.

Nikitina E, "Russia Climate Policy Formation and Implementation during 1990s", Climate Policy, Elsevier, Vol. 1, No. 3, 2000.

Nordhaus W.D. Z.Yang, "A General Dynamic, General Equillibrium Model of alternative Climate Change Strategies", American Economics Review, 1996, 86(4), pp. 741-765.

Nordhus William D. "The Cost of Slowing Climate Change", The Energy Journal-1991b, 12(1): 37-65.

Oberthur S. Otth, "The Kyoto Protocol International Climate Policy for the 21st Century", Springer Berlin, 1999.

Ohki Hiroshi, "International Cooperation in Combating Global Warming", Chairman Special Committee on Global Environmental Issue, 2001.

Organization for Cooperation and Development, Climate Change mobilizing Global effort, Paris, OECD, 1997.

Parson E.A. and D.W. Keith, "Fossil Fuels without CO_2 Emissions: Programs Prospects and Policy Implication", Science 1998, pp. 1053-54

Paterson Mathew and Michael Grubb eds. 1996, "Sharing the Effort: Options for Differentiating Commitments on Climate Change", London, UK, The Royal Institute of International Affairs.

Pearce David, Anil Markendya and Edward B. Barbier, "Blue Print for Green Economy", London, Earth Scan Publication, 1989.

Quiggin John and John K. Horowitz, "The Impact of Global Warming on Agriculture", A Ricardian Analysis; Commant American Economic Review, 1999, 89(4), pp. 1044-45.

Rahman A. Robins N and Ronecerel A., "Consumption versus Population which is the Climate Bomb", Exploiting the Population myth, Climate Network, Europe, 1993.

Rabkin Jeremy, "greenhouse Politics", Washington, AEI Publications, January 2000, pp. 1-3.

Rasmussen T.N., "Modeling the Economics of greenhouse Gas Abatement: An overlapping Generation Perspective", Review of Economic Dynamics, 2003, 6, pp. 99-119.

Reid W. V. and Goldenburg. J, "Developing Countries are Combating Climate Change Actions in Developing Countries that slow Growth in Carbon Emission", Energy Policy Vol. 26, No.3, 1997, pp. 233-37.

Riahi B. Schamadiner, Y. Yamagata, J. Yam and J.P. Vanypersole, "Managing Climate Risk", Science 294 no-5534, 26 October 2001, pp. 786-87.

Ridgley Mark, "Fair Sharing of greenhouse gas Burdens", Energy Policy 1996, 24(6), 517-29.

Ringi Lasse, Asbjam Torvanger and Bharh Holtsmark, "Can Multi Criteria Rules Fairly Distribute Climate Burdens", Energy Policy 26 (10), pp. 777-93.

Rosenwing Cynthis and Daniel Hillel, "Potential of Climate Change on Agriculture and Food Supply", National and Exploration, Vol. 1, No. 2, pp. 5-12

Robkin Jermy, "greenhouse Politics in the Issue American Enterprise Institute", (AEI), Washington, November 1997, p. 1.

Rose Adam, "Reducing Conflict in Global Warming in Energy Policy", 1990, 18(10), 927.

Rose Adam, Brandit Stevens, Jac Edwards and Marshal Wise, "International in Global Warming Policy : An Application to Tradeble Emission Permits", Environmental and Resources Economics, 1998, 12(1), p. 25-51.

Rosenzweig C, and Parry M.L., "Potential Impact of Climate Change on World Food Supply", Nature Vol. 367, 1994, pp. 133-38.

Sandalow D., Bowles I.A. "Fundamentals of Treaty on Climate Change", Science Vol. 292, 2001, pp. 1839-40.

Schelling Thomas C., "The Cost of Combating Global Warming Facing the Trade offs", Foreign Affairs, November & December 1997, p. 8-14.

Schmalensee Richard, " Comparing greenhouse Gases for Policy Purposes: The Energy Journal, 1993a, 14(1), p. 245-55.

Schmalensee Richard, "Symposium on Global Warming Change: Journal of Economics Perspectives", 1993b, ed., 7(4)Fall, p. 3-10.

SEAP, "Climate Change and greenhouse Effect", H.P./www.globalchange. com/ berry.html, 27.3.2004, p. 1.

Segan Carl, "Segan's View Point of Global Phenomena Feeling the Heat", US, SEN/26.05.1990, p. 6.

Seidel Stephenm, "Can We delay a greenhouse Warming", Washington DC, US Government Printing Office, 1983.

Seidel, S. Chapter an effectiveness of Energy Policies for Controlling CO_2, Washington DC, 1983.

Serageldin .I, "Population Dynamics Environment and Conflict", INTERI, 1997. Population, Environment and Development, Multiplexus, India, 1997.

Shogren Jason and Michael Toman, "Climate Change Policy"; in Paul. R. Portney and Robert N. Stavins eds., Public Policies for Environmental Protection, 2nd Edition, Washington DC., Resources for the Future 2000, pp. 125-68.

Sokana, Y,H, Safemul, "Climate View Point from the South", p. 1.

Spyres Jully, "Global Warming and Coastal Land Forester Communications", US, 1999-2001, p. 1.

Stevene .W.K. "The Change in Weather, People and Science of Climate", New York Random House, 1999.

Steward Kristin, " The Problem of Global Warming", Georgetown University School of Foreign Science: Science Technology and international Affairs, Vol. 1, 1998.

Storey Mark, Kyoto Beyond issue and options in the Global Response to Climate Change : Stockholm Swedish EPA, 15 November, 2002.

Sturges W.T. et.al. 2000, Extension of heat trapping gases and aerosols. A potent greenhouse gases identified in the atmosphere SF-5, CF-13, Science 289, p. 611-613.

Tol. Richard S.J. "The Damage cost of Climate Change toward more Comprehensive Calculations", Environmental Development Economics, 1995, 5, pp. 353-74.

Toman Michael, "Establishing and Operating clean Development Mechanism", RFF, Climate issue Brief, 22 Washington DC, Resources for the Future 2000.

Toronff E., "Gobal Climate Change : The Role of US Foreign Assistance", Report for the Congress Congressioanl Research Service, Washngton DC., 21 November 1997.

Treyur M.C., Kosloff L.H., "The 1997 Kyoto Protocol What does it mean for Project based Climate Mitigation and Adoption Strategies" 3(1), 1, 1998.

Trivedi R.N. "A Text of Environmental Science", Chapter-32, A greenhouse Effect a Continuing Catastrophe, New Delhi, Anmol, 1997, pp. 204-05.

Turner J.A., "A Realizable Renewable Energy Future", Science Vol. 285, 30 July 1999.

Varon J.L. "greenhouse Gas Emissions and Reductions by technology Transfer to Developing Countries", EA Coal, Research CCC/59.2002.

Victor .D., "The Collaspe of Kyoto Protocol and Struggle to Control Global Warming : Council on Foreign Relation", New York, 2001.

Vroli JK. C, "The Potential Size of Clean Development Mechanism", Presented at the International Conference, Emerging market for Emissions Trading, London, 26-27 April, 1997.

Welsch Heinz, "A CO_2 Agreement Proposal with Flexible quotas", Energy Policy, 21 July 1993, p.748.

WEPA, Eddystone Pennsylvania, "Global Warming the High cost of Kyoto Protocol", National and State Impacts, 1998.

Wiemer Jonathan, "Global Environmental Regulation", Instrument choice in Legal context Yalelaw Journal 1999, 108(4), pp.677-800

Wigley T.M.L and S.C.B. Raper, "Implications for Climate and Sea Level" Revised IPCC Emissions Scenarios Nature 1992, 35.7, pp.293-300.

Winer Jonathan, "Policy Design for International Gas Control", RFF, Climate Issue Brief, 6-Revised July 2000, Washington DC, Resources for the Future.

Wiser Glenn, " Kyoto Costs and Compliance" A Public Interest Lawers view of CoP-6, Washington DC., 2001.

Yan J., Alvforsp. Eldenstent and Svedberg G. "A Future for Biomass: Mechanical Engineering", October 1997.

Yan Jinyue, "Global Warming and Climate Change Mitigation Technology", Sweden, Royal Institute of Technology.

Zhang Z.X., "Estimating the Size of the Potential Market for all Three Flexbility Mechanism under Kyoto Protocol", Final Report Prepared by Asian Development Bank, 1999.

Zhang Zhong Xiang, "Is China Taking Action to Limit its greenhouse Emissions : Past Evidence and Future Prospectus", Mimeo,1998

BOOKS

Abrahamson. D. E., Eds., 1989: The Challenge of Global Warming. Island Press, Washington, D.C., pp. 358 .

Agrawala and S. Narain, "Global Warming in an unequal World". A Case of Environmental Colonialism: New Delhi, Centre for Science and Environment, 1992.

Agrawala, A. Narain, S. Sharma, A(editors) "Boiling Point in Green politics". Global Environmental Negotiations : New Delhi, Centre for Science and Environment, Vol. 1, 1999, pp. 16-121.

Alley, Richard B., The Two-Mile Time Machine: Ice Cores, Abrupt Climate Change, and Our Future. Princeton, NJ: Princeton University Press, 2002. SL QC 884 A55 2002.

Alvin Silverstein, "Global Warming", et.al., Twenty-First Century Books, Brookfield, CT(2003).

Archibald, J.D., 1996, Dinosaur extinction and the end of an era: What the fossils say: New York, NY, Columbia University Press, 237p, {TRC QE734.5. A73 1996]

Athanasious, Tom and Baer, Paul, Dead Heat: Global Justice and Global Warming, Seven Stories Press, 2002.

Bailey, Ronald. Global Warming and Other Eco Myths: How the Environmental Movement Uses False Science to Scare Us to Death, Prima Lifestyles, 2002. TRL

Balling, R. C. 1992; The heated debate: greenhouse predictions versus climate reality. Pacific Research Institute for Public Policy, San Francisco, 195.

Bartsh Ulrich and Benito. Miller, "Fossil Fuels in a Changing Climate Impacts of the Kyoto Protocol and Developing Country Participation", Oxford University Press : Oxford, 2000.

Benarde, M. A., 1992: Global Warning... Global Warming. John Wiley & Sons, New York, pp. 317.

Battan, L. 3., 1983: Weather in Your Life. W.H. Freeman and Company, San Francisco, 230 pp.

Bender & Leone, "Global Warming Opposing view point" San Diego, CA: Greenhouse Press; 1997, p. 16.

Benedict Richard Elliott, "Ozone Diplomacy : New Dimension in Safeguarding Planet" Harvard University Press, 1998.

Beniston, Martin, ed. Climatic Change: Implications for the Hydrological Cycle and for Water Management. Boston, MA: Kluwer Academic Publishers, 2002. SLQC981.8.C5C628 2002.

Bernard. H, W. J., 1993: Global Warming Unchecked: Signs to Watch for. Indiana University Press, Bloomington,

Bras, Rafael, ed. The World at Risk: Natural Hazards and Climate Change, Cambridge, MA 1992. New York: American Institute of Physics, 1993.GF85 .W67 1993 SWAIN

Brown, Lester Russell., Plan B: Rescuing a Planet under Stress and a Civilization in Trouble. Norton, 2003.TRL

Brown, Neville G., History of Climate Change. London: Routledge, 2001.

Bruce, James, P., et al, eds, Climate Change 1995: Economic and Social Dimensions of Climate Change. Cambridge, UK: Cambridge University Press, 1996. SL QC 981.8 C5 . C5 128 1996.

Buck Susan, "The Global Commons", Washington DC, Island Press, 1998.

Carpenter, Clive. "The greenhouse Effect." The Changing World of Weather. Middlesex: Guinness Publishing, Ltd., 1991, pp. 96-111.

Chambers, Nicky, Simmons, Craig; and Wackernagel, Mathis, Sharing Nature's Interest. Earthscan Publications 2000

Changnon, Stanley, A., and Gerald D. Bell, eds., El Nino, 1997-1998: The Climate Event of the Century. New York: Oxford University Press, 2000. SL GC 296.8 E54 2000.

Christopher Flavin and Odil Tunali, "Climate of Hope: New Strategic for Stabilizing the World's Atmosphere", World watch Institute, Washington, DC, 1996.

Climate Change: The IPCC Response Strategies. Washington, DC: Island Press, 1991. SL QC 981.8 C5 157 1990.

Comber, Mary, "Global Warming." World Almanac For Kids. Ed. Judith S. Levey. Mahwa: Reference Corporation, 1999, pp. 92-93.

Dauncey, Guy and Patrick Mazza. Stormy Weather. New Society Publishers, 2003, TRL

Dolan, E. F., 1990: Drought: The Past, Present and Future Enemy. Franklin Watts, New York, pp. 144.

Downing, Thomas E. Climate Change and World Food Security Heidelberg: Springer, 1996. QC981.8 .C5 C5145 1996 BUS/SPEA

Eisma, Doeke. Climate Change: Impact on Coastal Habitation. Boca Raton: Lewis Publishers, 1995. GE105 .C54 1995 BUS/SPEA

Environment Global Warming and greenhouse Effect. World Almanac 2000, Mahwah : World Almanac Books, 2000.

Essex, Christopher, and McKitrick, Ross. Taken By Storm: The Troubled Science, Policy and Politics of Global Warming, Key Porter Books, 2003

Fardon, John. "Global warming," 4000 Things You Should Know. Ed. Essex: Books are Fun, 2000. pp. 94.

Feldman, David L., ed. Global Climate Change and Public Policy. Chicago: Nelson-Hall, 1994. QC981.8 .C5 G647 1994 BUS/SPEA

Fleming, James Rodger. Global Changes: History, Climate, and Culture. New York: Oxford University Press, 1998. AJT9230 GEO-MAP

Gale, Zachary. "Is Global Warming a Real Problem?" Global Warming Debate. 2001 <http://www.youdebflte.com/DEBATES/GLQBAL WARMING.HTM > (Oct. 2001)

Gay, K., 1986: The greenhouse Effect. Franklin Watts, New York, 87 pp.

Gelbspan, R., 1997: The Heat is On: The High Stakes Battle over Earth's Threatened Climate. Addison-Wesley, Reading, Massachusetts, pp. 278.

Gelbspan, Ross. Bolting Point: How Politicians, Big Oil and Coat, Journalists and Activists Are Fueling the Climate Crisis~-And What We Can Do to Avert Disaster. Basic

Ghan, S. J., ed. Regional Impacts of Global Climate Change: Assessing Change and Response at the Scales that Matter Columbus, OH: Battelle Press, 1996. QC981.8 .C5 H253 1993 BUS/SPEA

Gille, John C. "greenhouse Effect." World Book Encyclopedia. Ed. Dale W.Jacobs. Chicago: World Book," Inc., 1996, p. 383.

Godrej, Dinyar, "Future is Now," New Internationalist. 1999 <http: //www. oneworld. org/ ni/ issue319 / rurure.htm> (Oct.2001)

Godrej, Dinyar. The No-nonsense Guide to Climate Change. Oxford: New Internationalist Publications , 2001. SL QC981.8.C5 G666 2001.

Gopal Bhargava, "Global Warming and Climate Change : Transparency and Accountability(in 3 Vols.)", Gyan Books Pvt. Ltd, New Delhi, October 2004.

Gore, A., 1992: Earth in the Balance: Ecology and the Human Spirit. Houghlon Mifflin, New York, pp. 497.

Graedel, T. E. and P. J. Crutzen, 1995: Atmosphere, Climate, and Change. W.H. Freeman, pp. 196.

greenhouse Effect." Concise Science Dictionary. Ed. Alan Isaacs, John Daintith, Elizabeth Martin. New York: Oxford University Press, 1991, p. 301.

Gregory, K. J., and Benito. G., 2003, Palaeohydrology; Understanding global change: Chichester. UK, John Wiley and Sons Ltd., p. 396.

Gribbin, 3. and M. Kelly, 1989: Winds of Change: Living in the Global greenhouse. Headway, Hodder & Stoughton, pp. 162.

Haimson. Leonine, "A History of Climate Change Negotiations", 1999, p. 1.

Harrison. P, " The Third Revolution, Population, Environmental and a Sustainable World," Penguin Books,1992, p. 368.

Hartmannn D. L., 1994: Global Physical Climatology. Academic Press. San Diego, 411pp. Houghton, J. T., 1994: Global Warming: The Complete Briefing. Lion Publishing. Oxford, pp. 192.

Hehner, Barbra " Global Warming." Blue Planet. Toronto, Ontario, Canada: Somerville House Publishing,1992, pp. 37-39.

Hocking, C, C. Sneider, J. Erickson and R. Golden, 1990; Global Warming and the greenhouse Effect, Lawrence Hall of Science, Berkeley, pp. 174.

Hoel Micheal, "How Should International greenhouse Gas Agreements be designed. In Partha Dasgupta; Karlgoran Maler and Alessandra Vercelli; eds. The Economics of Transitional Commons", Clarendon Press: Oxford, 1997, pp. 172-191.

Holper P.N., "greenhouse Gas and Science of Uncertainty", London/ New York: Cambridge University Press, 1994, p.81.

Houghtn John, " Global Warming" The Complete Briefing 2nd ed. New York, Cambridge University Press, 1997.

Houghton J.T., B.B. Callander and S.K. Varney eds., " Supplementary Report to the IPCC Scientific Assessment," New York, Cambridge University Press, 1992.

Houghton, J. T., L. G. Meira Filho, B. A. Callander, N. Harris, A. Kattenberg, and K. Maskell. Eds., 1996. Climate Change 1995: The Science of Climate Change. Intergovernmental Panel on Climate Change, Cambridge, pp. 572.

Houghton, J.T., et al, eds., Climate Change 1995: The Science of Climate Change. Cambridge, UK: Cambridge University Press, 1996. SL QC 981.8 C5 C5128 1996.

Houghton, J.T., et al, eds., Climate Change, 1994: Radiative Forcing of Climate Change and an Evaluation of the IPCC IS92 Emission Scenarios. Cambridge, UK: Cambridge University Press, 1995. SL QC 981.8 C5 C5125 1995.

John Ryan, "Over Our Heads: A Local Look at Global Climate", Northwest Environment Watch, Seattle, WA(1997).

Joint Implementation and Transaction Costs Under the Climate Change Convention, Organization for Economic Cooperation and Development (OECD), Environment

Kothari Rajani, " Environment Technology and Ethics" in J. Ronald Engel and John Gibb; Engel ed. Ethics of Environment and Development, London, Belhaven Press; A Division of Printer Publishers, 1990, p. 30.

Laurence Pringle, "Global Warming : the Threat of Earth's Changing Climate", Sea Star, New York, NY, (2001).

Lawrence Hall, " Global Warming & the greenhouse Effect", Science University of California: Berkeley, Berkeley, CA(1990).

Lee, Henry, ed. Shaping National Responses to Climate Change: A Post-Rio Guide. Washington, DC. Island Press, 1995. GE170 .S48 1995 BUS/SPEA

Leggett, Jeremy, K. The Carbon War: Global Warming and the End of the Oil Era, Routledge, 2001. TRL

Lyman, F., 1990: The greenhouse Trap: What we're doing to the atmosphere and how we can slow global warming. Beacon Press, Boston, 190 pp.

Lynas, Mark. High Tide: The Truth about our Climate Crisis. Picador, St. Martins Press, 2004. TRL

MacLeod. N., and Keller, G., eds., 1996, Cretaceous-Tertiary Mass Extinctions: Biotic and Environmental Changes: New York, W.W. Norton, p. 575.

McKibben B., "The End of the Nature", (10th Anniversary ed.,)New York, Anchor, 1999/

Mclntosh, Roderick J, et. al. The Way the Wind Blows: Climate, History, and Human Action. New York: Columbia University Press, 2000. SL QC981.8.C5 W395 2000

Metz, Bert, ed., Methodological and Technological Issues in Technology Transfer. Cambridge, UK: Cambridge University Press for the IPCC, 2000. SL T174.3 M475 2000.

Metz, Bert, et al, eds., Climate Change 2001: Mitigation: Contribution of Working Group III to the third assessment report of the Intergovernmental Panel on Climate Change. Cambridge, UK: Cambridge University Press, 2001. SL QC 981.8 C5 C511343 2001.

Michaels, Patrick. Meltdown: The Predictable Distortion of Global Warming by Scientists, Politicians, and the Media, Cato Institute, 2004. TRL

Microsoft Encarta- "Global Warming." Microsoft Encarta Encyclopedia Deluxe 2000. Redmond: Microsoft Corporation, 1993-1999.

Minger. T. J., Eds., 1990: greenhouse Glasnost: The Crisis of Global Warming. Ecco Press New York, pp. 292.

Moore, Thomas. "The Effects of Global Warming." Climate of Fear, Why We Shouldn't Worry about Global Warming. Washington, D.C.: CATO Institute, 1998, pp. 113-128.

Motavalli, Jim, Feeling the Heat: Dispatches from the Front Lines of Climate Change, Routledge, 2004, TRL.

Munasinghe, Mohan, ed. Global Climate Change: Economic and Policy Issues. Washington, DC: World Bank, 1995. QC981.8 .C5 G6474 1995 BUS/SPEA

Nicholas et.al., "Observed Climate Variability and Change in Houghton et.al.", Climate Change 1995, Cambridge, UK, Cambridge University Press, 1996.

Nordhaus William D, "Economic Approaches to greenhouse Warming in Robert Dombusch and James Poterba eds., Global Warming Economic Policy Responses, Cambridge MIT Press, 1991, 33-67

Nordhaus, William D. Managing the Global Commons: The Economics of Climate Change. Cambridge: MIT Press, 1994. QC981.8.C5N66 1994

Norman Anderson, "Ozone", Kendall/Hunt Publishing Company, Dubuque, IA.(1996).

O' Riordan Tim and Jagar Jill, "The Politics of Climate Change", A European Perspective: London, Routledge Press, 1996.

O' Riordan Tim and Jagar Jill, "History of Climate Change Science and Politics", London, New York, Routledge Press, 1996.

Olson Mancur, "The Logic of Collective Action", Cambridge Harvard University Press, 1965.

Oppenheimer M. and Boyle R. Dead Heat: The race against greenhouse effect, New York, Basic Books, 1990.

Ostrom Elimor, "Managing the Commons", New York, Cambridge University Press, 1990.

Paterson Matthew, "Global Warming and Global Politics", London and New York, Routlege, 1996.

Permetta, John. Impacts of Climate Change on Ecosystems and Species: Implications for Protected Areas. Gland, Switzerland: US-EPA, SIDA and RIVM, 1994. QC981.8 .C5 14772 1994 BUS/SPEA

Pleming J.R., 1998, Historical perspectives on climate change: New York, Oxford University Press. p. 194.

Pringle, Laurence. "Global Warming," Global Warming. New York: Sea star Books, 2001, pp. 46-52.

Pringle, Laurence. "Signs of a Warming Earth." Global Warming, The Threat of Earth's Changing Climate. New York: Sea Star Books, 2001, pp. 17-20.

Ramesh Chandra, "Global Terorism : A Threat to Humanity", Gyan Books Pvt.Ltd, New Delhi, October 2004.

Rayner S. Malone, " Human Choice and Climate Change", Columbus, OH battle Press, 1998, p. 297.

Rebecca Johnson, " The greenhouse Effect", Lerner Publication Company, Minneapolis, MN(1990).

Reconstructing Climate Policy: Beyond Kyoto (American Enterprise Institute Press, 2003) (with Richard B. Stewart).

Revkin, Andrew. "Business As Usual." Global Warming, Understanding The Forecast. Ed. Susan Costello. New York: Abbeville Press, 1992, pp. 119-123.

Romm, Joseph J., The Hype About Hydrogen: Fact and Fiction in the Race to Save the Climate, Island Press, 2004.

Rosenzweig, Cynthia. Climate Change and the Global Harvest: Potential Impacts of the greenhouse Effect on Agriculture. New York: Oxford University Press, 1998. AJT4342 GEO-MAP

Ruth Caplan, "Our Earth Ourselves", Bantam Books, New York, NY (1990).

Sally Morgan, "Global Warming", Reeds, Chicago, IL(2003).

Samir Dasgupta(ed), Kalyani Independent "The Changing Face of Globalization", Sage India, 2004.

Sandler Todd, " Global Challenges", An approach to Environmental, Political and Economic problems, New York, Cambridge University Press, 1997.

Schneider Stephen H., "Global Warming Are We Entering in the greenhouse Century", San Francisco, CA, Sierra Club Books, 1989.

Schneider, Stephen H. "The greenhouse Effect" Global Warming. San Francisco: Sierra Club Books, 1989, pp. 18-35.

Schneider, Stephen H., et. al. eds. Climate Change Policy: A Survey. Washington, DC: Island Press, 2002. SL QC981.8.C5 C511416 2002.

Sharma A., "Another Crawl for Mankind", New Delhi ; Down to Earth, Centre for Science and Environment , 15 December 1999, pp. 20-23.

Sinton Jonathan and David Fridley, "Hot Air and Cold Water", The unexpected Fall in China's Energy Use: China Environmental Series, Issue 4, Washington DC, Woodrowwilson Centre(in Press), 2001.

Smith, Joel B., ed. Adapting to Climate Change: An International Perspective. New York: Springer, 1996. QC981.8 .C5 A32 1996 BUS/SPEA

Somerville, R. C. 1996: The Forgiving Air Understanding Environmental Change. University of California Press, pp. 216.

Special Report on Emissions Scenarios: A Special Report of Working Group III of the Intergovernmental Panel on Climate Control. Cambridge, UK: Cambridge University Press, 2000. SL TD 885.5 G73 S7 2000.

Speth, James Gustave, Red Sky at Morning: America and the Crisis of Global Environment yale University Press, 2004.? TRL

Stevens, William K. "The greenhouse Experiment, Is the World Warming?' The Change in the Weather. New York: Delacorte Press, 1999, pp. 129-170.

Strzepek, Kenneth M. As Climate Changes: International Impacts and Implications. New York: Cambridge University Press, 1995. QC981.8.C5 A86 1995 GEO-MAP

Sujata K. Dass, "Global Climate and Sustainble Development", Gyan Books Pvt.Ltd, New Delhi, October 2004.

Suzuki, David and Holly Dressel. Good News for a Change: How Everyday People are Helping the Planet. Greystone Books, 2002 TRL.

Tennesen, Michael, Complete Idiot's Guide to Global Warming (Complete Idiot's 2004 TRL.

Watson, Robert T., et al, eds, Land Use, Land-Use Change and Forestry: A Special Report of the 1PCC. Cambridge, UK: Cambridge University Press, 2000. SL SD 390.7 C55 L36 2000.

Weart, Spencer R. The Discovery of Global Warming. Harvard University, 2004. TRL.

Wilson, EdwardO., The Future of Life. Alfred A. Knopf, 2002? TRL.

Zhang, Zhihong (2003); "The Forces behind China's Climate Change Policy: Interests, Sovereignty, Prestige' in Harris P.G.(ed). Global Warming and East Asia: the Domestic and International Politics of Climate Change, London and New York: Routledge, pp. 66-85.

Zhang, Zhong Xiang(1999a): "The Role of China in Combating Global Climate Change" in The Brown Journal of World Affairs. Summer/Fall 1999, Vol.VI, Issue 2, pp. 63-76.

INDEX

V

W

Y